Ancient Views on What Is Music

Books by David Whitwell

The Sousa Oral History Project
The Art of Musical Conducting
The Longy Club: 1900–1917
La Téléphonie and the Universal Musical Language
Extraordinary Women
A Concise History of the Wind Band
Essays on the Modern Wind Band
Essays on Performance Practice
A New History of Wind Music
The College and University Band
The Early Symphonies of Mozart
Music of the French Revolution
Stories from the Podium

On Composers
Wagner on Bands
Berlioz on Bands
Chopin: A Self-Portrait
Liszt: A Self-Portrait
Schumann: A Self-Portrait in His Own Words
Mendelssohn: A Self-Portrait in His Own Words

On Education
Philosophic Foundations of Education
Foundations of Music Education
Music Education of the Future

Aesthetics of Music
Aesthetics of Music in Ancient Civilizations
Aesthetics of Music in the Middle Ages
Aesthetics of Music in the Early Renaissance
Aesthetics of Music in Sixteenth-Century Italy, France and Spain
Aesthetics of Music in Sixteenth-Century Germany, the Low Countries and England
Aesthetics of Baroque Music in Italy, Spain, the German-Speaking Countries and the Low Countries
Aesthetics of Baroque Music in France
Aesthetics of Baroque Music in England

The History and Literature of the Wind Band and Wind Ensemble Series

Volume 1 The Wind Band and Wind Ensemble Before 1500
Volume 2 The Renaissance Wind Band and Wind Ensemble
Volume 3 The Baroque Wind Band and Wind Ensemble
Volume 4 The Wind Band and Wind Ensemble of the Classical Period (1750–1800)
Volume 5 The Nineteenth-Century Wind Band and Wind Ensemble
Volume 6 A Catalog of Multi-Part Repertoire for Wind Instruments or for Undesignated Instrumentation before 1600
Volume 7 Baroque Wind Band and Wind Ensemble Repertoire
Volume 8 Classical Period Wind Band and Wind Ensemble Repertoire
Volume 9 Nineteenth-Century Wind Band and Wind Ensemble Repertoire
Volume 10 A Supplementary Catalog of Wind Band and Wind Ensemble Repertoire
Volume 11 A Catalog of Wind Repertoire before the Twentieth Century for One to Five Players
Volume 12 A Second Supplementary Catalog of Early Wind Band and Wind Ensemble Repertoire
Volume 13 Name Index, Volumes 1–12, The History and Literature of the Wind Band and Wind Ensemble

Ancient Voices

Ancient Views on Music and Religion
Ancient Views on the Natural World
Ancient Views on What Is Music
Contemporary Descriptions of Early Musicians
Early Views of Music and Ethics
Early Thoughts on Performance Practice
Music Performance in Ancient Societies

Renaissance Voices

Essays on Renaissance Philosophies of Music
Renaissance Men on Music

www.whitwellbooks.com

David Whitwell

Ancient Voices
Views on Music by Ancient and Medieval Writers

Ancient Views on What Is Music

EDITED BY CRAIG DABELSTEIN

WHITWELL PUBLISHING • AUSTIN, TEXAS, USA

Ancient Voices: Views on music by ancient and medieval writers
Ancient Views on What Is Music
Dr. David Whitwell

WHITWELL PUBLISHING
AUSTIN, TX 78701
WWW.WHITWELLPUBLISHING.COM

© 2013 by David Whitwell
All rights reserved. First edition 2013

Composed in Bembo Book.
Published in the United States of America.
All images used in this book are in the public domain except where otherwise noted.

ISBN-13: 9781936512744

Cover design by Daniel Ferla.

Contents

	Foreword	ix
	Acknowledgement	xi

Part 1 What Is Music?

1	Ancient Voices Ask: What Is Music?	3
2	On Ancient Gods of Music	19
3	On Ancient Muses and Myths	31
4	On Divine Inspiration	49
5	Is Music Math?	61
6	Is Music Theory or Performance?	75

Part 2 Understanding versus Feeling

7	Early Voices Argue: Reason versus Experience	93
8	Early Voices Struggle to Explain the Emotions	103
9	Animals and Music	125
10	Is Man Ruled by Reason or Emotion?	145
11	Some Early Voices Intuit the Bicameral Mind	161
12	The Secret Agenda: Right-Hand Preference	171

Part 3 What Music Is

13	Music is the Ruler of the Passions of the Soul	181
14	On the Doctrine of the Affections	209
15	Music is Truth	233
16	Music as the Language of Truth	243
17	The End of Music: Catharsis	265
	Bibliography	277
	About the Author	297
	About the Editor	299

Foreword

As it appears to all philologists that music is older than speech, so it is no surprise that one finds music mentioned and discussed in the earliest forms of written languages. We would suppose that the first fascination about music among early people was that it was something which could be felt with strong impact yet could not be seen. It was most likely this mysterious characteristic which caused nearly every early society to associate music so closely with religion. It is this general subject which the reader will find explored in Part I.

Part II follows with the early Church's attempt to rid the new Christian of all forms of emotion, which led to the slight-of-hand of making music a branch of mathematics. No doubt it was pressure from intellectuals within the Church which led to the Church replacing this nonsense with a new dogma in which music was divided into two distinct divisions, the academic (theory, composition and physics) and actual performance. This might also be viewed as a separation between that which is easy to teach and that which is not (emotions being not easily subject to rational discussion). Everyone will notice that this separation is operative to the present day.

Part III begins with the long story of philosophers trying to explain our twin natures, the rational and the experiential, and music's role therein. Recent decades of clinical brain research has made these studies much easier to understand, but society does not yet recognize our twin natures as being of equal value. Part III concludes with philosophers' thoughts regarding the most obvious definition of music, that it is a special language for our otherwise mute experiential self (the right hemisphere of the brain) to communicate. In turn, the greatest reward to mankind through listening to music is catharsis, the discovery of the real us.

David Whitwell
Austin, Texas

Acknowledgments

I am indebted to my friend and colleague, Craig Dabelstein, for his help in preparing this book for publication.

David Whitwell
Austin, Texas

PART I
WHAT IS MUSIC?

Ancient Voices Ask: What Is Music?

*Music is a science of the phenomena of Love
in application to harmony and rhythm.*[1]
Plato (427–347 BC)

Music does not exist.
Sextus Empiricus (second century AD)

THE TWO QUOTATIONS ABOVE are representative of the difficulty philosophers have always had in defining and classifying music. When Plato joins 'science' and 'love' in his definition of music he is telling us that very early philosophers had already recognized that music had both rational and non-rational characteristics. This 'split-personality' would be given new labels by early Church philosophers, who divided music into 'Speculative' and 'Practical.' By the late Middle Ages and early Renaissance we find still new names in the expression, 'the art and science of music,' as we see, for example, in the fourteenth-century theorist, Marchetto of Padua:

> Music is an art [*ars*] both admirable and delightful; it resounds in heaven and on earth.
> Moreover, music is that science [*scientia*] which consists in numbers, proportions, consonances, intervals, measures, and quantities.[2]

In today's music schools we make a division of Music into the two branches, 'Theory' and 'Performance.' Much contemporary confusion is caused by the fact only one of the two is actually music, although we call both of them music.

The reader may be astounded that anyone could conclude that music does not exist. But one must recall that for nearly the first one thousand years of the Christian Era there was no notation; one could neither 'see' music on paper or in the air and this was a period when philosophy placed exclusive importance on information confirmed by the eyes (we still say 'seeing is believing'). Add to this the fact that the Church, in a clever slight-of-hand, made music a branch of mathematics[3] and you begin to understand the possibility of one concluding there was no such thing as music.

---

[1] *Symposium*, 187b. The first century BC poet, Bion, writes that No, 'music is sweeter even than love.' [Fragment XVIII]. Pliny the Younger, at the end of the first century AD. He writes of the daughter of Calpurnia Hispulla,

> She has even set my verses to music and sings them, to the accompaniment of her lyre, with no musician to teach her but the best of masters, love.

[2] Marchetto of Padua, *Lucidarium*, trans. Jan W. Herlinger (Chicago: Univeristy of Chicago Press, 1985), I, 5, ii and iii.

[3] This will also be the subject of a separate chapter.

One of those who claimed that music did not exist was the second-century philosopher, Sextus Empiricus. In his treatise, 'Against the Musicians,' he begins by acknowledging the recognized basic natures of music, that it is a science and also a performance skill, and even adds the interesting observation that 'music,' is sometimes used to describe other arts. 'Thus we speak of a work as "musical," even though it be a piece of painting.'[4]

Empiricus' plan was to present the characteristics which he found most people associated with music and then argue to the contrary. For example, he points to the belief that music helps in 'regulating human life and repressing the passions of the soul.' Here he quotes a story that Pythagoras once calmed some youths, who 'were in a state of Bacchic frenzy' from drinking, by having an aulos player perform a 'spondean' melody, whereupon they suddenly became sober. But Empiricus says, no, music does not have this power nor does any melody have, in itself, any particular quality, 'that some tunes are in their nature stimulating, others repressive.'

> In the case of musical tunes it is not by nature that some are of this kind and others of that kind, but it is we ourselves who suppose them to be such. Thus the same tune serves to excite horses, but not at all to excite men who hear it in a theater.

And, he says, it may not actually excite the horses, only distract them. This becomes his principle refutation, that music only distracts. Thus the drunken youths, in the Pythagoras story, only experienced a momentarily moderating influence of the music, soon thereafter to return to their original state.

> As to Pythagoras, in the first place he was foolish in desiring to render drunkards sober at the wrong moment, instead of quitting the place; and secondly, by trying to reform them in this way he confesses that aulos players have more influence than philosophers for the reforming of morals.

And so it goes until finally, Empiricus concludes with a bit of circuitous nonsense, the kind of philosophizing which the early Christian writers complain about,—philosophy which proves nothing. If music exists, says Empiricus, everything must be based on the individual note. He then offers the following reasoning illustrating that notes do not exist. The Cyrenaic philosophers say only feelings exist, nothing else. Democritus says sense-objects do not exist, hence neither sound. If sound exists, it must be either incorporeal or corporeal and the Stoics prove it is not the former and the Peripatetics demonstrate it is not the latter. He continues in this vein and finally concludes,

> Now, then, as sound does not exist, neither does the note ... and when the note does not exist, neither does the musical interval exist, nor symphony [harmony], nor melody, nor the Genera formed by these. Therefore, Music does not exist either.[5]

---

4   Sextus Empiricus, 'Against the Musicians,' in *Against the Professors*, trans. R. G. Bury (Cambridge: Harvard University Press, 1949), VI, 14.

5   Ibid., VI, 58. Another writer, the seventeenth-century Frenchman, Fenelon, in his *The Adventures of Telemachus*, has King Inachus conclude that since you can't see music, perhaps it is an odor!

In spite of the difficulty in defining music, nearly all early philosophers understood music to be something very powerful, made more significant by the fact that it was the only art you could not see and therefore often associated with religion or the divine. Some tried to investigate deeper into the very nature of music and found the definition of music in its function, as for example, 'to soothe.' Others found the definition of music in its ability to be a special language of the emotions. Some more specifically found music to be a special form of Truth representing the emotional or experiential aspects of man. Still other philosophers found the definition of music in its physiological properties.

Music *is* difficult to define, in part because it is all of the above.

The focus of the present chapter is on those early philosophers and musicians who attempted a broad general definition of music. We begin with the earliest large body of philosophical discussion of music, the writings of Plato (427–347 BC), which in turn are mostly a record of the dialogs of his teacher, Socrates.

When one synthesizes all the discussion of music by Socrates one is struck by how modern sounding the problems are and how similar are the values of the highest art music. In Socrates' ideal world, music meant live performance, not something found on paper or taken on a conceptual level. It was performance listened to by quiet, contemplative listeners. Both composer and performer were inspired not by 'rules of art,' but by divine inspiration. The purposes of the music were love of beauty and to move the emotions of the listeners, something music could do since it represented a form of Truth and because listeners had a genetic understanding of music. One cannot help but wonder how different our world today would be if we knew only music which would have been found appropriate by Socrates.

Judging by the writings of Plato, there seems to have been a consensus that the role of music in education was to form the character of the child. It was an idea which seems to have been not only widely shared but an idea already long held. From Plato's perspective, indeed from the perspective of nearly all early Greek philosophy, the key word is the 'soul.' The Greeks often used the analogy of the string instrument, the lyre, to illustrate the relationship of body and soul. One can see the lyre, as a material object like the body, but music is unseen, like the soul. They added to this analogy the word harmony, using it to express not only the unity of the various elements of music, but also to express the soul in its ideal state. Plato believed music was given to man by the Gods for this purpose, and not for the more common use of it as entertainment.

> Harmony, which has motions akin to the revolutions of our souls, is not regarded by the intelligent votary of the Muses as given by them with a view to irrational pleasure, which is deemed to be the purpose of it in our day, but as meant to correct any discord which may have arisen in the courses of the soul, and to be our ally in bringing her into harmony and agreement with herself.[6]

---

[6] *Timaeus*, 47d.

It follows, therefore, that Plato introduces the core of the ideal educational system with the following statement.

> Education has two branches,—one of gymnastic, which is concerned with the body, and the other of music, which is designed for the improvement of the soul.[7]

Another idea found in the writings of Plato was also carried down for centuries, although it took on somewhat a life of its own. In *Alcibiades I* (108d), Plato makes the statement, 'Musically is the very name for correctness in the art of music.' We believe that the intended emphasis was exactly what Plato wrote, on 'the *art* of music,' not the *science* of music. We think Socrates meant that 'musically,' when applied to *correctness in the art* of music (meaning performance, of course) was a reference to the aesthetic values so often found in Plato's writings, that music is Truth, that it is inspired and that it is intended to create an emotional catharsis in the listener, not entertain him. In a word, we believe that to Socrates 'musically,' or *correctness in the art of music*, was an idea closely related to philosophy itself. We believe it must be the same idea Socrates had in mind when he uttered the otherwise curious statement that 'philosophy is the noblest and best of music.' Socrates made this statement at the end of his life, while waiting in prison. At this time he confides a reoccurring dream that he should 'Set to work and compose music.' He apparently did compose at least one hymn in prison, thus perhaps he not only became a performer late in life but a composer as well. With this in mind, together with his philosophical view of '*correctness in the art of music*,' perhaps we can understand why he interpreted his dream as meaning he should concentrate on philosophy.

> I had imagined that this was only intended to exhort and encourage me in the study of philosophy, which as been the pursuit of my life, and is the noblest and best of music.[8]

Aristotle (b. 384 BC), perhaps the most rational man who ever lived, had to confess, 'It is not easy to determine the nature of music.'[9] Indeed he avoids attempting to define what music really is and, instead, makes his focus the uses of music. He acknowledges the powers of music but wonders if it is possible to obtain its benefits by listening, rather than by playing. His block here was the fact that in his day performers had become slaves.

> We call professional performers vulgar; no freeman would play or sing unless he were intoxicated or in jest.[10]

---

[7] *Laws*, 795d.

[8] *Phaedo*, 60e. The always well-read Beethoven must have found this passage for he answered, 'Music is a more lofty revelation than all wisdom and philosophy.'

[9] *Politica*, VIII, 5, 1339a, 14ff.

[10] Ibid., 1339b, 7ff.

Aristotle did accept the idea that music should be included in the schools for the purpose of developing character. The logic in this he found from his own experience, that the emotions experienced through music are very similar to the real emotions and can therefore shape the young listener.

> [The emotions] and of the other qualities of character, which hardly fall short of the actual emotions, as we know from our own experience, for in listening to such [music] our souls undergo a change.[11]

It is interesting that he specifies that the children are not to be taught music just to understand it, but to be able to actually perform it.[12] In another place he testifies again, 'No doubt after a man has learned music his soul has undergone a certain change.'[13]

The next influential person who struggles to define music is St. Augustine, of the fourth century, in a little known book, *On Music*. Augustine begins by asking, 'Where is music?' Is it [1] in the sound itself, [2] in the perception of the listener, [3] in the performer, or [4] in the memory?

Regarding the first, he suggests that everyone would accept the possibility of a sound, such as a drop of liquid, existing where there is no listener to hear it.[14] The second, of necessity, requires the first.

Number three, the performance, Augustine does not consider as fundamental as the first two, for we can hear music in our minds where there is no sound or performance at all. This kind of listening is, of course, closely related to the fourth, memory. The subject of memory was of great concern by the early philosophers because not only could you not see music, there was no notated form and it 'disappeared' when the performance was concluded. Thus for it to be considered as existing necessarily depended on memory. We find this point stressed by Aristotle's student, Aristoxenus, who was born ca. 379 BC.

> For the apprehension of music depends on these two faculties, sense-perception and memory; for we must perceive the sound that is present, and remember that which is past. In no other way can we follow the phenomena of music.[15]

At this point Augustine suddenly thinks of a fifth possible answer to the question, 'Where is Music?' Here he refers to a view which can be found in several other places in his works, the possibility of a kind of innate template for judging music.

---

[11] Ibid., 1340a, 21ff.

[12] Ibid., 1340b, 31ff.

[13] *Prior Analytics*, II, xxvii.

[14] Augustine is wrong, of course. The answer to the famous riddle, 'If a tree falls in the forest when there is no one there to hear it, does it make a sound?,' is no.

[15] Aristoxenus, *The Elements of Harmony*, trans. Henry S. Macran (Hildesheim: Georg Olms Verlag, 1974), 41.

> I believe, while we were discussing these things, a fifth kind appeared from somewhere, a kind in the natural judgment of perceiving when we are delighted by the equality of numbers or offended at a flaw in them.[16]

Augustine concludes this discussion by observing that of these, now five, possible descriptions of music only the God-given template form, which he now names 'the judicial,' is undying. The others 'either pass away when they are made or are stricken out of the memory by forgetfulness.'[17] This idea of genetic music information in man is a very important one, which we have discussed elsewhere.[18]

When Church administration replaced the fallen Roman Empire, part of its agenda to rid Rome of 'heathen' influences was to close the schools. When they finally allowed schools to reopen it was in response to the argument of more enlightened clerics who pointed out that the Christian must have some education in order to understand the Church service and its teachings. This is the point made by the Venerable Bede:

> We are to be initiated in *grammatica*, then in *dialectia*, afterward in *rhetorica*. Equipped with these arms, we should approach the study of philosophy. Here the order is first the quadrivium, and in this first *arithmetica*, second *musica*, third *geometria*, fourth *astronomia*, then holy writ, so that through knowledge of what is created we arrive at knowledge of the Creator.[19]

We see here the curriculum of the 'Dark Ages' and we find music among the sciences. Moreover, due to the paranoia of the Church on the subject of 'the emotions,' music had been officially classified by the Church as a branch of mathematics and thus for the next one thousand years all music treatises would be written by mathematicians and not by musicians. All this is by way of introducing the next influential writer on the definition of music, the famous mathematician, Boethius (475–524 AD).

Boethius made two arguments which would influence music education for centuries. The first, indeed, hangs over our heads as a form of prejudice even today. He states that the study of music is of higher value than the performance of music.

> Now one should bear in mind that every art and also every discipline considers reason inherently more honorable than a skill which is practiced by the hand and the labor of an artisan. For it is much better and nobler to know about what someone else fashions than to execute that about which someone else knows; in fact, physical skill serves as a slave, while reason, rules like a mistress. Unless the hand acts according to the will of reason, it acts in vain. How much nobler, then, is the study of music as a rational discipline than as composition and performance![20]

---

[16] St. Augustine, *On Music*, trans. Robert Taliaferro in *Writings of Saint Augustine* (New York: Fathers of the Church), VI, iv.

[17] Ibid., VI, vii.

[18] See another book in this series, *Music and the Natural World*.

[19] *De elementis philosophiae*, quoted in Nan Cooke Carpenter, *Music in the Medieval and Renaissance Universities* (Norman: University of Oklahoma Press, 1958), 20, fn. 12.

[20] Ibid., I, xxxiv.

Boethius is wrong, of course. This line of thought today, now called 'concept music teaching,' has caused the decline of music education all over the United States. Our Doctors of Education just don't get it. Students want the experience of music; they are not interested to just learn *about* music. So they come to our schools with a natural love of music and then promptly drop out of our music classes because they find our music classes are not really *music* classes.

The attempt by Boethius to define music resulted in a classification system which also had far reaching influence on music education. Boethius first ranks types of music into three species, in an apparent descending order of aesthetic importance.[21] The most important, presumably representing God directly, is Cosmic Music, in particular the 'Music of the Spheres.'[22] Next, in order of importance, is Human Music, which is to say, Vocal Music.

> Whoever penetrates into his own self perceives human music. For what unites the incorporeal nature of reason with the body if not a certain harmony and, as it were, a careful tuning of low and high pitches as though producing one consonance? What other than this unites the parts of the soul, which, according to Aristotle, is composed of the rational and the irrational? What is it that intermingles the elements of the body or holds together the parts of the body in an established order?

The third kind of music is Instrumental Music, music which he curiously seems to suggest exists in the instruments themselves. For the modern reader, the thought that music exists anywhere but in the vibrations in the air and their reception by the ear of the listener is quite odd. The eventual breakthrough which enabled philosophers to understand the correct solution to this question came through observations made by listening to echoes, in which case one could hear sounds *not* directly made by an instrument.

A contemporary of Boethius, and fellow Roman, was Cassiodorus. He divided philosophy into two branches, Speculative Philosophy and Practical Philosophy. Practical Philosophy, 'is that which seeks to explain advantageous things,' and includes only Moral, Economic and Political subject matters.[23]

Speculative Philosophy 'is that by means of which we surmount visible things and in some degree contemplate things divine and heavenly, surveying them with the mind alone, inasmuch as they rise above corporeal eyes.' This main branch of philosophy is made up of three sub-branches: Natural, Theoretical, and the Divine. Music is found under 'Theoretical,' together with Arithmetic, Geometry, and Astronomy.

Thus we see he thought of music not as a 'practical,' but as a 'speculative' art, 'something we contemplate with the mind,' and that it is clearly included in the category of mathematical-based disciplines. He saw music most closely related to arithmetic and indeed it is together with this subject that he defines it.

---

[21] Boethius, *Fundamentals of Music*, trans. Calvin Bower (New Haven: Yale University Press), I, ii.

[22] This is discussed further in I, xxvii.

[23] Cassiodorus, 'On Dialectic,' in *An Introduction to Divine and Human Readings*, trans. Leslie Jones (New York, Octagon Books, 1966).

> *Arithmetic* is the science of numerable quantity considered in itself. *Music* is the science which treats measure in relation to sound.

Future generations would take the labels, Speculative and Practical, and apply them almost exclusively to music meaning Theory and Performance.

The few philosophical works which survive from the next four hundred years suggest that the classification of music by Boethius had become firmly accepted. Aurelian of Reome, in his *Musica Disciplina* (ca. 843 AD), follows the celestial, human and instrumental divisions. Regarding the second of these, he maintains that the role of music is to join the rational and irrational facets of man, or quoting Aristotle, 'binding together the parts of the soul and body of man.'[24]

Aurelian acknowledges that music has the power to move the emotions of men, but in speaking of the musicians themselves his emphasis is on conceptual knowledge. This, he says, is what makes a musician, whereas in the case of the player who has only a mere skill, he is not called a musician but is rather named after his instrument—he is a flute player, etc.

> There is as much difference between a musician and a singer as there is between a grammarian and a mere reader, or between physical skill and intellect ... But a musician is one who has with well-weighed intellect attained the science of singing not by the servitude of labor, but by the rule of contemplation ... Musician and singer seem to differ as much as teacher and pupil ... And the singer seems to stand before the musician like a prisoner before the judge.[25]

A very interesting play from the tenth century, *Paphnutius*, written by a nun, Hrotswitha, also follows the ideas of Boethius. In this play a Disciple asks, 'What *is* music?' Paphnutius, a monk teacher, following the definition by Boethius, begins by telling the students that music is divided into three species: the celestial, the human, and that made with instruments. When the students want to know more about the music of the spheres (celestial music), Paphnutius begins to speak in the complex mathematical language of Boethius. The students object to this conceptual language and respond, 'What has this got to do with *music*?,' implying, we presume, that music has instead to do with feelings and emotions, not mathematics. The teacher's answer is, 'But that is how you *talk* about music!' The students wanted the *experience* of music and the teacher was talking at them about the *data* of music. Does this sound familiar?

Another tenth-century treatise, the *Enchiridion musices* by Odo of Cluny also has a Disciple who asks, 'What is music?' But the answer here is quite different, for Odo takes the ancient phrase of Plato, 'Musically is the very name for correctness in the art of music,' which was addressed to the philosophy of performance of live music, reforms the phrase to make it reflect the knowledge of music and has the teacher answer, 'Music is the science of singing correctly.' This is the earliest treatise in which letters are used as symbols for pitch in the modern sense and is a work written specifically to teach church singers to read music. This was one of the

---

[24] Aurelian of Reome, *The Discipline of Music*, trans. Joseph Ponte (Colorado Springs: Colorado College Music Press, 1968), III. The Aristotle reference is apparently to the *Nicomachean Ethics*, I, 13.

[25] Ibid., VII. His absurd and false line of thought would suggest that if one's goal were to learn to tango, one need only contemplate on the subject and not bother with learning by actual dancing.

most significant moments in all of music history for now music became something that one performed *from the page*; music became for the *eye* and not the *ear*. This forever changed how people would define music.

St. Bernhard (thirteenth century), used the identical phrase to define music, 'Music is the science of singing correctly,'[26] as does Philippe de Vitry in his famous treatise, *Ars Nova*. In this herald of the Renaissance, however, de Vitry does seem to cast the phrase into one leaning more toward performance than science, 'Music is the knowledge of accurate singing, or an easy means of achieving perfection in singing.'

One of the most interesting efforts in defining music during the latter Middle Ages was made by the Englishman, Roger Bacon (b. ca. 1214), who studied at both Oxford and Paris. He begins by dividing the world of music into two broad categories, 'one part of music deals with what is audible, the other with what is visible.'[27]

Audible Music he recognizes as being of two divisions, vocal music and instrumental music. In vocal music, in turn, Bacon finds four subdivisions.

> For one part concerns melody, as in singing; the second concerns meters, and considers the nature and properties of all songs, meters, and feet; the third concerns rhythm, and considers every variety of relations in rhythms; the fourth concerns prose and considers accents and other aforesaid things in prose discourse. For accent is a kind of singing; whence it is called accent from *accino, accinis* [I sing, thou singest], because every syllable has its own proper sound either raised, lowered, or composite, and all syllables of one word are adapted or sung to one syllable on which rests the principal sound. Thus length and shortness and all other things required in correct pronunciation are reduced to music.

This is a very interesting discussion for several reasons. First, these thoughts come at the end of at least two thousand years during which poetry was sung. When Bacon says 'every syllable has its own proper sound either raised, lowered, or composite,' we wonder if there was a commonly recognized, but now lost, tradition in the performance of sung poetry. Did the text, perhaps, 'compose' the music? We also find fascinating his statement, 'For accent is a kind of singing.' This comment, seven hundred years before our age, reminds us that among ancient peoples singing preceded language. Can we not see a trace here of that distant period when pitch fluctuation preceded, and perhaps turned into, the sounds we call consonants?

Bacon is not so expansive on instrumental music, noting only that the subject deals with 'the structure of the instruments and their use.' However, he also adds the extraordinary qualification that the theologian must also know the 'numberless mystical meanings' of the instruments. We wish he had elaborated more on this idea for it suggests some concepts now entirely lost. It would be even more valuable to know his full thoughts on this subject for he has made it clear in previous passages that he takes the Old Testament references to instruments literally, and not metaphorically as did most of the earlier Church philosophers.

---

[26] 'De Revisione Cantus Cistercienis,' trans. Francisco Guentner (American Institute of Musicology, 1974), 44.

[27] 'Causes of Error,' XVI in *The Opus Majus of Roger Bacon*, trans. Robert Burke (New York: Russell & Russell, 1962), I, 259.

It is Bacon's recognition of a category of music which he calls 'visual music' which is of most significance. The ancient Greek philosophers never discussed this topic at length, but there are sufficient hints in their descriptions of choral performance to suggest that the inevitable movements by the singers were thought of not as a kind of dance, but as the part of music you could see. One must remember that the Greeks placed considerable significance in the fact that one cannot *see* music and it was for this reason that music was so closely associated with religion (whose principal mysteries also cannot be seen). The significance of Bacon's discussion is that it is an early one which supplies important insights into this ancient association of music and movement.

> Music, moreover, consisting in what is visible, is necessary; and that it is such is evident from the book on the *Origin of the Sciences*. For whatever can be conformed to sound in similar movements and in corresponding formations, so that our delight may be made complete not only by hearing, but by seeing, belongs to music. Therefore dances and all bendings of bodies are reduced to gesture, which is a branch of music, since these are conformed to sound in similar movements and corresponding formations, as the author of the aforesaid book maintains. Therefore Aristotle says in the seventh book of the *Metaphysics* that the art of dancing is not complete without another art, that is, without another kind of music to which the art of dancing is conformed.

Bacon mentions the Old Testament reference to the dancing by the sister of Moses and recommends that theologians need to study this aspect of music (dance) in order that in preaching on these passages they might,

> know how to express all their properties, so that they may give utterance to all the spiritual senses of an angelic devotion.

De Vitry's Italian contemporary of the early fourteenth century, Marchetto of Padua offers a new classification of music, leaving behind the old music of the spheres. He categorizes music as being either 'harmonic, organic or rhythmic.'[28] Harmonic music is that which is produced by the voice. Organic music is that produced by breath, but not of the voice. Here he includes trumpets, shawms, pipes and organs.[29] Rhythmic music is that produced without breath, including the monochord, psaltery and bells.[30]

We find particularly interesting Marchetto's comments on altered tones. These he says are called 'chromatic,' from *chroma*, or 'color' in Greek, and have 'the color of beauty, because it is on account of the elegance and beauty of the dissonances that the whole tone is divided.'[31] We find this so interesting because it suggests a much greater use of dissonance in early Renaissance music than the surviving written forms suggest. And if this is true it follows that there must have been a greater employment of improvisation than music texts admit.

---

[28] Marchetto of Padua, *Lucidarium*, I, 8, 11ff.

[29] Ibid., I, 12, ii.

[30] Ibid., 14, ii.

[31] Ibid., treatise 2, I, 8, vi.

Another writer who heralds the Renaissance was Johannes de Grocheo. In his *De Musica* (ca. 1300) his definition of music is extraordinary: that music is a principal means of the intellect explaining itself. Also significant here, is the importance given to performance. When he says, yes, numbers may define the form of music, but it is of the nature of music to be performed, he has left Boethius far behind.

> Certain people, considering its form and material, describe music by saying that it is a science of number related to sound. Others, looking at its performance, say that it is an art devoted to singing. We, however, intend to take it in both ways, just as it is made known as a tool and ought to be made known as an art. Just as natural warmth is a first tool through which the soul exercises its functions, so as an art [music] is a principal tool or rule through which the practical intellect explains and exposes its functions. We may say, therefore, that music is an art or science concerning numbered sound taken harmonically, designed for singing easily. I say also a *science*, insofar as it treats of the knowledge of principles, an *art*, insofar as it rules the practical intellect in performing, concerning *harmonic sound*, since it is this basic material around which it is performed. By *number* its form is defined. But by *singing* performance is touched upon, to which it is properly *designated*.[32]

Turning now to the classification of music, Grocheo mentions the three genre of Boethius: Music of the Spheres, Human Music, and Instrumental Music. Although music theorists had accepted this classification without comment for half a millennium, Grocheo now blasts Boethius into oblivion. He courageously attacks the faulty logic, the pseudo-science, the beliefs of the Church and, let us admit it, the nonsense which Boethius had put forth.

> Those who make this kind of division either invent their opinion or they wish to obey the Pythagoreans or others more than the truth, or they are ignorant of nature and logic.[33]

Grocheo proposes to bring music down from the spheres and instead will use the practical classifications practiced by 'the men in Paris,' for it is there that the principles of all liberal arts are 'sought out diligently.' Therefore, to replace the three classifications of Boethius, Grocheo presents three new ones:

1. Civic or simple music, which they call vulgar [*vulgus*: of the masses] music.
2. Composed or regular music by rule, which they call measured music.
3. Ecclesiastic music, designed for praising the Creator, made from the first two and to which these two are best adapted.[34]

In the late Renaissance, in the *Musica* (1537) of Nicholaus Listenius, a student at Wittenberg when Luther was teaching there, we find an entirely new goal in the definition of music, one which combines the musicality of the Renaissance with the old catharsis principle found in the *Poetics* of Aristotle. In his Foreword, Listenius provides a moving review of the purpose and virtue of music.

---

32 Johannes de Grocheo, *De Musica*, trans. Albert Seay (Colorado Springs: Colorado College Music Press, 1967), 9.
33 Ibid., 10.
34 Ibid., 11.

> Many great and serious reasons are established by learned and intelligent men, for all men of genius particularly free princes, must be versed in music and habituated to it. It influences souls to humanity, suavity, even-temper; it restrains all immoderate affections, grief, wrath; it represses violence and obscene desires, for it calms them; as in sounds and songs, so in all the actions of life we may conserve harmony.[35]

Listenius begins his book with one of the old medieval definitions, 'Music is the science of singing correctly and well.' However, in his next sentence he clearly dates himself in the Renaissance by stating that the knowledge of music consists of three kinds: theoretical, practical and *poetic*. The theoretical is concerned only with understanding the subject. Hence, he says, the 'theoretical musician' is content in this knowledge and 'presents no example of his work in performance.'

His definition of practical music, which he divides into Choral and Figured, or Mensural, goes considerably beyond the usual definitions given in the university circles in France, England, and Italy, where the term is given to mean little more than simply performance itself. Listenius speaks of something beyond skill and says the performer teaches the listener something more than mere appreciation.

> Practical, whose goal is doing, is that which delights not only in the intricacies of skill, but extends into performance itself, leaving out no part of the act of performance. Hence the practical musician, who teaches others something more than the recognition of art, trains himself in it for the goal of any performance.[36]

His third kind of knowledge is an aesthetic definition quite new to the Renaissance. Here he is thinking of the meaning left with the listener when the performance is concluded. This he calls '*total* performance.' It is most important and enlightening that he observed that the practical and the poetic always include the theoretical, 'but the reverse is not true.'

> Poetic is that which is not content with just the understanding of the thing nor with only its practice, but which leaves something more after the labor of performance, as when music or a song of musicians is composed by someone whose goal is total performance and accomplishment. It consists of making or putting together more in this work which afterwards leaves the work perfect and absolute, which otherwise is artificially like the dead.[37]

The point Listenius makes here is of the greatest significance. He means the performer makes the compositions come alive through the addition of his own feelings, as opposed to merely playing the notes on paper. One often hears music critics say, 'Just play what the composer wrote' (that which is on paper). Curiously, in music's cousin, drama, where there is also a written form and a performance form, no one has ever said, 'Just speak the lines the author wrote!'

---

35 Nicolaus Listenius, *Musica*, trans. Albert Seay (Colorado Springs: Colorado College Music Press, 1975), 1.

36 Ibid., 3.

37 Ibid.

With the arrival of the Baroque, discussions of the definition of music begin to look quite different. The German, Johann Mattheson, as a composer himself, begins by observing that it is not sufficient to define music as simply playing or singing well for 'the noblest part of music [is] composing.'[38] Indeed, he points out that in Italy a singer is called *Musico*, an instrumentalist, *Suonatore*, but only the composer, 'who often has the least to say about his work,' is called *Maestro*! His basic definition of music is:

> Music is a science and an art of placing proper and pleasing sounds prudently, uniting them correctly with one another, and presenting them sweetly, to promote God's honor and all virtue through their euphony.[39]

He follows this by observing that 'nothing is accomplished by science alone; art is required as well.' By this he means you cannot speak of music without speaking of performance.

Next Mattheson turns to the classifications of music and begins with a review of the medieval classifications of 'universal music' (music of the spheres, etc.), 'human music' (having to do with the soul, etc.) and 'actual music.' Since the first two classifications cannot be actually heard, he explains he will discuss only 'actual music.'[40] The goal of actual music, he says, is that,

> which would through the instrument of the ears please the sense of hearing which dwells in the soul, and would thoroughly move or stir the heart or soul.[41]

With the expression, 'move the heart,' Mattheson epitomizes the Baroque itself, a period of fervent search for how music affects the emotions. We find this same emphasis in the definition of music by his famous French contemporary, Marin Mersenne.

> The song, or air, is a derivation of the voice, or of other sounds, by certain intervals either natural or artificial, which are agreeable to the ear and to the spirit, and which signify joy, or sadness, or some other passion by their movements.[42]

The Baroque, with its concentration on the emotions in music, put an end to the old scholastic ideas of earlier Church music. Now hardly ever do we hear the term 'speculative music' and it is very rare when someone wants to define music as a science. Indeed, the most noticeable pursuit of a 'speculative' nature during the Baroque was the attempt to make a 'science' of the way music reflected the emotions. This became the 'Doctrine of the Affections,' and a

---

[38] Johann Mattheson, *Der vollkommene Capellmeister* (1739), trans. Ernest Harriss (Ann Arbor: UMI Research Press, 1981), I, ii, 11ff.

[39] Ibid., I, ii, 15.

[40] Ibid., I, ii, 21ff.

[41] Ibid., I, ii, 24.

[42] Marin Mersenne, *Harmonie universelle* [1636], Treatise Three, Book Two ('Second Book of Songs') of the *Traitez de la Voix et des Chants* ..., trans. Wilbur F. Russell (Princeton: Westminster Choir College, unpublished dissertation, 1952), III, ii, 1.

dozen highly scholarly treatises appeared. Nothing came of them because what is important to man on his experiential side is not describable by his rational side, as anyone who has ever tried to write a love letter knows.

We find it very interesting that one philosopher of the Baroque, the Englishman, Roger North, seemed to understand this. He specifically contends that music does not stimulate the rational or conceptual side of man, as we see in the final sentence when he concludes his definition of music by adding that the two primary purposes of music are to please and to communicate emotions.

> Therefore in order to find the criteria of Good Music we must look into Nature itself, and the truth of things. Music hath two ends. First to please the sense, and that is done by the pure Dulcor of harmony, which is found chiefly in older music … Secondly, to move the affections, or excite the passion; and that is done by measures of time joined with the former [the affections]. And it must be granted that pure impulse, artificially acted and continued, hath great power to excite men to act, *but not to think*.[43]

He now expands on these ideas, making this point again as he focuses particularly on the importance of the emotions. Regarding the latter, it is most interesting to see that after three thousand years of philosophers telling man that 'Reason must rule,' North says, no, *feelings* must rule.

> I must sever the virtue of time in music, from the music itself, as having another scope and effect; and may be said to stir up comfortable actions, *but not to excite thinking* or please the sense.
>
> And as to all of music, besides the bare pleasing the sense, it must be referred to a power, by similar sounds, of bringing to our minds or memory the state of joy or grief, or of less important affections, as may be conform to what we hear. As for instance, who can hear the miserable clamor of one in affliction, without compassion? And whence that, but from a sensible reflection or memory of the same or like circumstances? And music by its sounds doth the same, and through the same operation of mind; for a savage, or brute, that hath no reflex thoughts, is not at all moved by compassionate sounds … I have instanced grief, but the case is the same in all the various states of humanity; for by hearing certain sounds that are like what men commonly use by way of expressing their then present condition, our minds are affected accordingly …
>
> But as to the point of better or worse intrinsically, reason may determine, but feeling [*humour*] must govern and pronounce. For the states of Humanity are infinitely various, and admit of all degrees of good and evil, important or frivolous, sane or distracted. And it must be granted that music which excites the best, most important and sane thinking and acting is, in true judgment, the best music; and this will fall upon the ecclesiastical style.

North's definition of music includes quite a new look to the classification of music. He finds four types of music: solitary, social, ecclesiastical and theatrical. By solitary music he means the music one makes for oneself, either for amusement or for solace.

---

43 John Wilson, *Roger North on Music* (London: Novello, 1959), 291ff.

> With respect to amusement, and relief of an active mind distressed either with too much, or too little employment, nothing under the sun hath that virtue, as a solitary application to music. It is a medicine without any nausea or bitter, and is taken both for pleasure and cure.[44]

His most interesting comments on 'social music' are relative to goals which the composer should attempt to achieve.

> People are apt to censure the whole according to the first and last relish.
>
> ......
>
> Whether the subject be merry or sad, the beginning of a work ought to be serious, and as much as may be majestic.
>
> ......
>
> There should be a continual regard to Humanity; for if there be in Nature any means to move the passions and affections, which were never denied to music, those ought to be pursued, as the best or rather the only means to please.

Church music, more than any kind of music, satisfied two of North's preferences—it was completely solemn ('all levities are excluded') and it was composed of a large sound, with an accompanied full chorus. Here, he says, 'is a body of melody and harmony to fulfill the sharpest appetite to music.' It is interesting that he also mentions the aesthetic advantage given the music by the architecture of the building in which it is performed.

North laments a serious shortage of singers available for church choirs and for this reason he recommends that perhaps the time has come to admit female singers into the choir.

> One might without a desperate solescisme maintain that if females were taken into the choirs instead of boys, it would be a vast improvement of choral music, because women come to a judgment as well as voice, which the boys' do not arrive at before their voices perish ... But both text[45] and morality are against it; and the Roman usage of castration is utterly unlawful, and a scandalous practice where it is used.

Regarding music for the theater, North objected to a tendency for melody to be common in style, vulgar he says, and because of the emphasis on melody the inner parts tended to have little purpose. This music, he says, should be left to its proper owners, the ordinary musicians. Such popular music 'is most apt for driving away thinking, and letting in dancing.'

The fascination with the role of emotion during the Baroque, not to mention the leaving behind of the rational processes, led some to return to thinking of a divine connection in music. The Englishman, Sir Thomas Browne, found the divine even in popular music.

---

[44] Ibid., 257ff.

[45] I Corinthians 14:34:
>As in all the churches of the saints, the women should keep silence in the churches.

> For myself … even that vulgar and tavern music, which makes one man merry, another mad, strikes in me a deep fit of devotion, and a profound contemplation of the first composer. There is something in it of divinity more than the ear discovers: it is an hieroglyphical and shadowed lesson of the whole world, and creatures of God.[46]

In the nineteenth century this 'divine connection' takes the form of a return to the ancient discussion of the soul and of the spiritual qualities of man. For example, Robert Schumann once observed, 'Music is to me the perfect expression of the soul.' And Wagner wrote, 'Music is the revelation of the inner vision of the Essence of the world.'[47]

And so the definition of music comes full circle. After having been side-tracked by the Church's emphasis on the science of music, music was once again something speaking from and to the soul. Since this return to ancient values was also accompanied by such great music during the eighteenth and nineteenth centuries, it makes it even more unimaginable that in the twentieth century composers and music educators would elect to return to the discredited notion of making music a science, or an art synonymous with concepts. Future music teachers will be hard pressed to explain the twentieth century.

This return of medieval scholasticism in the twentieth century, with its emphasis on reason, numbers and concepts, has discouraged any further discussion of the role of music in the formation of character. This role of music was believed by philosophers and educators for more than three thousand years, until our own time. In our time, however, no music educator will dare discuss this role. Are we surprised at our present society and its music?

---

[46] *Sir Thomas Browne's Works*, ed. Simon Wilkin (London: Pickering, 1836), II, 106ff.

[47] *Richard Wagner's Prose Works*, trans. William Ashton Ellis (New York: Broude), V, 108. George Bernard Shaw once observed, 'You use a glass mirror to see your face; you use works of art to see your soul.'

On the Ancient Gods of Music

Whom God loves not, that man loves not music.
Henry Peacham (1576–1643)
The Complete Gentleman

FOR THE ANCIENT CIVILIZATIONS OF GREECE AND ROME we are fortunate to have a considerable extant literature to help us judge what these ancient peoples themselves thought about music and music practice. Even in the case of the ancient Hebrew peoples we have the Old Testament which, even though it has its limits as an historical document, provides clues to the use of a wide variety of music.

With respect to Egypt and the countries of the Eastern Mediterranean there is very little extant literature, save clay tablets. Here we must call upon deduction based on iconography, but no matter how logical are conclusions seem, we must remember these icons represent thousands of years of experience which we really can never know.

A common characteristic of most of the oldest civilizations is that music was always associated with the gods.[1] It is clear that the earliest peoples did not associate music with the other arts, such as painting and sculpture, as we do today. Perhaps it was simply that music is the only art you cannot see. It is easy to understand how painting, for example, could be thought of as a craft, for in looking at a painting you can immediately see the craft. But music is different. While it cannot be seen, it can be immediately understood on an experiential level even by people with no training in music and, moreover, people living in environments far less attractive to the senses than our modern world. All this made music something very different from ordinary life and not uncommonly associated with the gods.

The area of the Near East which we call Mesopotamia consisted first of isolated city-states, among the oldest of which were Ur, Susa and Kish. The area known as Babylonia consisted of Sumeria to the south and Akkad to the north. During the third millennium BC these peoples were united by the Semitic king, Sargon I.

Based on the surviving evidence, Sumeria, ca. 3,000 BC, is the oldest civilization we know which developed a sophisticated tradition of music. Since they believed music was of divine origin, they created temples for a number of gods, all of whom they believed had to be enter-

---

[1] Alfred Sendrey, in *Music in the Social and Religious Life of Antiquity* (Rutherford: Fairleigh Dickinson University Press, 1974), 31, points out that among the most ancient civilizations, only China and the Hebrews did not ascribe music to divine origin. The fact that there is a disproportionate amount of information about temple music of the ancient world only reflects the fact that 'history' was for the most part written by priests.

tained, to keep them in good spirits, by singing and playing of instruments.[2] Among these gods was one called *Enlil*, the father of humanity, who governed with a musical instrument called *al*.

Soon after the beginning of the second millennium the Amorites invaded Sumeria, ending the Sumerian Empire. From the Sumerian capital, Babylon, we take the name of the people of the next period. The Babylonians (2,000–562 BC) were extraordinary people, excelling in mathematics, astronomy, geography and medicine. They founded schools in which they taught cuneiform writing and they first introduced the 354-day calendar with 12-hour days.

With respect to culture, the Babylonians seemed to have little of their own and we can therefore understand that they absorbed completely that of the Sumerians, including their musical traditions. We find a new god, however, *Ea*, who was god of the mysteries and arts, especially associated with the flutist-psalmist.

The Assyrians (750–606 BC), who took their name from the god *Ashur*, were a fierce and warlike collection of tribes who conquered Babylonia. They built the great capital city of Nineveh and began to develop unusual skills in the art of sculpture.[3] But, if it were not for the great stone-reliefs now in the British Museum this empire would probably never be mentioned today, for after their defeat in 612 BC they disappeared from history.

Aside from the stone-reliefs, we can see these feared warriors had also some appreciation for music in the fact that whenever they put a city to the sword, they spared the musicians who, with the rest of the valuable booty, were sent back to Nineveh.[4]

In Egypt (2,686–52 BC), as in other ancient civilizations, the spiritual nature of music caused it to be linked in myth with the gods. We find this especially interesting with respect to the limited hieroglyphic language of Egypt. For example, the symbol which represents the god who created earth is also used to represent the god *Hesu*, who created music.[5] Another dual god, *Hathor*, was both the goddess of love and the goddess of music. A hymn to Hathor found in the temple of Dandera, seems to refer to the 'music of the spheres,' a familiar notion among the ancient philosophers, most notably Pythagoras.

> To thee, the heaven and its stars make music,
> Sun and moon sing praises to thee,
> The whole earth is making music for thee.[6]

There is an extraordinary painting from the more recent Graeco-Roman temple at Medamund, north of Thebes, which includes a complete hymn to the god Hathor. We see a group of female musicians, with harp, drum, and lute, beneath a hieroglyph description:

---

[2] Sendrey, *Music in the Social and Religious Life of Antiquity*, 31.

[3] Carl Engel, *The Music of The Most Ancient Nations* (London: Reeves, 1909), 24ff.

[4] Henry G. Farmer, 'The Music of Ancient Mesopotamia,' in *The New Oxford History of Music* (London: Oxford University Press, 1966), 237.

[5] Sendrey, *Music in the Social and Religious Life of Antiquity*, 37.

[6] Quoted in Lise Manniche, *Music and Musicians in Ancient Egypt* (London: British Museum Press, 1991), 12.

> The members of the choir take up their instruments and play them. The songstreses in full number adore the Golden Goddess and make music to the Golden Goddess: they never cease their chanting.

The text of the hymn is written behind the lutanist and a singer. We take notice especially of the aesthetic aim of this music, 'nourishment for the heart.'

> Come, O Golden Goddess, the singers chant
> for it is nourishment for the heart to dance the *iba*,
> to shine over the feast at the hour of retiring
> and to enjoy dance at night.
>
> Come! The procession takes place at the site of drunkenness,
> this area where one wanders in the marshes.
> Its routine is set, the rules firm:
> nothing is left to be desired.
>
> The royal children satisfy you with what you love
> and the officials give offerings to you.
> The lector priest exalts you singing a hymn,
> and the wise men read the rituals.
>
> The priest honors you with his basket,
> and the drummers take their tambourines.
> Ladies rejoice in your honor with garlands
> and girls with wreaths.
>
> Drunkards play tambourines for you in the cool night,
> and those they wake up bless you.
> The bedouin dance for you in their garments,
> and Asiatics with their sticks.
>
> The griffins wrap their wings around you,
> the hares stand on their hind legs for you.
> The hippopotami adore with wide open mouths,
> and their legs salute your face.[7]

In yet another painting celebrating Hathor, no fewer than twenty-nine female musicians are pictured with percussion instruments.

Another goddess, *Merit*, was considered to be the personification of music. And then there was the strange dwarf god *Bes*, usually associated with childbirth but who, nevertheless, is usually pictured playing a variety of musical instruments. All in all, what we see in these myths is a special significance given to music from the earliest of times.

In the oldest tomb paintings, of the Old Kingdom (2,686–2,181 BC), we can see musicians included in scenes associated with the worship of the gods. In later periods we learn the names of such musicians who are also identified as having positions related to the worship of these gods. One of these, Amenemhab, who appears several times in the Eighteenth Dynasty is

---

7   Ibid., 61.

described in a stela as having 'followed the king's footsteps in foreign lands.' He is identified as holding a very high office, 'overseer of the singers of the North and South,' and he describes his role as a performer in the temple:

> I purify my mouth. I adore the gods. I exalt *Horus* who is in the sky. I adore him. The *Ennead* listens, the inhabitants of the Underworld rejoice. They appear at my voice.

In one tomb painting he is called, 'chief of singers of Amun,' and appears singing to the sun god the following beautiful song.

> Praise to you millions and millions of times!
> I have come to you, adoring your beauty.
> Your mother Nut [the sky] embraces you.
> You are joyful as you traverse the sky and the earth.
> May the gods of the Underworld [as the sun passes underneath the earth] worship you and sing your praise when you hear my words which worship you every day,
> So that you endow me with a burial in peace after enduring old age and my *ba* being among my ancestors, following the king.[8]

When female musicians appear in the New Kingdom Period (1,567–1,085 BC), some of them also have apparent positions in the temple, with titles such as 'Chief of the Singers.' The tomb paintings tell us of music in the temple by both solo and choral singers, dances accompanied by instruments, and processions around the altar. The tendency toward string instruments in temple scenes leads Sendrey to speculate regarding the character of the temple music:

> We must consider its character solemn and sedate; from this we may conclude that their sacred music must have been rigid and formal, similar to the ceremonies of their ritual.[9]

The literature of the most recent period speaks of observances of a religious-cult which were much less somber. The early historian, Herodotus, for example, describes two such festivals.

> When they travel to Bubastis, this is what they do. They sail thither, men and women together, and a great number of each in each boat. Some of the women have rattles and rattle them, others play the aulos through the entire trip, and the remainder of the women and men sing and clap their hands. As they travel on toward Bubastis and come near some other city, they edge the boat near the bank, and some of the women do as I have described. But others of them scream obscenities in derision of the women who live in that city, and others of them set to dancing, and others still, standing up, throw their clothes open to show their nakedness. This they do at every city along the riverbank. When they come to Bubastis, they celebrate the festival with great sacrifices, and more wine is drunk at that single festival than in all the rest of the year besides. There they throng together, man and woman (but no children), up to the number of seven hundred thousand, as the natives say.[10]

......

---

[8] Quoted in Farmer, 'The Music of Ancient Mesopotamia,' 59.

[9] Sendrey, *Music in the Social and Religious Life of Antiquity*, 49.

[10] *The History of Herodotus*, trans. David Grene (Chicago: University of Chicago Press, 1987), 157.

> On the eve of the festival of Dionysus, each one of them cuts the throat of his pig in front of the doorway and then gives it, to take away, to the swineherd who has sold it to him. For the rest of the festival in honor of Dionysus, except for the dance choruses, the Egyptians celebrate it almost in everything like the Greeks. But instead of phalluses they have another invention, which are eighteen-inch-high images, controlled by strings, which the women carry round the villages; these images have a penis that nods and in size is not much less than all the rest of the body. Ahead there goes an aulos player, and the women follow, singing in honor of Dionysus.[11]

Athenaeus,[12] speaking of the period of Ptolemy (285–246 BC), quotes a reference to a 'choral band of 600 men,' with three hundred harp players participating in the music for such a festival.

A fragment by the Greek philosopher and poet, Xenophanes (570–480 BC) seems to criticize the epic poets Homer and Hesiod saying they have, 'attributed to the gods all things which are disreputable and worthy of blame when done by men.'

Among the Alexandrian poets, Bion says music is sweeter even than love![13] We especially like, among these love poems, one by Hermesianax about a teacher, Aristippus, who left his school and job to chase his love, Lais, 'whose loveliness has never been described.'

> To her he fled; and so he left behind
> The lecture hall and audience as well;
> Unto his love he clung with heart and mind.

We mention this poem also because it later reveals to us that the Greek god, *Zeus*, guards all who serve the Muse!

Plutarch (46–127 AD) wrote that 'some have thought that God himself played upon the aulos.'[14] He was probably referring to Apollo, into whose rites he had been initiated.

In the Old Testament we are told that the Hebrew god was also a musician. Zechariah 9:14 tells us God was a trumpet player, although Psalm 105 describes him as a choral conductor.[15]

Among the Roman poets of the early Christian era there were some who still gave credit for their inspiration to the gods, as we see in Ovid.

> Now, since a god inspires my lips, I will dutifully follow the inspiring god; I'll open Delphi and the heavens themselves and unlock the oracles of the sublime mind. Great matters, never traced out by the minds of former men, things that have long been hidden, I will sing.[16]
>
> ......

---

[11] Ibid., 152.

[12] Athenaeus, in *Deipnosophistae*, V, 201.

[13] 'Fragment XVIII,' in Henry H. Chamberlin, *Last Flowers* (Cambridge: Harvard University Press, 1937), 61.

[14] 'Concerning Music.' In 'The Banquet of the Seven Wise Men,' he points out that 'the Gods are better pleased with the sounds of panpipes and the aulos than with the voice of men.'

[15] The early Church father, Clement of Alexandria, also referred to 'the Choir-master, the Lord,' in 'The Miscellanies,' trans. William Wilson (Edinburgh: T & T Clark, 1884), VI, xi.

[16] Ovid, *Metamorphoses*, XV, 143.

> Be kind, ye fair, to the poetic choir.
> Whom Muses love and deities inspire.
> God's in us and with heaven we discourse,
> In springs divine our instinct has its source.[17]

A poem of Tibullus warns the ladies to have respect for the poets who are favored by the gods.

> But you, my girl, watch out; the gods love poets;
> I warn you, have respect for a sacred bard
> singing of Messalinus, who drives before him
> whole conquered cities—the victor, battle-scarred
> and crowned with bay, while round him his bay-wreathed soldiers
> deafen the crown with their wild triumphal song.[18]

The poet, Statius (45–96 AD) has a grim and pessimistic poem, 'Thebaid,' in which evil gods arrange for the murder of sleeping Thebans, including a musician.

> Alert Ialmenus, now never to see the dawn,
> had played his lyre to the last stars, singing the paean
> of Thebes. The god pressed his weakened neck to the left,
> and his head lay heedlessly against the lyre.
> Agylleus thrust a sword through his chest and impaled
> his right hand, ready-poised on the hollow lyre-shell,
> his fingers quivering on the strings.[19]

In a similar dark mood, Ovid tells of one poet who was *not* protected by the gods, in fact he was murdered in the act of performance!

> And poor Lampetides—he had been summoned
> To no such revels, only to play the lute,
> To grace the feast with song, and so he stood there
> Holding the ivory quill, surely no fighter,
> And Pettalus mocked him: 'Sing that song in Hell,
> The rest of it, at least!' and pierced his temple,
> And as he fell, the dying fingers struggled,
> To play once more, and made only a discord.[20]

Perhaps this contributed to Ovid finally indicating he had lost faith in the gods. He reveals this in an interesting passage, while nevertheless mentioning again that the poets, who were also singers at this time, are favored by the gods.

---

[17] Ovid, *The Love Poems*, III, 547.
[18] Tibullus, *Poems*, II, v. In the Poem III, iv, Apollo says 'Gods love all poets.'
[19] Statius, *Thebaid*, X, 304.
[20] Ovid, *Metamorphoses*, V, 111ff.

> We bards are classed as holy, heaven's care;
> Divinity, they say, flows in our veins.
> But every holy thing brash death profanes;
> There's nothing that his murky clutches spare.
>
> Orpheus' great parents—what did they avail?
> Or song whose magic power the beasts subdued?
> To sad reluctant lyre in the wild wood
> 'Ah, Linus, Linus' went his father's wail.
>
> And Homer too, whose founts of song inspire
> The Muses' streams on poets' lips for ay,
> Sank to Avernus' depths on his last day:
> Verse, verse alone escapes the insatiate pyre.
>
> In poetry the toils of Troy live on,
> And that slow web night's cunning would unwind.
> So Nemesis and Delia fame will find,
> Who last and first their poet's worship won.
>
> What use is that Egyptian ritual,
> Those timbrels, these long nights of chastity?
> When evil fate dooms good men, may I be
> forgiven if I've no faith in gods at all![21]

Although not one of the ancient gods or muses, one of the Christian saints, St. Cecilia, has become in the English-speaking world, in effect, a modern god of music. The oldest account of St. Cecilia is found in the 'Martyrologium Hieronymianum' and her feast day has been celebrated since the fourth century. By an early date this celebration fell on 22 November, on which it is still commemorated today.

Since the fourteenth century she has been pictured with an organ near by, or is represented as playing on the organ, evidently based on an incorrect translation of *organis*, 'instruments.' In any case this began the association with music and this has resulted in many poems and compositions in her honor.

Among the English Restoration poems are several dedicated to the honor of St. Cecilia's Day, which had become a traditional day to honor music. Joseph Addison has written two such poems.[22] In his 'A Song for St. Cecilia's Day,' he begins in praise of the patron saint.

> Let all Cecilia's praise proclaim,
> Employ the echo in her name,
> Hark how the flutes and trumpets raise,
> At bright Cecilia's name, their lays;
> The organ labors in her praise.
> Cecilia's name does all our numbers grace,

---

[21] Ovid, *Amores*, III, 9.

[22] Joseph Addison (1672–1719) was a fellow at Magdalen College, Oxford, and was very active in politics, eventually becoming Secretary of State.

> From every voice the tuneful accents fly,
> In soaring trebles now it rises high,
> And now it sinks, and dwells upon the base.
> Cecilia's name through all the notes we sing,
> The work of every skillful tongue,
> The sound of every trembling string,
> The sound and triumph of our song.

Now he turns to the purposes of music, including the emotions and character development:

> For ever consecrate the day,
> To music and Cecilia;
> Music, the greatest good that mortals know,
> And all of heaven we have below.
> Music can noble hints impart,
> Engender fury, kindle love;
> With unsuspected eloquence can move,
> And manage all the man with secret art …

He concludes with a poetic reference to the Day of Judgment.

> When time itself shall be no more,
> And all things in confusion hurled,
> Music shall then exert its power,
> And sound survive the ruins of the world.

The second poem on this subject by Addison is called 'Ode for St. Cecilia's Day,' written in 1699 and set to music by Daniel Purcell. In this work he concentrates on aesthetic characterizations of the violin, flute, organ and trumpet and eventually mentions improvisation ('divisions') in church music.

> First let the sprightly violin
> The joyful melody begin,
> And none of all her strings be mute;
> While the sharp sound and shriller lay
> In sweet harmonious notes decay,
> Softened and mellowed by the flute.
>
> Next, let the solemn organ join
> Religious airs, and strains divine,
> Such as may lift us to the skies,
> And set all Heaven before our eyes.
>
> Let then the trumpet's piercing sound
> Our ravished ears with pleasure wound.
> The soul overpowering with delight,
> As, with a quick uncommon ray,
> A streak of lightening clears the day,

> And flashes on the sight.
> Let Echo too perform her part,
> Prolonging every note with art,
> And in a low expiring strain
> Play all the concert over again …
>
> And now the choir complete rejoices,
> With trembling strings and melting voices.
> The tuneful ferment rises high,
> And works with mingled melody.
> Quick divisions run their rounds,
> A thousand trills and quivering sounds
> In airy circles over us fly,
> Till, wafted by a gentle breeze,
> They faint and languish by degrees,
> And at a distance die.

As in the above case, most of these St. Cecilia Odes were set to music. William Congreve wrote a poem, 'A Hymn to Harmony,' in honor of St. Cecilia's Day of 1701, which was set to music of 'John Eccles, Master of Her Majesties Musick.' John Oldham's (1653–1683) 'Ode for an Anniversary of Musick on St. Cecilia's Day,' was set to music by 'Dr. Blow.'

> Begin the song, your instruments advance
> Tune the voice, and tune the flute,
> Touch the silent, sleeping lute,
> And make the strings to their own measures dance.

After a nice phrase, this Ode summarizes the values of music:

> How dull were life, how hardly worth our care,
> But for the charms that musick lends!
>   ……
>
> Musick's the cordial of a troubled breast,
> The softest remedy that grief can find;
> The gentle spell, that charms our care to rest,
> And calms the ruffled passions of the mind.
> Musick does all our joys refine,
> It gives the relish to our wine,
> 'Tis that gives rapture to our love,
> And wings devotion to a pitch divine;
> 'Tis our chief bliss on earth, and half our heaven above.[23]

---

[23] In *The Works of John Oldham* (London: Bettenham, 1722), II, 254.

Alexander Pope also contributed an 'Ode to St. Cecilia's Day,' one which begins with a call to the Muses:

> Descend, ye Nine! descend and sing;
> The breathing instruments inspire.[24]

Next Pope offers a catalog of the purposes and virtues of music.

> By Music, minds an equal temper know,
> Nor swell too high, nor sink too low.
> If in the breast tumultuous joys arise,
> Music her soft, assuasive voice applies;
> Or when the soul is pressed with cares,
> Exalts her in enlivening airs.
> Warriors she fires with animated sounds;
> Pours balm into the bleeding lover's wounds:
> Melancholy lifts her head,
> Morpheus rouses from his bed,
> Sloth unfolds her arms and wakes,
> Listening Envy drops her snakes;
> Intestine war no more our Passions wage,
> And giddy Factions hear away their rage.
>   ……
> Music the fiercest grief can charm,
> And fate's severest rage disarm:
> Music can soften pain to ease,
> And make despair and madness please.

Jonathan Swift has written an ode which reflects the instruments of the French court which had accompanied the restoration of Charles II.

> Grave Dean of St. Patrick's, how comes it to pass,
> That you, who know music no more than an ass,
> That you who so lately were writing of drapiers,
> Should lend your cathedral to players and scrapers [violinists]?
> To act such an opera once in a year,
> So offensive to every true Protestant ear,
> With trumpets, and fiddles, and organs, and singing,
> Will sure the Pretender and Popery bring in,
> No Protestant Prelate, his lordship or grace,
> Durst there show his right, or most reverend face:
> How would it pollute their crosiers and rochets,
> To listen to minims, and quavers, and crotchets![25]

---

[24] 'Ode on St. Cecilia's Day,' in *The Works of Alexander Pope* (New York: Gordian Press, 1967), IV, 397ff.

[25] 'Dr. Swift to Himself on St. Cecilia's Day.'

The most important purpose of music is to express emotions and we have an extraordinary testimonial to this purpose in one of John Dryden's (1631–1700) most famous odes, his 'A Song for St. Cecilia's Day, 1687,'[26] a work which was set to music by Giovanni Draghi. He begins by suggesting that the earth and man were created in harmony[27] by God.

> From Harmony, from heavenly Harmony
> This universal frame began:
> From Harmony to Harmony
> Through all the compass of the notes it ran,
> The Diapason closing full in Man.

But he quickly turns to the emotional essence of music, in a burst of enthusiasm, 'What Passion cannot Musick raise and quell!' Now he presents a remarkable survey of the emotional qualities which he associates with various musical instruments, expressed in his most vivid choice of words.

> The TRUMPETS loud clangor
> Excites us to arms
> With shrill notes of anger …
> ……
>
> The double double double beat
> Of the thundering DRUM …
> ……
>
> The soft complaining FLUTE
> In dying Notes discovers
> The woes of hopeless lovers,
> Whose dirge is whispered by the warbling LUTE.
> ……
>
> Sharp VIOLINS proclaim
> Their jealous pangs, and desperation,
> Fury, frantick indignation,
> Depth of pains, and height of passion …
> ……
>
> But oh! what Art can teach
> What human voice can reach
> The sacred ORGANS praise?
> Notes inspiring holy love,
> Notes that wing their heavenly ways
> To mend the choirs above.

---

[26] The best known ode which Dryden wrote for the celebration of St. Cecilia's Day (in 1697) carries the title 'Alexander's Feast or The Power of Music.' It is more celebrated as poetry, but is no less valuable for our purposes as it is an allegorical work which brings to life several ancient Greek gods. We read of 'flying fingers' on the lyre addressed to Jove and of trumpets, drums and hautboys in praise of Bacchus.

[27] It is interesting that research in physics has found that each organ of the body produces a specific pitch.

Dryden concludes with a reference to the music of the spheres and the trumpet of the Day of Judgment, whose 'Musick shall untune the sky.'[28]

---

[28] *The Works of John Dryden*, ed. Edward Hooker (Berkeley: University of California Press, 1956), III, 201ff.

Of Ancient Muses and Myths

Grant me music, Mercury, as you did when
Stones moved into place for Amphion singing;
Bear my song, O tortoise-shell deftly strung with
Seven strings sounding ...[1]

THE READER HAS FOUND IN THE PREVIOUS CHAPTERS evidence of how difficult it was for earlier men to explain exactly what music was. As they resorted instead to associate music with religion and ancient gods, so also the ancient Greek myths fall into this category. In this case it was often performers who, not being able to explain where their musical ideas and talent came from, often attributed their inspiration to mythical figures. Such was the case of the prayer above uttered by Horace to the god Mercury to provide musical inspiration. This tradition, at least as represented in literature, continued until fairly modern times.

The Greek myths and mythical gods are actually an important chapter in our civilization's history. These myths, while only colorful stories to us, were for the early Greeks not fables, but at the very least an important handed down oral tradition from a period before the arrival of Greek writing. While we can't think of them as genuine oral history, yet there may be embedded in these stories small nuggets of historical possibilities. Consider, for example, the myth of the sea god, Triton, and his 'invention' of the trumpet. He, we are told, in the war against the giants, blew into a sea conch producing sounds so new and frightening that the giants, thinking they had encountered a terrible and ferocious monster, took flight. Well, if we leave out the part about the giants, it certainly is easy to imagine this as a possible scenario for the discovery of the trumpet-type instrument. That is to say, some distant man walking along the shore, picking up a large conch and blowing through it to remove the water and sand, may have produced a frightening sound.

Similarly, when Ovid relates a mythical musical contest between Pan and his panpipes and Apollo with his lyre,[2] a contest which the latter wins, could not this be viewed as an allegorical testament to the transformation of Greek music from more ancient rural roots to the much more sophisticated music of the lyric poets?[3]

The lyric poets, of the seventh and sixth centuries BC, felt a particular relationship to the mythical figures we call the 'Muses.' Bacchylides (sixth century BC), for example, defined his music as a gift of the Muses,

---

[1] Horace, *Odes*, I, 12.

[2] *Metamorphoses*, Bk. XI.

[3] Athenaeus, in *Deipnosophistae*, IX, 390, quotes Chamaeleon of Pontus as saying, 'The men of old devised the invention of music from the birds singing in solitary places; by way of imitating them, men instituted the art of music.'

a monument not made with hands, [that it] might be a common joy for mankind.⁴

From the lyric poets we read several times of the importance of their being inspired. In Pindar (b. ca. 518 BC) for example,

> Pisa too enjoins
> My speech, for from her bidding come to men
> The songs inspired of heaven …⁵

and in Bacchylides.

> … for the inspired prophet of the violet-eyed Muses is ready to sing.⁶

This special relationship the lyric poets felt with the gods and muses, addressing pleas to their gods for inspiration, finds common ground centuries later when Bach would sometimes pen a note at the top of his manuscripts asking for God's help.

Pindar adds that this inspiration from the gods is a gift for which the poet must maintain respect.

> For to insult the gods is a fool's wisdom,
> A craft most damned, and unmeasured boasting
> Is music for mad minds. Let no voice babble
> Such follies.⁷

We begin our discussion with those Muses who have enjoyed associations with music, both among ancient and more recent writers.

CLIO, THE MUSE OF HISTORY.

One of the nine daughters of Jupiter and Mnemosyne (Memory), they also include:

Calliope, Muse of Epic Poetry
Euterpe, Muse of Lyric Poetry
Melpomene, Muse of Tragedy
Terpsichore, Muse of Choral Dance and Song
Erato, Muse of Love Poetry
Polyhymnia, Muse of Sacred Poetry
Urania, Muse of Astronomy and
Thalia, Muse of Comedy.

---

4 Ode for an Athenian, Winner of the Foot Races at Isthmus.
5 Ode to Theron of Acragas, Winner of the Chariot Race.
6 Ode for Automedes of Philius, Victor in the Pentathlon at Nemea.
7 Ode for Epharmostus of Opous, Winner of the Wrestling Match.

Horace (65–8 BC) addressed a plea for subject matter to the Muse Clio.

> Come, what man or demigod shall you choose to
> Hymn with lyre or high-shrilling pipe, Muse Clio,
> Or what god? Whose name shall be lifted up and
> Sportively echoed
>
> Down the shaded glens of Mount Helicon or
> On the slopes of Pindus or snow-capped Haemus?
> There the forests crowded to follow singing
> Orpheus, whose music
>
> (Taught him by his mother) made rushing rivers
> Cease their flow and blustering winds be silent,
> All so sweetly sounding to strings of lyre that
> Ears grew on oak trees.[8]

MERCURY

A son to Jupiter and Maia, said to be of sweet voice and persuasive in speech, inventer of the lyre and aulos and forerunner of mathematicians and astronomers.

Tertulian (b. ca. 160 AD), one of the early Church fathers, assigns the invention of the aulos to Minerva. Mercury, having invented letters, he calls the god of music notation.[9]

To Mercury, Horace addresses a plea for musical inspiration.

> Grant me music, Mercury, as you did when
> Stones moved into place for Amphion singing;
> Bear my song, O tortoise-shell deftly strung with
> Seven strings sounding.[10]

Here we have an example of how myths may reflect historical events from long before any form of written history. In this instance, Mercury is said to have invented, a few hours after birth, the lyre by stretching sheep-gut strings over the hollow of a tortoise shell. He was also the god of athletics and a 'master' of language, all of which are mentioned by Horace.

> Nimble-spoken Mercury, Atlas' grandson,
> Who by speech astutely advanced mankind from
> Brute and worked a comeliness into him by
> Grace of gymnastics,
>
> You I sing, great Jupiter's herald bearing
> Words of gods, first founder of song and lyre-shell …[11]

---

8 Horace, *Odes*, I, 12.

9 Tertullian, 'Spectacles,' trans. Rudolph Arbesmann in *Disciplinary, Moral and Ascetical Works* (New York: Fathers of the Church, 1959), X, 8.

10 Horace, *Odes*, III, 11.

11 Ibid., I, 10.

This myth is mentioned again by Cassiodorus (490–585 AD) in a letter to the famous Boethius (480–524 AD). His purpose in writing was to ask Boethius to find a harp player to fulfill a request by Clovis, king of the Franks, whom Cassiodorus suggests has 'heard of the fame of my banquets.'

> It is the talking loom of the Muses, with speaking wefts and singing warps, on which the plectrum shrilly weaves sweet sounds. Now this instrument Mercury is said to have discovered, modeling it on the mottled tortoise. As the bringer of such benefits, astronomers have believed it should be sought among the stars, urging that music must be heavenly, since they can detect the shape of a lyre placed among the constellations.[12]

CALLIOPE, Muse of Epic Poetry

Plato (427–347) mentioned Calliope in relating a discussion by Socrates which centered on an ancient fable about a grasshopper which illustrates the power of music to carry away the listener. We are pleased to find Socrates' assurance here that the Muses know who among us honors them!

> SOCRATES. A lover of music like yourself ought surely to have heard the story of the grasshoppers, who are said to have been human beings in an age before the Muses. And when the Muses came and song appeared the grasshoppers were ravished with delight; and singing always, never thought of eating and drinking, until at last in their forgetfulness they died. And now they live again in the grasshoppers, who, as a special gift from the Muses, require no nourishment, but from the hour of their birth are always singing, and ever eating and drinking; and when they die they go and inform the Muses in heaven which of us honors one or other of the Muses. They win the love of Terpsichore for the dancers by their report of them; of Erato for the lovers, and of the other Muses for those who do them honor, according to the several ways of honoring them;—and to Calliope the eldest Muse and Urania who is next to her, they make a report of those who honor music of their kind, and spend their time in philosophy; for these are the Muses who are chiefly concerned with the heavens and with reasoning, divine as well as human, and they have the sweetest utterance.[13]

A plea for inspiration is addressed by Horace to the Muse, Calliope ('beautiful voiced').

> Calliope, descend from the skies, O queen,
> And sing your flute a lingering melody,
> Or lift your lovely voice alone, or
> Sing to the lyre or the harp of Phoebus.[14]

---

[12] Letter to Boethius, in *Variae*, trans. Thomas Hodgkin (London: Frowde, 1886) II, xl.

[13] *Phdaerus*, 259c.

[14] Horace, *Odes*, III, 4.

MELPOMENE, Muse of Tragedy.

In another ode, to commemorate the death of his friend Quintilius, Horace appeals to another of the Muses, Melpomene, for help.

> Could shy reticence set limits to grief for so
> Fondly cherished a head? Teach me your saddest strains,
> Muse Melpomene,[15] whom All-father blessed with pure
> Voice along with the lyre he gave …
>
> Say you drew from the lyre lovelier tones than did
> Thracian Orpheus when trees harkened to hear him play.[16]

JOVE, another name for Jupiter.

Supreme ruler of the universe, wisest of the divinities, Jupiter was the gatherer of clouds and snow, dispenser of rains, winds and thunder. Under the name of Zeus, he was the patron god of the Roman State.

Ovid describes a professional singer who begins his song with an appeal to Jove for inspiration. Before this, however, he gives us a rare reference to the musician tuning up, with a specific indication of some kind of harmony.

> And when he had tried the chords by touching them with his thumb, and his ears told him that the notes were in harmony although they were of different pitch, he raised his voice in this song: 'From Jove, O Muse, my mother—for all things yield to the sway of Jove—inspire my song! Oft have I sung the power of Jove before; I have sung the giants in a heavier strain, and the victorious bolts hurled on the Phlegraean plains. But now I need the gentler touch, for I would sing of boys beloved by gods, and maidens inflamed by unnatural love and paying the penalty of their lust.'[17]

APOLLO, also known as Phoebus, son to Jupiter (Zeus)

Apollo was the patron of music, poetry and medicine. This is the beginning of the long association between music and medicine.

Tibullus (54–19 BC) attributes to Apollo not only the usual association with music, but also emphasizes his powers of prophesy. We remind the reader that all poetry at this time was sung.

> His long robes hid the hallowed form from sight,
>   and the hem seemed to ripple round his feet.
> At his left side a lyre hung, worked with skill
>   that made it gleam with gold and tortoise-shell,
> and while he sang, he plucked it with a quill.

---

[15] Melpomene, 'Songstress,' from the Greek *melos*, or *melody*.
[16] Horace, *Odes*, I, 24.
[17] Ovid, *Metamorphoses*, X, 143.

> But O the warning sung at that song's end!
> 'Gods love all poets,' he said, 'and such men find
> Bacchus, Apollo, and each Muse a friend.'
> Yet those wise sisters and the god of wine—
> they lack the power to see the future plain.
> Jove's gift of foresight is not theirs but mine.
> To me, inevitable fate is clear.[18]

Tibullus mentions prophesy in association with Apollo in another poem, although here he goes under the name Phoebus.

> Your blessing, Phoebus; a new priest enters your temple.
> Be gracious, greet his coming with voice and lyre,
> and when your fingers set the strings to sounding,
> let it be loyalty that they inspire.
> Come, be among us while we heap the altars,
> your brow encircled with a wreath of bay—
> comb your long hair, put on your treasured raiment,
> O come, god bright and beautiful as the day!
> Be as you were when you sang of Jove's triumph
> with Saturn finally driven from the throne.
> Prophet, the priest who serves you learns the meaning
> of the notes of that bard to which the future is known.
> You guide the lots as they fall; you show the augur
> what marks of the god to read in the entrails;
> with you as master, the Sibyl's six-metered strophes
> have given us counsel whose wisdom never fails.[19]

According to Greek mythology, Apollo killed Cyclops, forger of the thunderbolts of Zeus, to avenge the death of his son at the hands of Zeus. In return, Zeus forced Apollo to serve for a time as a herder for the mortal king, Admetus. It is in this role that we see Apollo, in Ovid's (43 BC–17 AD) *Metamorphoses*, living the life of a shepherd and playing on panpipes.

> … for Apollo
> Could never change the will of Jove: moreover,
> Even if he could, he was not there, but living
> In Elis at the time, where he had taken
> A shepherd's cloak, a pipe of seven reeds,
> A forest wand for staff, and all his thinking
> Of love and playing music, so his cattle
> Went wandering off and Mercury saw them, stole them,
> Drove them into a forest where he hid them.[20]

---

[18] Tibullus, *Poems*, III, iv.

[19] Ibid., II, v. Propertius, in Poem II, 31, tells of visiting a temple built to honor Apollo by Caesar Augustus. He describes seeing a marble statue of Apollo, posed as singing with his lyre.

[20] Ovid, *Metamorphoses*, II, 677ff.

Tibullus also mentions this aspect of the Apollo myth, with interesting musical references. Here Apollo himself speaks,

> It is not told in mockery that I
> served as Admetus' shepherd, long ago,
> and lost the will to play the lyre, or try
> new harmonies for voice and strings to share—
> but used an unstopped pipe, in my despair …[21]

In another place, Tibullus also attributes to Apollo, who was also the god of medicine, the power to heal the sick through music.

> Come near, Apollo, come and make me well—
> heal me, Apollo of the flowing hair …
> Be near me, holy presence; bring your songs
> and all your delicacies that soothe the sick.[22]

Lucian of Samosata (b. ca. 125 AD) mentioned Apollo in the context of a fictional banquet of the gods:

> Apollo harped, Silenus danced his wild measures, the Muses uprose and sang to us from Hesiod's Birth of Gods, and the first of Pindar's odes.[23]

In discussing the proverb, 'Babys plays the [aulos] even worse,' Erasmus (1466–1536) mentions a Greek myth we have not read elsewhere.

> Babys, they say, was a brother of Marsyas, the man who was not afraid to challenge Apollo himself to a musical contest. When he was defeated, he was suspended by Apollo from a pine-tree upside down, and flayed. Then, when Apollo was preparing to destroy Babys too, Pallas interceded for him, saying that his aulos playing was so unsuccessful and unskillful that clearly he was quite negligible; 'Babys' she said 'plays even worse.' Apollo was impressed by her words, and treated Babys with such disdain that he did not even think him worthy of punishment, but judged it better to abandon him to his incompetence.[24]

As the patron of music, Apollo has attracted the attention of numerous later poets. We find him, for example, in Shakespeare's *Cymbeline*. In a scene intended to be humorous, Cloten arranges a morning serenade by a group of string players in an attempt to woo Imogen.

---

[21] Tibullus, *Poems*, III, iv.

[22] Ibid., III, x.

[23] Lucian, *Icaromenippus*.

[24] 'Adages,' in Ibid., XXXIV, 18.

CLOTEN. It's almost morning, is't not?
1. LORD. Day, my lord.
CLOTEN. I would this music would come. I am advised to give her music o' mornings; they say it will penetrate

Enter Musicians.

Come on; tune. If you can penetrate her with your fingering, so; we'll try with tongue too: if none will do, let her remain; but I'll never give o'er. First, a very excellent good-conceited thing; after, a wonderful sweet air, with admirable rich words to it: and then let her consider.

Song

> Hark! hark! the lark at heaven's gate sings,
> And Phoebus 'gins arise,
> His steeds to water at those springs
> On chalic'd flowers that lies;
> And winking Mary-buds begin
> To open their golden eyes:
> With everything that pretty is,
> My lady sweet, arise:
> Arise, arise!

The influence of the ancient lyric poets of Greece is still much in evidence among the seventeenth-century English poets. Even surrounded by the Puritan threats, one still finds the poet appealing to the Muses for inspiration, as for example Robert Herrick (1591–1674) in his 'To Apollo. A short Hymn,'

> Phoebus! when that I a Verse,
> Or some numbers more rehearse;
> Tune my words, that they may fall,
> Each way smoothly Musical.[25]

DIANA, TWIN SISTER TO APOLLO, AND DAUGHTER TO ZEUS AND LATONA.

Diana, despising the weakness of love, imposed upon her nymphs vows of perpetual maidenhood. Associated with hunting, when weary of the chase she turned to music and dancing.

We have a hymn to Diana by Horace which begins,

> Raise your hymn, tender girls, sing of Diana now,
> Hymn the Cynthian,[26] lads, god of the unshorn locks,
> Sing Latona as well, most
> Deeply loved by the heart of Jove.[27]

---

[25] Quoted in L. C. Martin, *The Poetical Works of Robert Herrick* (Oxford: Clarendon Press, 1963), 122.
[26] This refers to Apollo, who according to tradition was born on Mount Cynthus.
[27] Horace, *Odes*, I, 21.

NEPTUNE, ONE OF THE GREAT GODS, FOUNDER OF THE YOUNGER DYNASTY OF THE WATERS.

Horace begins a poem in praise of Neptune and then progresses to several other deities as well.

> I shall start with a song about
> Neptune's might and his nymphs green-haired within the sea;
> You shall then take the lyre and sing
> Of Latona and swift Cynthia's whetted darts;
> Hers my song who with swan-yoked car
> Visits Paphus and rules Cnidus and all the isles
> Of the glittering Cyclades;
> Lastly, we will salute Night with a lullaby.[28]

ORPHEUS, CHIEF REPRESENTATIVE OF SONG AND THE LYRE.

Taught by Apollo to play the lyre, Orpheus journeyed to Egypt to study the gods and their rites. Returning with the knowledge of these orgiastic rites, some consider him the founder of the Dionysian celebrations. He also reached a high degree of influence because he was believed to have discovered mysteries, purification from sins, cures of diseases and the means of averting divine wrath.

In the most familiar myth of Orpheus, he goes to Hades to look for Eurydice, who has been killed by a snake. Orpheus is killed there, but his ghost remains with his beloved Eurydice. Ovid, in his *Metamorphoses*, has Orpheus killed on earth. This passage, while violent, has numerous and interesting references to music.

> While with such songs the bard of Thrace drew the trees, held beasts enthralled and constrained stones to follow him, behold, the crazed women of the Cicones, with skins flung over their breasts, saw Orpheus from a hill top, fitting songs to the music of his lyre. Then one of these, her tresses streaming in the gentle breeze, cried out: 'See, see the man who scorns us!' and hurled her spear straight at the tuneful mouth of Apollo's bard; but this, wreathed in leaves, marked without harming him. Another threw a stone, which, even as it flew through the air, was overcome by the sweet sound of voice and lyre, and fell at his feet as if it would ask forgiveness for its mad attempt. But still the assault waxed reckless: their passion knew no bounds; mad fury reigned. And all their weapons would have been harmless under the spell of song; but the huge noise of the Berecyntian flutes, mixed with discordant horns, the drums, and the breast-beatings and howlings of the Bacchanals, drowned the lyre's sound; and then at last the stone's were reddened with the blood of the bard whose voice they could not hear. First away went the multitudinous birds still spellbound by the singer's voice, with the snakes and the train of beasts, the glory of Orpheus' audience, harried by the Maenads; then these turned bloody hands against Orpheus and flocked around like birds when in the day they see the bird of night wandering in the daylight; and as when in the amphitheater in the early morning of the spectacle the doomed stag in the arena is the prey of dogs. They rushed upon the bard and hurled at him their wands wreathed with green vines, not made for such use as this. Some threw clods, some branches torn from trees, and some threw stones. And, that real weapons might not be

---

[28] Ibid., III, 28.

wanting to their madness, it chanced that oxen, toiling beneath the yoke, were plowing up the soil; and not far from these, stout peasants were digging the hard earth and sweating at their work. When these beheld the advancing horde, they fled away and left behind the implements of their toil. Scattered through the deserted fields lay hoes, long mattocks and heavy grubbing tools. These the savage women caught up and, first tearing in pieces the oxen who threatened them with their horns, they rushed back to slay the bard; and, as he stretched out his suppliant hands, uttering words then, but never before, unheeded, and moving them not a whit by his voice, the impious women struck him down. And (oh, the pity of it!) through those lips, to which rocks listened, and to which the hearts of savage beasts responded, the soul, breathed out, went faring forth in air.

The mourning birds wept for thee, Orpheus, the throng of beasts, the flinty rocks, and the trees which had so often gathered to thy songs; yes, the trees shed their leaves as if so tearing their hair in grief for thee. They say that the rivers also were swollen with their own tears, and the naiads and dryads alike mourned with disheveled hair and with dark bordered garments. The poet's limbs lay scattered all around; but his head and lyre, O Hebrus, thou didst receive, and (a marvel!) while they floated in mid-stream the lyre gave forth some mournful notes, mournfully the lifeless tongue murmured, mournfully the banks replied. And now, borne onward to the sea, they left their native stream and gained the shore of Lesbos near the city of Methymna. Here, as the head lay exposed upon a foreign strand, a savage serpent attacked it and its streaming locks still dripping with the spray. But Phoebus at last appeared, drove off the snake just in the act to bite, and hardened and froze to stone, just as they were, the serpent's widespread, yawning jaws.

The poet's shade fled beneath the earth, and recognized all the places he had seen before; and, seeking through the blessed fields, found Eurydice and caught her in his eager arms.[29]

Seneca (3 BC–65 AD) mentions Phoebus [Apollo] with his 'unequal pipes' [the panpipes, as opposed to the aulos][30] and the frequently told tale of Orpheus using music to conquer nature.

Orpheus born of the melodious Muse, whose plectrum evoked chords at which torrents halted and winds fell silent, at whose music the birds left off their song and with the whole woodland attending followed the singer ...[31]

An extraordinary variant of this myth reappears in a thirteenth-century collection of fables known as *Gesta Romanorum*. Here an emperor, faced with a wild elephant in his forest, finds two beautiful virgins who are musicians and sends them naked into the forest to tame the elephant. Sure enough, their music causes the elephant to fall asleep, with his head on one of the girl's lap (!), whereupon the other girl cuts it off![32]

Desiderius Erasmus (1469–1536) was the greatest humanist, scholar and writer of prose of the sixteenth century. He was born near Rotterdam and left an orphan while still a teenager. The executor of his parents estate, in order obtain everything for himself, gave Erasmus over to a monastic career.

---

[29] Ovid, *Metamorphoses*, XI, 1ff.

[30] Seneca, *Hippolytus*. Phoebus is mentioned again in *Oedipus*, 494.

[31] Seneca, *Medea*, 620, also 350.

[32] *Gesta Romanorum*, trans. Charles Swan (London: C. and J. Rivington, 1824), II, 128.

He quotes the great testimonials of music found in ancient literature, but sometimes he seems to miss their true meaning and sometimes he distorts them. An example is the story of Orpheus taming wild beasts with music. The purpose of the myth was to illustrate that music can affect and improve the nature of man. Erasmus, who surely knew better, offers two outrageously false explanations:

> Take those wild men sprung from hard rocks and oak trees—what power brought them together into a civilized society if not flattery? This is all that's meant by the lyre of Amphion and Orpheus.[33]
>
> ......
>
> The same poets record that Orpheus, poet and lute player, moved the hardest of stones with his singing. What did they mean? They meant to show that men as unfeeling as stone, who were living after the manner of wild beasts, were rescued from promiscuity by this wise and eloquent hero and initiated into the holy ways of marriage.[34]

Shakespeare uses the Orpheus tale in two of his important plays. Conforming to the purpose of music most frequently mentioned by earlier writers, its ability to soothe the listener or player, we see in *Henry VIII* the rejected queen Katherine calling for music to soothe her feelings.

> QUEEN. Take thy lute, wench; my soul grows sad with troubles;
> Sing and disperse 'em, if thou canst. Leave working.
>
> *Song*
>
> Orpheus with his lute made trees,
> And the mountain tops that freeze,
> Bow themselves, when he did sing:
> To his music plants and flowers
> Ever sprung, as sun and showers
> There had made a lasting spring.
>
> Every thing that heard him play,
> Even the billows of the sea,
> Hung their heads, and then lay by.
> In sweet music is such art,
> Killing care and grief of heart
> Fall asleep or, hearing, die.[35]

In one case, Shakespeare points to the effectiveness of music to express melancholy, an emotion much dwelled upon in sixteenth-century England. In *The Two Gentlemen of Verona*, Proteus pretends to help his rival, Thurio, court Silvia by encouraging him to organize a serenade, by which he can impress her with the sincerity of his melancholy.

---

33 'Praise of Folly,' [1503] in *The Collected Works of Erasmus* (Toronto: University of Toronto Press, 1992), XXVII, 101.
34 'On the Writing of Letters,' [1522] in Ibid., XXV, 135.
35 *Henry VIII*, III, i.

> For Orpheus' lute was strung with poets' sinews,
> Whose golden touch could soften steel and stones,
> Make tigers tame and huge leviathans
> Forsake unsounded deeps to dance on sands.
> After your dire-lamenting elegies,
> Visit by night your lady's chamber-window
> With some sweet consort; to their instruments
> Tune a deploring dump; the night's dead silence
> Will well become such sweet-complaining grievance.[36]

PAN, SON TO MERCURY AND A WOOD-NYMPH, GOD OF WOODS AND FIELDS, FLOCKS AND SHEPHERDS.

Pan lived in caves and danced and made love to the Dryads. Fond of music, he invented the syrinx (panpipe) and was a master performer on this instrument. The unreasonable fear of Pan by travelers at night caused his name to be used in coining of the term 'panic.'

In Virgil's *Georgics,* a commemoration of the country life he knew as a youth, we sense his attraction for this god.

> Now we shall sing the shepherds' rural gods,
> Recall Apollo's role in guarding herds,
> And sing the woods and rivulets of Pan.
> All other themes are stale, diverting tunes
> To while the time away.[37]

A poem by Tibullus confirms, by its description, that the panpipe known by the ancient Romans was shaped as the one we know today.

> A milk-drenched Pan stood in the ash-tree's shelter,
>   and Pales graced a rough-carved wooden shrine;
> a pipe, its thin voice stilled, from a branch might dangle,
>   the shepherd's pledge for favors a god would show—
> with its range of reeds from the largest to the lesser,
>   joined by way in an ever-dwindling row.[38]

Ovid, in his *Metamorphoses*, has the god Mercury tell the story of the invention of the panpipe, the instrument always associated with Pan and known to the ancients as the *Syrinx*.

> And Mercury came flying
> On winged sandals, wearing the magic helmet,
> Bearing the sleep-producing wand, and lighted

---

[36] *The Two Gentlemen of Verona*, III, ii, 78ff.

[37] Virgil, *Georgics*, III, 1ff.

[38] Tibullus, *Poems*, II, v.

On earth, and put aside the wings and helmet
Keeping the wand. With this he plays the shepherd
Across the pathless countryside, a driver
Of goats, collected somewhere, and he goes
Playing a little tune on a pipe of reeds,
And this new sound is wonderful to Argus.
'Whoever you are, come here and sit beside me,'
He says, 'This rock is in the shade; the grass
Is nowhere any better.' And Mercury joins him,
Whiling the time away with conversation
And soothing little melodies, and Argus
Has a hard fight with drowsiness; his eyes,
Some of them, close, but some of them stay open.
To keep himself awake by listening,
He asks about the pipe of reeds, how was it
This new invention came about?

The god began the story:
'On the mountain slopes
Of cool Arcadia, a woodland nymph
Once lived, with many suitors, and her name
Was Syrinx. More than once the satyrs chased her,
And so did other gods of field or woodland,
But always she escaped them, virgin always
As she aspired to be, one like Diana,
Like her in dress and calling, though her bow
Was made of horn, not gold, but even so,
She might, sometimes, be taken for the goddess.
Pan, with a wreath of pine around his temples,
Once saw her coming back from Mount Lycaeus,
And said—'and Mercury broke off the story
And then went on to tell what Pan had told her,
How she said *No*, and fled, through pathless places,
Until she came to Ladon's river, flowing
Peaceful along the sandy banks, whose water
Halted her flight, and she implored her sisters
To change her form, and so, when Pan had caught her
And thought he held a nymph, it was only reeds
That yielded in his arms, and while he sighed,
The soft air stirring in the reeds made also
The echo of a sigh. Touched by this marvel,
Charmed by the sweetness of the tone, he murmured
This much I have! and took the reeds, and bound them
With wax, a tall and shorter one together,
And called them Syrinx, still.[39]

---

39 Ovid, *Metamorphoses*, I, 671ff.

One of the more frequently told myths of Greece involved a musical contest between Pan with his panpipes and Apollo with his lyre. Apollo, as a god of music, of course wins in every retelling. The adjudicator, in this version by Ovid, is a mountain god, Tmolus. Midas is the famous king who came to hate gold by having too much of it.

> But Midas, hating wealth, haunted the woods and fields, worshiping Pan, who has his dwelling in the mountain caves. But stupid his wits still remained, and his foolish mind was destined again as once before to harm its master. For Tmolus, looking far out upon the sea, stands stiff and high, with steep sides extending with one slope to Sardis, and on the other reaches down to little Hypaepae. There, while Pan was singing his songs to the soft nymphs and playing airy interludes upon his reeds close joined with wax, he dared speak slightingly of Apollo's music in comparison with his own, and came into an ill-matched contest with Tmolus as the judge.
>
> The old judge took his seat upon his own mountain-top, and shook his ears free from the trees. His dark locks were encircled by an oak-wreath only, and acorns hung around his hollow temples. He, looking at the shepherd-god, exclaimed: 'There is no delay on the judge's part.' Then Pan made music on his rustic pipes, and with his rude notes quite charmed King Midas, for he chanced to hear the strains. After Pan was done, venerable Tmolus turned his face toward Phoebus [Apollo]; and his forest turned with his face. Phoebus' golden head was wreathed with laurel of Parnasus, and his mantle, dipped in Tyrian dye, swept the ground. His lyre, inlaid with gems and Indian ivory, he held in his left hand, while his right hand held the plectrum. His very pose was that of an artist. Then with trained thumb he plucked the strings and, charmed by those sweet strains, Tmolus ordered Pan to lower his reeds before the lyre.[40]

VENUS (APHRODITE), GODDESS OF LOVE AND BEAUTY, DAUGHTER TO JUPITER AND DIONE.

The fourth book of *Odes* by Horace begins with a kind of love song to Venus, the god of love. Although he is now too old for the 'warfare' of love, he imagines in this poem a temple to Venus, to be constructed by an aristocrat, Paulus Maximus, a friend of Ovid and confidant of the emperor.

> He will set you in marble shape
> Under a cedarwood roof out by the Alban lakes.
> There your nostrils will breathe the sweet
> Wafted incense in clouds, there Berecynthian
> Flutes and lyres will afford delight
> Intermingled with hymns, not without reedy pipes;
> There twice daily your goddess-self
> Shall in dances be praised, dances of lads and girls
> Treading three-quarter meters like
> Those of Salian priests, nimbly on gleaming feet.[41]

---

[40] Ibid., XI, 147ff. In XIII, 780, Ovid introduces the giant, Cyclops, playing a great panpipes consisting of one hundred pipes. The sound it made was proportionally large:

> All the mountains felt the sound of his rustic pipings; the waves felt it too.

[41] Horace, *Odes*, IV, 1.

THALIA, THE MUSE OF COMEDY.

John Milton (1608–1674) mentions Thalia in his description of the gods' contribution to an entertainment scene.

> It is no wonder, then, that through you three gods, their powers divine coordinated, brought to birth songs so sweet. Now the Thracian lyre, too, with its fretted gold, sounds for you, touched softly by an artist hand. Amid the hanging tapestries is heard the lyre that with its skillful dancing measures guides the feet of the maidens. Let sights so glorious detain *your* Muse at least, and let them call back whatever inspiration enervating indulgence in wine drives away. Believe me, while the ivory shall send forth its strains, and the holiday-making throng of dancers, keeping time to the *plectrum*, shall fill the vaulted, perfumed chambers, you will know full well that Phoebus is making his way, voicelessly, through your heart, even as some sudden glow of warmth makes its way through your very marrow; and through the maidens' eyes, and through their fingers as they sound forth their strains, Thalia will glide swiftly into your bosom, and master it utterly.[42]

Given the colorful personalities of the Muses and gods, some writers created scenes in which a number of them are pictured together, as we see in an example by Ausonius (310–395 AD).

> Clio, singing of famous deeds, restores times past to life. Euterpe's breath fills the sweet-voiced flutes. Thalia rejoices in the loose speech of comedy. Melpomene cries aloud with the echoing voice of gloomy tragedy. Terpsichore with her lyre stirs, swells, and governs the emotions. Erato bearing the plectrum harmonizes foot, song and voice in the dance. Urania examines the motions of the heaven and stars. Calliope commits heroic songs to writing. Polymnia expresses all things with her hands and speaks by gesture. The power of Apollo's will enlivens the whole circle of these Muses: Phoebus sits in their midst and in himself possesses all their gifts.[43]

Martianus Capella, of whom little is known, composed in the middle of the fifth century a remarkable allegorical work describing a heavenly wedding called 'The Marriage of Mercury and Philology,' or the Marriage of Eloquence and Learning, in which the seven bridegrooms were the seven disciplines of the liberal arts and the guests were various Greek gods, together with a dozen famous earlier philosophers.[44] A final poetic passage describes an extraordinary concert by the gods.

> For Eratine, daughter of the Cyprian, and Himeros, attendant of Cupid, and Terpsis, one of the household servants of Dione, were the first to enter, singing in pleasing harmony; but the lad [Hymen?] was playing on a single aulos. Next came Persuasion, Pleasure, and the Graces, singing to the accompaniment of a lyre and dancing hither and thither with the rhythmic beat. At the same time companies of heroes and of philosophers with flowing locks were moving along in the vanguard, to the left and the right, all chanting in soft and sweet tones, many of them singing hymns and praises of the gods, others singing melodies they had just learned. In the middle were some rustic and tuneful

---

[42] 'Elegia Sextat,' in *The Works of John Milton*, ed. Frank Patterson (New York: Columbia University Press, 1931–1938), I, 211.

[43] Ausonius, *Ausonius*, trans. Hugh G. Evelyn White (London: Heinemann, 1921), II, 281.

[44] *Martianus Capella and the Seven Liberal Arts*, trans. William Harris Stahl and Richard Johnson (New York: Columbia University Press, 1977), II, 10.

> demigods, playing on appropriate instruments, the Goat-Footed one [Pan] on a pandura, Silvanus on a reed pipe smoothed of knots, and Faunus on a rustic flute. A company of heroes that followed after, attracted great wonder and surprise; for Orpheus, Amphion, and Arion, most skillful musicians, were harmoniously playing a moving melody on their golden lyres.[45]

One philosopher who had grown tired of the Muses and gods was Voltaire. He seemed particularly disturbed that librettists and composers relied on such things as the ancient myths, rather than legitimate plots, to attract the audience.

> An Asiatic, who should travel to Europe, might well consider us as pagans; our week days bear the names of Mars, Mercury, Jupiter, and Venus; and the nuptials of Cupid and Psyche are painted in the pope's palace; but, particularly, were this Asiatic to attend our opera, he would not hesitate in concluding it to be a festival in honor of the pagan deities.[46]
>
> ……
>
> At the opera, and in more serious productions, the gods are introduced descending in the midst of tempests, clouds, and thunder; that is, God is brought forward in the midst of the vapors of our petty globe. These notions are so suitable to our weak minds, that they appear to us grand and sublime.[47]

On the other hand, many later writers took the original gods and Muses and created new mythical traditions. Among the more interesting of these are tales of the invention of various musical instruments. Several of these involve a musician called Terpander of Lesbos, who flourished ca. 710–670 BC and is said to have won the first music contest at the Feast of Carneius, in Sparta, in 676 BC, and to have invented the practice of lyre singing.[48] Plutarch, however, passes on to us the older belief that the invention of this practice belonged to the gods.

> Heraclides in his *Compendium of Music* asserts, that Amphion, the son of Jupiter and Antiope, was the first that invented playing on the lyre and lyric poetry, being first instructed by his father; which is confirmed by a small manuscript, preserved in the city of Sicyon, wherein is set down a catalog of the priests, poets, and musicians of Argos.[49]

Plutarch also comments, in passing, that Terpander, by the power of his music, once appeased a sedition among the Lacedaemonians.[50]

---

45 Ibid., 351.

46 *Philosophical Dictionary*, 'Contradictions,' in *The Works of Voltaire* (New York: St. Hubert Guild, 1901), VII, 264.

47 *Philosophical Dictionary*, 'Heaven of the Ancients,' in Ibid., X, 17.

48 W. Chappell, *The History of Music* (London: Chappell), 32. We can assume this practice was actually much older, in view of the icons we seen in the Egyptian tombs.

49 Plutarch, in 'Concerning Music.'

50 Ibid.

Several early writers, including Strabo and Plutarch, also credit Terpander for being the one who introduced the seven-string lyre, replacing the earlier three- and four-string instruments.[51] Pindar, however, gave credit to Apollo for this instrument.

> Yet for these men the Muses' peerless choir
> Glad welcome sang on Pelion, and with them
> Apollo's seven-stringed lyre and golden quill.[52]

Pliny the elder (23–79 AD) gives the following history of the invention of instruments, information he has gathered from unnamed sources available to him.

> The bronze trumpet [was invented] by Pysaeus son of Tyrrhenus ... Amphion [was responsible for the invention of] music, Pan son of Mercury the flute and single aulos, Midas in Phrygia the slanted flute, Marsyas in the same nation the double aulos, Amphion the Lydian modes, Thracian Thamyras the Dorian, Marsyas of Phrygia the Phrygian, Amphion, or others say Orpheus and others Linus, the harp. Terpander first sang with seven strings, adding three to the original four, Simonides added an eighth, Timotheus a ninth. Thamyris first played the harp without using the voice, Amphion, or according to others Linus, accompanied the harp with singing; Terpander composed songs for harp and voice. Ardalus of Troezen instituted singing to the aulos.[53]

There were also myths which carried meaning relative to the daily life of these early peoples. One, the myth of Arion, appealed to the fear of falling from a ship. An early version of this myth is found in Herodotus of Halicarnassus (ca. 484–425 BC), whom some call the 'father of history.' He traveled extensively and his writing is valuable for his commentary on what he observed. In his history,[54] he tells the mythical story of Arion who was forced to jump ship and was rescued by a dolphin. The ship's crew was the audience for a song by Arion, before he jumped, and they seem to be described as genuine listeners.

> They for their part thought what a pleasure it would be for them to hear the greatest singer in the world, and so they retreated from the stern of the boat to amidships.

Finally, a charming Greek myth concerns the use of music at the time of one's death. Philetaerus, in the fourth century BC, cites a myth that if one goes to Hades, but is a recognized lover of good music, one is permitted 'to revel in love affairs,' whereas 'those whose manners are sordid, having no knowledge of music,' are condemned to spend eternity carrying water

---

[51] Gregory Nagy, *Pindar's Homer* (Baltimore: Johns Hopkins University Press, 1982), 89; *The Geography of Strabo*, trans. Horace L. Jones (Cambridge: Harvard University Press, 1960), XIII, 2, 4.

[52] Ode for Pytheas of Aegina, Winner of the Youths' Pankration.

[53] Pliny the Elder, *Natural History* VII, lxi, 204ff.

[54] Book I, 24.

in a fruitless effort to fill 'the leaky jar.'[55] Thus Philetaerus exclaims, 'Zeus, it is indeed a fine thing to die to the music of the aulos!' By this he meant arranging to have these musicians playing as one dies so as to demonstrate to the gods that one truly appreciated good music.

It is in the context of this myth that we understand a line in Menander's play, *Old Cantankerous*. The character, Getas, enters the stage from a shrine as an aulos player begins to play for him. Getas tells the aulos player to stop playing, 'I'm not ready for you yet!'

And this is why before Jesus could perform one of his miracles, that of raising a girl from the dead, he had to first chase the aulos players out of the house, saying, 'Depart, for the girl is not dead but sleeping.'[56]

For many people, even university educators, our ancient history is given little attention with respect to its value for our modern world. But what do we lose when we lose civilization's accumulated knowledge? The author of an important early book on the Greek myths, Charles Mills Gayley, in his *The Classic Myths* (1893), was one who worried.

> It is incumbent upon our universities and schools [that] the Greek and Latin classics shall be reinstated in their proper place as a means of discipline, a humanizing influence, the historic background against which our present appears. For, cut off from the intellectual and imaginative sources of Greece and Rome, the state and statesmanship, legislation and law, society and manners, philosophy, religion, literature, art, and even artistic appreciation, run readily shallow and soon dry.

---

55 Philetaerus, *The Aulos Lover*, quoted in Athenaeus, *Deipnosophistae*, XIV, 633.

56 Matthew 9:24. As usual, aulos here incorrectly appears in English translation as 'flute.'

On Inspiration

IN THE PREVIOUS ESSAYS the reader has seen the close connection between music and religion among the most ancient civilizations. Both music and religion held significant mysteries for the ancient average (non-privileged) person, the priest in his rituals and the musician performing the only art which could not be seen.

The ancient musicians themselves, far from understanding the powers of their own art, also turned to the mystery of religion in explaining the source of their inspiration. In this chapter the reader will find a few illustrations of the evolution of this divine connection as the ancient world gave way to the Christian era.

Toward the end of the ancient Roman period, even the normally very rational Cicero (106–43 BC) could not help but accept the view that the very performances of poets, who were also singers, and musicians seemed to document a connection with the divine.

> The human soul is in some degree derived and drawn from a source exterior to itself. Hence we understand that outside the human soul there is a divine soul from which the human soul is sprung …
>
> And poetic inspiration also proves that there is a divine power within the human soul.[1]

However, the emotional power of the performances which Cicero had apparently observed left him with a serious doubt whether the average person had the background, or was even entitled, to deal with such strong impressions.

> But do you see what harm the poets inflict? They introduce great heroes wailing, they enfeeble our souls, and on top of that are so agreeable that they are not only read by actually learned by heart. So when to bad home upbringing and a sheltered and dainty way of life the poets are added as well, they crush all the sinews of virtue. So Plato was right to expel them from the society which he framed in his search for the best character and the best political constitution.[2]

Part of Cicero's concern in the above passage may have been the sheer volume of activity. Horace, at least, complained that everyone now thought they were poets.

> The fickle public has changed its taste and is fired throughout with a scribbling craze; sons and grave sires sup crowned with leaves and dictate their lines. I myself, who declare that I write no verses, prove to be more of a liar than the Parthians: before sunrise I wake, and call for pen, paper, and writing-case. A man who knows nothing of a ship fears to handle one; no one dares to give southernwood to the sick unless he has learnt its use; doctors undertake a doctor's work; carpenters handle carpenters' tools; but, skilled or unskilled, we scribble poetry, all alike.[3]

---

1   Cicero, *De Divinatione*, xxxii, 70 and xxxvii.
2   Cicero, *Tusculan Disputations*, II, 27.
3   Horace, *Epistles*, II, 1, 117.

Horace complained of the poet, Cassius, who delighted himself in writing two hundred lines before breakfast and another two hundred after dinner! Sniffed Horace,

> Of him they say that his books and their cases supplied all the fuel needed to cremate him after his death.[4]

Another reason why this body of poetry, known as the Augustan Lyric Poetry, was so popular was because it was music. It was poetry fashioned after the style of the old lyric poets of Greece and like that earlier poetry this poetry was sung. There is abundant evidence of this, as one can see in Propertius' comment that he 'took to the lyre & sang.'[5] Horace is even more specific.

> You have no cause to think that *the words which I*,
> By far-resounding Aufidus born, *compose*
> *For singing to the lyre*, in meters ...

Some of the greatest of the early Roman writers contributed to this body of lyric poetry. Virgil (70–19 BC), Horace (66–8 BC), Tibullus (54–18 BC), Propertius (50–16 BC), and Ovid (43 BC–17 AD) were apparently singers. In addition to Horace, documented above we know that Ovid once sang at a wedding,[6] Propertius played the lyre and sang,[7] and Virgil in his youth played and sang shepherd songs.[8]

It is apparent that the Roman lyric poetry was inspired by the earlier Greek lyric poets and indeed Horace observes that of all the Greek writers, it was these older lyric poets who were the best.[9] The extent to which these Roman lyric poets knew the Greek poets and their literature is documented by repeated references to it.

Like those poets of ancient Greece, these later poets of Rome, no doubt in part as a manifestation of the spirit of lyric poetry itself, also looked to the muses and gods as the source of their ability and inspiration. Horace, for instance, provides a perfect illustration of this heartfelt association.

> By the race of the Romans, earth's
> Greatest, I have been deemed worthy of rank among
> Noble choirs of its singing bards;
> Thus I now am the less hounded by Envy's fang.
> O my Muse of the golden shell,

---

4   Horace, *Satires*, I, 10, 61. There were two poets of this name and it is not known which Horace referred to. One of them, by the way, was one of the slayers of Caesar.

5   Propertius, *Poems*, I, 3.

6   Ovid, *Letters in Exile*, I, 2.

7   Propertius, *Poems*.

8   Virgil, *Georgics*, IV, 564.

9   Horace, *Epistles*, II, 1, 28. He also adds here that one should not attempt to compare the Greeks and Roman lyric poets, as that would be like comparing apples and oranges, as we would say today (he said 'olives and nuts'). In any case, says Horace, we, the Romans, 'have much more skill than the well-oiled Greeks.'

> You who modulate sweet sounding of harmonies,
> Who could grant even toneless fish
> Gifts of song like the swan's, were you so willed to do,
> All of this is a gift from you:
> Having passers-by point fingers at me as Rome's
> Lyric singer; if what I write
> Pleases, yours were the thoughts, yours was the pleasure's source.[10]

And in another place,

> Phoebus has inspired me, and Phoebus gave me
> Technical skill in song and the name of poet.[11]

Some of these Augustan lyric poets felt the gods reciprocated by protecting the poets. Thus, a poem of Tibullus warns the ladies to have respect for the poets who are favored by the gods.

> But you, my girl, watch out; the gods love poets;
> I warn you, have respect for a sacred bard
> singing of Messalinus, who drives before him
> whole conquered cities—the victor, battle-scarred
> and crowned with bay, while round him his bay-wreathed soldiers
> deafen the crown with their wild triumphal song.[12]

It was in the belief of this special relationship that we find Ovid making the interesting observation that poets are more susceptible to love because of the emotions that have invested in their love poetry. Whereupon he reminds the ladies (prostitutes) that poets have associations with the gods and for this reason it is really not appropriate to ask for money from a poet!

> Guile too in poet's nature hath no part;
> Our characters are molded by our art.
> No lust of place or riches weighs us down,
> We love our shady couch and spurn the town.
> But quickly caught, by passions strong we're burnt,
> Too well the lesson of true love we've learnt.
> Our hearts are softened by our gentle trade,
> And by our calling is our conduct swayed.
> Be kind, ye fair, to the poetic choir
> Whom Muses love and deities inspire.
> God's in us and with heaven we discourse,
> In springs divine our instinct has its source.

---

[10] Horace, *Odes*, IV, 3.

[11] Ibid., IV, 6.

[12] Tibullus, *Poems*, II, v. In the Poem III, iv, Apollo says 'Gods love all poets.' In the actual experience of love, like Ovid, Tibullus reveals, in Poem I, iv, a lack of confidence.

> Spare me, I beg you; let me not be railed at
> as one who tried to teach an art he failed at!

> It's sin to look for payment from the bard,
> A sin, alas, that women never regard.[13]

Ovid had his doubts about the reality of this special protection and indeed points to one poet who was *not* protected by the gods, in fact he was murdered in the act of performance!

> And poor Lampetides—he had been summoned
> To no such revels, only to play the lute,
> To grace the feast with song, and so he stood there
> Holding the ivory quill, surely no fighter,
> And Pettalus mocked him: 'Sing that song in Hell,
> The rest of it, at least!' and pierced his temple,
> And as he fell, the dying fingers struggled,
> To play once more, and made only a discord.[14]

Perhaps this contributed to Ovid finally indicating he had lost faith in the gods, particularly those of Egyptian heritage. He reveals this in an interesting passage, while nevertheless mentioning again that the poets are favored by the gods.

> We bards are classed as holy, heaven's care;
> Divinity, they say, flows in our veins.
> But every holy thing brash death profanes;
> There nothing that his murky clutches spare.
>
> Orpheus' great parents—what did they avail?
> Or song whose magic power the beasts subdued?
> To sad reluctant lyre in the wild wood
> 'Ah, Linus, Linus' went his wail.
>
> And Homer too, whose founts of song inspire
> The Muses' streams on poets' lips for ay,
> Sank to Avernus' depths on his last day:
> Verse, verse alone escapes the insatiate pyre.
>
> In poetry the toils of Troy live on,
> And that slow web night's cunning would unwind.
> So Nemesis and Delia fame will find,
> Who last and first their poet's worship won.

---

[13] Ovid, *The Art of Love*, III, 539. As it turned out, it was not love, but the love poems which got Ovid in trouble. He wrote, in *The Cures for Love*, 361,

> For lately people have attacked my poems;
> They blame my Muse as bawdy and immoral.
> So long as I give fun and I am world famous,
> If one or two decry me, I shan't quarrel.

Unfortunately it only took one, Augustus, to decry him and he was sent off in exile!

[14] Ovid, *Metamorphoses*, V, 111ff.

> What use is that Egyptian ritual,
> Those timbrels, these long nights of chastity?
> When evil fate dooms good men, may I be
> forgiven if I've no faith in gods at all!¹⁵

With the arrival of the Christian era and the Middle Ages, some Church philosophers continued to honor the idea that poet-singers had a certain divine connection. St. Justin Martyr mentions this, when he recalls a comment by a poet-musician in Homer, 'God inspired me with melodies.'[16] A third-century Church philosopher, Origen, provides a more extended explanation of the nature of this 'divine connection.' The 'spirit of madness' he mentions is often called the 'divine frenzy' and is best thought of as a great state of excitement.

> There are besides ... certain special energies of this world, spiritual powers, which bring about certain effects ... there being, for example, a peculiar energy and power, which is the inspirer of poetry; another, of geometry; and so a separate power, to remind us of each of the arts and professions of this kind. Many Greek writers have been of opinion that the art of poetry cannot exist without madness; whence also it is several times related in their histories, that those whom they call poets were suddenly filled with a kind of spirit of madness ... Now these effects we are to suppose are brought about in the following manner: As holy and immaculate souls, after devoting themselves to God with all affection and purity, and after preserving themselves free from all contagion of evil spirits, and after being purified by lengthened abstinence, and imbued with holy and religious training, assume by this means a portion of divinity, and earn the grace of prophecy, and other divine gifts ... And the result of this is, that they are filled with the working of those spirits to whose service they have subjected themselves.[17]

The official position of the Church was that Reason must rule man, and not the emotions one associates with music. The second-century Church philosopher, Clement of Alexandria reflects this as he provides a new interpretation of the 'divine connection.'

> There is in man reasoning; and there is a divine Reason.
> Reason is implanted in man to provide for life and sustenance,
> But divine Reason attends the arts in the case of all.
> Teaching them always what it is advantageous to do.
> For it was not man that discovered art, but god brought it;
> And the Reason of man derives its origin from the divine Reason.[18]

---

[15] Ovid, *Amores*, III, 9.

[16] Saint Justin Martyr, *The Monarchy or The Rule of God*, trans. Thomas B. Falls (New York: Christian Heritage, Inc.), 455.

[17] Origen, *De Principiis*, trans. Frederick Crombie, in *The Writings of Origen* (Edinburgh: T. & T. Clark, 1871), III, iii.

[18] Clement of Alexandria, *The Miscellanies*, trans. Alexander Roberts, in *Ante-Nicene Christian Library* (Edinburgh: T. & T. Clark, 1869), XII, Book V, Pg. 290. In Book VI, Clement quotes Plato and Democritus regarding the 'divine conection' of poets.

He also gives, in passing, a little indication of the Church's hostility to pagan entertainments.

> We must not aspire to please the multitude. For we do not practice what will please them, but what we know is remote from their disposition.[19]

During the later Dark Ages traditional secular philosophy had almost completely disappeared. Only one important thinker from this period is familiar to us today, the ninth century Irishman, Joannes Scotus Eriugena, who reflects a new dogma on the part of the Church. Now the Christian is told that the emphasis is not on the work of art, or the artist, but on God who created the artist. It is a kind of reverse form of the 'divine connection.'

> As the understanding [*intellectus*] of the artist precedes the understanding of the art, and the understanding of the art precedes the understanding of what is in it and made by it, so the understanding of the Father, the Artificer, precedes the understanding of His Art, i.e., His Wisdom, in which He created all things. Next the knowledge of everything made in and by that Art follows the understanding of the Art itself. Whatever true reasoning finds prior in any sense must precede according to natural sequence.[20]

The musicians we most associate with the late Middle Ages are the troubadours. We think of them as part of the Pre-Renaissance because with them genuine important secular art begins to surface again after the long dark ages. The inspiration for their songs comes often from Spring, but most often from Love, as we see in the lyrics for a song by Raimbaut d'Orange.

> I sing not for bird or flower, not for snow or for ice and not even for cold or for warmth, nor for the meadow's growing green again; and for no other pleasure do I sing, nor have I ever sung, but for my mistress for whom I long, because she is the most lovely in the world.[21]

Some of the most poignant songs are inspired not by the joy of love, but by the grief and pain which often accompany love. A song of Borneil is one of many which mention this confluence of emotions.

> I grieve inwardly while outwardly I sing, so that this would seem like churlish inconstancy in me if I were not so firmly bound by Love, which teaches me that a sincere lover achieves perfection in his discouragement and that I should pretend to be cheerful and joyful and should suffer patiently; for the most precious riches are to be gained from noble suffering and fear.[22]

---

[19] Clement of Alexandria, *The Miscellanies*, trans. William Wilson (Edinburgh: T. & T. Clark, 1884), I, 378.

[20] Joannes Scotus Eriugena, *Periphyseon on the Division of Nature*, trans. Myra Uhlfelder (Indianapolis: Bobbs-Merrill, 1976), III, 3.

[21] 'Non chant per auzel,' in Alan Press, *Anthology of Troubadour Lyric Poetry* (Austin: University of Texas Press, 1971), 113.

[22] 'Chans em broil,' in Ruth Sharman, *The Cansos and Sirventes of the Troubadour Giraut de Borneil* (Cambridge: Cambridge University Press, 1989), 147. Troubadour poems of similar inspiration are: Ventadorn, 'Per melhs cobrir'; Vidal, 'Per miehs sofrir'; Borneil, 'Mas, com m'ave,' 'Quar non ai' and 'De chantar, Ab deport'; and trouvère poems by Bethune, 'Si voirement'; Couci, 'L'an que rose,' 19; and Brule, 'De bone amour,' 'Desconfortez, plains d'ire' and 'Ire d'amors.'

Another song of Borneil begins much more pessimistically, it being inspired by pain without hope.

> I lament and sigh and weep and sing, but my song brings me no pleasure; for, instead, the more I sing, the more sad I become and the more I weaken my heart and my reason. And I do not wonder that a man who is saddened by song—which usually drives away pain and sorrow—should fear to see his mind and his affairs gravely altered![23]

We see the other side of the coin in a similarly inspired song by a rare female troubadour, La Comtessa de Dia (fl. ca. 1160).

> It will be mine to sing of that which I would not desire,
> I am so aggrieved by the one to whom I am the friend,
> for I love him more than anything that can be.
> Pity does not help me toward him, nor courtliness,
> nor my beauty, nor my good name, nor my wit;
> and so I am cheated and betrayed as much
> as I'd deserve to be if I were ugly.[24]

If, through this contest between joy and pain, the outcome should be a happy ending, then, of course, there is a burst of new inspiration. Such a song was composed by de Nesle.

> I must sing, for I have won joy again
> that always fled from me and stayed far away;
> I have paid with pain and sadness many a day—
> now it is my time to be free of pain;
> for the beautiful lady whom I have loved so long,
> who used to war against me for her love,
> has lately come to terms with me.[25]

But, on the other hand, if love is lost, then, as in this example by Ventadorn, there is no inspiration at all and the voice of the singer is stilled.

> I want all those who ask me to sing to know the truth, if I have occasion or leisure for it. Let him sing who wants to. I have not been able to do it since I lost my happiness through my dark destiny.[26]

---

[23] 'Plaing e sospir,' in Ibid., 411.

[24] 'A chantar m'er,' in Ibid., 185.

[25] 'Chanter m'estuet,' in Ibid., 369.

[26] 'Tuih cil que'm,' in Stephen Nichols, *The Songs of Bernart de Ventadorn* (Chapel Hill: The University of North Carolina Press, 1965), 174.

There must have been many occasions when the troubadours found their only inspiration in being forced by necessity to write for monetary purposes. One song by Borneil begins by admitting that he must, 'put great effort into composing a song that I owe for my lodging'[27] The trouvère, Colin Muset (fl. 1230), complains rather bitterly over the failure of his noble patron to provide the wages he feels entitled to.

> There's poor provisions in my bag,
> There's nothing in my wallet.[28]

No doubt a frequent source of inspiration, although it is rarely mentioned, was the delight which the composer himself received from his own art[29] and, on the other hand, some simply found meaning in their duty to the court they worked for.[30] While a position as a court musician meant one's obligation was to a very small circle of patrons, nevertheless we see in the late medieval repertoire indications that some musicians were beginning to think of their broader reputations and even of fame. Borneil, observes that, 'fair renown, once acknowledged, lasts and never varies in hue.'[31] In another song, he advises a colleague,

> Why compose poetry if you do not wish everyone to know your poem immediately? For song brings no other reward.[32]

It is also interesting that in this same singer one can see clear evidence of the beginning of awareness that his reputation depends on aesthetic values in contrast to the usual repertoire needed for mere entertainment purposes.

> Then it is right that I sing in order to make entreaty as well as on command. But now they will say that it would be far better if I strove to sing in the light style. And yet this is not true, for poetry deep with meaning, rich and rare, brings and bestows fine reputation, just as unbridled nonsense detracts from it. But I firmly believe that a song is not worth as much to begin with, as later when a man understands it.[33]

And in this regard it is important for him to have a listener who is educated enough to appreciate his efforts.

---

27 'En un Chantar,' in Sharman, *The Cansos and Sirventes of the Troubadour Giraut de Borneil*, 300.
28 'Sire Cuens,' in Frederick Goldin, *Lyrics of the Troubadours and Trouveres* (Garden City: Anchor Books, 1973, 427.
29 'De chantar,' in Sharman, *The Cansos and Sirventes of the Troubadour Giraut de Borneil*, 250.
30 'Ne me sont,' in Hendrik van der Werf, *The Chansons of the Troubadours and Trouvères* (Utrecht: A. Oosthoek, 1972), 106.
31 'S'es chantars,' in Sharman, *The Cansos and Sirventes of the Troubadour Giraut de Borneil*, 427.
32 'Era'm platz', in Ibid., 396.
33 'La flors,' in Ibid., 172.

> Churlish men of base lineage consider many of my fine songs as idle nonsense, though no excellent man of noble birth, if he succeeded in catching their meaning, ever excused himself from listening to them or belittled the pleasure they afforded. And is a man who takes no pleasure in joy and song not thoroughly despicable?[34]

But apparently he found during his time in the early thirteenth century that a decline in the quality of aristocratic life in general made his life as a musician become less and less satisfying. Two of his works give us a clear description of the changes taking place and of his consequently returning to God for the inspiration for his music.

> If it were not for [God] who tells me that I should sing and be cheerful, I could never be stirred by the gentle season when the grass grows, nor by meadow or bough or woodland or flower, or hard-hearted lord or vain love. But I comply with his request, for since joy fails and fades, renown and knighthood are in decline, and since the great rulers have forsaken joy, nothing that the worst among them does has been praised by me. For I have resolved not to seek the favor of any rich and powerful man who is an evil ruler.
>
> The world was good in the days when joy was welcomed by everyone, and when that man was well liked in whom joy most abounded, and when reputation and noble rank went hand in hand. For now the most vicious are called virtuous and the man sunk in deepest melancholy is held to be the best, and the man who takes the most he can from other people will be envied the most …
>
> I have seen a time when a man valued songs and found pleasure in dance melodies and lays. Now that courtly pleasures and gracious deeds are forsaken, and true lovers, in all their concerns, have left the straight path for the crooked, I see that all sense of right has fled …[35]
>
> ……
>
> To the honor of God I return to my song, from which I had taken my leave and departed, and not to the calls and cries of the birds, nor to the leaf on the bough do I return, nor do I find any joy in singing. On the contrary, I am angry and full of sorrow, for in many writings do I see and recognize that sin is strengthening its hold, so that trust and faith are failing and wickedness flourishes.
>
> And I wonder greatly when I think of how the world has fallen [spiritually] asleep.[36]

Another class of poet singers in the late Middle Ages were the Goliards, consisting of mostly wandering clerical students. They frequently looked to wine for their inspiration and in one surviving song the poet confesses that the quality of his song is directly related to the quality of the wine.

> Special gifts for every man
> Nature will produce,
> I, when I compose my verse,
> Vintage wine must use,
> All the best the cellar's casks

---

[34] 'De chantar, Ab deport,' in Ibid., 458. Similar references to the esteem which comes from the composer's work are found in Ventadorn, 'Tant ai mo cor'; Borneil, 'Alegrar mi volgr'en,' 'Quar non ai,' 'De chantar,' and 'Be m'era bels chanters'; and Adam de la Halle, 'Merveille est.'

[35] 'Si per mon Sobre-Totz,' in Sharman, *The Cansos and Sirventes of the Troubadour Giraut de Borneil*, 477.

[36] 'A l'honor Dieu,' in Ibid., 417.

> Hold of these libations.
> Such a wine calls forth from me
> Copious conversations.
>
> My verse has the quality
> Of the wine I sip,
> I can not do much until
> Food has passed my lip,
> What I write when starved and parched
> Is of the lowest class,
> When I'm tight, with verse I make
> Ovid I surpass.
>
> As a poet n'er can I
> Be appreciated
> Till my stomach has been well
> Filled with food and sated,
> When god Bacchus gains my brain's
> Lofty citadel
> Phoebus rushes in to voice
> Many a miracle.[37]

With the arrival of the Renaissance, we begin to find the discussion of poetry sounding much like our present age. Boccaccio, as an example, provides an expansive survey of the uses of poetry, while still maintaining its divine connection.

> This poetry, which ignorant triflers cast aside, is a sort of fervid and exquisite invention, with fervid expression, in speech or writing, of that which the mind has invented. It proceeds from the bosom of God, and few, I find, are the souls in whom this gift is born; indeed so wonderful a gift it is that true poets have always been the rarest of men. This fervor of poesy is sublime in its effects: it impels the soul to a longing for utterance; it brings forth strange and unheard-of creations of the mind; it arranges these meditations in a fixed order, adorns the whole composition with unusual interweaving of words and thoughts; and thus it veils truth in a fair and fitting garment of fiction. Further, if in any case the invention so requires, it can arm kings, marshal them for war, launch whole fleets from their docks, nay, counterfeit sky, land, sea, adorn young maidens with flowery garlands, portray human character in its various phases, awake the idle, stimulate the dull, restrain the rash, subdue the criminal, and distinguish excellent men with their proper need of praise: these, and many other such, are the effects of poetry.[38]

Having given this wide functional use of poetry, he apparently felt it necessary to remind his readers that nevertheless poetry is an art.

> Now since nothing proceeds from this poetic fervor, which sharpens and illumines the powers of the mind, except what is wrought out by art, poetry is generally called an art. Indeed the word poetry has not the origin that many carelessly suppose, namely *poio*, *pois*, which is but Latin *fingo*, *fingis*; rather

---

37 In 'Estuans intrinsecus,' in *Vagabond Verse*, trans. Edwin H. Zeydel (Detroit: Wayne State University Press, 1966), 67.

38 *Genealogia Deorum Gentilium*, quoted in *Boccaccio on Poetry*, trans. Charles Osgood (New York: The Liberal Arts Press, 1956). XIV, viiff.

it is derived from a very ancient Greek word *poetes*, which means in Latin exquisite discourse (*exquisita locutio*). For the first men who, thus inspired, began to employ an exquisite style of speech, such, for example, as song in an age hitherto unpolished, to render this unheard-of discourse sonorous to their hearers, let it fall in measured periods …

He strengthens this defense of the art by quoting Cicero,

> We have it on the highest and most learned authority, that while other arts are matters of science and formula and technique, poetry depends solely upon an inborn faculty, is evoked by a purely mental activity, and is infused with a strange heavenly inspiration.[39]

---

[39] Ibid.

Is Music Math?

Music is the daughter of Arithmetic.
Anonymous, *Scholia enchiriadis* (ca. 900 AD)

READING THE ABOVE QUOTATION, perhaps it should be no surprise that much of our modern music notation system is characterized by simple arithmetic. This anonymous treatise, written at the very dawn of the creation of our modern music notation system, also epitomizes the central problem which all earlier philosophers had with music and which confuses music educators today. In a word, how do you make music, whose essence and values are non-rational, fit into a rational world? The answer for modern music educators is to ignore the inherent values in music and focus instead on teaching about music. For the early philosophers the answer was to simply ignore the characteristics of music they couldn't explain and take what they could understand and declare music Rational.

> [Music is] the rational discipline of agreement and discrepancy of sounds according to numbers in their relation to those things which are found in sounds ... Because everything comprehended by these disciplines exists through reason formed of numbers and without numbers can be neither understood nor made known.[1]

On the other hand, for musicians of today, and the past, music is characterized more by pitches we hear, not numbers that we count. It follows that the symbols representing these pitches constantly remind us that music is for the ear. It is also very important to remember that for a very long time there was no notation of music at all. The ancient Egyptians had none and the ancient Greeks didn't even have names for the individual pitches.

For the ancient philosophers music was a special problem. They understood, through observing its impact on listeners, that it was important, but they could not see it and they had built a philosophical world in which the eye was the most important of the senses (we still say, 'Seeing is believing!'). But music obviously dwelt with the emotions, a topic which always made early philosophers uncomfortable because they could not generalize about them and because emotion seemed to them the antithesis of Reason.

Once the ancients discovered they could use numbers to describe musical sounds they were delighted, for now they could bring music into their world of Reason. The early Church was also delighted, for now it could admit music into the curriculum as a branch of mathematics and entirely avoid discussion of the emotions in music, a very sensitive topic since they had for so long preached that the emotions were 'the first step toward sin!'

---

[1] Anonymous, 'Of Symphonies,' in Oliver Strunk, *Source Readings in Music History* (New York: Norton, 1950), 135.

The origin of the idea of using numbers to describe music is usually attributed to Pythagoras (580–500 BC). Like much of ancient Greek culture, however, perhaps some of his ideas came from the older society of Egypt. Iamblichus tells us, for example, that Pythagoras spent twelve years in Egypt where he studied 'arithmetic, music and all the other sciences.'[2] Since nothing by his own hand has survived, and because there is a lot of nonsense attributed to Pythagoras, it is difficult to determine exactly his role in music history. He certainly was not the first to discover the overtone series, but he may have been the first to use numbers as symbols to represent the intervals between the lower pitches of the series.[3] One can see how the relationship between mathematics and music followed.

Aristotle found here a fundamental theory for looking at the world.

> The so-called Pythagoreans, who were the first to take up mathematics, not only advanced this study, but also having been brought up in it they thought that its principles were the principles of all things. And since of these principles numbers are by nature the first, and in numbers they seemed to see many resemblances to the things that exist and come into being—more than in fire and earth and water ... since again, they saw that the modifications and the ratios of the musical scales were expressible in numbers—since, then, all other things seemed in their whole nature modeled on numbers, and numbers seemed to be the first things in the whole of nature, they supposed the elements of numbers to be the elements of all things, and the whole heaven to be a musical scale and a number.[4]

Following this line of thought, one can understand how medieval philosophers could come to the hypothesis that perhaps the organization of the planets was related to the intervals of the overtone series and that one could therefore study astronomy (in a time with no adequate telescopes) through studying music. But we are perhaps more surprised to discover that some early philosophers found a connection between music and grammar, as Sextus Empiricus (second century AD) did,

> For this is a feature of arts which are conjectural and subject to accidents such as navigation and medicine; but Grammar is not a conjectural art but akin to Music and Philosophy.[5]

We find this association again one thousand years later in Roger Bacon (b. ca. 1214), who not only found a relationship between music and grammar but now added the field of logic!

> Now the accidental parts of philosophy are grammar and logic. Alpharabius makes it clear in his book on the sciences that grammar and logic cannot be known without mathematics. For although grammar furnishes children with the facts relating to speech and its properties in prose, meter, and rhythm, nevertheless it does so in a puerile way by means of statement and not through causes or reasons. For it is the function of another science to give the reasons for these things, namely, of that science, which must consider fully the nature of tones, and this alone is music, of which there are numerous

---

[2] Iamblichus (ca. 250–325 AD), 'The Life of Pythagoras.'

[3] Thus his greatest contribution to mankind, the idea that numbers could represent abstract thought was the beginning of all higher mathematics.

[4] *Metaphysics*.

[5] Sextus Empiricus, 'Against the Professors,' trans. R. G. Bury (Cambridge: Harvard University Press, 1949), I, 72.

> varieties and parts. For one deals with prose, a second with meter, a third with rhythm, and a fourth with music in singing. And besides these it has more parts. The part dealing with prose teaches the reasons for all elevations of the voice in prose, as regards differences of accents and as regards colons, commas, periods, and the like. The metrical part teaches all the reasons and causes for feet and meters. The part on rhythm teaches about every modulation and sweet relation in rhythms, because all those are certain kinds of singing, although not so treated as in ordinary singing ... Therefore grammar depends causatively on music.
>
> In the same way logic ... Alpharabius especially teaches this in regard to the poetic argument, the statements of which should be sublime and beautiful, and therefore accompanied with notable adornment in prose, meter, and rhythm ... And therefore the end of logic depends upon music.[6]

The reader will forgive us if we pause to reflect that much of what we call music theory functions like grammar. As a result some music theory teachers teach only the grammar of music and not music at all. Consequently we also have a tradition of analysis in which we analyze only the grammar and discover nothing of the great truths of music—a form of analysis that happens in no other discipline. One cannot imagine, for example, an English literature course where the study of Shakespeare's *Hamlet* ended with the analysis of the grammar of his English.

Following Aristotle's observation, quoted above, that numbers were to be thought of as the basis of nature, we can see that by the sixth century AD virtually all of science was now incorporated into mathematics. This is clearly expressed in a letter by Cassiodorus (480–573 AD) to the famous mathematician, Boethius (475–524 AD).

> You have thoroughly imbued yourself with Greek philosophy. You have translated Pythagoras the musician, Ptolemy the astronomer, Nicomachus the arithmetician, Euclid the geometer, Plato the theologian, Aristotle the logician, and have given back the mechanician Archimedes to his own Sicilian countrymen. You know the whole science of Mathematics.[7]

Boethius certainly considered that music was within his expertise as a mathematician, leaving his readers to choke on musical description such as this:

> But since the nete synemmenon to the mese (3,456 to 4,608) holds a sesquitertian ratio—that is, a diatessaron—whereas the trite synemmenon to the nete synemmenon (4,374 to 3,456) holds the ratio of two tones.[8]

Aurelian of Reome, in his *Musica Disciplina* of ca. 843 AD, treats the relationship of mathematics and music as if the numbers of the intervals were subject to weighing and not hearing.

---

6   *Opus Majus*, in *The Opus Majus of Roger Bacon*, trans. Robert Burke (New York: Russell & Russell, 1962), II. See also XVI for his views on the relationship of music to both mathematics and theology.

7   Letter to Boethius, in *The Letters of Cassiodorus* (London: Frowde, 1886), 169.

8   Boethius, *Fundamentals of Music*, trans. Calvin Bower (New Haven: Yale University Press), IV, ix.

> Music has the greatest correspondence to mathematics and encompasses that part of mathematics that compares one quantity with another.[9]

In another place, he says if one wishes to become more versed in music,

> let him turn his eyes to the harmony of proportions, to the contemplation of intervals, and to the exactitude of mathematics.[10]

One of the most important philosophers at the end of the Middle Ages was the Englishman, Roger Bacon (b. ca. 1214), who studied at Oxford and at the University of Paris. Perhaps reflecting the power of the Church at this time, he was outspoken in his disrespect for the masses, the 'unenlightened throng,' the 'ignorant multitude,' whom he says can never rise to the perfection of wisdom.[11] For this reason, he maintains, the wise have always been an elite segment of society, separated from the masses. He found this true in religion ('as with Moses so with Christ the common throng does not ascend the mountain') and well as in the universities. He cites a book by A. Gellius in which the author maintained that the great Greek philosophers had discussions among themselves at night, so as to 'avoid the multitude.'

> In this book he says that it is foolish to feed an ass lettuces when thistles suffice him. He is speaking of the multitude for whom rude, cheap, imperfect food of science is sufficient. Nor ought we to cast pearls before swine.

Johannes de Grecheo, in his *De Musica*, ca. 1300, makes it sound more like a matter of professional jealousy,

> Many speculative thinkers make a secret of their calculations and their discoveries, not wishing to reveal them to others.[12]

In his discussion of the Liberal Arts, Bacon first comments that while the ancients knew of the various sciences, they only actually used two: astronomy for the calendar, and music for worship.[13] Mathematics, he calls the 'gate and key' for the other Liberal Arts[14] and he specifically recommends that for children the study of mathematics should come before the study of music.

---

9   Aurelian of Reome, *The Discipline of Music*, trans. Joseph Ponte (Colorado Springs: Colorado College Music Press, 1968), VI.

10 Ibid., X.

11 Nicholas of Cusa (1401–1464), in 'Compendium,' XIV, trans. William Wertz, Jr., in *Toward a New Council of Florence* (Washington, D.C.: Schiller Institute, 1993), 539ff, says the uneducated man is nothing but an animal.

12 Johannes de Grocheo, *De Musica*, trans. Albert Seay (Colorado Springs: Colorado College Music Press, 1967), 2.

13 *Opus Majus*, XIV.

14 Ibid., 'Mathematics,' I.

> The natural road for us is to begin with things which befit the state and nature of childhood, because children begin with facts that are better known by us and that must be acquired first. But of this nature is mathematics, since children are first taught to sing, and in the same way they can learn the method of making figures and of counting, and it would be far easier and more necessary for them to know about numbers before singing, because in the relations of numbers in music the whole theory of numbers is set forth by example, just as the authors on music teach, both in ecclesiastical music and in philosophy.[15]

With the beginning of the Renaissance we find a representative treatise by one of the ars antique, Jacques de Liege. His treatise is called a 'music treatise,' *Speculum Musicae* (1313), but the first five of its seven books deal with mathematics. We see the importance of 'numbers' in music when he complains that he is being attacked by the younger generation, the ars nova, for his belief that music should be based on the number 3, a purely rational construction based on Church dogma. His contemporary, Jean de Muris (ca. 1290–1350), takes the same position and offers some 'proof' for the importance of the number 3. He includes not only the Trinity, but the 3 aspects of time of celestial bodies, the 3 attributes of the stars and sun, the 3 attributes of the elements, the 3 intellectual operations, the 3 terms in the syllogism and many more.[16] De Muris also points to the relationship of music and geometry when he observes that 'the wiser ancients long ago agreed and conceded that geometrical figures should be the symbols of musical sounds.'[17] This he follows with an extraordinary omission, which, had he filled it, would be more interesting to us today than the rest of his entire treatise. It also reminds us that theory and notation always follow the actual practice of music.

> For reasons which we shall pass over, their symbols did not adequately represent what they sang.

One of the more respected theorists of the Middle Renaissance was Johannes Tinctoris (1435–1511) who, once again, had actually made his reputation as a mathematician. In the Prologue to his own treatise *Concerning the Nature and Propriety of Tones*, Tinctoris identifies himself as one who professes 'the mathematical sciences.'[18] In this same work, in speaking of Church modes he says these were named,

> according to arithmetic, without which it is obvious no famous musician escapes.[19]

---

[15] Ibid., III. See also XVI for more on the relationship of music to both mathematics and theology.
[16] Strunk, *Source Readings*, 173.
[17] Ibid., 175.
[18] *Concerning the Nature and Propriety of Tones*, trans. Albert Seay (Colorado Springs, 1976), 1.
[19] Ibid., 3.

During his tenure in Naples under Ferdinand I, Tinctoris must have been exposed not only to Italian Humanism, but to a wide variety of secular art music of high quality. Yet he assigns little space to these things in his treatises and, as an official of the Church, concluded Jesus Christ to have been the greatest singer. His main testimony of the new values in music is found in his complaints over composers who were breaking the old mathematical rules.

> As a result of this tempest, the musical ability of our time has undergone such an increase that it seems to be a new art ...
>
> But alas! I wonder not only at these but even at many other famous composers, for while they compose so subtly and so ingeniously with incomprehensible smoothness, I have known them to ignore entirely musical proportions or to signify incorrectly those which they do know. I do not doubt that this results from a lack of arithmetic, without which no brilliant achievement in music escapes, for proportion is produced from its entrails.[20]

What Tinctoris called the 'new art' was a return to the ancient idea that music should communicate emotions rather than mathematical principles. In his treatise Tinctoris refers to an incident which must be regarded as a hallmark of this change, although we doubt that Tinctoris recognized it as such. He tells us that in response to his old-fashioned treatise on the importance of mathematics in music a singer, a representative of the new Humanistic focus on the emotions, wrote to Tinctoris telling him he was going to make him eat his treatise:

> ... has not been afraid to menace me with a violent meal of this little book if ever I should return to my native land.

In sixteenth-century Italy, in spite of the activity of the Humanists, we still find some curiously old-fashioned views. In Galilei's *Fronimo*, a book dealing with intabulating for the lute, the author comes upon his friend, Fronimo, a distinguished lutanist. His friend is sitting outdoors on a stump, playing for himself, and Galilei describes him not lost in the rapture of his performance, but absorbed in the mathematics of music.

> He has not yet seen me, so intent is he on considering the proportions of the musical intervals.[21]

It will seem curious to the modern reader that for a long time the interval of the sixth was considered a dissonance, long after its inversion, the third, had become considered a consonant. This judgment was made on the basis of the 'proportions of the intervals,' which is what Fronimo was listening to, rather than by the ear. Therefore, it is a harbinger of a new era when theorists begin to accept the ear's judgment over mathematics. We see an excellent illustration of this process in Girolamo Cardano (1501–1576), an important mathematician and writer on almost every subject.[22] He personally recognizes that the sixth sounds consonant and he admits

---

[20] *Proportionale Musices*, trans. Albert Seay in *Journal of Music Theory* 1 (1957): 27.

[21] Vincenzo Galilei, *Fronimo* [1584], trans. Carol MacClintock (Neuhasen-Stuttgart: Hanssler-Verlag, 1985), 32.

[22] In his own catalog of his works, his music treatise is found together with those on mathematics.

'why should we reject what the ear already approves,' even if the mathematical ratios do not agree. He seems a bit frustrated that he cannot explain mathematically why it should sound good and finally concludes that it is just a matter of time before it is understood.

> So it is necessary to consider why a connection of tones which is pleasing to the ears does not have a rational explanation. Accordingly, the usefulness of the aural sense is clear, but its rationale is found in the discovery of many things which are not yet fully known through experience.[23]

Another harbinger of our times, sad to say, is the fall of music from being a science. While maintaining that geometry and arithmetic are 'vital instruments for the search of Truth,' Vives in his important treatise, *On Education*, now finds the role for music to be, 'for relaxation and recreation of the mind through the harmony of sounds.'[24] It is noteworthy that Vives finds this the primary purpose of music in education.

> In music we have deteriorated much from the older masters, on account of the dullness of the ear which has utterly lost all discrimination of subtle sounds, so that now we no longer distinguish even the long and short sounds in common speech; and for this reason we have lost some kinds of meters, and that primitive harmony of tones, the effects of which the ancient writers testify were vast and marvelous. Young men should receive theoretical instruction in music, and should also have some practical ability. Only let the pupil practice pure and good music which, after the Pythagorean mode, soothes, recreates, and restores to itself the wearied mind of the student; then let it lead back to tranquility and tractability all the wild and fierce parts of the student's nature.[25]

As with France and Italy, it was not to the universities of the German-speaking countries that one could look for new ideas in music. Here also they remained locked in the old medieval Scholastic notion that music belonged to mathematics. Thus, in 1505, the University of Leipzig appointed Sebastianus Muchelon as 'lector musicae et aritmetice,'[26] a document of the University of Köln in 1515 specifies the teaching of 'the books on mathematics, that is geometry, arithmetic, music and astronomy' and in 1558 the University of Heidelberg employed a lecturer in mathematics who was expected to include music in his teaching. Johannes Cochlaeus, a professor at Köln, in his *Tetrachordum Musices* of 1511, still finds music firmly attached to mathematics.

> Arithmetic is concerned with absolute numerals, music with numerals related to each other ...[27]

---

[23] Quoted in Clement Miller, *Hieronymus Cardanus, Writings on Music* (American Institute of Musicology, 1973), 104.

[24] Juan Vives, *Vives: On Education*, trans. Foster Watson (Cambridge: University Press, 1913), I, v. He classifies all poetry under the heading of music.

[25] Ibid.

[26] Nan Cooke Carpenter, *Music in the Medieval and Renaissance Universities* (Norman: University of Oklahoma Press, 1958), 251. Carpenter documents the association with mathematics extensively.

[27] Johannes Cochlaeus, *Tetrachordum Musices*, trans. Clement Miller (American Institute of Musicology, 1970), 21.

In one of the works of Erasmus (1469–1536) we again find the harbinger of the modern age when the ear begins to receive equal billing, so to speak, with the eye. It is an interesting discussion and concludes with a memorable phrase. Erasmus defines the common usage of an old Greek proverb, 'Double diapason,' to mean any two things very far apart. In the course of his musical discussion he seeks to make the principal point that the range of two octaves is a kind of natural furthermost limit, with respect to the ear hearing the mathematical proportions in music. Clearly concerned that he was writing on a subject which he had limited experience, he tells us that as he was writing, a famous philosopher, Ambrogio Leone of Nola, just happened to walk in and thus he attributes to this man the remainder of the discussion. Leone finds two reasons for calling the double octave the natural limit. First, he has observed that the [male] voice can not reach beyond the fifteenth without becoming forced and artificial. The second argument is because Reason and the senses must work together. While Reason can comprehend numbers of any size, hence, for example, the possibility of a distance of a thousand octaves, the senses do not distinguish relationships beyond two octaves.

> But the physical senses have had their own limits prescribed for them by nature, and if they transgress these, they gradually become misty and wandering, and can no longer judge with certainty as they used to do, but through a cloud, as they say, or in a dream. It was not fitting that principles of art should be drawn from an uncertainty of judgment. But since the ancients understood that beyond the fifteenth note of the scale the judgment of the ears began to fail, they decided to fix the bounds of harmony there, so that no one could have any reason to bring up that adage of yours, 'unheard music is useless.'[28]

There was one theorist who was far ahead of his time and attacked the whole idea of the inclusion of mathematics in the teaching of music. Adrian Coclico was a Flemish man teaching at Wittenberg in 1545 when he arrived at the thoughts he expressed in his *Compendium Musices* of 1552, a treatise intended as a manual for the teaching of singing to choir boys. Tine and time again he advises the reader to forget the 'books of the musician-mathematicians' and comes very strongly to the aesthetic basis of music—the listener.

> As a singer, [the boy] will study especially how to please the ears of men and how to inspire pleasure in them, as well as admiration and favor for himself. He will also be continually guided by the judgment of his ears. The ears easily understand what is done correctly or badly and are truly the masters of the art of singing.[29]

It is a treatise of practical music, not the theory of music, and he attributes his viewpoints to his own teacher, the 'most noble musician, Josquin,' from whom he learned 'incidentally, from no book.'

---

[28] 'Adages,' in *The Collected Works of Erasmus* (Toronto: University of Toronto Press, 1992)., XXXI, 202ff. Erasmus discusses the last phrase in a discussion of the proverb, 'Hidden music has no listeners [and is thus worthless]' in Ibid., XXXII, 117ff.

[29] Adrian Coclico, *Musical Compendium*, trans. Albert Seay (Colorado Springs: Colorado College Music Press, 1973), 6.

During the sixteenth century the English remained married to the old scholastic, mathematical world of music. Thus even Shakespeare, always a mirror of real (aristocratic) life in London, found it necessary to introduce a music teacher as a man 'Cunning in music and the mathematics.'[30]

With the dawn of the Baroque these views continued, as for example we see in the definition of music by William Wooten (1666–1727) found in his *Reflections upon Ancient and Modern Learning* (1694),

> Musick is a Physico-Mathematical Science, built upon fixed rules, and stated proportions.

Wooten finds it particularly objectionable that musicians do not respect, and do not even read, the great treatises of the past.

> Whereas all modern mathematicians have paid a mighty deference to the ancients; and have not only used the names of Archimedes, Apolonius and Diophantus, and the other ancient mathematicians with great respect; but have also acknowledged, that what further advancements have since been made, are, in a manner, wholly owing to the first rudiments, formerly taught. Modern musicians have rarely made use of the writings of Aristoxenus, Ptolemee, and the rest of the ancient musicians; and, of those that have studied them, very few, unless their editors have confessed that they could understand them. Others have laid them so far aside, as useless for their purpose; that it is very probable, that many excellent composers have scarce ever heard of their names.

Even so remarkable a mind as Isaac Newton, in formulating his ideal university curriculum, has the 'mathematics lecturer' teaching music.[31] Newton, by the way, labored for years in an attempt to correlate the numbers representing the vibrations of musical pitches with the numbers representing the light waves of the colors of the visual realm. When he died he left a drawing, a kind of chart, in which he has created his hypothetical correspondence of tones and colors, but he left no text to describe how he arrived at these findings and no one has ever been able to make sense of them.[32]

The great French treatise of the Baroque, the *Harmonie universelle* of 1636, is again the work of a mathematician, Marin Mersenne (1588–1648). There is much fascinating reading here, but with regard to the topic at hand, music and mathematics, there is one new proposal of note. He invented a new notation system consisting entirely of numbers, which he regarded as useful primarily in correspondence.

---

[30] *The Taming of the Shrew*, II, ii, 57.

[31] We do, however, support his position that the faculty should be given lifetime supervision of the alumni!

> All Graduates without exception found by the Proctors in Taverns or other drinking houses, unless with travelers at their Inns, shall at least have their names given in to the Vice-Chancellor who shall summon them to answer for it before the next Consistory.

[32] The reader can find this chart reproduced in *The Correspondence of Isaac Newton* (Cambridge: University Press, 1959), I, 377.

> This manner of composing can be used by learned theoreticians, who wish to compare and send their compositions to each other, or who wish to have their compositions printed without using the [normal musical] notes of practice, which not every printer has.[33]

The reader must remember that the seventeenth century was also the beginning of The Enlightenment and was a period of fervent activity in inventions of all kinds. This climate produced another work related to new notation and it is found in the ten books on music of the *Musurgia Universalis* (1650) by the German born Athanasius Kircher (1601–1680). In Book Three, 'Arithmetical,' Kircher presents a system of 'musical arithmetic,' through which the rules of addition, subtraction, multiplication and division of intervals are represented by special characters.

And perhaps another experiment of this sort is found by Gottfried Leibniz (1646–1716), a system which might be of profit to student composers!

> Music is subordinate to Arithmetic and when we know a few fundamental experiments with harmonies and dissonances, all the remaining general precepts depend on numbers; I recall once drawing a harmonic line divided in such a fashion that one could determine with the compass the different compositions and properties of all musical intervals. Besides, we can show a man who does not know anything about music, the way to compose without mistakes.[34]

On the other hand, it is among the German writers of the Baroque that we find the first clear documentation of a new era of philosophy in music, a philosophy not based on mathematics. The most important discussion on this view has come down to us is by Johann Mattheson (1681–1764). In his *Neu-Eröffnete Orchestre* Mattheson attacks the old notion of mathematics-based theory in music by going directly to the elements upon which the older theorists had based their reasoning, in particular the nature of the intervals. In his discussion of whether the interval of the fourth should be regarded as a consonance or dissonance, Mattheson concludes it is not a matter of mathematics, but rather a matter of the ear, that is how the fourth is used. The reader should particularly notice, as a hallmark of the Baroque's movement away from music based on concepts to music based on feeling, that Mattheson specifies here that music communicates with 'the inner soul.'

> Numbers in music do not govern but merely instruct. The Hearing is the only channel through which their force is communicated to the inner soul of the attentive listener … The true aim of music is not its appeal to the eye, nor yet altogether to the so-called 'Reason,' but only to the Hearing, which communicates pleasure, as it is experienced, to the Soul and the 'Reason.' Hence, if the testimony of the ear is followed, it will be discovered that in its relation to the surrounding sounds and harmony, the fourth will be either consonant or dissonant.[35]

---

33 Treatise IV, book iv, 17.

34 Leibniz, untitled manuscript, known as 'Precepts for Advancing the Sciences and Arts' (1680), in *Leibniz Selections*, ed. Philip Wiener (New York: Scribner's, 1951), 42ff.

35 Johann Mattheson, *Das Neu-Eröffnete Orchestre* (Hamburg, 1713), 126ff. Mattheson also writes at length in opposition to the old dogma that mathematics is the basis of music in his book, *Das Forschende Orchestre* of 1721.

Such views, which would seem obvious to most modern readers, were nevertheless a direct attack on the old mathematics-based theories of music and resulted in letters and books attacking Mattheson for his views. Johann Buttstedt, an organist in Erfurt, attacked Mattheson in a book, *Ut, Mi, Sol, Re, Fa, La, Tota Musica et harmonia Aeterna … entgegen gesetzt Dem neu-eröffneten Orchestre* in which he contends that since German music is now practiced only by craftsmen [*Spielmanns-Wesen*] the current musicians are not even educated in the older rules.

> How many musicians will one find today who have real knowledge? Most of them do not even know how many styles and modes there are and what music is suitable for ecclesiastical or motet styles. The knowledge of such styles is almost entirely lost … Why? [Modern music] is hard to understand and not well paid for. And so, instead of correct knowledge mere Galanterie suffices, just as the finery of ladies once consisted of pearls and golden chains but now of mere ribbons and laces.[36]

To defend himself, Mattheson published a new book, *Das Beschützte Orchestre*, in which he appealed to a number of distinguished German musicians to join in the debate over mathematics versus feelings, and some distinguished musicians came to the defense of Mattheson. Handel wrote Mattheson at this time, taking a very practical approach to the debate.

> The question seems to me to reduce itself to this: whether one should prefer an easy & most perfect Method to another that is accompanied by great difficulties capable not only of disgusting pupils with Music, but also making them waste much precious time that could better be employed in plunging deeper into this art & in the cultivation of one's genius?[37]

Johann Heinichen, in language much stronger than Mattheson's, ridiculed the old-fashioned theorists as having wasted their entire life in pursuit of *rudera antiquitatis*.

> All will be sheer Greek to those steeped in prejudices when nowadays they hear that a moving music composed for the ears requires even more subtle and skillful rules—to say nothing of lengthy practice—than the heavily oppressive music composed for the eyes which the cantors of even the tiniest towns maltreat on innocent paper according to all the venerable rules of counterpoint … And we Germans alone are such fools as to jog on in the old groove and, absurdly and ridiculously, to make the appearance of the composition on paper, rather than the hearing of it, the aim of music.[38]

Johann Kuhnau also was strong in his support of Mattheson.

> As regards the great controversy that the gentleman of Erfurt has brought upon you, I do not believe that, save for him, anyone will disapprove of your *Orchestre*. This is especially true of your point of view in matters of the solmisation and the old ecclesiastical modes; for you wrote your *Orchestre* for a galant-homme who, being no professional musician, has not the least interest in amusing himself with innumerable old freaks which are usually outmoded at best and worth—virtually nothing.[39]

---

[36] Quoted in Beekman Cannon, *Johann Mattheson, Spectator in Music* (Archon Books, 1968), 135ff.

[37] George Friedrich Handel, letter to Johann Mattheson, February 24, 1719, quoted in Piero Weiss, *Letters of Composers Through Six Centuries* (Philadelphia: Chilton, 1967), 63.

[38] Quoted in Cannon, *Johann Mattheson, Spectator in Music*, 141ff.

[39] Quoted in Ibid., 142.

In his *Der vollkommene Capellmeister* of 1739 Mattheson returns to this question.[40] Here he begins with the basic point that mathematics is an aid to music, as it is to most disciplines. However, 'they are wrong who believe or want to teach others that mathematics is the heart and soul of music' or that it is responsible for changes in emotion in the music. He begins his argument with the concept of proportions in general, which he finds in natural, moral, rhetorical and mathematical relationships. For the first three of these, natural, moral and rhetorical relationships, Mattheson maintains no precise mathematical measure is possible. One cannot, for example measure the distance from the earth to the sun precisely because the flames leaping out from the sun render no fixed edge. His comment regarding precision in language is quite perceptive. Everyone would agree, he supposes, that 'life' is a positive, happy word. But if one says 'life is denied,' the meaning is changed. Thus, 'the heart's emotion no longer has its basis in mere sounds and words.'

Turning to music, he proposes two rhetorical questions:

1. If someone wants to be a sound musician, must he not attain this through mathematics?
2. Cannot one become an admirable composer and musician without thorough knowledge of the arts of measuring?

> Now if someone says yes to the first question, and no to the second, then he contradicts ancient and modern experience, indeed, his own eyes, ears, hands, the combined senses of all mankind, and shuts the only door through which his intelligence gives him what he has. Whereas if he answers no to the first question and yes to the second, then mathematics cannot possibly be the heart and soul of music.

From this he concludes mathematics can measure, but not determine the essence of a thing. 'Everything that goes on in music is based on mathematical relationships of intervals just about as much as seamanship is based on anchors and cables.'

> However one defines the mathematical relationships of sounds and their quantities, no real connection with the passions of the soul can ever be drawn from this alone.

Mathematics is only the 'science, theory and scholarship' of music. To introduce what exists beyond this he quotes Andreas Papius.

> The mere cognition of the ratio of a step, a half step, a comma, the consonances, etc., will bring the name virtuoso or artistic prince to no one, but rather the minute examination according to the laws of nature of the various works which are produced by great artists: from this we can understand the composer's soul, in regard to how and to what extent, in his particular work, one thing more than another masters the human mind and emotions, which is the highest pinnacle of the discipline of music.

Again, his point here is that mathematics can measure the elements of music, but not how these elements are used. It is the latter, not the former, which concern feelings in music.

---

40 Johann Mattheson, *Der vollkommene Capellmeister* [1739], trans. Ernest Harriss (Ann Arbor: UMI Research Press, 1981), Foreword, VI.

> A perfect understanding of the human emotions, which certainly are not to be measured by the mathematical yardstick, is of much greater importance to melody and its composition than the understanding of tones ... This is certain: it is not so much good proportion, but rather the apt usage of the intervals and keys, which establishes the beautiful, moving and natural quality in melody and harmony. Sounds, in themselves, are neither good nor bad; but they become good and bad according to the way in which they are used. No measuring or calculating art teaches this.

How then does one describe the role mathematics plays in music, together with its other elements? Mattheson offers following metaphor:

> The human mind is the paper. Mathematics is the pen. Sounds are the ink; but Nature must be the writer.

Mattheson points out that sculptors know and can measure the proportions of the human body, but 'heart and soul ... and beauty is not on this account to be found in such mathematical measuring; but only in that force which God put in Nature.' Similarly, in painting, when 'mathematics ceases entirely, true beauty really first begins.' And so with music,

> A composer can succeed quite well without special mathematical skills. Many who virtually climbed to the pinnacle of music can hardly name or interpret all parts of mathematics; not to mention anything more ... However, the best mathematician, as such, if he were to want to compose something, could not possibly achieve this with mere logic.
>
> Let it be said once in fact for all: Good mathematical proportions cannot constitute everything: this is an old, stubborn misconception.

The point, he says, is this: 'music draws its water from the spring of Nature; and not from the puddles of arithmetic.' The composer expresses something understood from Nature. Only then can this be mathematically expressed, but not the other way around. When Mattheson speaks here of Nature, he is also thinking of God.

> Mathematics is a human skill; nature, however, is a divine force ... Now the goal of music is to praise God in the highest, with word and deed, through singing and playing. All other arts besides theology and its daughter, music, are only mute priests. They do not move hearts and minds nearly so strongly, nor in so many ways ...
>
> Music is above, not in opposition to mathematics.

In conclusion, Mattheson cannot resist taking a shot at those remaining exponents of the old mathematics-based polyphony.

> I have occupied myself with music, practical as well as theoretical, with great earnestness and ardor for over half a century already: I have also met many very learned Mathematici in this not insubstantial time who thought they made new musical wonders out of their old, logical writings; but they have, God knows! always failed miserably. On the other hand, I have quite certainly and very often experienced that not a single famous actor, musician, nor composer, not only in my time but as far as

I can remember having read or heard about, has been able to construct even a simple melody which was of any value on the feeble foundations of mathematics or geometry ... What will happen in the future is yet to be seen.

We might also add that in his biographical work, *Ehrenpforte* (Hamburg, 1740), in reference to a person who had claimed both a goal of making 'music a scientific or scholarly pursuit' and an association with Bach, Johann Mattheson adds that Bach certainly did not teach this man 'the supposed mathematical basis of composition.' 'This,' Mattheson testifies, 'I can guarantee.'[41]

And so the stage was set for a century and a half of the greatest, most heart-felt musical compositions ever written, the innumerable great Classical Period and Romantic Era compositions by the German and Austrian composers. They are a powerful rebuttal to three thousand years or so of philosophical arguments on the mathematical basis of music.

Nothing more was heard of mathematics until the twentieth century when the serial composers appeared. The Twelve-Tone Era lasted about fifty years (the same length as the Classical Period) and is now dead.[42] It produced music the public did not want to hear and does not want to hear today. It was a failed experiment by composers who were ignorant of history's demonstration that great music is based neither on concepts nor numbers.

'But,' these composers say, 'we are not of this world; it is in the future when our compositions will be understood and appreciated.' We can see nothing to suggest this will be the case. Actually, as we survey concert programs here and abroad, we do not find a single serial composition which can be said to be 'in the repertoire.'

---

41 Quoted in Hans T. David and Arthur Mendel, *The Bach Reader* (New York: Norton, 1966), 440.

42 A musician we admire told us, 'Thank God I lived long enough to see the death of Communism and Twelve-Tone music!'

Is Music Theory or Performance?
(Musica speculativa vs Musica practica)

How would one define love? We beg the reader's indulgence to consider which of the two following definitions seems more to the point.

1. Love is something one comes to understand and define on the basis of his personal experience with various kinds of love throughout the course of his life.
2. Love is a concept you learn about from reading books.

Nearly everyone, we would guess, would pick the first and would conclude that love is experiential and not conceptual.

Common sense would suggest that a similar distinction in definitions of music would produce a similar answer.

1. Music is something one comes to understand and define on the basis of his personal experience with hearing and/or playing music throughout the course of his life.
2. Music is a concept you learn about from reading books.

But if you assume the first answer is self-evident you may be surprised to learn that the academic world has handed down from antiquity a contention that says, 'No! Music is a science you learn from books.' This wrong-headed prejudice is at the heart of American music education today. How has the academic world come to such a conclusion, ignoring the fact that millions of persons all over the world love to listen to and perform music even though they 'know nothing' about it? Who could contend that when we say, 'Music is the International Language,' we are making reference to reading material?

This prejudice which makes music a conceptual discipline, rather than an experiential one, has its origin in the central premise of nearly all early philosophers, that man must be governed by Reason. This was closely supported by the argument that the eye is the most important of the five senses, the consequences of which for ear-dependent music are obvious. It then followed that 'knowing about' something was a higher accomplishment than actually 'doing' something. The usual example given was the architect, who deserves more credit than the mere stone mason or carpenter. The point here was that one thinks and the others merely craft with their hands. Aurelian, in his *Musica Disciplina* of 843 AD, points out that this is why instrumentalists are not even called 'musicians,' but are rather named for their instruments (tools, as it were) as in 'flute players,' etc.[1]

---

[1] Marchetto of Padua (fourteenth century) therefore concludes the singer is only the 'tool' of the musician. See *Lucidarium*, trans. Jan W. Herlinger (Chicago: University of Chicago Press, 1985), treatise 16, I, iv.

One of the earliest examples of this line of thought is found in Plato. He has Socrates discussing various musical performers with a student and Socrates asks, 'But can a man who does not know a thing, know that the thing is right?'[2] He meant, even though the musician sounds very pleasing, how can he (we) judge if he is doing the right thing if he (we) knows nothing of the theory and science of music? Some fifteen centuries later this same belief was stated by John [Cotton?] in his treatise *On Music* written ca. 1100 AD. He seems perplexed that he hears nice music played by musicians who know nothing.

> Thus we sometimes see jongleurs and actors who are absolutely illiterate composing pleasant-sounding songs.

Amazingly, to the uneducated listener he says, You may enjoy what you hear but you can't know if it is good unless you master the science and theory of music.

> For whoever devotes unremitting labor to it, and perseveres without pausing or wearying, can gain from it this reward, that he will know how to judge the quality of song.[3]

And again, performing well brings you no credit, only knowing about performance brings credit!

> We said 'having a knowledge of music' because even if one unversed in the subject does what he does correctly, still, because he does it unwittingly, he is little esteemed.[4]

And finally, he suggests that the musician who performs without 'knowing' what he is doing is nothing but a beast!

> From the musician to the singer how immense the distance is;
> The latter's voice, the former's mind will show what music's nature is;
> But he who does, he knows not what, a beast by definition is.[5]

Some three hundred years later we find this paraphrased by the great theorist, Tinctoris (1435–1511).

> There is a big difference between musicians and singers.
> These know, those talk about, what music is.
> And he who doesn't know what he talks about is considered an animal.[6]

---

[2] *Laws*, 668c.

[3] John, 'On Music,' in *Hucbald, Guido, and John on Music*, trans. Warren Babb (New Haven: Yale University Press, 1978), 51.

[4] Ibid., 77.

[5] John gives the source as the *Micrologus*, but it actually comes from the beginning of Guido's *Regulae rhythmicae*.

[6] *Dictionary of Musical Terms*, trans. Carl Parrish (New York: Free Press of Glencoe, 1963), 45.

But this logic was carried even further, for St. Augustine (fourth century) declares that audience members who listen to music without understanding the 'science' of music are also beasts!

> AUGUSTINE. And what's more, aren't those who like to listen to [performers] without this science to be compared to beasts?[7]

The argument here is that animals, lacking Reason, can hear sounds, but not 'music.' Following this line, the fifteenth-century theorist, Tinctoris, reflecting on those listeners he has known who prefer even poor singers to simple theory [moderate rationalities], thinks God should turn them into animals!

> I think these people worthy to have their human faces with their stupid ears changed by divine intervention into those of an ass.[8]

This kind of thinking can still be found at the end of the seventeenth century, as we see in William Wotton's (1666–1727), *Reflections upon Ancient and Modern Learning* (1694). He distinguishes between what he calls the 'skilled' listener and the 'common' listener and tries to make his point by analogy with painting. The expert, he says, finds his enjoyment in the detail, the technique and, for all we can tell, never sees the entire painting!

> For, in making a judgment of Musick, it is much the same thing as it is of pictures. A great judge in Painting does not gaze upon an exquisite piece so much to raise his passions, as to inform his judgment, as to approve, or to find fault. His eye runs over every part, to find out every excellency; and his pleasure lies in the reflex act of his mind, when he knows that he can judiciously tell where every beauty lies, or where the defects are discernible: which an ordinary spectator would never find out.

Likewise in music, says Wotton, the common man has his 'passions raised,' without any contribution to his 'understanding.'

> So likewise in Musick; He that hears a numerous Song, set to a very moving tune, exquisitely sung to a sweet instrument, will find this passions raised, while his understanding, possibly, may have little or no share in the business. He scarce knows, perhaps, the names of the notes, and so can be affected only with an Harmony, of which he can render no account. To this man, what is intricate, appears confused; and therefore he can make no judgment of the true excellency of those things, which seem fiddling to him only, for want of skill in Musick.

The end of this kind of reasoning would presume that a man could just sit and enjoy contemplation of the 'science' of music without ever bothering to actually go hear musicians perform. Is it possible anyone could ever advocate such an idea? Yes! As we see in the following contention by the famous Petrarch, the fourteenth-century poet and musician.

---

7   *On Music*, trans. Robert Taliaferro in *Writings of Saint Augustine* (New York: Fathers of the Church), I, iv.

8   *Concerning the Nature and Propriety of Tones*, trans. Albert Seay (Colorado Springs, 1976), 5.

> A deaf person can know the tones and numbers characterizing the intervals of fifth and octave, as well as the other proportions of the musical scale with which musicians work. Although one does not hear the sounds of the human voice, of strings or the organ, he nevertheless may understand in his mind their fundamental canon and, doubtless, will prefer the intellectual pleasure to a mere titillation of the ear.[9]

The emphasis on music as a 'science,' rather than as an experiential practice, received a further boost from the early Church fathers who, in their paranoia about the emotions, through some smoke and mirrors allowed music to be taught in their schools only if it were transformed into a branch of mathematics. And so from approximately the sixth to the sixteenth centuries, one thousand years, virtually all music treatises were written by mathematicians. The result was descriptions of music such as this passage from Boethius (475–524 AD).

> But since the nete synemmenon to the mese (3,456 to 4,608) holds a sesquitertian ratio—that is, a diatessaron—whereas the trite synemmenon to the nete synemmenon (4,374 to 3,456) holds the ratio of two tones …[10]

Is this music? We must pause to point out that there were a few rays of light to be found, a few writers who were able to separate music from the dogma to some degree. Hucbald, in his *De harmonica institutione* (ca. 895 AD) seems to make a distinction between what one hears on the basis of 'judgment' and by 'ear.'[11] And Guido of Arezzo, in his *Epistola de ignoto cantu* (1030–1032 AD) points out that he has not followed the model of Boethius, 'whose treatise is useful to philosophers, but not to singers.'[12] Even Boethius, himself, for all his mathematical description of music had to admit, however reluctantly, that there was something in music which greatly moved ordinary, uneducated people. This characteristic of music is so strong, he writes, that we cannot free ourselves from it even if we try. For a brief moment he is writing about music, and not math.

> Why is it that mourners, even though in tears, turn their very lamentations into music? This is most characteristic of women, as though the cause for weeping might be made sweeter through song …
> Someone who cannot sing well will nevertheless sing something to himself, not because the song that he sings affects him with particular satisfaction, but because those who express a kind of inborn sweetness from the soul—regardless of how it is expressed—find pleasure. Is it not equally evident that the passions of those fighting in battle are roused by the call of trumpets? If it is true that fury and wrath can be brought forth out of a peaceful state of mind, there is no doubt that a more temperate mode can calm the wrath or excessive desire of a troubled mind. How does it come about that when someone voluntarily listens to a song with ears and mind, he is also involuntarily turned

---

[9] 'Remedies for Fortune Fair and Foul,' trans. Conrad Rawski (Bloomington: Indiana University Press, 1991), II, xcvii, 241.

[10] Boethius, *Fundamentals of Music*, trans. Calvin Bower (New Haven: Yale University Press), IV, ix.

[11] Hucbald, 'Melodic Instruction' in *Hucbald, Guido, and John on Music*, trans. Warren Babb (New Haven: Yale University Press, 1978), 119b/1.

[12] Ibid., 125.

toward it in such a way that his body responds with motions somehow similar to the song heard? How does it happen that the mind itself, solely by means of memory, picks out some melody previously heard?

From all these accounts it appears beyond doubt that music is so naturally united with us that we cannot be free from it even if we so desired.[13]

The old difficulty in defining music, with its twin rational and non-rational characteristics, received new attention at the time the first modern universities were founded in Europe. The Scholastic doctors who taught at Oxford and Paris, beginning in the thirteenth century, were accustomed by long precedent to discuss music as a conceptual subject. For one thousand years it had been a branch of mathematics and a member of the seven Liberal Arts. But these professors were also very much aware that the actual performance of music which they heard included elements, such as feeling, which were not easily represented or explained by numbers, or any other conceptual symbols.[14]

Hence they simply divided the discipline of Music at this time into two branches: *musica speculativa* and *musica practica*. They said, in effect, 'We will teach the first, and leave to you, the performers on the street, the second.' Thus, the prejudice we have seen in the medieval music treatises concerning 'science' versus 'practice' now, with the appearance of the new, modern universities, becomes institutionalized and proposition becomes dogma. Thus, for example, at the university in Oxford, one finds in the fourteenth century new treatises by Walter Odington and Simon Tunstede which are organized on the basis of musica speculativa and musica practica.[15] Of the six books which constitute Odington's treatise, by the way, the first three are purely mathematical.

One can understand, therefore, how important an harbinger it was when the first treatises on musica practica began to appear. One of the first was the *Practica musicae* by Franchino Gaffurio (1451–1518). He begins by making reference to the use of music in moral education in ancient Greece.

> It is readily apparent, illustrious Prince, how much influence the profession of the art of music had and with what veneration it was held among the ancients. We know this both from the example of the greatest philosophers, who, when they were very old, devoted themselves to this discipline as if in it they put the finishing touch to their studies, and from the practice of the strictest governments, which with the utmost diligence saw to it that whatever was harmful to public morals should be eliminated. Not only did these states not banish the art of music; they cultivated it with the utmost zeal as the mother and nurse of morals.[16]

---

[13] Boethius, *Fundamentals of Music*, I, i.

[14] Even today we have no independent symbols of music notation dedicated to feeling.

[15] Nan Cooke Carpenter, *Music n the Medieval and Renaissance Universities* (Norman: University of Oklahoma Press, 1958), 86.

[16] *The Practica musicae of Franchinus Gafurius*, trans. Irwin Young (Madison: University of Wisconsin Press, 1969), 3.

He continues by pointing out that no other subject is so universally approved and suggests that it may also be the oldest of the liberal arts. It is here also that he begins to introduce the musica practica branch (performance) and makes the point that it is only the practical side, and not the theory side, that influences morals, a practice given much emphasis by the ancient Greeks.

> Now music is not, like the other learned disciplines, merely a speculative pursuit: it reaches out into practice, and as was said previously, is connected with morality. I would not have fulfilled my duty if I had remained in the field of research only, serving a few without toiling diligently for the public good also.
>
> Thus this field of music theory is valuable not only because of the knowledge it gives music itself, but also because its roots extend very far; it aids other disciplines. This has been verified by the testimony of very influential men who have acknowledged that they learned literature from music above all else. Fabius Quintilian declares, on the authority of Timagenes, that this art 'is the most ancient of all studies in liberal education.'[17]

Gaffurio begins the main body of his text with the accurate observation that most previous theorists had concentrated on musica speculativa, rather than musica practica. Since it seems also to have been his observation that most practicing musicians had ignored the treatises on musica speculativa, he is astonished that musicians could nevertheless understand such things as harmony. We know today that it is perfectly reasonable that one can know music without knowing about music, as proven by modern clinical brain research and is most perfectly demonstrated in the child prodigy[18] and many popular artists who 'know nothing' about music and, in some extraordinary cases, do not even read music.

> Even though the majority of scholars have pursued the science of harmony, while neglecting its practical application, far more extensively than those who have studied the practical application of the science—after all, the science of harmony is the domain of the theoretician—nevertheless, it is incredible that musicians could have attained the practical skill in harmony which they did attain without any study of theory.[19]

Gaffurio's explanation for this 'incredible' fact is the correct one: musicians learn the fundamentals of music experientially. It is this same explanation, we reiterate, that accounts for the fact that the world is filled with musicians who have never taken our music classes!

Now speaking of the practical musicians, Gaffurio represents it as their view that knowledge is useless unless it is put into practice. Further, he seems to suggest that the speculative scholar cannot really understand the theoretical nature of music unless he actually hears these principles in use and even in performing them.

---

[17] Ibid., 5ff.

[18] Music is the only field of man's endeavors in which it is possible to have a child prodigy, due to the amount of musical information which comes to all genetically..

[19] Ibid., 11.

> There are also those who hold things valueless if they are not put to use. These people feel that the practice of vocal music has contributed most to the development of harmony, not because of the multitude of possibilities inherent in practice, but because it exhibits perfection itself.
>
> The mechanics of music are found in the movement of sounds producing consonances and melody. It is true that these sounds are assembled in vain by theory and science unless they are expressed in practice. Hence one must become thoroughly conversant with the highness, lowness, and the combinations of these sounds not only through one's mind and reason but also through the habit of listening to and articulating them.[20]

Having suggested, above, that the practical musicians' claim that it was their practice which contributed most to theory, he now makes the most interesting comment that in the middle Renaissance singers were singing things for which there was as yet no means of notation!

> Further, sounds which cannot be written down are committed to memory by usage and practice so that they will not be lost, for their delivery flows imperceptibly into the past.[21]

Gaffurio concludes his treatise, *Practica musicae*, by once again observing that after having written two treatises on musica speculativa, the kind of books he knows the readers are weary of, he felt compelled to add a volume on musica practica.

> Now, most gracious reader, I have presented my thoughts on musical practice with perhaps no less talent and industry than you wished for, though your wish was unspoken. For of course, since you must have grown weary reading my books on theory, you needed this just as some sharp foods are needed to revive and refresh the taste. Nor did I think I could escape blame if, when I taught the art of music and unveiled its innermost secrets (if I may use the phrase), I held back in silence from this part as well, which is called practica and consists of and is perfected by the actual practice of music itself.[22]

As the Renaissance progressed with growing sophistication in both composers and performers, there appears nevertheless to have been some return of the old debate relative to the respective importance of theory and performance. The greatest mind of the middle Renaissance, Leonardo da Vinci, said, 'Words are of less account than performances.'[23] While he appears to put 'science' in a lower category, he does not forget its importance.

> Those who devote themselves to practice without science are like sailors who put to sea without rudder or compass and who can never be certain where they are going. Practice must always be founded on sound theory.[24]

---

[20] Ibid., 12.

[21] Ibid., 18.

[22] Ibid., 266.

[23] *The Literary Works of Leonardo da Vinci*, ed. Jean Paul Richter (London: Phaidon, 1970), I, 78.

[24] Anthony Blunt, *Artistic Theory in Italy, 1450–1600* (Oxford: Clarendon Press, 1959), 28.

Actually, Leonardo believed that experience was the real teacher. Therefore, for him, both performance and science were based on experience.

> Good judgment is born of clear understanding, and a clear understanding comes of reasons derived from sound rules, and sound rules are the product of sound experience—the common mother of all the sciences and arts.[25]

During the sixteenth century the debate over the relative importance of theory and performance continued. The Italian theorist, Zarlino, almost seems to be pleading for more respect for theory, employing a nice analogy of going to the doctor.

> But just as it is necessary that sense and reason concur in order to make judgment in things of music, so it is necessary that he who wants to judge anything pertaining to art have two capabilities: first, that he be expert in things of science, that is, of speculation; and second, that he be expert in things of art, which consists of practice …
>
> Accordingly, just as it would be insane to rely on a physician who does not have the knowledge of both practice and theory, so it would be really foolish and imprudent to rely on the judgment of [a musician] who was solely practical or had done work only in theory.[26]

In another place, Zarlino tries to show how both the theorist and the performer fail without a more complete knowledge of music.

> Theory without practice is of small value, since music does not consist only of theory and is imperfect without practice. This is obvious enough. Yet some theorists, treating of certain musical matters without having a good command of the actual practice, have spoken much nonsense and committed a thousand errors. On the other hand, some who have relied only on practice without knowing the reasons behind it have unwittingly perpetrated thousands upon thousands of idiocies in their compositions.[27]

Bottrigari also takes the view that practice cannot be respected without theory, but his argument looks back to the medieval dogma that the person who 'knows' is to be respected more than the person who 'does,' or, the mind must be judged higher than the hand. After a discussion of the complexities of tuning based on the old tetrachord system, the character Desiderio asks,

> I was thinking about asking you if it is necessary for all musicians, such as those of today who compose madrigals and motets, to know these things, and if they do know them, or if simple practice suffices.[28]

---

[25] Ibid., I, 119.

[26] Gioseffo Zarlino, *On the Modes*, trans. Vered Cohen (New Haven: Yale University Press, 1983), 106.

[27] Gioseffo Zarlino, *The Art of Counterpoint*, trans. Guy Marco and Claude Palisca (New Haven: Yale University Press, 1968), 226ff.

[28] Hercole Bottrigari, *Il Desiderio*, trans. Carol MacClintock (American Institute of Musicology, 1962), 35.

Benelli answers, yes, every musician should know these things, but it is also possible to succeed without knowing and understanding the theoretical explanations, although some honor must be withheld.

> If, then, simple practice is sufficient to such composers to compose madrigals or motets or other kinds of cantilene, I will answer 'yes'; since I see and feel that most of them succeed with great applause, and in a short time even youths nowadays do marvelous miracles. But I will add also that it does not seem to me to be a great honor to accomplish things and not to be able to give the reasons for them.[29]

Vincenzo Giustiniani, whose writings reflect the end of the sixteenth century, believed that no one had sufficient native talent to compose great music without a firm knowledge of theory.

> In order that a musical composition succeed in gaining esteem it is necessary that it be composed according to the proper and true rules of this profession and, in addition, with new and difficult restrictions which may not be known to all musicians in general; and not only madrigals and compositions to be sung by several voices, but even in others in counterpoint, and canons, and that which seems more marvelous, the same arias to be sung easily by a single voice. And to succeed in this task the inclination given to many by nature will not be sufficient; there is required also study and application of mind and body. For possessing the rules and the just proportions of numbers, joined with those of the voice or of sound and the knowledge of the effects which are caused by these in the souls of men, not only in general but in particular corresponding to the individual inclinations of everyone and to the taste which prevails in different periods, one may be able to apply skill and experience to his own times, to human inclinations in general, and to the particular tastes of each person. And to attain this ability much application of the intellect is required, and much discussion is necessary to come to some conclusion about the work when the principles have been worked out beforehand.[30]

Due to the sense of intellectual freedom accompanying the significant religious and civic upheavals following Luther in sixteenth-century Germany, we are not surprised to find wide differences in opinion among the authors of music treatises regarding the relative importance of theory and performance. In the case of Andreas Ornithoparchus' *Musice active micrologus*, of 1517, we find an almost hostile view of performers. Ornithoparchus first admits that speculative understanding of music judges not by the ears, but by 'wit and reason,' but he is quick to point out that this is hard work 'and should not be lightly esteemed.'[31]

Next he argues for three categories of musician: performers, poets and critics (those who judge music only by 'speculation and reason'). It is the first category which he discusses at length, following the old Church prejudices against musicians who are 'merely' performers,

---

[29] Ibid., 36.

[30] Vicenzo Giustiniani, *Discorso sopra la Musica* [ca. 1628], trans. Carol MacClintock (American Institute of Musicology, 1962), 67ff.

[31] Ornithoparchus, *Musicae active mirologus* and Dowland, *Introduction: Containing the Art of Singing* (New York: Dover, 1973), 123.

craftsmen who engage in performance while understanding nothing they do. One would like to think that this is the last time we shall confront this relic of the worst of medieval Scholastic values, but alas this attitude is still found in some universities today.

> The first category deals with instruments, such as harpists, organists and all others who prove their skill by instruments. They are removed from the intellectual part of music, being as servants, and using no Reason, void of all speculation and following their sense only. Now though they may seem to do things with learning and skill, yet it is plain that they have no knowledge, because they do not comprehend what they profess. Therefore we deny that they have Music, which is the Science of making melody. One can have knowledge without practicing and this is a greater end than being an excellent practitioner. We do not associate nimbleness of fingers with Science, which resides in the soul, but rather to practice. If it were otherwise the more one knew about the Art, the more he would automatically become swift in his fingerings.[32]

Ornithoparchus includes singers among instrumentalists, which is to say performers, and again he says their performance means nothing if it is without 'the rules of Reason.' Thus, as regards the speculative versus the practical musician (theoretical versus performer), Ornithoparchus accepts the old Church dogma that it is more honorable to know than to do. Supposing the reader may wonder about the performers in the Old Testament, Ornithoparchus quickly adds that, well, they were also prophets and wise men!

Given this very limited definition of what a true musician is, one can understand Ornithoparchus' concern that the old Church style was dying out.

> Hence it is, that excepting those which are, or have been in the chapels of princes, there are none, or very few true musicians. Whereupon the Art itself doth grow into contempt, being hidden like a candle under a bushel, the praising of the almighty Creator of all things decreases and the number of those which seek the overthrow of this Art increases daily throughout Germany.

Ornithoparchus returns to the subject of the importance of musicianship based on theoretical learning in his discussion of polyphonic music. Now it is the composer who is the object of his attention and he lashes out at those who compose without 'following the rules.' In mid-stream he suddenly recalls having heard some effective music by composers not trained in theoretical knowledge, which is something he cannot quite explain.

> I cannot but scorn certain composers (for so they will be called, though indeed they are Monsters of Music), who, though they know not so much as the first elements of the art, yet proclaim themselves 'the musicians' musician,' being ignorant in all things, yet bragging of all things and do ... disgrace, corrupt and debase this art, which was in many ages before honored and used by many most learned, most wise men. They use any signs at their pleasure, neither reckoning of value, nor measure, seeking rather to please the ears of the foolish with the sweetness of the melody ... I know such a man, who has been hired to be the organist at the castle in Prague, who though he know not (and I conceal his greater faults) how to distinguish a perfect time from an imperfect, yet maintains publicly that he is writing from the very depth of music ... Many more have violently inundated the art of music, as

---

32 Ibid., 123.

> those which are not compounders of harmonies, but rather corruptors, children of the furies rather than the Muses, not worthy of the least grace I may do them. For their songs are ridiculous, not grounded on the principles of the art, though perhaps true enough. For the artist does not grace the art, but the art graces the artist. Therefore a composer does not grace music, but the contrary. There are some who make true songs not by art, but by custom, as having happily lived among singers all their life, yet do not understand what they have made, knowing that such a thing is, but not what it is.[33]

We have no doubt that he was aware of the attacks of the humanists on the old polyphonic Church style and, indeed, there were many later during the sixteenth century who greatly discounted this old scholastic style of composition. Perhaps for the same reason, he also sensed that his treatise would not receive universal praise.

> I doubt not that there will be some who will snarl at it and backbite it, condemning it before they read it and disgracing it before the understand it. Some would rather seem, than be, musicians, not obeying authors, or precepts or reasons, but whatsoever comes into their hair-brain Cockscomb … To whom I beg you (gentle Readers) to lend no ear … for it is in vain to harp before an ass.[34]

Another German writer who would have certainly found no value in the views of Ornithoparchus was Adrian Coclico, who wrote a treatise, *Compendium Musices* in 1552 intended as an aid in the training of boy singers. He almost completely rejects the old speculative tradition and his book is filled with comments such as the following which begins his discussion of scales.

> I have wished to train boys in music through but few words and precepts on that account, so that no youth running to the books of musician-mathematicians will waste his life in reading them and never arrive at the goal of singing well.[35]

This is really the first book which advocates the values of performance with almost no importance given to theory. We can understand this perspective because this author came to his conclusions on the basis of his own experience in having been a student under the great Josquin.

> In Belgian cities, where prizes are given to singers and, because of the prizes to be gained, no procedure or labor is undertaken unless it pertains to the goal of singing well, no music is written down or prescribed by precept.
> My teacher, Josquin des Pres, never rehearsed or wrote out any musical procedures, yet in a short time made perfect musicians, since he did not hold his students back in long and frivolous precepts, but taught precepts in a few words at the same time as singing through exercise and practice.[36]

---

[33] Ibid., 169.

[34] Ibid., 211.

[35] Adrian Coclico, *Musical Compendium*, trans. Albert Seay (Colorado Springs: Colorado College Music Press, 1973), 10, Seay writes, 'Music by 1550 was less and less of a liberal art and more and more a fine art, while theory had begun to lose most of its speculative character in favor of the purely practical.'

[36] Ibid., 16.

Rather than theoretical background, Coclico looked for enthusiasm, zeal and love of music in a prospective student.

> First, adolescents or better, boys ... should bring to their teacher a great zeal and desire for learning music, together with their natural enthusiasm, so that they may listen as eagerly and attentively as possible to whoever teaches and guides ... He, however, who is possessed by a certain single-minded zeal for learning ..., this person I hold myself committed that he will be an excellent musician. In a Greek proverb it is beautifully stated: Love teaches music.[37]

This natural enthusiasm he felt was particularly necessary in the case of the student who desired to compose.

> [The Student] should be led to composing by a great desire, and by a certain natural impulse he will be driven to composition, so that he will not taste food nor drink until his piece is finished, for, since this natural impulse so drives him, he accomplishes more in one hour than others in a whole month. Composers to whom these unusual motivations are absent are useless.[38]

By way of contrast, Henry Peacham (1576–1643), of England, in his *The Complete Gentleman*, a publication intended as a guide for the education of a noble, finds remarkable enthusiasm for the speculative branch of music.

> Infinite is the sweet variety that the theoric of music exerciseth the mind withal, as the contemplation of proportion, of concords and discords, diversity of moods and tones, infiniteness of invention, etc. But I dare affirm there is no one science in the world that so affecteth the free and generous spirit with a more delightful and inoffensive recreation, or better disposeth the mind to what is commendable and virtuous ...
>
> Yea, in my opinion, no rhetoric more persuadeth or hath greater power over the mind.[39]

With the arrival of the Baroque with its concentration on the role of emotion in music we see the pendulum begin to swing toward the importance of performance over the theoretical. Johann Mattheson still writes that one should employ both the speculativa and the practical in performance and like Leonardo he argues that theory should be employed at the service of performance, and not the other way around as earlier theorists suggested.

> That type of contemplation or theory is however to be preferred to all others which does not delve so deeply into shallow, mental considerations that action is forgotten; but turns its main aim toward actual practice and usage ... Whoever wants to make good use of both aspects must never separate them, but keep them fast together, like body and soul.

---

[37] Ibid., 5ff.

[38] Ibid.

[39] Henry Peacham, *The Complete Gentleman*, ed. Virgil Heltzel (Ithaca: Cornell University Press, 1962), 115ff.

In another place Mattheson becomes rather critical of the theoretical aspect of music because of the impression it renders to the ordinary person. His argument is that emphasis of the theory side of music gives the impression to the layman that they know nothing about music if they have not had this training. Mattheson knew by observation what we have learned today through clinical brain research. The fact is all men are born with the knowledge to understand this language of music. Of the conceptual music teacher Mattheson concludes,

> For they are persuaded that this beautiful and perfect creation, which a beneficent God has given us men for our pleasure, and likewise as a model of the eternal, harmonious Splendor, depends solely upon deep learning and laborious knowledge. To prove this, they dispense their philosophical rules and scholarly vagaries, not only with great authority, but likewise with such obscurity that one has a rightful aversion for the stuff, and would rather remain in permanent ignorance than to go through such horrenda.[40]

Mattheson, having been a performer, knew that rational concepts cannot well describe the experience of music. Thus he advises the pursuit of performance, after the necessary foundation, as a means of finding a 'healthy idea of music, purified of all unnecessary school-dust.'

We know we are in a new era with the regard to the recognition of performance when François Couperin contended,

> Just as there is a difference between grammar and declamation, so there is an infinitely greater one between musical theory and the art of fine playing.[41]

Roger North, of England, at this time also refers to the 'grammar' of music and suggests that he found a distinction between theoretical studies and what he calls the 'real knowledge' necessary to being a performer.

> The teaching of music and languages are very different, although the masters of the former [follow] the methods used by them of the other; that is, a sort of grammar to be [learned] by heart, whether it be or be not understood. The difference lies in this, that languages are mere memory, and come from the arbitrary use of nations, and may be as well one way or another; and this use grammarians endeavor to reduce to rule, which must be learnt and remembered. But music is taken from nature itself, and depends on body in a physical sense, even as the mathematical sciences do, and takes place finally in our imagination and fancy; and therefore should be taught by explaining it to the understanding as well as by giving the rules to which the practice of it is reduced. And for this reason it is that in the musical science the rules are very few, and those but introductory as it were to show what the subject matter is, that the learner might not have the trouble of being an original inventor of the whole science … And yet the real knowledge that belongs to music is dilated enough, and it is through that, that a man must learn the skill of a musician, whether he be showed it, or gathers it

---

[40] Johann Mattheson, *Das Neu-Eroffnete Orchestre* (Hamburg, 1713), 2ff. Mattheson also writes at length in opposition to the old dogma that mathematics is the basis of music in his book, *Das Forschende Orchestre* of 1721.

[41] François Couperin, *L'Art de toucher* (Paris, 1717, reprinted Wiesbaden: Breitkopf & Härtel, 1933), Preface.

of himself by observation, as generally is done ... As for children, I think easier ways might be found than the soured and mysterious Gamut, which they must rehearse antrorsum & retrorsum, without the least proffer to them of an explanation of it.[42]

Descartes observed that the performer, since his art is practiced live before an audience, automatically has a kind of check and balance in his decisions which the theorist escapes.

> For the consequences of the [practical study] will soon punish the man if he judges wrongly, whereas the [speculative study] has no practical consequences and no importance for the scholar except that perhaps the further they are from common sense the more pride he will take in them, since he will have had to use so much more skill and ingenuity in trying to render them plausible.[43]

Voltaire ridicules the old scholastic emphasis on 'conceptual music' in his fictional debate among the inmates of the hospital Quinze Vingt.

> A deaf man reading this short history, acknowledged that these blind people were quite wrong in pretending to judge of colors; but he continued firmly of the opinion that deaf people were the only proper judges of music.[44]

After the Baroque it seems quite clear in retrospect that for most persons 'music' meant performance, and not theory. The first modern school of music, the Paris Conservatoire, established in 1792, was a school of performance. The only study not related to one's instrument was weekly solfeggio courses and apparently a harmony course taught by Catel.

In 1865 Wagner was asked by King Ludwig II of Bavaria for advice in the establishment of a 'German Music School to be founded in Munich.' Wagner responded with an essay of some length and he concluded that it must be performance which is the 'invisible bond' of the curriculum. He goes further and maintains that the only true way to teach aesthetics and music history is through performance.

> The invisible bond, uniting the various branches of study, will always have to be [in] performance ... In keeping with the whole plan of our Music school, this cannot be pursued upon an abstract scientific path, mayhap through academic lectures and the like; but here, too, we must strike the purely practical path of direct artistic exercise, under higher guidance for the performance ...
> The true aesthetics and the sole intelligible history of music ... we must teach in no other way but by beautiful and correct performances of works of classical music.[45]

It is also probably fair to suggest that all the great nineteenth-century composers believed that music only really existed in performance, not in the score. Perhaps the reason for this was best expressed in the often quoted observation by Mahler, 'The best things in music are not found in the notes.' So much for any conceptual philosophy of music! Liszt once wrote,

---

[42] Quoted in John Wilson, *Roger North on Music* (London: Novello, 1959), 59.
[43] 'Discourse on the Method' (1637), I, 9ff.
[44] 'The Ignorant Philosopher,' in *The Works of Voltaire* (New York: St. Hubert Guild, 1901), XXXV, 293.
[45] *The Prose Works of Wagner*, trans. William Ashton Ellis, IV, 197ff.

> Unfortunately it is not with music as it is with painting and poetry: body and soul alone are not enough to make it comprehensible; it has to be performed, and very well performed too, to be understood and felt.[46]

He espresses the same thought in a letter thirteen years later,

> What is the good of anything that is written on paper, if it is not comprehended by the soul and imparted in a living manner?[47]

Wagner had once written to Liszt expressing this same thought:

> Only the performer is the real, true artist. All that we create as poets and composers expresses a wish but not an ability: only the performance itself reveals that ability or art.[48]

After the testimony of two hundred years by some of the greatest composers and greatest minds who ever lived, in the mid-twentieth century American music educators took it upon themselves to turn the clock again back to a medieval emphasis on teaching the 'science' of music, today called the conceptual aspects of music. Any objective observer would conclude that this approach has once again failed. Just compare the small numbers of students per capita in music classes, compare the relative level of spending by the school on music, compare the content of writing in educational journals—compare anything you want to compare.

The fundamental reason why conceptual teaching in music is doomed to failure, if the goal is music education, is because conceptual teaching is not the teaching of music. Aristotle reminds us that the written word, 'cat,' is not the real thing, it is only a symbol of the spoken word. And the spoken word, 'cat,' is not the real thing either. Thus, when we write, 'cat,' we are two generations away from the real thing. It is the same in music and it is the flaw that makes nonsense of the entire concept of conceptual teaching. The notion of conceptual teaching in music is based on the mistaken belief that what is on paper is music. Any child can tell you it is not.

Subsequently, for the most part this kind of teaching in music begins and ends with teaching only the grammar of music. This does not happen in any other field of education. In English Literature, for example, the study of Shakespeare's grammar is noted but it is not the core of the studies; the great moral truths are. Conceptual music teachers very rarely go beyond the grammar to discuss Truth in music. It is what makes the Mahler quote so illuminating, 'The most important things in music are not found in the notes!' We are simply not teaching 'the important things.' And we wonder why more students are not in our classes; we wonder why the financial support has disappeared and we wonder why the school board makes calculus a core subject when hardly anyone will ever use it in their lifetime.

---

[46] Letter to Abbe de Lemennais, Marseille, April 28, 1845.
[47] Letter to Rosa von Milde, Weimar, August 25, 1858.
[48] Letter to Franz Liszt, Zurich, July 20, 1850.

Let us be clear. Music theory has its place but music theory is not music. If we say we are going to teach music, then don't teach music theory. Teach music.

Let us repeat this using the terms of the early universities. We have inherited two forms of music, a speculativa form, which includes notation and all of theory and much of modern music education, which we can talk and write about, and which we learn by eye, and a practica form which is mostly learned by ear (the private studio teacher says, 'No, it goes like this').

But in truth, the speculativa form does not exist. It is only the conceptual symbolic language which represents the practica form, which is the real music! Thus, when music schools teach the conceptual form, while they call it music, they are not really teaching music. Harmony as it is usually taught, for example, is not music and might better be identified as the grammar of music, or perhaps even as another symbolic language.

In terms of pure education there are further very significant reasons for the poverty of the current conceptual philosophy of teaching. Two come to mind immediately. First, conceptual theory joins most of the rest of education in presenting the child with rational information. But rational information is by nature secondary and makes the child like every other child on the planet. Music, if taught experientially, has the potential to reach and teach the real child, the unique, individual being.

Second, conceptual music teaching, by its very nature, will always present to the class the teacher's experience in music, not the individual student's experience. That is backward. Because music is experiential, it must be based in the child. It is the child's experience which should be the goal of education.

Music is one of very few subjects in the school which can reach the class at an individual level. It is the greatest argument for music education and holds the greatest potential for financial and parental support. Why are we throwing away this remarkable advantage we have over the other subjects in school? Why don't we understand that we cannot have it both ways—we cannot obtain the educational rewards of teaching *music* if we only teach *about* music.

PART 2
UNDERSTANDING VERSUS FEELING

Early Voices Argue: Reason versus Experience

In works of music that man who judges by rules,
judges wrong.

Voltaire[1]

THE FRAGMENTS OF GREEK PHILOSOPHY which have survived from the period before Socrates and Plato are characterized by an intellectual attempt to understand the material world. Of what elements is the universe composed? How did man and animal life evolve? What happens after death? These are the kinds of questions discussed in the fragmentary remains of their work.

As a natural extension of this line of inquiry, we find the fifth century BC philosophers beginning to think about how the mind is organized and unanimous in finding no alternative but that man must be ruled by Reason. But no matter how strongly these early philosophers argued that man must be ruled by Reason, common observation told them there was more to the story. In particular, emotions and the experience gained from the practical endeavors of life clearly played a role which could not be ignored. Their problem was that they couldn't talk or write about the emotions and much of 'experience,' so they tended to just create categories of relative importance, Reason, of course, always being the most important. Democritus,[2] as an example, wrote,

> There are two forms of knowledge, one legitimate, one obscure; and the following all belong to the obscure form, sight, hearing, smell, taste, and touch.[3]

They, like us, had great difficulty talking about non-rational things. We, at least, have some advantage as a result of clinical brain research in knowing that not only is the right hemisphere of the brain mute, but the rational areas tend to deny its very existence.[4]

---

[1] 'Remarks on M. Pascal's Thoughts,' in *Philosophical Dictionary*, 'Taste,' in *The Works of Voltaire* (New York: St. Hubert Guild, 1901), XXI, 250, 256.

[2] The exact dates of Democritus are not known, but we understand him to be earlier than Plato as Aristoxenus, in *Historical Notes*, tells us that Plato wanted to burn the entire works of Democritus.

[3] Quoted in Milton C. Nahm, *Selections from Early Greek Philosophy* (New York: Appleton-Century-Crofts, 1964), 197.

[4] The first important research was conducted by Dr. Roger Sperry, who was awarded the Nobel Prize in Medicine for his findings in the organization of the right and left hemispheres of the brain.

The real problem for any philosophy which generalizes that Reason must rule is that in the end the rational side of ourselves is not the real us. Everything understood by the rational areas of our brain is second-hand information. Someone tells us, 'two plus two is four,' and we memorize it. This fact has been recognized, if not talked about, for a very long time. Aristotle (b. 384 BC) states this in the very first sentence of his *Posterior Analytics*.

> All teaching and learning that involves the use of reason proceeds from pre-existent knowledge.[5]

Clearly, this side of ourselves cannot be the real us, it is all someone else. By simple observation, as we said, and common sense the early philosophers sensed this and in order to account for 'the rest of us,' they tended to center much of their thought in the concept of the 'soul,' dividing the soul into regions to contain the emotions, the senses, and reason.

Toward the end of the sixth century, BC, several philosophers began to isolate the separate natures of reason and experience. Gorgias, in particular, was on the correct path in coming to understand that we cannot really know something unless we experience it ourselves. This same philosopher was also the author of one of the most frequently quoted statements of the fifth century:

> He who deceives is more honest than he who does not deceive
> and he who is deceived is wiser than he who is not.

He was speaking of the theater and meant that one can be more honest with fiction, not running the personal risk involved in telling the truth in non-fiction. The member of the audience, it followed, was 'wiser' as a consequence.

Theages, as probably most early philosophers, equated Wisdom as the end of reason. Today we would say knowledge is the end of reason; Wisdom is the end of experience.[6] The difference between the two is the story of some of the most interesting writing by earlier philosophers, those courageous men who understood the importance of defending the whole us against the tyranny of Reason. This is fundamental background reading for those who desire to understand the importance of music.

In modern society, especially in the field of education, we still suffer from the singular value the early philosophers awarded to 'Reason.' How familiar sounding is this warning by Parmenides (second half of the sixth to the first half of the fifth century BC), founder of the Eleatic School of philosophy. The senses, and experience, are real, but it is Reason, and not they, that is to be trusted.

---

5   Trans. Hugh Tredennick (Cambridge: Harvard University Press, 1960).

6   As did Leonardo da Vinci, who observed, 'Wisdom is the daughter of Experience.' *The Literary Works of Leonardo da Vinci*, ed. Jean Paul Richter (London: Phaidon, 1970), II, 240.

> You must debar your thought from this way of search, nor let ordinary experience in its variety force you along this way, allowing the eye, sightless as it is, and the ear, full of sound, and the tongue, to rule.[7]

Why, knowing what we know, does this judgment still control education? Probably for the same reasons that frustrated the early philosophers: we find it difficult to 'talk' about the non-rational parts of our experience, no matter how important they are. The modern tyranny is 'accountability.' How can we defend what we cannot talk about? And so, in the case of music education, we abandon the value of the genuine experience and focus our teaching on what we can talk about—concepts. Concepts can be graded and accounted for. Too bad that in our so doing the subject of music is once again removed from the real us. Too bad that in so doing we are teaching about music and not music itself.

There were some early philosophers who refused to simply take Reason as the unquestioned master. Even Plato in one place seems to suggest that some form of personal experience may be a pre-requisite of 'knowledge.'

> But then, certain professors of education must be wrong when they say that they can put knowledge into the soul which was not there before, like sight into blind eyes.[8]

Plutarch also pointed out that sometimes Reason grows out of experience, and he provided an example from his own life.[9]

> Upon which that which happened to me, may seem strange, though it be true; for it was not so much by the knowledge of words, that I came to understanding of things, as by my experience of things I was enabled to follow the meaning of words.

The Roman philosopher, Lucretius (99–55 BC), focused on the dependence of Reason on the senses, asking in one place,

> Can anyone
> Explain what bodily sensation is
> Unless he trusts his own experience of it?[10]

This philosopher also noticed the curious characteristic of the feeling sense that we call today 'phantom limb.' This is the perception that one can feel a leg, for example, in that case where the leg in fact no longer exists. Reason, of course, had no explanation for this phenomenon so vividly illustrated by Lucretius:

---

7   Fragment seven, quoted in Giovanni Reale, *A History of Ancient Philosophy* (Albany: State University of New York Press, 1987), 88.
8   *Republic.*, VII, 518c.
9   'Life of Demosthenes.'
10 *The Way Things Are*, III, 351.

> It is said scythe-bearing battle chariots,
> Red-steaming from their killing course, can cut
> Limbs off so quickly you can see them tremble
> Or quiver on the ground, before their soldier
> Has any inkling what has happened to him.
> His fighting spirit pushes his attack
> With what equipment he still has; he'll charge
> And never know his left arm and his shield
> Are swept off with marauding chariot-wheels
> And scythes and horses, while near by, a comrade
> Lifts his right arm to scale a wall, and sees
> His right arm isn't there, or attempts to rise
> While his leg is kicking at him from the ground.[11]

We find one extraordinary argument that experience gives meaning to that most rational representative of Reason, grammar. In his treatise on 'Mathematics,' Roger Bacon (b. ca. 1214 AD) contends that the theologian must have training in music in order to understand the Scriptures.[12] One reason, of course, is simply to be able to fully understand the many references to music in the Old Testament. The second reason is relative to the many kinds of meters found in the old Hebrew text. Here he notes that while the grammarian may teach the practical rules, only music gives 'the reasons and theories' for these meters. In the same manner, he points to the issue of pronunciation, as the Scripture is filled with 'accents, longs, shorts, colons, commas, and periods.'

> All these belong causally to music, because of all these matters the musician states the reason, but the grammarian merely the fact.

This idea is worthy of thought when one remembers that all philologists today believe that music preceded speech in early man.

Bacon, by the way, is sometimes credited as being the first to clearly point to the separate hemispherical functions of the brain. He does this in a passage where he argues that Reason is never certain until it tests its contentions by experience.

> For there are two modes of acquiring knowledge, namely, by reasoning and experience. Reasoning draws a conclusion and makes us grant the conclusion, but does not make the conclusion certain, or does it remove doubt so that the mind may rest on the intuition of truth, unless the mind discovers it by the path of experience.[13]

---

[11] Ibid., III, 641.

[12] This entire discussion is found in 'Mathematics,' in *The Opus Majus of Roger Bacon*, trans. Robert Burke (New York: Russell & Russell, 1962), I, 259.

[13] Ibid., 'Experimental Science,' I.

Early Voices Argue: Reason versus Experience   97

This idea, that Reason cannot rest until it has been proven by experience, is one often used by those who doubted the primacy of Reason. This was a point made frequently by Leonardo da Vinci (1452–1519).

> No human investigation can be called true science without passing through mathematical tests; and if you say that the sciences which begin and end in the mind contain truth, this cannot be conceded, and must be denied for many reasons. First and foremost because in such mental discourses experience does not come in, without which nothing reveals itself with certainty.[14]
>
> ……
>
> To me it seems that all sciences are vain and full or errors that are not born of experience, mother of all certainty, and that are not tested by experience, that is to say, that do not at their origin, middle or end pass through any of the five senses.[15]
>
> ……
>
> Experience does not err.[16]

Voltaire agreed, writing in an essay, 'The Ignorant Philosopher,'

> We know nothing in the world but by experience.

Geoffrey Chaucer (1340–1400) went even further writing that we should trust Reason only in the absence of personal experience. 'We should honor and believe these old books, where there is no test other than experience.'[17] Indeed, in numerous places Chaucer clearly states that various kinds of knowledge is proven only by experience. For example, with regard to the fact that there is a limit to one's lifespan, Chaucer says we need no authority for this, as it is proven by experience.[18] Or regarding the significance of dreams, 'This has been well founded by experience.'[19] Even, Chaucer says, where the Bible does not suffice, experience will teach you.

> And yf that hooly writ may nat suffyse,
> Experience shal the teche.[20]

Michel Montaigne (1533–1592), after first suggesting that it is only when reason fails us that we make use of experience, makes a comment similar to the previous one by Chaucer:

> Were I a good pupil there is enough, I find, in my own experience to make me wise.[21]

---

[14] *The Literary Works of Leonardo da Vinci*, ed. Jean Paul Richter (London: Phaidon, 1970), I, 31ff.

[15] Ibid., I, 33ff.

[16] Ibid., II, 240.

[17] 'The Legend of Good Women,' line 27.

[18] 'The Knight's Tale,' 3001.

[19] 'The Nun's Priest's Tale,' 4168.

[20] 'L'Envoy de Chaucer a Bukton,' 21. For additional references to understanding being proven by experience, see 'The Wife of Bath's Tale,' 468; 'The Friar's Tale,' 1517; 'The Sumner's Tale,' 2057; 'The Merchant's Tale,' 2238; 'Troilus and Criseyde,' III, 1283; 'The House of Fame,' II, 370; and 'Romaunt of the Rose,' 5553.

[21] Michel de Montaigne, *Essays*, trans. M. A. Screech (London: Penguin, 1993), III, xiii, 1218.

We must add that there were still some philosophers, especially Churchmen, who refused to recognize the importance of experience. A case in point is St. John of the Cross, an old style Church philosopher so severe the he seems to us to belong in the darkest of the Dark Ages. He begins his major treatise, 'The Ascent of Mount Carmel,' by declaring that in his writings he will not rely on his own experience or on science, 'for these can deceive us.' All answers will come from the Scriptures![22]

Some writers found cases in which direct experience was more valuable than extended rational study, as we see, for example, in Giraldi Cinthio's *Discorso intorno al comporre dei romanzi* of 1549.

> To a man not of dull or of weak intellectual capacity, one day's conversation with a man who is learned, prudent, and expert in composing and who will talk of things related to it will do more than a year's study.

A similar remark was made by Voltaire in a letter to Père Porée. Voltaire contends that the artist learns by experience, and not from books.

> No matter how many books are written on the technique of painting by those who know their subject, not one of them will afford as much instruction to the pupil as will the sight of a single head by Raphael.[23]

In particular, when it came to 'doing' things, the actual exercises of one's life or profession, a number of early philosophers were quick to place more value on personal experience than on Reason or learning. Socrates, in taking this stand, pointed to the example of midwives. Speaking of the fact that only women who have had child-bearing experience should act as midwives, we read,

> SOCRATES. It is said that Artemis was responsible for this, because though she is the goddess of childbirth, she is not herself a mother. She could not, indeed, allow the barren to be midwives, because human nature cannot know the mystery of an art without experience.[24]

Aristotle took an even broader view, with respect to 'doing' and he went on to contend that it is from these direct experiences that character is formed.

> Of all the things that come to us by nature we first acquire the potentiality and later exhibit the activity (this is plain in the case of the senses; for it was not by often seeing or often hearing that we got these senses, but on the contrary we had them before we used them, and did not come to have them by using them); but the virtues we get by first exercising them, as also happens in the case of the arts

---

[22] 'The Ascent of Mount Carmel,' in *The Collected Works of St. John of the Cross*, trans. Kieran Kavanaugh and Otilio Rodriguez (Washington, D.C.: Institute of Carmelite Studies, 1979), 70. Juan de Yepes y Alverez (1542–1591), known as St. John of the Cross, was imprisoned for a time by the Inquisition for his liberal views, although the modern reader is hard pressed to find such views in his surviving works.

[23] Letter to Père Porée (1730), quoted in Barrett Clark, *European Theories of the Drama* (New York: Crown, 1959), 279.

[24] *Theaetetus*, 149c.

as well. For the things we have to learn before we can do them, we learn by doing them, e.g. men become builders by building and lyre players by playing the lyre; so too we become just by doing just acts, temperate by doing temperate acts, brave by doing brave acts ...

It is from the same causes and by the same means that every virtue is both produced and destroyed, and similarly every art; for it is from playing the lyre that both good and bad lyre players are produced ... For if this were not so, there would have been no need of a teacher, but all men would have been born good or bad at their craft. This, then, is the case with the virtues also ... Thus, in one word, states of character arise out of like activities. This is why the activities we exhibit must be of a certain kind; it is because the states of character correspond to the differences between these. It makes no small difference, then, whether we form habits of one kind or another from our very youth; it makes a very great difference, or rather all the difference.[25]

Giovanni Boccaccio (1313–1375) would appear to agree completely with Aristotle when he maintains that it is a man's personal experience, not merely knowledge, which makes him productive. In this passage he seems to infer that experience and the man become one.

It is difficult for anyone to accomplish anything in which he has not had any experience ... This is the reason a worker is able to use his tools—a man is known according to his inner nature.[26]

Girolamo Cardano (1501–1576), one of the most prolific philosophers of the Renaissance, testified,

I have been more aided by experience than by my own wisdom or by the faith in the power of my art.[27]

......

Perhaps someone will quite rightly ask whether the same people who know these rules also play well or not. For it seems to be a different thing to know and to execute ... The same question arises in other discussions. Is a learned physician also a skilled one? In those matters which give time for reflection, the same man is both learned and successful, as in mathematics, jurisprudence, and also medicine ...

But in those matters in which no time is given and guile prevails, it is one thing to know and another to exercise one's knowledge successfully, as in gambling, war, dueling, and commerce. For although acumen depends on both knowledge and practice, still practice and experience can do more than knowledge.[28]

Cardano's suggestion above that a learned physician may or may not be a skilled one reminds us of a similar discussion by Montaigne, who recalled that Plato[29] once wrote that we should never submit ourselves to a doctor unless he himself had had the same illness and cured himself. This leads Montaigne to make the observation,

---

[25] 'Ethica Nicomachea' 1103a.25 and following.
[26] 'A Warning against Credulousness,' in *The Fates of Illustrious Men*, trans. Louis Hall (New York: Ungar, 1965), 25.
[27] Quoted in Oystein Ore, *Cardano The Gambling Scholar* (New York: Dover, 1953), 47.
[28] *The Book on Games of Chance*, trans. Sydney Gould (New York: Dover, 1953), 225.
[29] *Republic*, III, 408 D–E.

> If doctors want to know how to cure syphilis it is right that they should first catch it themselves![30]

There is one more story regarding medicine and experience which we should mention, found in the correspondence between Descartes and the Princess Elizabeth of Bohemia. In 1645, the princess was suffering from 'a slow fever and a dry cough.' Descartes wrote her that the commonest cause of slow fever was sadness and its cure was the mastery of reason over the passions.[31] But when Elizabeth challenged Descartes, pointing out that she found it necessary to make decisions on the basis of her experience, and not on Reason, Descartes quickly retreated.

> I do not doubt that your Highness' maxim is the best of all, namely that it is better to guide oneself by experience in these matter than by reason. It is rarely that we have to do with people who are as perfectly reasonable as men ought to be, so that one cannot judge what they will do simply by considering what they ought to do; and often the soundest advice is not the most successful.[32]

To return to the subject of 'doing,' we might also point out that Izaak Walton, in his *The Compleat Angler*, mentions an author, a Mr. Hales, who was ridiculed for writing a book on fencing. This was, Walton points out, because 'that art was not to be taught by words, but practice.'[33] Leonardo da Vinci found that even writing, an essentially rational occupation, was based on experience.

> They will say that I, having no literary skill, cannot properly express that which I desire to treat of; but they do not know that my subjects are to be dealt with by experience rather than by words; and experience has been the mistress of those who wrote well.[34]

The sixteenth-century Spanish playwright, Fernando de Rojas, suggested that it was experience which made the difference in all professions, observing that 'Experience makes men artists in their profession.'[35] The most famous Spanish playwright of this period, Lope de Vega, pauses to remind his listeners that Love is something which can be understood only by experience.

> Let no man speak Love's name that has not felt his power.[36]

---

[30] Michel de Montaigne, *Essays*, trans. M. A. Screech (London: Penguin, 1993), III, xiii, 1218.

[31] Quoted in *Descartes Philosophical Letters*, trans. Anthony Kenny (Oxford: Clarendon Press, 1970), 161.

[32] Letter to Elizabeth, May, 1646, quoted in Ibid., 195. Elizabeth (1618–1680) was a princess Palatine of Bohemia.

[33] Izaak Walton, *The Compleat Angler* (London: Oxford University Press, 1935), 6. Izaak Walton (1593–1683) is best known for his biographies of contemporary English writers.

[34] Quoted in *The Literary Works of Leonardo da Vinci*, ed. Jean Paul Richter (London: Phaidon, 1970), I, 116.

[35] Fernando de Rojas, *Celestina*, trans. James Mabbe (New York: Applause Publishers, 1986), 37.

[36] Lope de Vega, *The Knight from Olmedo*, trans. Jill Booty, in *Lope de Vega, Five Plays* (New York: HIll and Wang, 1961), 179.

The early philosophers also often point to music as something which must be learned by experience, not from books. We have seen, above, Aristotle observe, 'lyre players learn by playing the lyre,' and in a similar vein we find,

> The art of music causes the man to be a musician.[37]
> Boethius (475–524)

> For in any art those things which we know of ourselves are much more numerous than those which we learn from a master.[38]
> Guido of Arezzo, Micrologus (1026–1028)

> For it seems impossible that anyone should become a builder who has not first built something; or that anyone should become a harpist who has not first played the harp.[39]
> Thomas Aquinas (1224–1274)

> Practice is the best teacher of any subject. One learns music by playing.[40]
> Erasmus (1469–1536)

> Who is it that procured you that judgment in music? It was the application of mind in observing musicians.[41]
> François de Salignac de La Mothe-Fenelon (1651–1715)

And even in the case of composition we find some writers who question the value of the written rules. Charpentier, the seventeenth-century French composer, concludes his book on the rules of composition by admitting,

> Practice teaches more about this than all the rules.

To which Voltaire added,

> The composer of Armide and Issé [Lully], and the worst of composers, worked according to the same musical rules.[42]

He perhaps would have given one reason why in the case of music the 'rules' do not make the difference:

---

37 Boethius, *Consolatione Philosophiae*, trans. Samuel Fox (London: George Bell, 1895), XVI, iii.
38 Quoted in Strunck, *Source Readings in Music History*, 117.
39 *Commentary on the Metaphysics of Aristotle*, trans. John Rowan (Chicago: Henry Regnery, 1961), 684–685 (IX.L.7:C 1850).
40 'Adages,' in *The Collected Works of Erasmus* (Toronto: University of Toronto Press, 1992), XXXII, 25.
41 Fenelon, *The Adventures of Telemachus, Son of Ulysses*, Book XII, (London: Garland Publishing, 1979, facsimile of the 1720 edition), Book XXIV, Op. cit., II, 270.
42 Letter to Père Porée (1730), quoted in Barrett Clark, *European Theories of the Drama* (New York: Crown, 1959), 279.

> Is it not an amusing thing, that our eyes always deceive us, even when we see very well, and that on the contrary our ears do not?[43]

Finally, in the Pre-Renaissance, beginning in the twelfth century, the 'dark ages' finally begins to give way to a new spirit of hope and optimism. This helped fuel a great improvement in secular music which led to widespread hiring of individual musicians by courts and cities. This was followed by the arrival of Humanism in the Renaissance, which finally brought emotions back into music and ended the Church Era during which music was categorized as a branch of mathematics. This made possible an era of great enthusiasm for the performance of music, documented in the Renaissance music we all know. Curiously, according to one very important observer of the early Renaissance music scene, Johannes de Grecheo, the theorists, the last protectors of Reason in music, seem to have retreated.

> At the present time it happens that many people seek the practical side of this art, but few pay attention to its speculative character. And, for this reason, many speculative thinkers make a secret of their calculations and their discoveries, not wishing to reveal them to others.[44]

---

43 *Philosophical Dictionary*, 'Prejudice,' in *The Works of Voltaire* (New York: St. Hubert Guild, 1901), XII, 290.

44 Johannes de Grocheo, *De Musica* (ca. 1300), trans. Albert Seay (Colorado Springs: Colorado College Music Press, 1967), 2.

Early Voices Struggle to Explain the Emotions

The work of getting anybody to cheerfully undertake the monotony and drudgery of teaching must be effected not by pay merely, but by a skillfully worked-up appeal to the emotions as well.[1]

Pliny the Younger (61–113 AD)

THE PHILOSOPHERS OF THE ANCIENT WORLD were nearly unanimous in arguing that Reason must govern a man's actions and it was fairly easy for most of them to assume that the brain was the seat of Reason. Not having our advantage in knowing that we have, in fact, *two* quite different hemispheres of the brain, they were generally at a loss to explain where, if Reason was in the brain, the seat of the emotions was. Thus we most often read of the emotions being housed in either the soul or the heart.

Since, by their understanding, Reason occupied the brain, it seemed to follow logically that the emotions must be something of a lesser order. This appeared to be confirmed by ordinary experience, for one could observe that lower animals had some form of emotions, but not Reason, as the reader will see in the following chapter.

No matter how much they minimized the emotions, their logic was always stopped by something else commonly observed in man and that was the fact that the emotions could, on occasion, completely shut down Reason. Everyone had experienced this to some degree with respect to Love. Aristotle, like many others, knew Reason could not compete with love, especially sexual love. 'For no one,' he says, 'could think of anything while absorbed in this.'[2] The same conclusion is found in the writings of John of Salisbury (first half, twelfth century), who phrased it this way:

> It is impossible to surrender oneself to the lusts of the flesh, and at the same time to dedicate oneself to philosophy.[3]

While Aristotle shared the frustrations of his contemporary philosophers in trying to explain the emotions, in one respect he understood a fundamental truth about them, that they are universal. We know today that the basic emotions are universal and genetic to all men. Aristotle expresses this in a very famous passage in which he also points out that the spoken and written word is only a symbol of something more fundamental.

---

[1] Letter V, to Pompeius Saturninus.
[2] 'Ethica Nicomachea,' 1152b.18.
[3] *The Metalogicon*, trans. Daniel McGarry (Berkeley: University of California Press, 1955), 218ff.

> Words spoken are symbols or signs of affections or impressions of the soul; written words are the symbols of words spoken. As writing, so also is speech not the same for all races of men. But the affections themselves, of which these words are primarily signs, are the same for the whole of mankind.[4]

Another common observation about the emotions by the early philosophers had to do with oratory. Many writers point out that if the orator will engage the emotions of his listeners he will win them over, regardless of whether the actual content of his speech is true or not. Plutarch (46–119 AD) believed this was the very purpose of Rhetoric.

> Rhetoric, or the art of speaking, is ... the government of the souls of men, and that her chief business is to address the affections and passions, which are as it were the strings and keys to the soul, and require a skillful and careful touch to be played on as they should be.[5]

Aristides Quintilianus, who lived sometime between the first and fourth century AD, in his treatise, *De Musica*,[6] assigns the emotions to the soul, where he divides them into male and female qualities. This same duality he finds in nature as well, in plants, minerals, and spices, expressed through their qualities of color or texture and their opposites.

> Passions arise in the soul out of its affinity with the male or the female or with both. Thus the female is seriously lacking in restraint, and with it the appetitive part [of the soul] is in accord, while the male is violent and energetic, and the spirited part [of the soul] resembles it. In the female—both the female type of soul and the female branch of humanity—griefs and pleasures are rife, anger and recklessness in the male. Couplings of these passions arise too: of griefs with pleasures and of anger with recklessness, of recklessness with pleasure and grief, of anger with both, and indeed of each with any one or more of the others. One could find a thousand different varieties of these emotions if one studied them in all their complexity.

Aristides acknowledges that each person has his own unique emotional makeup and that this affects perception. Also the objects of our perception have their own emotional characteristics. Thus when the soul encounters an object, through perception, it 'obtains an impression' of the object and compares it to the emotions of itself. By this he means first comparing it to the male and female natures.

> We distinguish as belonging to the female those colors and shapes that are vivid and decorative, and to the male those that are subdued and conducive to mental reflection. Secondly, among the objects of hearing, we associate sounds that are smooth and gentle with the female, rougher ones with its opposite. To avoid mentioning everything individually, one may assert that it is quite generally true, in all cases, that those objects of perception which naturally invite us to pleasure and to the gentle relaxation of the mind are to be adjudged female, those that stimulate us to thought and arouse activity are to be assigned to the province of the male.

---

[4] 'On Interpretation,' I, trans. Harold P. Cook (Cambridge: Harvard University Press, 1962).

[5] 'Life of Pericles.'

[6] Aristides discussion begins Book II. All our quotations are from the translation by Andrew Barker, *Greek Musical Writings* (Cambridge: Cambridge University Press, 1989), II, 457ff.

Most early philosophers were not so complacent with regard to the emotions. Cicero (106–43 BC), for example, was more typical with his warning that the emotions, which he divides into four basic classes, were something to be avoided!

> The emotions of the mind, which harass and embitter the life of the foolish (the Greek term for these is *pathos*, and I might have rendered this literally and styled them 'diseases,' but the word 'disease' would not suit all instances; for example, no one speaks of pity, nor yet anger, as a disease though the Greeks term these pathos. Let us then accept the term 'emotion,' the very sound of which seems to denote something vicious, and these emotions are not excited by any natural influence. The list of the emotions is divided into four classes, with numerous subdivisions, namely sorrow, fear, lust, and that mental emotion which the Stoics call by a name that also denotes a bodily feeling, *hedone*, 'pleasure,' but which I prefer to style 'delight,' meaning the sensuous elation of the mind when in a state of exultation), these emotions, I say, are not excited by any influence of nature; they are all of them mere fancies and frivolous opinions. Therefore the Wise Man will always be free from them.[7]

And again, in his treatise *On Duties*, he emphasizes that any display of emotions suggests that we are not in control of ourselves. The more highly developed person, he with a 'greater soul,' must especially observe this warning. It is also important to note here the implication that Cicero understood on some level the bicameral nature of our mind, or as he puts it, *thought* versus *passion*.

> We must be careful that the movements of our soul do not diverge from nature, and the care must be all the greater as the soul is greater. We shall achieve this if we are careful not to reach states of extreme excitement or alarm and if we keep our minds intent on the preservation of *decorum*. The movements of our souls are of two kinds: some involve thought, others involve passion. Thought is mostly expended in seeking out the truth, passion urges men to action.[8] Therefore we must take care to expend thought on the best objects and to make clear that our passions are obedient to our intellect ...
>
> Throughout a man's life the most correct advice is to avoid agitations, by which I mean excessive commotions in the soul that do not obey intelligence ... Whenever passionate feelings disturb our activities, we are, of course, not acting with self-control and those around us cannot approve what we do.[9]

In another place Cicero expresses himself even more strongly, picturing the life of the man who falls victim to his emotions:

> The man whom we see on fire and raging with lusts frantically pursuing everything with insatiable desire, and the more lavishly he swallows down pleasure from all quarters, the worse and more burning his thirst—would you not be entitled to call him most unhappy? The man who is carried away with frivolity and empty euphoria and uncontrolled desires, is he not the more wretched the happier he *thinks* he is?

---

7 Cicero, *De Finibus*, III, x, 35.

8 This reminds us of a comment made about Rousseau at the time of the French Revolution. It was said of him that, 'He made madmen of people who would otherwise only have been fools.'

9 Cicero, *De Officiis*, 131ff.

> So just as these people are wretched, so are those happy whom no fears alarm, no distresses gnaw, no lusts arouse, no pointless euphoria dissolves in languorous pleasure. Just as the sea is recognized as calm when not even the slightest breeze ruffles the waves, so a state of mind can be accounted calm and peaceful, when there is no disturbance by which it can be agitated.[10]

In his recommendation that one should carefully study the emotions in the face of another, Cicero seems to imply that emotions are universal and genetic.

> Just as in lyre playing the ears of musicians perceive even the smallest details, so we should acquire the habit of making important deductions from trivial details if we want to become sharp and untiring critics. From the stare, from the raising or lowering of the eyebrows, from sadness, from joviality, from a laugh, from a spoken phrase, from a significant silence, from a raised voice, from its lowering, from other similar indications we shall begin to judge quickly which of these actions is in tune, which of them clashes with moral duty and nature.[11]

The Roman philosopher, Quintilian (30–96 AD), divides emotions into two classes, as did Aristides, but now with important new labels, *pathos* and *ethos*. He begins by attempting to convey the meaning of these Greek terms to his Latin readers.

> Emotions however, as we learn from ancient authorities, fall into two classes; the one is called *pathos* by the Greeks and is rightly and correctly expressed in Latin by *adfectus* (emotion): the other is called *ethos*, a word for which in my opinion Latin has no equivalent: it is however rendered by *mores* (morals) and consequently the branch of philosophy known as *ethics* is styled *moral* philosophy by us. But close consideration of the nature of the subject leads me to think that in this connection it is not so much *morals* in general that is meant as certain peculiar aspects; for the term *morals* includes every attitude of the mind. The more cautious writers have preferred to give the sense of the term rather than to translate it into Latin. They therefore explain *pathos* as describing the more violent emotions and *ethos* as designating those which are calm and gentle: in the one case the passions are violent, in the other subdued, the former command and disturb, the latter persuade and induce a feeling of goodwill.[12]

He agrees with some authors who maintain that while the *ethos* is continuous, *pathos* is more momentary in character. On the other hand, *pathos* and *ethos* are sometimes of the same nature, differing only in degree.

> Love for instance comes under the head of *pathos*, affection of *ethos*; sometimes however they differ, a distinction which is important for the peroration, since *ethos* is generally employed to calm the storm aroused by *pathos*.

---

[10] Cicero, *Tusculan Disputations*, V, 15ff.

[11] Ibid., I, 146.

[12] Quintilian, *The Education of an Orator (Institutio Oratoria)*, trans. H. E. Butler (London: Heinemann, 1938), VI, ii, 8 through 36.

Quintilian now goes into greater detail with respect to the profession of the orator-lawyer. We find particularly interesting his argument that the orator employs *pathos*, or emotion, when he wishes to create empathy in the listener.

> The aim of appeals to the emotion is not merely to show the bitter and grievous nature of ills that actually are so, but also to make ills which are usually regarded as tolerable seem unendurable, as for instance when we represent insulting words as inflicting more grievous injury than an actual blow or represent disgrace as being worse than death.

But how does the orator do this? Quintilian now tells us that he will reveal to us 'secret principles of this art.' What follows is a precursor of Stanislavsky's 'method acting,' through which one learns to re-experience the emotions one has to convey from the stage. Among the performing arts only musicians are spared such processes, for in music the emotions expressed *are* the real ones. Nevertheless, Quintilian's discussion should remind musicians that true emotional communication must be founded on genuine emotions.

> The prime essential for stirring the emotions of others is, in my opinion, first to feel those emotions oneself. It is sometimes positively ridiculous to counterfeit grief, anger and indignation, if we content ourselves with accommodating our words and looks and make no attempt to adapt our own feelings to the emotions to be expressed. What other reason is there for the eloquence with which mourners express their grief, or for the fluency which anger lends even to the uneducated, save the fact that their minds are stirred to power by the depth and sincerity of their feelings? Consequently, if we wish to give our words the appearance of sincerity, we must assimilate ourselves to the emotions of those who are genuinely so affected, and our eloquence must spring from the same feeling that we desire to produce in the mind of the judge. Will he grieve who can find no trace of grief in the words with which I seek to move him to grief? Will he be angry, if the orator who seeks to kindle his anger shows no sign of laboring under the emotion which he demands from his audience? Will he shed tears if the pleader's eyes are dry? It is utterly impossible …
>
> Accordingly, the first essential is that those feelings should prevail with us that we wish to prevail with the judge, and that we should be moved ourselves before we attempt to move others. But how are we to generate these emotions in ourselves, since emotion is not in our own power? I will try to explain as best I may. There are certain experiences which the Greeks call *avradias*, and the Romans *visions*, whereby things absent are presented to our imagination with such extreme vividness that they seem actually to be before our very eyes. It is the man who is really sensitive to such impressions who will have the greatest power over the emotions … It is a power which all may readily acquire if they will.

Quintilian attributes his own fame to his ability to do this.

> Again, when we desire to awaken pity, we must actually believe that the ills of which we complain have befallen our own selves, and must persuade our minds that this is really the case. We must identify ourselves with the persons of whom we complain that they have suffered grievous, unmerited and bitter misfortune, and must plead their case and for a brief period feel their suffering as though it were our own, while our words must be such as we should use if we stood in their shoes. I have often seen actors, both in tragedy and comedy, leave the theater still drowned in tears after concluding the performance of some moving role …

> I have frequently been so much moved while speaking, that I have not merely been wrought upon to tears, but have turned pale and shown all the symptoms of genuine grief.

One early philosopher, Longinus (first century AD), in discussing oratory mentions some types of what he calls 'false emotion.' These include such categories as exaggeration, puerility (childish) and parenthyrsus (empty, or no emotion).[13]

One of the most striking discussions of emotions by an early writer is by the famous medical authority, Galen (second century AD). The ancient writers often give the chief purpose of music as its ability to soothe the emotions. If Galen's descriptions here of a passionate man were typical, then perhaps we can understand how important to society this purpose of music would have been to the ancients.

> Whenever a man becomes violently angry over little things and bites and kicks his servants, you are sure that this man is in a state of passion.
>
> ……
>
> I watched a man eagerly trying to open a door. When things did not work out as he would have them, I saw him bite the key, kick the door, blaspheme, glare wildly like a madman, and all but foam at the mouth like a wild boar.[14]

St. Augustine (fourth century) believed there were four classes of emotions, desire, joy, fear and sorrow, each of which could be divided into subordinate species. Indeed, he observed, 'Yet are the hairs of [a man's] head easier to be numbered than are his feelings....'[15] He experienced some frustration in trying to understand the role of memory in relation to the emotions.

> The same memory contains also the affections of my mind, not in the same manner that my mind itself contains them, when it feels them; but far otherwise, according to a power of its own. For without rejoicing I remember myself to have joyed; and without sorrow do I recollect my past sorrow. And that I once feared, I review without fear; and without desire call to mind a past desire. Sometimes, on the contrary, with joy do I remember my fore-past sorrow, and with sorrow, joy … How is it that when with joy I remember my past sorrow, the mind hath joy, the memory hath sorrow … Does the memory perchance not belong to the mind?[16]

Augustine also had some doubts over the relative power of Reason and the emotions, but he finally concluded, 'I feel that the power of the mind must be greater than desire for the very reason that it is only right and just that it should hold sway over desire.'[17] But, regarding the power of the mind, he would have been surprised at the power of music given in an anecdote by Guido of Arezzo (eleventh century):

---

13   Longinus, *On the Sublime*, trans. W. Rhys Roberts (Cambridge: University Press, 1935), III, 1ff.

14   Galen, 'On the Passions and Errors of the Soul,' trans. Paul W. Harkins (Columbus: Ohio State University Press), 29, 38.

15   *The Confessions*, Book IV.

16   Ibid., Book X.

17   *The Free Choice of the Will*, trans. Robert P. Russell (Washington, D.C.: The Catholic University of America Press), x.

> A man was roused by the sound of the cithara to such lust that, in his madness, he sought to break into the bedchamber of a girl, but, when the cithara player quickly changed the mode, was brought to feel remorse for his libidinousness and to retreat abashed.[18]

We know today that the right hemisphere of the brain supplies emotional context to the speech of the left hemisphere (Reason). Bartholomew Anglicus (thirteenth century) remarks on the effect on the listener of this emotional coloring.

> Now it is known by these foresaid things, how profitable is a merry voice and sweet. And contrariwise is of an unordinate voice and horrible, that gladdeth not, neither comforteth; but is noyful and discomforteth and grieveth the ears and the wit.[19]

Roger Bacon (b. ca. 1214) quoted Seneca to the effect that to achieve the most lofty speech the emotional context had to go beyond that recognized as 'sane.'

> The mind cannot reach the realms of the sublime while it remains sane. It must leave the beaten track, dash forth, take the bit in the teeth, and carry the rider where he would have feared to mount himself.[20]

One medieval philosopher who wrote extensively on the emotions was Thomas Aquinas (1224–1274). First he organizes the emotions in a series of pairs:

> We are now in a position to arrange all of the emotions in the order of their actual occurrence. First come love and hatred; second, desire and aversion; third, hope and despair; fourth, fear and courage; fifth, anger; sixth and last, joy or sadness, which come after all the emotions. From what we have said it is clear that, within these pairs, love has precedence over hatred, desire over aversion, fear over courage, and joy over sadness.[21]

He is not sure where exactly the emotions are located in the body, but assumes they are related to the intellect, on the basis that the Scriptures also mention love and joy with respect to God and the angels.[22] His speculation leads to some weird-science, including his belief that the physical changes for an emotion such as anger, is caused by the 'overheating of the blood around the heart'[23] and his conclusion that astrology affected our emotions.

---

[18] *Hucbald, Guido, and John on Music*, trans. Warren Babb (New Haven: Yale University Press, 1978), 160.

[19] Quoted in *Medieval Lore*, trans. Robert Steele (London: Stock, 1893), 64.

[20] Roger Bacon, *The Opus Majus of Roger Bacon*, trans. Robert Burke (New York: Russell & Russell), II, 786. The Seneca passage is found in *De Tranquillitate Animi*, XVII.

[21] *Summa Theologiae* (London: Blackfriars, 1971), XIX, 55.

[22] Ibid., 13.

[23] Ibid., XIX, 13.

> [The heavenly bodies] may make impressions on our own body, and when the body is affected movements of the passions arise; either because such impressions make us liable to certain passions; for instance the bilious are prone to anger.[24]

Aquinas is ambiguous on the question of whether the emotions have a moral quality, stating in one place that they do[25] and in another place that they do not.[26] He believed that Reason must control the emotions and that this control separates man from the animals. But he was also aware that the emotions can 'blind reason completely,'

> as happens when vehement rage of concupiscence makes a man beside himself or out of his mind; this may come also from some physical disorder. Passion, remember, goes with physiological change. In this condition men become like the beasts, driven of necessity by passion; they are without the motion of reason, and, consequently, of will.[27]

In another recourse to weird-science, Aquinas found that the power of the emotions varied from man to man according to the temperament controlled by the 'humors.'

> If the nature of a given individual be considered, in terms of his unique temperament, again anger is more natural than desire. Anger is easily aroused as a result of a natural, temperamental inclination to irascibility, more easily than desire or any other emotion. An irascible disposition is characteristic of a choleric temperament and choler is more quickly aroused than other humors; it is said to be like fire. Thus a person who by temperament has a naturally irascible disposition will become angry more readily than one who has a pleasure-loving disposition will have his desires aroused. For this reason, too, Aristotle holds that anger is more likely to be inherited from one's parents than desire.[28]

With the arrival of the Renaissance there was a new impetus for philosophers to comment on the emotions, driven by the emphasis on emotions in the secular music of the 'Pre-Renaissance' and rediscovery of the works of the ancient writers which contributed to the new Humanistic movement. The French poet, Machaut (b. 1300) in his *Voir Dit* describes the requirements necessary to fine Poetry, Reason, Rhetoric and Music. But there is another requirement for composition which was clearly of the greatest importance to Machaut. The composer's work must come from the most genuine, heart-felt feelings. In a letter to Peronnelle, he explains, 'There is nothing so just and true as experience … He who does not create out of real feeling, counterfeits his words and songs.'

> Qui de sentement ne fait, Son dit et son chant contrefait.[29]

---

[24] *Summa Contra Gentiles* (London, Burns Oates & Washbourne, 1923), LXXXV.

[25] *Summa Theologiae*, XIX, 43.

[26] Ibid., XXXV, 23.

[27] Ibid., XVII, 91.

[28] Ibid., XXI, 99.

[29] *Le Livre du Voir-Dit de Guillaume de Machaut* (Paris: Paulin Paris, 1875), 61.

And we have a glimpse of what 'real feeling' meant to Machaut in another poem:

> Then, like one accustomed to sighing, I uttered a lament and sigh from the depths of my heart, accompanied by weeping and washed in tears; and with great effort I turned toward her my flushed, pale, sad, sorrowful, and weeping face, full of suffering. But I said nothing to her because I was unable to speak; instead, I gazed fixedly at her.[30]

John Gower (1330–1408) comments on the great capacity of the face to express the emotions one feels; a number of earlier philosophers incorrectly attributed this to the eyes alone.

> The face expresses the state of one's mind and displays the wrath of a heart strongly aroused. For in the event that one express himself silently, no index of the mind can be more reliable than the face.[31]

The Spanish poet, Fernando de Rojas (1477–1541), understood correctly that the basic emotions are universal, as we read in his most famous poem,

> Examine, then, your inner self, inspect your feelings well,
> And by your heart you'll judge how others' passions surely go.[32]

The greatest French writer of the sixteenth century, Michel Montaigne (1533–1592), left a number of interesting observations on the perception of the emotions during the Renaissance. First, with a little weird-science, he suggests that the strong emotions of the gentleman, in contrast to the common man, somehow weaken him physically.

> Experience shows that gross, uncouth men make more desirable and vigorous sexual partners; lying with a mule-driver is often more welcome than lying with a gentleman. How can we explain that except by assuming that emotions within the gentleman's soul undermine the strength of his body, break it down and exhaust it, just as they exhaust and harm the soul itself?[33]

Montaigne, who often supports the positions of the Church, was well aware of the Church's demand that Reason must rule the emotions. Montaigne leaves the impression that he could easily do this.

> With very little effort I stop the first movements of my emotions, giving up whatever begins to weigh on me before it bears me off. If you do not stop the start, you will never stop the race. If you cannot slam the door against your emotions you will never chase them out once they have got in.[34]

---

[30] Guillaume de Machaut, 'Remede de Fortune,' trans. James Wimsatt and William Kibler (Athens: The University of Georgia Press, 1988), 254.

[31] John Gower, *The Voice of One Crying*, trans. Eric Stockton in *The Major Latin Works of John Gower* (Seattle: University of Washington Press, 1962), IV, iii.

[32] Fernando de Rojas, *La Celestina*, trans. J. M. Cohen (New York: New York University Press, 1966), 565.

[33] Michel de Montaigne, *Essays*, trans. M. A. Screech (London: Penguin, 1993), II, xii, 547ff.

[34] Ibid., III, x, 1150.

He is prompt to add an amendment to this boast when it comes to carnal pleasure, observing that 'when its force is at its climax it overmasters us to such an extent that reason has no way to come into it.'[35] He mentions that some men were so disturbed over their loss of Reason due to the emotions of love that they castrated themselves and that others applied compress of cold things such as snow on the offending member.[36]

Taking a different position from most philosophers, Montaigne doubts whether the face really is a true mirror of one's feelings.

> Anyone can put on a good outward show while inside he is full of fever and fright. They do not see my mind: they only see the looks on my face.[37]

Extending this line of thought, Montaigne apparently mistakenly concluded that our separate body parts have their own emotions, uncontrolled by our mind. He points to facial expressions which give away thought we wish to keep secret, to our hands going where we do not tell them and our voices failing when *they* want to. The most compelling evidence, he points out, is the penis, 'which thrusts itself forward so inopportunely when we do not want it to, and which so inopportunely lets us down when we most need it.' He recommends putting it on trial for rebelliousness.[38]

This subject causes him to remind the reader again that he was never carried away by love against his will:

> When I was young I resisted the advances of love as soon as I realized that it was getting too much hold over me; I took care that it was not so delightful to me that it finally took me by storm and held me captive entirely at its mercy.[39]

His views on this subject in old age were more ironic.

> In former days youth and pleasure never made me fail to recognize the face of vice within the sensuality: nor does the distaste which the years have brought me make me fail to recognize now the face of pleasure within the vice.[40]

In a broader view of the emotions of pleasure, Montaigne warns,

> Most pleasures, tickle and embrace us only to throttle us, like those thieves whom the Egyptians call *Philistae*. If a hangover came before we got drunk we would see that we never drank to excess: but pleasure, to deceive us, walks in front and hides her train.[41]

---

35 Ibid., II, xi, 481.

36 Ibid., II, xxxiii, 825.

37 Ibid., II, xvi, 710. In another place, however, he observes that in speaking, facial expressions and the voice 'lend value to things which in themselves are hardly worth more than chatter.' [Ibid., II, xvii, 726]

38 Ibid., I, xxi, 115.

39 Ibid., III, x, 1147.

40 Ibid., III, ii, 919.

41 Ibid., I, xxxix, 275.

The Spanish philosopher known as St. John of the Cross (1542–1591) finds four basic emotions: joy, hope, sorrow and fear. He finds little for which man should experience joy, not riches, goods, titles or general prosperity.[42] 'Neither, indeed, is there any reason for joy in children ... Indeed, it would also be vanity for a husband and wife to rejoice in their marriage, when they are uncertain whether God is being better served by it.'

According to St. John of the Cross, man suffers by even reflecting on the emotions. The solution he recommends is to erase from the mind all memory of pleasure deriving from appetites, for 'When all things are forgotten, nothing disturbs the peace or stirs the appetites.'[43]

One finds similar conservative views from Erasmus, who always could be found near the views of the Church. Thus Erasmus begins with the Church dogma,

> First of all, it's admitted that all the emotions belong to Folly, and this is what marks the wise man off from the fool; he is ruled by reason, the fool by his emotions.[44]

He finds two general categories of emotions. After stating that Reason must play the role of king, he names some emotions as nobles to the king-Reason, including love of parents, kindness towards friends and compassion for the afflicted. Those, however, which are sensuous in nature he places in quite a different category.

> As for those passions of the soul that are furthest removed from the dictates of Reason and are debased to the lowliness of beasts, consider these to be like the lowest dregs of the masses. Of this kind are lust, debauchery, envy, and similar disorders of the mind, which should all without exception be consigned to forced labor like vile and wicked slaves, so that, if they are able, they may produce the work and services required of them by their master, or, if not, at least not cause any harm.[45]

In another place he describes physical love in much stronger terms.

> These are obscene, bestial pleasures, altogether unworthy of man, which make wild animals of us; they are impure as well, containing more bitterness than sweetness.[46]

Here, as was the case with a great many early Churchmen, Erasmus places most of the blame on women,

> the hateful vices of the female sex, how few good, modest women there are to be found, how few men who do not regret that they entered upon wedlock. [The writer] will expose to view these all too common experiences, that wives are quarrelsome, impudent, shameless, and ... drive husbands to their death.[47]

---

[42] 'The Ascent of Mount Carmel,' in *The Collected Works of St. John of the Cross*, trans. Kieran Kavanaugh and Otilio Rodriguez (Washington, D.C.: Institute of Carmelite Studies, 1979),., 241ff.

[43] Ibid., 222.

[44] 'Praise of Folly,' [1503] in *The Collected Works of Erasmus* (Toronto: University of Toronto Press, 1992), XXVII, 104.

[45] 'Enchiridion,' 'The Handbook of the Christian Soldier,' [1503] in Ibid., LXVI, 42.

[46] 'On the Writing of Letters,' [1522] in Ibid., XXV, 36.

[47] Ibid., XXV, 147.

In a letter to a young man, Erasmus advises,

> Above all, avoid all strong emotion, excessive joy, unrestrained laughter, too much walking, excessive study, and anger especially.[48]

As a defense against the emotions Erasmus recommends scholarly studies, which 'do not change us from men into wild animals, but from men into gods.'[49]

Henry Agrippa (1486–1536), in his early *De occulta philosophia*, reflects the ancient Church view that Pleasure is the source of most evil. He ties the general subject of the emotions to this idea, maintaining that depraved appetites arise from four passions: oblectation, effusion, vaunting and loftiness, and envy, with,

> these four passions arising from a depraved appetite of pleasure, the grief or perplexity of produces many contrary passions, as horror, sadness, fear, and sorrow.[50]

The basic emotions, he says, are nothing else but certain motions or inclinations proceeding from the apprehension of anything, as of good or evil. In total he finds eleven basic emotions, existing in contrary pairs, except for the last. These are, love, hatred; desire, horror; joy, grief; hope, despair; boldness, fear; and anger.[51]

Although some of the early Reformation leaders were much more severe than Luther in all aspects of the Christian life, Zwingli, who was one of these, nevertheless recognized that some pleasures must be allowed.

> I am so far from condemning joy in moderation that I think he who takes it away from the pious will have to restore it with interest.[52]

During the Renaissance English philosophers were particularly interested in melancholy. In view of this, we note an interesting passage in Shakespeare which finds categories of this single emotion.

> I have neither the scholar's melancholy, which is emulation; nor the musician's, which is fantastical; nor the courtier's, which is proud; nor the soldier's, which is ambitious; nor the lawyer's, which is politic; nor the lady's, which is nice; nor the lover's, which is all these. But it is a melancholy of mine own, compounded of many simples, extracted from many objects, and indeed the sundry contemplation of my travels, in which my often rumination wraps me in a most humorous sadness.[53]

---

[48] Quoted in Ibid., V, 390.

[49] 'On the Writing of Letters,' [1522] in Ibid., XXV, 36.

[50] Agrippa, *De occulta philosophia* in Donald Tyson, *Three Books of Occult Philosophy* (St. Paul: Llewellyn Publications, 1993), I, lxi.

[51] Ibid., I, lxii.

[52] Ulrich Zwingli, 'Refutation of the Tricks of the Baptists' [1523], in *Ulrich Zwingli, Selected Works*, ed. Samuel Jackson (Philadelphia: University of Pennsylvania Press, 1901), 71.

[53] *As You Like It*, IV, i, 10ff. In *Two Gentlemen of Verona*, III, ii, 78ff, one preparing a serenade hopes to impress the lady with the sincerity of his melancholy.

Of particular interest to us is Shakespeare's use of the metaphor of out of tune music for a character's emotional unbalance, a device earlier writers also employed. In *The Comedy of Errors*, a character speaks of 'my feeble key of untuned cares'[54] and in *Much Ado About Nothing*, Hero asks Beatrice,

> Do you speak in the sick tune?[55]

In *Hamlet,* Ophelia uses the same metaphor.

> And I, of ladies most deject and wretched,
> That sucked the honey of his music vows,
> Now see that noble and most sovereign reason,
> Like sweet bells jangled, out of tune and harsh.[56]

With the period we call the Baroque we find ourselves in an era obsessed with the emotions, but there were still representatives of the old Church view present. Baltasar Gracian (1601–1658), for example, reflects the old Church dogma that the emotions were the gateway to sin. And it was here that he connected the emotions with art, observing,

> Art would be deficient if it merely taught you to conceal the limits of your talent. It must also teach you to disguise the impetus of your emotions …
> Discovering someone's emotions is like opening a breach in the fortress of his talent.[57]

In another place, he gives a variant of this last sentence:

> The emotions are the breaches in the defenses of the mind.[58]

A philosopher with similar severe views was Spinoza who divides the mind into active, or adequate, ideas and passive, or inadequate, ideas. The emotions he classifies as passive or 'confused ideas.'[59] His actual definitions of various emotions are all related to man's moral state. A sampling,

> Love is nothing else but Pleasure accompanied by the idea of an external cause. Hate is nothing else but Pain accompanied by the idea of an external cause.[60]

……

---

54 *The Comedy of Errors*, V, i. 315.

55 *Much Ado About Nothing*, II, iv, 35.

56 *Hamlet*, III, i, 155ff.

57 Gracian, *A Pocket Mirror for Heroes*, trans. Christopher Maurer (New York: Currency Doubleday, 1996), 7.

58 Gracian, *The Oracle*, Nr. 98.

59 Spinoza, 'General Definition of the Emotions' in *The Ethics*, 'Of the Origin and Nature of the Emotions.'

60 Ibid., Proposition XIII.

> Hope is inconstant Pleasure, arising from the image of something future or past, whereof we do not yet know the issue. Fear is an inconstant Pain …
>
> If doubt is removed, Hope becomes Confidence and Fear become Despair …
>
> Joy is Pleasure arising from the image of something past whereof we doubted the issue. Disappointment is the Pain opposed to Joy.[61]

Among the more original philosophers of the Baroque we find the famous René Descartes (1596–1650), who imagined much weird-science on the subject of the emotions. Following his inclination to describe the body as a machine, he offers the organ as a metaphor for the basic body mechanism which results in the perception of the emotions.

> You can think of our machine's heart and arteries, which push the animal spirits into the cavities of its brain, as being like the bellows of an organ, which push air into the wind-chests; and you can think of external objects, which stimulate certain nerves and cause spirits contained in the cavities to pass into some of the pores, as being like the fingers of the organist, which press certain keys and cause the air to pass from the wind-chests into certain pipes. Now the harmony of an organ does not depend on the externally visible arrangement of the pipes or on the shape of the wind-chests or other parts. The functions we are concerned with here does not depend at all on the external shape of the visible parts which anatomists distinguish in the substance of the brain, or on the shape of the brain's cavities, but solely on three factors: the spirits which come from the heart, the pores of the brain through which they pass, and the way in which the spirits are distributed in these pores.[62]

The 'animal spirits' referred to here, Descartes defines as,

> The parts of the blood which penetrate as far as the brain serve not only to nourish and sustain its substance, but also and primarily to produce in it a certain very fine wind, or rather a very lively and pure flame, which is called the *animal spirits*.[63]

Descartes continues with his weird-science by finding the physical location of the emotions to be in the heart,[64] whence our emotional awareness comes through small nerves, scattered throughout the body.

> The nerves which go to the stomach, esophagus, throat, and other internal parts whose function is to keep our natural wants supplied, produce one kind of internal sensation, which is called 'natural appetite.' The nerves which go to the heart and the surrounding area, despite their very small size, produce another kind of internal sensation which comprises all the disturbances or passions and emotions of the mind such as joy, sorrow, love, hate and so on. For example, when the blood has the right consistency so that it expands in the heart more readily than usual, it relaxes the nerves scattered around the openings, and sets up a movement which leads to a subsequent movement in the brain producing a natural feeling of joy in the mind; and other causes produce the same sort of movement

---

[61] Ibid., Proposition XVIII, Note II.

[62] 'Treatise on Man,' in *The Philosophical Writings of Descartes*, trans. John Cottingham, Robert Stoothoff and Dugald Murdoch (Cambridge: Cambridge University Press, 1985). 166.

[63] Ibid., 129.

[64] Later he located some of the emotional activity in the pineal gland (more weird-science). See 'Treatise on Man,' 129, 'Meditations on First Philosophy,' VI and 'Principles of Philosophy,' IV, 316ff.

in these tiny nerves, thereby giving the same feeling of joy. Thus, if we imagine ourselves enjoying some good, the act of imagination does not itself contain the feeling of joy, but it causes the animal spirits to travel from the brain to the muscles in which these nerves are embedded. This causes the openings of the heart to expand, and this in turn produces the movement in the tiny nerves of the heart which must result in the feeling of joy ... Or again, if the blood is too thick and flows sluggishly into the ventricles of the heart and does not expand enough inside it, it produces a different movement in the same small nerves around the heart; when this movement is transmitted to the brain it produces a feeling of sadness in the mind, although the mind itself may perhaps not know of any reason why it should be sad. And there are several other causes capable of producing the same feeling. Other movements in these tiny nerves produce different emotions such as love, hatred, fear, anger and so on; I am here thinking of these simply as emotions or passions of the soul, that is, as confused thoughts, which the mind does not derive from itself alone but experiences as a result of something happening to the body with which it is closely conjoined. These emotions are quite different in kind from the distinct thoughts which we have concerning what is to be embraced or desired or shunned.[65]

In another place Descartes expands his views to the physiology of the emotions, explaining the physical manifestation associated with these basic passions,[66] excepting Wonder which is located only in the brain. In the case of Love,

> the pulse has a regular beat, but is much fuller and stronger than normal; we feel a gentle heat in the chest; and the digestion of food takes place very quickly in the stomach. In this way this passion is conducive to good health.

In Hatred,

> the pulse is irregular, weaker and often quicker; we feel chills mingled with a sort of sharp, piercing heat in the chest; and the stomach ceases to perform its function, being inclined to regurgitate and reject the food we have eaten, or at any rate to spoil it and turn it into bad humors.

In Joy,

> the pulse is regular and faster than normal, but not so strong or full as in the case of love; we feel a pleasant heat not only in the chest but also spreading into all the external parts of the body along with the blood which is seen to flow copiously to these parts; and yet we sometimes lose our appetite because our digestion is less active than usual.

In Sadness,

> the pulse is weak and slow, and we feel as if our heart had tight bonds around it, and were frozen by icicles which transmit their cold to the rest of the body. But sometimes we still have a good appetite and feel our stomach continuing to do its duty, provided there is no hatred mixed with the sadness.

---

[65] 'Principles of Philosophy,' in Ibid., IV, 316ff.

[66] 'The Passions of the Soul,' (1649), xcviff.

Desire,

> agitates the heart more violently than any other passion, and supplies more spirits to the brain. Passing from there into the muscles, these spirits render all the senses more acute, and all the parts of the body more mobile.

Descartes now elaborates on the physical manifestations associated with the passions.[67] We will cite only one as an example, those associated with Love.

> These observations, and many others that would take too long to report, have led me to conclude that when the understanding thinks of some object of love, this thought forms an impression in the brain which directs the animal spirits through the nerves of the sixth pair to the muscles surrounding the intestines and stomach, where they act in such a way that the alimentary juices (which are changing into new blood) flow rapidly to the heart without stopping in the liver. Driven there with greater force than the blood from other parts of the body, these juices enter the heart in greater abundance and produce a stronger heat there because they are coarser than the blood which has already been rarefied many times as it passes again and again through the heart. As a result the spirits sent by the heart to the brain have parts which are coarser and more agitated than usual; and as they strengthen the impression formed by the first thought of the loved object, these spirits compel the soul to dwell upon this thought. This is what the passion of love consists in.

Writers from among the aristocracy in Baroque France complain that they find the nobles superficial even in the emotions they feel for their departed friends. The Duchesse d'Orleans relates that after the funeral of the Dauphine, the court immediately resumed its card-playing, 'hunting in the afternoon, music at night.'

> If this were a matter of strength of character one might perhaps appreciate it and admire them for it, but that is not the reason, for as long as they see the sad spectacle they cry, but as soon as they leave the room they laugh again and forget all about it.[68]

This attitude is confirmed by the Duke of Saint-Simon who observes that even the death of Louis XIV, after having reigned seventy years, was little regretted and that few persons felt a sense of loss, apart from his personal servants.[69]

During the Baroque in England one encounters the rabid Puritan movement, which tended to take a gloomy view on the question of the emotions. Rev. Joseph Hall (1574–1656), in a discussion on the difference between anger and madness, offers this portrait of anger.

---

[67] Ibid., ciiff.

[68] Letter to the duchess Sophie, June 12, 1690, quoted in, *A Woman's Life in the Court of the Sun King*, trans. Elborg Forster (Baltimore: Johns Hopkins University Press, 1984), 69.

[69] *The Memoirs of the Duke of Saint-Simon*, trans. Bayle St. John (London: George Allen, 1926), III, 28.

> Raging madness is a short madness; what else argues the shaking of the hands and lips; paleness or redness or swelling of the face; glaring of the eyes; stammering of the tongue; stamping with the feet; unsteady motions of the whole body; rash actions ... distracted and wild speeches? And madness is nothing but continued rage.[70]

Later in this treatise he concludes 'he is a rare man that has not some kind of madness reigning in him.' The kinds of madness he had in mind were melancholy, pride, false devotion, ambition or covetousness, anger, laughing madness of extreme mirth, drunken madness, outrageous lust, curiosity and profaneness and atheism.[71]

For many English writers at this time interest on the emotions centered on melancholy. William Harvey, in his *Lectures on the Whole of Anatomy* of 1616, appeared interested in melancholy, but offered only weird-science by way of discussion. He mentions that 'physicians differ regarding the melancholy juice' and suggests melancholics lack pleasant disposition and talent and wonders if its origin were related to the 'splen-stone.'[72]

Robert Burton (1577–1640), author of *The Anatomy of Melancholy* of 1621, associates a transitory form of melancholy with mortality itself, for every man experiences it on some occasion. This form comes and goes with,

> every small occasion of sorrow, need, sickness, trouble, fear, grief, passion, or perturbation of the mind, any manner of care, discontent, or thought, which causes anguish, dullness, heaviness and vexation of spirit, any ways opposite to pleasure, mirth, joy, delight, causing forwardness in us, or a dislike. In which equivocal and improper sense, we call him melancholy, that is dull, sad, sour, lumpish, ill-disposed, solitary, any way moved, or displeased. And from these melancholy dispositions no man living is free ... Melancholy in this sense is the character of Mortality.[73]

William Shenstone (1714–1763) offered a rather unique, almost positive, view of melancholy.

> If Melancholy may be said to be fraught with any spirit at all as I believe it *may*; for I believe a pretty *Spirit* may be distilled from *Tears*.[74]

As this view differed from the Puritans, so he also argued against their attitude toward the subduing of the emotions.

---

[70] 'Holy Observations,' in *The Works of Joseph Hall, D.D.*, ed. Philip Wynter (New York: AMS Press, 1969), VII, 541.

[71] Ibid., 542.

[72] *The Works of William Harvey*, ed. Robert Willis (Reprinted New York: Johnson Reprint Corp., 1965), 93ff.

[73] Robert Burton, *The Anatomy of Melancholy*, ed. Floyd Dell (New York: Tudor Publishing Company, 1938), 125. In his 'Medical Remains' [*The Works of Francis Bacon* (Cambridge: Cambridge University Press, 1869), VII, 424], Bacon offers the recipe for making a 'wine against adverse melancholy, preserving the senses and the reason.' This involves roots of bugloss, misted with wine containing three ounces of refined gold, etc.

[74] Letter to Lady Luxborough, June 1, 1748, in *Letters of William Shenstone* (Minneapolis: University of Minnesota Press, 1939), 106.

> While we labor to subdue our passions, we should take care not to extinguish them. Subduing our passions, is disengaging ourselves from the world; to which, however, whilst we reside in it, we must always bear relation; and we may detach ourselves to such a degree as to pass an useless and insipid life, which we were not meant to do.[75]

David Hume (1711–1776) in attempting to analyze the operation of the emotions, begins with his division of human understanding into impressions (or sensation) and ideas (or reflections). Impressions he subdivides into original, which are the senses, and secondary, which are the passions.[76] The latter Hume further subdivides into calm and violent. But every emotion or passion has its own range of intensity.

> Of the first kind is the sense of beauty and deformity in action, composition, and external objects. Of the second are the passions of love and hatred, grief and joy, pride and humility. This division is far from being exact. The raptures of poetry and music frequently rise to the greatest height; while those other impressions, properly called passions, may decay into so soft an emotion, as to become, in a manner, imperceptible. But as in general the passions are more violent than the emotions arising from beauty and deformity.

Hume finds some passions occur as a single idea in the mind, but most are associated with additional emotions. For example, he says disappointment can give rise to anger, anger to envy and envy to malice. This suggests that man experiences a flood of near-simultaneous emotions, which Hume accounts for as follows:

> It is difficult for the mind, when actuated by any passion, to confine itself to that passion alone, without any change or variation. Human nature is too inconstant to admit of any such regularity. Changeableness is essential to it. And to what can it so naturally change as to affections or emotions, which are suitable to the temper, and agree with that set of passions, which then prevail?[77]

The great Francis Bacon (1561–1626), in Book Eight of his *Natural History*, discusses the physical effects of the passions on the body. Here he includes fear, joy, anger, light displeasure, shame, wonder, laughing, lust, grief and pain. Of the latter two, for example, he observes,

> Grief and pain cause sighing, sobbing, groaning, screaming and roaring, tears, distorting of the face, grinding of the teeth, sweating. Sighing is caused by the drawing in of a greater quantity of breath to refresh the heart that labors; like a great draught when one is thirsty. Sobbing is the same thing stronger ... Tears are caused by a contraction of the spirits of the brain; which contraction by consequence astringeth the moisture of the brain, and thereby sends tears into the eyes.[78]

---

75 William Shenstone, *Men and Manners* (Boston: Houghton Mifflin, 1927), 53.

76 *A Treatise of Human Nature*, II, i, 1. Like most early philosophers, Hume did not realize that pains in the body are not actually felt there, but rather in the brain.

77 Ibid., II, i, ¤5.

78 *The Works of Francis Bacon*, ed. James Spedding (Cambridge: Cambridge University Press, 1869), Century VIII, Section 714.

In Bacon's *History of Life and Death*, he discusses individual emotions from the perspective of their physical influence on the body. Among his more interesting contentions, we find,

> Great joys attenuate and diffuse the spirits, and shorten life; ordinary cheerfulness strengthens the spirits …
> Sensual impressions of joys are bad …
> Joy suppressed and sparingly communicated comforts the spirits more than joy indulged and published.[79]
> Grief and sadness, if devoid of fear, and not too keen, rather prolong life …
> Great fears shorten life.
> Suppressed anger is a kind of vexation, and makes the spirit to prey upon the juices of the body.
> Envy is the worst of passions, and preys on the spirits …
> A light shame hurts not, because it slightly contracts the spirits and then diffuses them …
> Love, if not unfortunate, and too deeply wounding, is a kind of joy …
> Hope is of all the affections the most useful, and contributes most to prolong life.[80]

Bacon correctly observes that the motions of the face 'disclose the present humor and state of the mind and will.'[81] For this reason, in another place he recommends that one maintain a 'steadfast countenance, not wavering, etc., in conversation.'[82]

Francis Hutcheson (1694–1746) appears to us to be the first philosopher to begin to understand the emotions in a way that corresponds with what we know today from clinical research. In a single sentence he correctly states that the emotions are part of the mind and that they are basic to human nature.

> The Nature of human actions cannot be sufficiently understood without considering the affections and passions; or those modifications or actions of the mind consequent upon the apprehension of certain objects or events, in which the mind generally conceives good or evil.[83]

Whereas Hutcheson had intended the previous chapter to focus on sensation, in Chapter Two he now considers Affections and Passions. Earlier philosophers had sometimes used these terms rather loosely, even as synonyms, but Hutcheson is careful to define them. Affection is what we would call the basic emotions, such as joy and sorrow, and they arise generally from sensation. Passion he considers a more outward, willful and much stronger form of emotion.

---

[79] Later [*History of Life and Death*, in Ibid., X, 144], he states that sudden grief or fear can produce sudden death. In addition, 'Many have died from great and sudden joys.'

[80] *History of Life and Death*, in Ibid., X, 98ff.

[81] *The Advancement of Learning*, in Ibid., VI, 238.

[82] 'Civil Conversation,' in Ibid., XIII, 309.

[83] *An Essay on the Nature and Conduct of the Passions*, I, i.

> When the word Passion is imagined to denote anything different from the Affections, it includes a strong Brutal Impulse of the Will, sometimes without any distinct notions of good, public or private ... and prolongs and strengthens the affection sometimes to such a degree, as to prevent all deliberate reasoning about our conduct.[84]

The great question for all earlier philosophers was, how does one control such passions? Hutcheson's solution is moral philosophy, rather than some abstract concept of 'Reason,' as the policeman of our passions.

He concludes this chapter with a plea for the goal of balancing our affections and passions. Earlier philosophers had contended that a man is constituted with a tendency toward a specific Temper, caused by a prevalence or absence of various fluids in the body. For Hutcheson, the point was that if this be true, then one is by nature unbalanced, rendering the goal of balance in emotions the more difficult.

> The sensations of anger in some Tempers are violent above their proportion; those of ambition, avarice, desire of sensual pleasure, and even of natural affection, in several dispositions, possess the mind too much, and make it incapable of attending to anything else. Scarce any one Temper is always constant and uniform in its passions ... Custom, Education, Habits and Company may often contribute much to this disorder.

Hutcheson finds five classifications of 'what excites our emotions other than self-interest.' For example, emotions can be awakened by moral sense or a sense of honor, inspired by others or by the public, etc. He also notes that the issue is not that we must control the emotion itself, but our opinions formed from it. Related to this is a section regarding the opinion of others. Here, under 'Judgment of Spectators,' he rhetorically offers two models.

> Let them see one entirely employed in Solitude with the most exquisite Tastes, Odors, Prospects, Painting, Musick; but without any Society, Love or Friendship, or any opportunity of doing a kind or generous action.

In contrast, let them see,

> A man employed in protecting the poor and fatherless, receiving the blessings of those who were ready to perish, and making the widow to sing for joy; a father to the needy, an avenger of oppression ... Which of the two would a Spectator choose? Which would he admire, or count the happier, and most suitable to human Nature?[85]

Alexander Pope (1688–1744) left a nice maxim on this subject:

> The world is a thing we must of necessity either laugh at or be angry at; if we laugh at it, they say we are proud; if we are angry at it, they say we are ill-natured.[86]

---

[84] Ibid., II, i.

[85] Ibid., V, iv.

[86] *The Works of Alexander Pope* (New York: Gordian Press, 1967), X, 553.

Another who commented on how we think *about* our emotions was Matthew Prior (1664–1721), a non-fiction writer of the Restoration. He paraphrases a Spanish maxim he had heard, as follows:

> When we are born our mind comes in at our toes, so goes upward through our legs, to our middle, thence to our heart and breast, lodges at last in our head and from thence flies away. The meaning of which is that childish sorts and youthful wrestlings, and trials of strength, amorous desires, courageous and manly designs, council and policy succeed each other in the course of our lives till the whole terminates in death. The consequence of it is obvious, our passions change with our ages, and our opinion with our passions.[87]

Anthony Cooper, Earl of Shaftesbury (1671–1713), a student of Locke, concluded that the emotions are in large part genetic by nature. Nevertheless, he believed that the various emotions have a certain inequality in their strength among individual men. It is interesting that he uses music, which is the very expression of emotions, as a metaphor to describe his views on this subject.

> Upon the whole, it may be said properly to be the same with the affections or passions in an animal constitution as with the strings of a musical instrument. If these, though in ever so just proportion one to another, are strained beyond a certain degree, it is more than the instrument will bear: the lute or lyre is abused, and its effect lost. On the other hand, if while some of the strings are duly strained, others are not wound up to their due proportion, then is the instrument still in disorder, and its part ill performed. The several species of creatures are like different sorts of instruments; and even in the same species of creatures (as in the same sort of instrument) one is not entirely like the other, nor will the same strings fit each. The same degree of strength which winds up one, and fits the several strings to a just harmony and consort, may in another burst both the strings and instrument itself. Thus men who have the liveliest sense, and are the easiest affected with pain or pleasure, have need of the strongest influence or force of other affections, such as tenderness, love, sociableness, compassion, in order to preserve a right balance within, and to maintain them in their duty, and in the just performance of their part, whilst others, who are of a cooler blood, or lower key, need not the same allay or counterpart, nor are made by Nature to feel those tender and endearing affections in so exquisite a degree.[88]

Several other English philosophers of this period were interested in various facets of the question of emotions varying with individuals. William Shenstone (1714–1763), for example, believed that talented persons had by nature stronger emotions.

> People of real genius have strong passions; people of strong passions have great partialities.[89]
>
> ……
>
> People of the finest and most lively genius have the greatest sensibility, of consequence the most lively passion.[90]

---

87 'Opinion,' in *The Literary Works of Matthew Prior* (Oxford: Clarendon, 1959), I, 578ff.
88 *Characteristics of Men, Manners, Opinions, Times*, 'Concerning Virtue or Merit,' II, iii.
89 William Shenstone, *Men and Manners* (Boston: Houghton Mifflin, 1927), 79.
90 Ibid., 60.

He was also not quite sure that pure friendship was possible between the sexes.

> There is no word in the Latin language, that signifies a female friend. 'Amica,' means a mistress; and perhaps there is no friendship between the sexes wholly disunited from a degree of love.[91]

Shenstone, by the way, also did not accept the idea that the emotions could be universal in character. The proof, for him, was obvious in the case of humor.

> Trifles will burst one man's sides, which will not disturb the features of another; and a laugh one cannot join, is almost as irksome as a lamentation.

Jonathan Swift (1667–1745), in writing about preaching to Englishmen, offers another consideration on how specific emotions can vary with individuals by way of introducing the subject of geography.

> But I do not see how this talent of moving the passions, can be of any great use towards directing Christian men in the conduct of their lives, at least in these Northern climates; where, I am confident, the strongest eloquence of that kind will leave few impressions upon any of our spirits, deep enough to last till the next Morning, or rather to the next meal.[92]

As a final illustration of those who sought individual associations with the emotions we must mention John Locke (1632–1704). In his famous treatise on education he contends that crying 'is a fault that should not be tolerated in children.' If it can't be stopped by 'a look, or a positive command … blows must.'[93]

---

[91] Ibid., 41.

[92] 'A Letter to a Young Gentleman,' in *The Prose Works of Jonathan Swift* (Oxford: Blackwell, 1957), IX, 69.

[93] 'Thoughts Concerning Education' in *The Works of John Locke* (London, 1823; reprinted in Aalen: Scientia Verlag, 1963), 102ff.

On Animals and Music

> *Ye famous ships, that on a day were brought to land at Troy by those countless oars, what time ye led the Nereids' dance, where the music loving dolphin rolled and gamboled round your dusky prows …*
>
> Euripides (480–406 BC), *Electra*

> *Where many a songful dolphin trips*
> *To lead the dark blue beaked ships …*
>
> Aristophanes (448–380 BC), *The Frogs*

> *Dolphins delight infinitely in music; they love it, and if any man sings or plays as he sails along in fair weather, they will quietly swim by the side of the ship, and listen till the music is ended.*
>
> Plutarch (46–120 AD)[1]

IN ANCIENT TIMES, AS WELL AS TODAY, man has seemingly always had a special fascination with dolphins, which may account in part for the frequent references in ancient literature of dolphins listening to music. But, in reading ancient literature one is also struck by the wide variety of animals which appear when the subject under discussion is music. In addition to dolphins, one reads of swordfish, elephants, horses, oxen, lions, tigers, bears, deer, wolves, asses, hogs, sloths, dogs, cats, silk-worms, flies, frogs, snakes, birds of many kinds, dragons and often just 'wild animals.'

Frequently when we read of the reactions of the animals, it seems we are really reading about the reactions of real people, as in the Plutarch quotation above which resembles the description of a contemplative listener. On the other hand, sometimes we find references in which the musical attributes are really those of the animal itself, as in the case of Kircher's seventeenth-century account of the Central American sloth.

> It perfectly intones as learners do, the first elements of music, *do, re, me, fa, sol, la, sol, fa, me, re, do*. Ascending and descending through the common intervals of the six degrees, insomuch that the Spaniards, when they first took possession of these coasts, and perceived such a kind of vociferation in the night, thought they heard men accustomed to the rules of music.

---

[1] Plutarch, 'The Banquet of the Seven Wise Men.' *The Geography of Strabo*, trans. Horace L. Jones (Cambridge: Harvard University Press, 1960), XV.2.12, on the other hand describes the use of trumpets to scare off whales.

Kircher concluded,

> If music were first invented in America, I would say that it must have begun with the amazing voice of this animal.[2]

For the most part, the value we find today in these animal references is in their potential for helping to illuminate the views of music among the early writers. The ancients had a difficult time with music. They understood through observation that music had powerful properties, something they often seem at a loss to explain. Above all, it was because they *could not see music* that they were so puzzled that music could be so influential. This last characteristic, that music is the only art you cannot see, is, we believe, why the ancients so often associated music with religion rather than with the other arts. Because music was (and is) therefore so difficult to talk about, we often have the impression that they were more comfortable in transferring the wonder of music to animals for observation, rather than trying to explain it in the domain of physiological man. This seems to us particularly the case in the many instances where there is a discussion of emotions expressed through the singing of birds. The thought process was that as animals clearly had no capacity for Reason yet could respond to the non-rational sounds of music, the study of the response of animals to music was a way of observing the nature of music disconnected from Reason, which was impossible for them to do in the case of man.

Also some insights are found in the use of animals and music in analogy, metaphor or as surrogates for various basic ideas. St. Augustine, for example, once offered a syllogism contending that as animals have no Reason, they cannot have art. But, animals are capable of imitation, which he concludes proves that imitation cannot be art.[3] Perhaps another example is related to the interest by the ancient Greeks in the correspondence of man with nature. Those passages in which we find man and animals *joining together* to make music carry, we believe, a symbolic reference to their common bond in nature. Thus, in Euripides we find a plea to a bird to help perform a dirge.

> Thee let me invoke, tearful Philomel, lurking 'neath the leafy covert in thy place of song, most tuneful of all feathered songsters, oh! come to aid me in my dirge, trilling through thy tawny throat, as I sing the piteous woes of Helen.[4]

---

[2] Athanasius Kircher, *Musurgia universalis* (1650), trans. Frederick Crane (unpublished dissertation, State University of Iowa, 1956), Book One, 'Anatomical.' Kircher gives a description of this animal which he says is named from the fact that in fifteen days it does not travel as far as one can throw a spear.

> No one knows what meat it feeds on ... they for the most part keep on the tops of trees ... [With their feet] they have such strength, that whatsoever animal they lay hold on they keep it so fast, that it is never after able to free itself from their nails, but it is compelled to die through hunger. On the other hand, this beast so greatly affects the men that are coming towards it by its countenance, that in pure compassion they refrain from molesting it, and easily persuade themselves not to be solicitous about that which nature has subjected to so defenseless and miserable a state of body.

[3] Augustine, *On Music*, trans. Robert Taliaferro in *Writings of Saint Augustine* (New York: Fathers of the Church), I, iv.

[4] Euripides, *Helen*, 1113ff.

One of the most frequently repeated stories about music in early literature is a story which makes the same point, here the joining of an insect with a performer on a string instrument to complete a performance. An anonymous version of the first century is found on the statue of a famous lyre player, Eunomus.

> Thou knowest, Apollo, how I, Eunomus the Locrian, conquered Spartis, but I tell it for those who ask me. I was playing on the lyre an elaborate piece, and in the middle of it my plectrum loosened one chord, and when the time came to strike the note I was ready to play, it did not convey the correct sound to the ear. Then of its own accord a cicada perched on the bridge of the lyre and supplied the deficiency of the harmony. I had struck six chords, and when I required the seventh I borrowed this cicada's voice; for the midday songster of the hillside adapted to my performance that pastoral air of his, and when he shrilled he combined with the lifeless chords to change the value of the phrase. Therefore I owe a debt of thanks to my partner in the duet, and wrought in bronze he sits on my lyre.[5]

In 'The Princess of Babylon,' Voltaire employs a pastoral scene, so often used in Renaissance and Baroque literature, as the setting for the singing of love songs. Here there is an ensemble of birds singing the soprano and alto parts, with shepherds singing the tenor and bass. One listener, with tears flowing from her eyes, calls the resulting music 'consolatory and voluptuous.'[6]

Another metaphoric use of animals by ancient writers addresses a topic not discussed at all today—the influence of the character of a musician on his music making. The Greeks, with their interest in unifying everything in nature, often asked, 'Can the music be good if the performer himself is a bad person?' Early writers always answered this question, 'No,' as we also see in one of the fables of Aesop (620–560 BC), 'The Kid and the Aulos Playing Wolf.'

> A kid had lagged behind the flock and was set upon by a wolf. The kid turned around and said to the wolf, 'I'm sure that I'm to be your dinner, but just so that I won't die ignominiously, play a tune on our aulos for me to dance to.' While the wolf played and the kid danced, the dogs heard and chased the wolf away. The wolf turned back and said to the kid, 'This is what I deserve. A butcher like me oughtn't to try to be an aulos player.'[7]

The moral of this story resonates in later centuries, as for example in the case of Albertus Magnus in his thirteenth-century treatise, *De animalibus*.

---

5   *The Greek Anthology*, trans. W. R. Paton (Cambridge: Harvard University Press, 1939), IX, 584. A poem from the first century BC also associates the cricket with the lyre.

> Noisy cicada, drunk with dew drops, thou singest thy rustic ditty that fills the wilderness with voice, and seated on the edge of the leaves, striking with saw-like legs thy sunburnt skin thou shrillest music like the lyre's. But sing, dear, some new tune to gladden the woodland nymphs, strike up some strain responsive to Pan's pipe, that I may escape from Love and snatch a little midday sleep. [Ibid., IV, 196]

Another nice retelling of this story is found in the sixth-century poet, Paulus Silentiarius, in Ibid., I, vi, 54.

6   'The Princess of Babylon,' in *The Works of Voltaire* (New York: St. Hubert Guild, 1901), III, 206.

7   *Aesop*, trans. Lloyd W. Daly (New York: Yoseloff, 1961), Nr. 97.

> The animosity between the wolf and sheep is so strong its influence extends to all of their anatomical parts; thus, musical strings made of sheep gut do not resonate in harmony with strings made of wolf gut.[8]

The sixteenth-century German, Henry Agrippa, makes the same point.

> Neither can the strings made of sheep's and wolf's guts be brought to any agreement, because their foundations are dissonant.[9]

It seems clear that nothing about music so impressed earlier philosophers as its ability to arouse strong emotions. But early writers (before the twelfth century) did not regard strong emotions in a man, taken by themselves, as a virtue. Perhaps, then, by illustrating music's ability to create strong emotions in animals, rather than in man, they believed they could appear to present this power of music more objectively. And similarly, loud music by animals appears sometimes a metaphor for the power of music, which seems the case in this example in Chaucer:

> Ful loude songen hire [their] affecciouns[10]

We will return to this subject below, but for the moment we mention the example found in early literature of the power of the military trumpet to inflame the passion of the horse. Consider this passage from the Old Testament:

> With fierceness and rage he swallows the ground; he cannot stand still at the sound of the trumpet.
> When the trumpet sounds, he says 'Aha!'
> He smells the battle from afar, the thunder of the captains, and the shouting.[11]

A similar description is found in Aeschylus.

> As some wild war-horse when the trumpets sound
> Stiffens and champs the curb and paws the ground.[12]

One can understand how a horse so trained could become a danger in peace time. In the sixteenth-century work by Sir Philip Sidney, *The Countesse of Pembrokes Arcadia*, a horse, trained to respond to the sound of the trumpet, upon hearing the instrument played leaped forward, causing the surprised rider to almost fall from the saddle.[13] It was for this reason that when

---

8   *De animalibus*, trans. James Scanlan (Binghamton, NY: Medieval & Renaissance Texts, 1987), 158.

9   Henry Cornelius Agrippa, *Of the Vanitie and Uncertaintie of Arts and Sciences*, ed. Catherine Dunn (Northridge: California State University, Northridge Press, 1974), II, xxv.

10 Chaucer, 'The Squire's Tale.'

11 Job 39:20.

12 *The Seven Against Thebes*, 386.

13 Book III, xiii.

court persons were to travel in a procession with horses, the court trumpeters were required to spend some time in the stable playing for the horses, to acclimate them to the sound so as not to pose a danger to the women in the party.

> … to goe often into the Stable, to acquainte the horses with the sound of the trumpet, and the noise of the drumme.[14]

A somewhat different illustration of the power of music to inflame the passion of horses is mentioned by Aelianus with regard to the performance of the aulos in Libya.

> This is the aulos music which throws mares into an amorous frenzy and makes horses mad with desire to couple. This in fact is how the mating of horses is brought about.[15]

The previous two examples have in common the idea that music can affect the behavior of animals. Polybius, writing of Rome in the second century BC, gives an extensive account of the use of music to control flocks.

> The impression that all the animals on the island of Corsica are wild arises from the following cause. The island is thickly wooded and the countryside so rocky and precipitous that it is impossible for the shepherds to follow their flocks and herds about as they graze. So, whenever they wish to collect them they take up position in some convenient place; from there they summon them by horn, and all the animals respond without fail to the instrument which they recognize. Now if any travelers who may touch at the island see goats and cattle grazing unattended and try to catch them, the animals will not come near them because they are not used to them and take to flight. Again, if the shepherd sees the strangers disembarking and sounds his horn, the herd will run off at full speed and gather round the horn. For this reason the animals give the appearance of being wild …
>
> There is nothing surprising in the fact that the animals should obey the sound of a horn, for in Italy those who are engaged in herding swine use exactly the same method. The swineherd does not follow the animals, as he does in Greece, but walks in front and sounds a horn at intervals, while the animals keep behind him and respond to the call. Indeed the pigs have become so accustomed to answering the particular instrument belonging to their herd that those who witness this practice for the first time are amazed and can hardly believe their ears. The fact is that because of the great size of the population and the abundance of food the droves of swine in Italy are very large, especially among the inhabitants of Tuscany and the Gauls, so that a single farrowing of a single herd may produce a thousand or even more piglets. The peasants therefore drive them out from their night sites to feed according to their litters and ages. Then if several droves are taken to the same place, they cannot keep the various groups apart, and so they become mixed up, either while they are being driven out, or as they are feeding, or on the way home. So the swineherds invented the horn call as the simplest method of separating them without labor or trouble when the litters had become mixed. And in practice whenever one of the swineherds leads off in one direction sounding his horn, and another turns away in another direction, the animals separate of their own accord and follow with such eagerness the sound of the individual horn which they know that it is impossible to check them or turn them back.[16]

---

[14] Paul Jones, *The Household of a Tudor Nobleman* (Urbana, 1918), 229.

[15] *On the Characteristics of Animals*, XII, 44.

[16] Polybius, *The Rise of the Roman Empire* (New York: Penguin, 1981), 430.

For a final example of the ancient use of a musical instrument to affect the behavior of an animal, one must mention an extraordinary passage in Herodotus, the great fifth century BC historian.

> The Scythians blind their slaves, a practice in some way connected with the milk which they prepare for drinking in the following way: they insert a tube made of bone and shaped like a flute into the mare's anus and blow; and while one blows, another milks. According to them, the object of this is to inflate the mare's veins with air and so cause the udder to be forced down. They make the blind men stand round in a circle, and then pour the milk into wooden casks and stir it; the part which rises to the top is skimmed off and is considered the best; what remains is not supposed to be so good.[17]

When early writers address the purpose of music, the most often given purpose is its ability to soothe the emotions. It seems clear that they gave a higher value to music's ability to soothe, rather than inflame, the passions. This, of course, is what one of the best-known Greek myths is all about, the tale of Orpheus using his skill in music to 'tame the savage beast.' In this famous myth, the 'savage beast' is once again really only a metaphor for man. Perhaps this myth is what Shakespeare was thinking of when he wrote of wild horses being calmed down, by a trumpet no less!

> For do but note a wild and wanton herd,
> Or race of youthful and unhandled colts,
> Fetching mad bounds, bellowing and neighing loud,
> Which is the hot condition of their blood;
> If they but hear perchance a trumpet sound,
> Or any air of music touch their ears,
> You shall perceive them make a mutual stand,
> Their savage eyes turned to a modest gaze
> By the sweet power of music: therefore the poet
> Did feign that Orpheus drew trees, stones, and floods;
> Since nought so stockish, hard, and full of rage,
> But music for the time doth change his nature.[18]

There is a passage in the *De animalibus* by Albertus Magnus (thirteenth century) in which he makes the observation that 'for some reason sheep eat better when they are soothed by the pleasant sound of music.'[19] Of course, we would not go so far as to suppose that sheep are a metaphor for school children (!), but we were reminded of a passage in Milton relative to the meal time in school.

---

[17] Herodotus, *The Histories* (New York: Penguin, 1977, 271 [IV, 1].

[18] *The Merchant of Venice*, V, i, 79ff.

[19] *De animalibus*, trans. James Scanlan, 169.

> The interim of unsweating themselves regularly, and convenient rest before meat may both with profit and delight be taken up in recreating and composing their travailed spirits with the solemn and divine harmonies of Musick heard or learned ... The like also would not be unexpedient after Meat to assist and cherish Nature in her first concoction, and send their minds back to study in good tune and satisfaction.[20]

With these references to eating, we might mention that one occasionally finds in early literature the suggestion that a singer might improve his tone by moistening his vocal cords with wine.[21] In a sixteenth-century Spanish poem a fly makes this same suggestion to a frog. At the same time he points out that the wine will lighten his dismal singing—so dismal he calls him the 'Dutchman's Nightingale.'

> Out of the Wine-Pot cry'd the Fly,
> Whilst the Grave Frog sat croaking by,
> Than live a Watery Life like thine,
> I'd rather choose to die in Wine.
>
> ......
>
> In Gardens I delight to stray,
> And round the Plants do sing and play:
> Thy Tune no Mortal does avail,
> Thou are the Dutchman's Nightingale:
> Wouldst thou with Wine but wet thy Throat,
> Sure thou would'st leave that Dismal Note;
> Lewd Water spoils thy Organs quite,
> And Wine alone can set them right.[22]

In some cases, we are told, becoming too soothed by music could create a danger for animals. Pliny the Elder, in the first century, finds that dolphins become so absorbed by music that they can then be captured.

> Dolphins are obviously able to hear; for dolphins are charmed even by music, and are caught while bewildered by the sound.[23]

Albertus finds the same is true with deer.

> This animal takes delight in all unusual sights and sounds; hence, wanting to be seen by itself and prone to being charmed by the sounds of pipes and song, it often falls into peril of capture or death.[24]

---

[20] 'On Education,' in *The Works of John Milton* (New York: Columbia University Press, 1931–1938)., IV, 288ff.

[21] There is an account of a Norwich Cathedral choir director in the 1920s, named Dr. Buck, who gave his boy singers water pistols filled with wine, which he instructed them to shoot into their throats to lubricate their performances.

[22] Francisco de Quevedo (1580–1645), 'Letrilla burlesca,' in *An Anthology of Spanish Poetry*, ed. John Crow (Baton Rouge: Louisiana State University Press, 1979), 113.

[23] Pliny the Elder, *Natural History*, L, 137.

[24] *De animalibus*, trans. James Scanlan, 94.

The most extraordinary tale in this regard is one from the second century AD.

> There is an Etruscan story current which says that the wild boars and the stags in that country are caught by using nets and hounds, as is the usual manner of hunting, but that music plays a part, and even the larger part, in the struggle. And how this happens I will now relate. They set the nets and other hunting gear that ensnare the animals in a circle, and a man proficient on the aulos stands there and tries his utmost to play a rather soft tune, avoiding any shriller note, but playing the sweetest melodies possible. The quiet and stillness easily carry [the sound] abroad; and the music streams up to the heights and into ravines and thickets—in a word into every lair and resting place of these animals. Now at first when the sound penetrates to their ears it strikes them with terror and fills them with dread, and then an unalloyed and irresistible delight in the music takes hold of them, and they are so beguiled as to forget about their offspring and their homes. And yet wild beasts do not care to wander away from their native haunts. But little by little these creatures in Etruria are attracted as though by some persuasive spell, and beneath the wizardry of the music they come and fall into the snares, overpowered by the melody.[25]

Cassiodorus, in the sixth century, informs us that it was the use of the Hypodorian mode, 'the lowest of all,' which was the most effective in soothing man and beast.

> These tones ... have been shown to possess such great usefulness that they calm excited minds and cause even wild animals and serpents and birds and dolphins to approach and listen to their harmony.[26]

Perhaps the most extraordinary tale of music soothing animals is found among the medieval 'Volsung and Niblungs' epics. Here a character manages to soothe a den full of snakes while using his feet to play as his hands were bound. Well—all but one snake!

> So Gunnar was cast into a worm-close, and many worms abode him there, and his hands were fast bound; but Gudrun sent him a harp, and in such wise did he set forth his craft, that wisely he smote the harp, smiting it with his toes, and so excellently well he played, that few deemed they had heard such playing, even when the hand had done it. And with such might and power he played, that all the worms fell asleep in the end, save one adder only, great and evil of aspect, that crept unto him and thrust its sting into him until it smote his heart; and in such wise with great hardihood he ended his life days.[27]

And finally, one of the most famous ancient tales which centers on music soothing the listeners is the story of the Sirens. Best known in Ovid's *Metamorphoses*, these mythological daughters of Phorcys, the sea god, lived on small rock islands off the southwest coast of Campania, where they lured sailors to their death on the rocks through their irresistibly sweet singing. While many ancient philosophers retold this tale, the early Christian writers, focus-

---

[25] Claudius Aelianus (second century AD), *Of the Characteristics of Animals*, XII, 46.

[26] Cassiodorus, 'On Music,' in *An Introduction to Divine and Human Readings*, trans. Leslie Jones (New York: Octagon Books, 1966), 8.

[27] 'The Story of the Volsungs and Niblungs,' trans. Eir'kr Magnœsson and William Morris in *Epic and Saga*, volume 49, *The Harvard Classics* (New York: Collier, 1910), 372.

ing on supremacy of Reason, maintained it was the *words* of the songs, not the music, which captured the sailors! As far as we know, no one before Albertus, in the thirteenth century, had ventured to give so detailed a description of these Sirens. In his version it must have been the music which attracted and calmed the sailors, because it clearly was not the physical appearance of these mythical daughters!

> SYRENAS (Sirens), popularized in poetic fable, are marine monsters whose upper body has the figure of a woman with long pendulous breasts with which it suckles its young; the face is horrible and it has a mane of long free-flowing hair; below they have eagle's claws, and above are aquiline wings, and behind a scaly tail used as a rudder to guide their swimming. Upon making an appearance, they hold out their young in full view, emit some sweet, alluring sounds by which they lull their hearers to sleep, and then tear the sleepers to pieces.[28]

With this terrible myth we move to the opposite end of the spectrum, where there are remarkable tales which seem to concentrate on the power of music to frighten. Hence, according to Albertus, in the thirteenth century, the dragon could only be captured when frightened by music. One never knows when one might need this information!

> Dragons are said to be afraid of thunder and prone to be struck by lightning, just as in a contrary sense the eagle among birds and the laurel among plants are said to be impervious to lightening; for this reason they say that when an enchanter seeks to charm a dragon with songs, he causes a great reverberating sound to be made by beating on a drum or stretched leather, and the dragon mistaking this for thunder cowers in fright and meekly allows the enchanter to mount its back.[29]

Another myth involving animals and percussion is found in the writings of Erasmus in the sixteenth century.

> They say that the tigress, if she hears the roll of drums all round her, is driven mad, and ends by tearing herself in pieces.[30]

For a final example in which animals are used as metaphors for the power of music we turn to the seventeenth-century Spanish playwright, Molina, and a charming tribute to the power of music to lift the spirits.

> Little songbirds,
> innocent flatterers,
> untaught musicians, idlers
> among reed-beds and wild thyme,
> cheer my sad spirits
> with your melodies;

---

[28] Albertus Magnus, *De animalibus*, trans. James Scanlan, 373. What reader who has traveled to Italy will not recall that the female gypsy pick-pockets also hold out their young as distractions.

[29] Ibid., 404. First-hand accounts of some listeners of the music of the French Revolution recall their fear on hearing the percussion instruments.

[30] 'Parallels,' [1514] in *The Collected Works of Erasmus* (Toronto: University of Toronto Press, 1992), XXIII, 175.

> with your gentle voices
> help me rise above my cares.[31]

Now we move to the subject of the use of animals to illustrate specific aspects of man and music, beginning with descriptions of the contemplative listener. First, we have a vivid description of a listener in a fourteenth-century poem by Machaut, listening to birds with as much quiet contemplation as if they were human singers.

> I dropped gently to the ground and hid myself as best I could beneath the trees, so it could not see me there, to listen to the very sweet melody of its delightful song. And I took more pleasure in listening to its sweet singing that ever I could tell.[32]

In another place, Machaut uses a story about birds to make the point that the required attention necessary to the contemplative listener is impossible if one is independently under emotional stress.

> And in more than thirty thousand places the birds, wide-throated, were trying to out-sing one another, as if it were a contest, making the whole orchard ring; and it's no lie that prior to Hope's visiting me in my need, my senses had been so distorted that I'd not noticed the birds or their music, or how merry they all were. But this should not be held against me, because there are two things that falsify the senses and cause them to react irrationally: these are great joy and great sadness.[33]

A very interesting passage which mentions animals listening to music is found in St. Augustine (fourth century). At this time music was admitted to the Liberal Arts only as a branch of mathematics. For this reason, several writers make the point that it is the 'knowing the numbers,' that is, knowledge of theory, which defines the musician. The person who understands music without this knowledge is, they say, only a beast, meaning an animal can hear the sound but not the 'music.' Augustine makes this point here as well as the observation that a gentleman should listen to music only for superficial relaxation, warning that he should not allow the experience to become meaningful.

> AUGUSTINE. Now tell me, then, don't [singers] all seem to be similar to the nightingale, all those which sing well under the guidance of a certain sense, that is, do it harmoniously and sweetly, although if they were questioned about the numbers or intervals of high and low notes they could not reply?
> STUDENT. I think they are very much alike.
> AUGUSTINE. And what's more, aren't those who like to listen to them without this science to be compared to beasts? For we see elephants, bears, and many other kinds of beasts are moved by singing, and birds themselves are charmed by their own voices. For, with no further proper purpose, they would not do this with such effort without some pleasure.
> STUDENT. I judge so, but this reproach extends to nearly the whole of human kind.

---

[31] *Damned for Despair*, III, iii.

[32] 'Le Jugement du roy de Behaigne,' trans. James Wimsatt and William Kibler (Athens: The University of Georgia Press, 1988), 60.

[33] 'Remede de Fortune,' trans. James Wimsatt and William Kibler, Ibid., 334.

AUGUSTINE. Not as much as you think. For great men, even if they know nothing about music, either wish to be one with the common people who are not very different from beasts and whose number is great; and they do this very properly and prudently. But this is not the place to discuss that. Or after great cares in order to relax and restore the mind they very moderately partake of some pleasure. And it is very proper to take it in from time to time. But to be taken in by it, even at times, is improper and disgraceful.[34]

In contrast to the Church philosophers, fortunately there were those in all earlier times who understood that music had important values in and of itself. This, of course, is what lies behind all accounts of the contemplative listener and particularly so in those cases where a crowd of people suddenly fall silent when a musician begins to perform. There is a fine description of such a moment when birds stop their singing to listen to the famous fourteenth century composer and performer, Landini.

> Now the sun rose higher and the heat of the day increased and the whole company remained in the pleasant shade; and as a thousand birds were singing among the verdant branches, someone asked Francesco to play the organ a little, to see whether the sound would make the birds increase or diminish their song. He did so at once, and a great wonder followed: for when the sound began many of the birds were seen to fall silent, and gather around as if in amazement, listening for a long time....[35]

Albertus, in the thirteenth century, makes a similar observation regarding nightingales.

> In my own observations of this bird I have remarked that it flies toward persons who are singing, provided they have a melodious voice; as long as these persons continue singing, the bird listens in silence; but as soon as they stop, the nightingale takes up the song, as if responding in a roundelay chorus. Furthermore, these birds duplicate the same process in response to one another, provoking each other to song.[36]

And speaking of animals listening to music, what are we to make of the claim by Giustiniani, of the sixteenth century, that silk-worms in Lombardy seemed to profit by listening to singing and playing? Why, he also wonders, when in fishing for swordfish, is it 'reputed necessary to sing, and what is more, to sing with Greek words?'[37] And speaking of fishing with music, Herodotus, the great fifth century BC historian, quotes a story told by the Persian king, Cyrus, to some ambassadors who were too late to gain his help.

---

34 *On Music*, trans. Robert Taliaferro in *Writings of Saint Augustine* (New York: Fathers of the Church)., I, iv.

35 Giovanni da Prato, *Paradiso degli Alberti* (1389).

36 Albertus Magnus, *De animalibus*, 315.

37 Vicenzo Giustiniani, *Discorso sopra la Musica* [ca. 1628], trans. Carol MacClintock (American Institute of Musicology, 1962), 75ff.

> An aulos player saw some fish in the sea and played his aulos to them in the hope that they would come ashore. When they refused to do so, he took a net, netted a large catch, and hauled them in. Seeing the fish jumping about, he said to them: 'It is too late to dance now: you might have danced to my music—but you would not.'[38]

In early literature one often finds stories of musical contests in pastoral settings. In one of these from the second century, cows are the adjudicators and like human listeners they gravitate toward the best musician.

> Once upon a time there was a beautiful girl who used to graze a great many cows in a wood. Now she was also very musical, and in her day cows enjoyed music. So she was able to control them without either hitting them with a staff or pricking them with a goad. She would simply sit down under a pine, and after crowning herself with pine-twigs would sing the story of Pan and the Pine, and the cows would stay close enough to hear her voice. A boy who grazed cows not far away, and who was also good-looking and musical, challenged her to a singing contest. Because of his sex, he was able to produce more volume than she could, and yet because he was only a boy, his voice had a very sweet tone. So he charmed away her eight best cows and enticed them into his own herd. The girl was annoyed at the damage done to her herd, and at being beaten at singing, and she prayed to the gods to turn her into a bird before she arrived home. The gods granted her prayer and turned her into this mountain bird, which is as musical as she was. And even now she still goes on singing, telling her sad story, and saying that she's looking for her missing cows.[39]

We find an occasional reference to animals, again like humans, who have a preference for a certain kind of music. According to Pliny the Elder, first century,

> The dolphin is an animal that is not only friendly to mankind but is also a lover of music, and it can be charmed by singing in harmony, but particularly by the sound of the water-organ.[40]

In this regard, it is interesting that in a recent research project psychologists found that rats had a strong preference for the music of Bach, when given a choice between Bach and rock music.[41]

We cannot leave the subject of music and dolphins without reminding the reader of one of the most retold stories of the ancient world, the rescue of the musician Arion by a dolphin. Here is the version of this tale as given by Herodotus the great historian of the fifth century BC.

> Most of his time Arion had spent with Periander, till he felt a longing to sail to Italy and Sicily. This he did; and after making a great deal of money in those countries, he decided to return to Corinth. He sailed from Tarentum in a Corinthian vessel, because he had more confidence in Corinthians than in anyone else. The crew, however, when the ship was at sea, hatched a plot to throw him overboard

---

38   Herodotus, *The Histories*, I, 142.
39   Longus, 'Daphnis and Chloe' trans. Paul Turner (London: Penguin Books, 1956), I, 37.
40   Pliny the Elder, *Natural History*, IX, viii, 25.
41   See http://www.soundtherapy.co.uk/research/musicresearch.php

and steal his money. He got wind of their intention and begged them to take his money, but spare his life. To no purpose, however; for the sailors told him either to kill himself if he wanted to be buried ashore, or to jump overboard at once.

Arion, seeing they had made up their minds, as a last resource begged permission to stand on the after-deck, dressed in his singing robes, and give them a song: the song over, he promised to kill himself. Delighted at the prospect of hearing a song from the world's most famous singer, the sailors all made their way forward from the stern and assembled amidships. Arion put on his full professional costume, took up his lute and, standing on the after-deck, played and sang a lively tune. Then he leapt into the sea, just as he was, with all his clothes on.

The ship continued her voyage to Corinth, but a dolphin picked up Arion and carried him on its back to Taenarum. Here Arion landed and made his way in his singing costume to Corinth, where he told the whole story. Periander was not too ready to believe it; so he put Arion under strict supervision, keeping the ship's crew meanwhile carefully in mind. On their return he sent for them and asked if they had anything to tell him about Arion. 'Oh yes,' they answered, 'we left him safe and sound at Tarentum in Italy.' But no sooner were the words out of their mouths than Arion himself appeared, just as he was when he jumped overboard. This was an unpleasant shock for the sailors. The lie was detected, and further denial useless.[42]

After the heterogeneous ensemble practice of the Middle Ages, listeners during the sixteenth century developed a strong preference for hearing music made by ensembles of the same kind of instrument, which was called a 'consort.' As we might expect, this preference was also transferred to animals in sixteenth-century literature. One Englishman recommends that the best equipped households will have their dogs organized in a consort!

> If you would have your kennels for sweetness of cry then you must compound it of some large dogs that have deep, solemn mouths ... which must as it were bear the bass in consort, then a double number of roaring and loud-ringing mouths which must bear the counter tenor, then some hollow, plain, sweet mouths which must bear the mean or middle part and so with these three parts of music you shall make your cry perfect.[43]

Can one take this seriously? Shakespeare, in his *A Midsummer Night's Dream*, gave a similar description. 'My hounds,' says Theseus, 'are,'

> Slow in pursuit, but matcht in mouth like bells,
> Each under each. A cry more tuneable
> Was never holla'd to, nor cheer'd with horn.[44]

And again a reference to the dog-consort principle in Sidney's *The Countesse of Pembrokes Arcadia*.

> Their cry being composed of so well sorted mouths, that any man would perceive therein some kind of proportion, but the skillful woodsmen did find a music.[45]

---

[42] Herodotus, *The Histories*, I, 24.
[43] Quoted in Elizabeth Burton, *The Pageant of Elisabethan England* (New York: Scribner's), 190.
[44] William Shakespeare, *A Midsummer Night's Dream* (IV, 1).
[45] Sir Philip Sidney, *The Countesse of Pembrokes Arcadia*, I, Book I, x.

We assume when we read here of Sidney's 'well sorted mouths' and Shakespeare's 'matcht in mouth like bells' that there was some arrangement of the dogs according to their vocal pitch, etc. With this in mind we were reminded of a description by Athanasius Kircher, of the seventeenth century, of a keyboard instrument made of cats!

> Not so long ago, in order to dispel the melancholy of some great prince, a noted and ingenious actor constructed an instrument such as this. He took live cats all of different sizes, and shut them up in a kind of box especially made for this business, so that their tails, stuck through the holes, were inserted tightly into certain channels. Under these he put keys fitted with the sharpest points instead of mallets. Then he arranged the cats tonally according to their different sizes, so that each key corresponded to the tail of one cat, and he put the instrument prepared for the relaxation of the prince in a suitable place. Then when it was played, it produced such music as the voices of cats can produce. For when the keys, depressed by the fingers of the organist, pricked the tails of the cats with their points, they, driven to a rage, with miserable voices, howling now low, now high, produced such music made of the voices of cats as would move men to laughter and even arouse shrews to dance.[46]

This practice of dogs in consorts, if it really existed, may have begun in the fifteenth century for we find a hunting book published in Portugal which praised the noise of the hounds by stating that not even Guillaume de Machaut made such beautiful concordance of melody.

> Guilherme de Machado nom fez tam fermosa concordanca de melodia, nem que tam bem pareca como a fazem os ca–es quando bem correm.[47]

Agrippa, sixteenth century, discusses the homogeneity in color, which lies at the heart of the consort principle, in a passage in which he uses animals as surrogates for bad singers.

> It is necessary that all consorts proceed from fit foundations, both in stringed instruments, in pipes, and vocal singing, if you would have them agree well together: for no man can make the roaring of lions, the lowing of oxen, the neighing of horses, the braying of asses, the grunting of hogs to be harmonious.[48]

There is extensive literature on the horse ballet, especially during the seventeenth century when this kind of entertainment became very popular in court celebrations. An early reference can be found in Pliny the Elder, who observes,

> The horses docility is so great that we learn that the entire cavalry of the army of Sybaris used to perform a sort of ballet to instrumental music [*symphoniae*].[49]

---

46 Kircher, *Musurgia universalis*, 138ff.
47 Quoted in Guillaume de Machaut, *Musikalische Werke*, ed. Friedrich Ludwig (Leipzig, 1926), II, 32.
48 *De occulta philosophia*, II, xxv.
49 Pliny the Elder, *Natural History*, VIII, lxiv, 157.

Horse dancing was a form of entertainment for the Greek soldiers and there are stories of the enemy obtaining the music used by some city for their horse dances and then playing this music in battle, causing the horses of the enemy to stand up and dance rather than attack. A seventeenth-century writer adds an interesting observation:

> The trumpets are the instruments best to use of horse dancing because they [the horses] can learn to breathe when the trumpets breathe. There is no instrument more agreeable to the horse, because it is martial, and the horse which is naturally generous, likes to be animated by its sound.[50]

The sixteenth-century writer, Michel Montaigne, mentions in passing a quotation from Flavius Arrianus regarding an elephant which was said to simultaneously dance and play cymbals.[51]

Before leaving the subject of dance, we must mention an account of dolphins performing a group movement, resembling a funeral procession, followed by a dance of joy, as told by Albertus in the thirteenth century.

> When the king of Caria captured a particular large dolphin, a teeming school of its mates followed the captive to the shore, forming a procession, like a funeral cortege of mourners. Seeing this, the king ordered the dolphin released, whereupon the entire assembly of dolphins welcomed their freed companion and performed a sort of leaping dance as they led it back to sea.[52]

To conclude, we must take special note of the descriptions of singing birds found in early literature, for they are by far the most frequently mentioned animal with respect to music. The range of birds and their music is, taken together, quite extraordinary. We might begin with a survey by Albertus Magnus, in his *De animalibus*.

> As a general rule, birds emit more vocal sounds than other animals, a manifestation of the levity of their spirits. This is particularly true of the smaller birds, many of whom sing a musical song and display a lightness of spirit reflected in the ease of their melodious outpourings. Birds sing most vocally during the mating season when the males warble in a more tuneful fashion than the females whose natural disposition is colder and more aloof.[53]

Among the most melodious of the birds he finds Finches,[54] Birds of Paradise,[55] and above all, the Blackbird.

---

[50] Claude Menestrier, *Des Ballets anciens et modernes, selon les regles du Theatre* (Paris, 1682), 238.

[51] Not to mention his discussion of the affinity of the tunny-fish for astrology, geometry and arithmetic! Michel de Montaigne, *Essays*, trans. M. A. Screech (London: Penguin, 1993), II, xii, 534.

[52] Albertus Magnus, *De animalibus*, 349.

[53] Ibid., 190.

[54] Ibid., 219.

[55] Ibid., 207.

> In the opinion of some writers, this bird was called 'modula' in ancient times, because it produces melodies [*modulos*] and songs [*melos*]. Some claim a black bird was once trained by human art to reproduce all nine notes of the scale that are used in the composition of every musical piece; moreover, the trained bird gloried so in its talent that it would often sing through its range of notes in melodious sequence for a human audience …
>
> This bird sings well in the springtime but during the winter makes a stuttering sound.[56]

Albertus' most extended, and interesting, discussion of a musical bird is devoted to that virtuoso, the Nightingale.

> PHYLOMENA (Nightingale) is a small, well-known bird, named from 'phylos' and 'menos,' which means sweet, because it loves sweet songs. Another possible derivation is from 'philos' and 'mene,' because in competing with another bird to produce the best song, the nightingale would rather run out of breath and expire than cease singing and give in to its opponent.
>
> Though small in body, the nightingale has a great store of breath wherewith it produces a range of sounds no less remarkable for its modulated tones as for the multiplicity of its notes. One minute it sustains a long note with one continuous breath, and then it varies the tone like the inflections of a human singing voice. Again, it separates the notes with staccato effect, all the while maintaining a connected melody, so that the song on its outgoing breath is continued with matching force on inhalation. At varying times its song is full basso profundo; treble; prolonged in a trill; soprano; or reduced to a whisper—in essence, representing almost all of the tunes made by musical instruments.[57]

There is an attractive passage in Chaucer's 'The Books of the Duchess,' in which he speaks of birds singing, some low and some high, with 'sweetness,' in tune, with 'so merry a harmony, so sweet strains' and observes 'nowhere was ever heard instrument or melody yet half so sweet or of half so well in accord.' When he also mentions that none merely pretended to sing, but all did not spare their voices, not to mention the reference to 'the most solemn service,' we are inclined to wonder if this passage were intended to reflect, not really a description of birds, but a representation of the best choral singing Chaucer had heard.

> With smale foules a gret hep
> That had affrayed me out of my slep,
> Thorgh noyse and swetness of her song.
> And, as me mette, they sate among
> Upon my chambre roof wythoute,
> Upon the tyles, overal aboute,
> And songen, everch in hys wyse,
> The moste solemne servise
> By noote, that ever man, y trowe,
> Had herd; for some of hem song lowe,
> Som high, and al of oon acord.
> To telle shortly, att oo word.
> Was never herd so swete a steven,—
> But hyt had be a thyng of heven,—

---

[56] Ibid., 305.

[57] Ibid., 315.

> So mery a soun, so swete entewnes,
> That certes, for the toun of Tewnes,
> I nolde but I had herd hem synge;
> For al my chambre gan to rynge
> Thurgh syngynge of her armonye.
> For instrument nor melodye
> Was nowhere herd yet half so swete,
> Nor of acorde half so mete;
> For ther was noon of hem that feyned
> To synge, for ech of hem hym peyned
> To fynde out mery crafty notes.
> They ne spared not her throtes.[58]

And, speaking of the sweet voices of birds, an eighth-century English poem called 'The Phoenix' praises an imaginary bird whose voice is sweeter than any musical instrument, including the human voice.

> The music of its voice
> is sweeter and more beauteous than any craft of song,
> winsomer than any melody;
> nor trumpets, nor horns, may equal that sound,
> nor strain of harp, nor the voice of man,
> of any man on earth, nor organ's tone,
> nor harmonious lay, nor feather of swan,
> nor any of the sounds that the Lord hath created
> for men's delight in this sad world.[59]

The sixteenth century, in particular, was a period of great advances in technology of all kinds, including many mechanical devices with musical associations. The water powered construction mentioned in Sidney's *The Countesse of Pembrokes Arcadia* we take to be a tribute to the singing of real birds.

> There were birds also made so finely, that they did not only deceive the sight with their figures, but the hearing with their songs; which the water instruments did make their gorge deliver.[60]

In George Peele's play, *The Arraignment of Paris*, there is another mechanical device called for which makes bird sounds. The cast includes a large number of Greek gods and the nine Muses and near the beginning of the play there occurs an extraordinary performance for

---

[58] 'The Book of the Duchess,' 295ff.

[59] *The Exeter Book* (Oxford University Press, 1958), 131ff.

[60] Sir Philip Sidney, *The Countesse of Pembrokes Arcadia*, in *The Prose Works of Sir Philip Sidney*, ed. Albert Feuillerat (Cambridge: Cambridge University Press, 1962), Book I, xiv.

double choir, a choir of gods on stage and the Muses off-stage. The stage direction describes their music as an echo to the song of birds heard shortly before and indicated by another stage direction, 'An artificial charm of birds being heard within.'[61]

Finally, there are some interesting references in early literature to music education among the birds. Some, such as St. Ambrose, say that 'some birds learn to sing by nature and others by training.'[62] Most writers, however, are concerned with the subject of birds teaching other birds to sing. We find a remarkable first-century account by Pliny the Elder on the singing of Nightingales and of their education of their young.

> Nightingales pour out a ceaseless gush of song for fifteen days and nights on end when the buds of the leaves are swelling—a bird not in the lowest rank remarkable. In the first place there is so loud a voice and so persistent a supply of breath in such a tiny little body; then there is the consummate knowledge of music in a single bird: the sound is given out with modulations, and now is drawn out into a long note with one continuous breath, now varied by managing the breath, now made staccato by checking it, or linked together by prolonging it, or carried on by holding it back; or it is suddenly lowered, and at times sinks into a mere murmur, loud, low, bass, treble, with trills, with long notes, modulated when this seems good—soprano, mezzo, baritone; and briefly all the devices in that tiny throat which human science has devised with all the elaborate mechanism of the aulos ... And that no one may doubt its being a matter of science, the birds have several songs each, and not all the same but every bird songs of its own. They compete with one another, and there is clearly an animated rivalry between them; the loser often ends her life by dying, her breath giving out before her song. Other younger birds practice their music, and are given verses to imitate; the pupil listens with close attention and repeats the phrase, and the two keep silence by turns: we notice improvement in the one under instruction and a sort of criticism on the part of the instructress ... Frequent cases have been seen before now of nightingales that have begun to sing when ordered, and have sung in answer to an organ, as there have been found persons who could reproduce the birds' song with an indistinguishable resemblance by putting water into slanting reeds and breathing into the holes, or by applying some slight check with the tongue. But these exceptional and artistic trills after a fortnight gradually cease, though not in such a way that the birds could be said to be tired out or to have had enough singing; and later on when the heat has increased their note becomes entirely different, with no modulations or variations.[63]

Montaigne agrees that if we observe carefully we can see this educational process taking place.

> Even nightingales born free do not all sing one and the same song: each one sings according to its capacity to learn. They make jealous classmates, squabbling and vying with each other so heartily that the vanquished sometimes drops down dead, not from lack of song but lack of breath. The youngest birds ruminate thoughtfully and then begin to imitate snatches of song; the pupils listen to the lessons of their tutors and then give an account of themselves, taking it in turns to stop their singing. You can hear their faults being corrected; some of the criticism of their tutors are perceptible even to us.[64]

---

61   Act I, scene one.

62   Saint Ambrose, 'Six Days of Creation: Five,' in *Hexameron, Paradise, Cain and Abel,* trans. John J. Savage (New York: Fathers of the Church, 1961), 200.

63   *Natural History,* X, xliiiff.

64   *Essays,* II, xii, 519ff.

With regard to Montaigne's reference to the birds 'vying with each other,' we recall that the sixteenth-century Italian, Giustiniani, also mentions that in the case of birds,

> they almost seem to compete among themselves to reach a greater perfection and to teach such skill to their young.[65]

We conclude these thoughts with a most remarkable story told by Montaigne, who gives Plutarch as his source.

> But strange indeed is the account of a female magpie vouched for by Plutarch, no less. It lived in a barber's shop in Rome and was wonderfully clever at imitating any sounds it heard. It happened one day that some musicians stopped quite a while in front of the shop, blasting away on their trumpets. Immediately the magpie fell pensive, mute and melancholic, remaining so all the following day. Everyone marveled, thinking that the blare of the trumpets had frightened and confused it, making it lose both hearing and song at the same time. But they eventually found that it had been deeply meditating and had withdrawn into itself; it had been inwardly practicing, preparing its voice to imitate the noise of those trumpeters. The first sound it did make was a perfect imitation of their changes, repetitions and stops; after this new apprenticeship it quit with disdain all that it was able to do before.[66]

---

[65] *Discorso sopra la Musica*, 75ff.

[66] *Essays*, II, xii, 519ff.

Is Man Ruled by Reason or Emotion?

*Anyone who sets reason aside and uses only his sensitive part
lives not as a man but as a beast.*

Dante

The understanding may err, but not feelings.

Robert Schumann

THE ANCIENT PHILOSOPHERS lacked the findings of modern clinical medical research which establishes that we are clearly bicameral in mind. Assuming there was just one mind it is easy for us to see how they concluded that Reason, among all our potentialities, must rule. Of course it is precisely because of our bicameral mind's composition that they had such difficulty in discussing our emotions, even though they never hesitated to acknowledge our emotions' power over us. The strongest testimonial to this difficulty are the repeated warnings, apparently unheeded generation after generation, that Reason must rule.

Heeded or not, centuries of philosophical writing, strongly seconded by the new Christian Church, could not be answered in kind by the right hemisphere of our brain because it is mute. As a consequence, today society has endless difficulties in dealing with emotions. The most frequent choice, and the worst, is to try to deal with them in the terms of the left hemisphere of the brain, the rational and intellectual side of us. A case in point is contemporary music education in America, where the professors have attempted to recast the nature of music into something conversant with the world of reason and intelligence. But this does not work now, just as it never worked in the ancient world. The sad fact is that the medical profession gave to music education professors the greatest possible gift in the clinical proof of the bicameral mind and the professors have failed to take advantage of this gift. But the truth is there and so now, in view of the lack of interest by music educators, the ball has returned to the field of medicine. It will be they who will make the case for music education in society and indeed one of their universities already has a science degree program in bio-musicology.

In general those ancient philosophers who had such difficulty in dealing with the emotions left descriptions of the emotional side of us which are, for the modern reader, often quite extraordinarily negative. Cicero (106–43 BC), as a case in point, could accept the idea that our senses were a natural part of nature, but he found the emotions were something quite different and clearly something to be avoided!

> The emotions of the mind, which harass and embitter the life of the foolish (the Greek term for these is *pathos*, and I might have rendered this literally and styled them 'diseases,' but the word 'disease' would not suit all instances; for example, no one speaks of pity, nor yet anger, as a disease though the

> Greeks term these pathos. Let us then accept the term 'emotion,' the very sound of which seems to denote something vicious, and these emotions are not excited by any natural influence. The list of the emotions is divided into four classes, with numerous subdivisions, namely sorrow, fear, lust, and that mental emotion which the Stoics call by a name that also denotes a bodily feeling, *hedone*, 'pleasure,' but which I prefer to style 'delight,' meaning the sensuous elation of the mind when in a state of exultation), these emotions, I say, are not excited by any influence of nature; they are all of them mere fancies and frivolous opinions. Therefore the Wise Man will always be free from them.[1]

And again, in his treatise *On Duties*, sounding like an early Church father or later Puritan, he emphasizes that any display of emotions suggests that we are not in control of ourselves. The more highly developed person, he with a 'greater soul,' must especially observe this warning. In spite of the strong warning he intends to give here, we cannot help noticing the indication that he had some awareness, no doubt through simple observation, that there are two sides of our being, those which here he calls thought and passion.

> We must be careful that the movements of our soul do not diverge from nature, and the care must be all the greater as the soul is greater. We shall achieve this if we are careful not to reach states of extreme excitement or alarm and if we keep our minds intent on the preservation of *decorum*. The movements of our souls are of two kinds: some involve thought, others involve passion. Thought is mostly expended in seeking out the truth, passion urges men to action. Therefore we must take care to expend thought on the best objects and to make clear that our passions are obedient to our intellect …
>
> Throughout a man's life the most correct advice is to avoid agitations, by which I mean excessive commotions in the soul that do not obey intelligence … Whenever passionate feelings disturb our activities, we are, of course, not acting with self-control and those around us cannot approve what we do.[2]

And since Cicero probably anticipated that his warning, that 'passions must be obedient to our intellect,' would fall on deaf ears, as a last desperate effort he now paints for us contrasting pictures of the man under the influence of emotion and the man who has succeeded in subjecting his emotions to Reason.

> The man whom we see on fire and raging with lusts frantically pursuing everything with insatiable desire, and the more lavishly he swallows down pleasure from all quarters, the worse and more burning his thirst—would you not be entitled to call him most unhappy? The man who is carried away with frivolity and empty euphoria and uncontrolled desires, is he not the more wretched the happier he *thinks* he is?
>
> So just as these people are wretched, so are those happy whom no fears alarm, no distresses gnaw, no lusts arouse, no pointless euphoria dissolves in languorous pleasure. Just as the sea is recognized as calm when not even the slightest breeze ruffles the waves, so a state of mind can be accounted calm and peaceful, when there is no disturbance by which it can be agitated.[3]

---

1 Cicero, *De Finibus*, III, x, 35.
2 Cicero, *De Officiis*, 131ff.
3 Cicero, *Tusculan Disputations*, V, 15ff.

Aristides Quintilianus, who lived between the first and fourth centuries AD and was one of the last of the ancient Greek philosophers, looked back and confessed that Reason was incapable of controlling the emotions.

> No cure could be found in Reason alone for those who were burdened by these emotions; for pleasure is a very powerful temptation, captivating even the animals that lack reason, and grief which remains unsolaced casts many people into incurable illnesses.[4]

He is one of many witnesses who speak of the ancient Greeks' use of music to mold character and he also points out that it was their belief that music could do what Reason could not, with respect to the control of the emotions. He tells us that the ancients made everyone cultivate music from childhood throughout their lives in order that the proper kind of music would have a positive impact on the soul. The effectiveness of music in doing this he compares to the 'diverting of a stream, which was rushing through impassable crags or dispersing itself in marshy places, into an easily trodden and fertile plain.' One of the chief concerns of the ancients, he tells us, was with regard to the misuse of music.

> Those who neglected music, melody and unaccompanied poetry alike, were utterly crude and foolish; those who had involved themselves in it in the wrong way fell into serious errors, and through their passion for worthless melodies and poetry stamped upon themselves ugly idiosyncrasies of character.

It was this concern, he recalls, which caused the authorities to assign 'educational music to as many as 100 days, and the relaxing kind [of music] to no more than 30.'

He does not entirely condemn entertainment music, but in granting its place he still does not waver from the principal value of music, to form character.

> We should not avoid song altogether just because it gives pleasure. Not all delight is to be condemned, but neither is delight itself the objective of music. Amusement may come as it will, but the aim set for music is to help us toward virtue.

He points to the success of the Greeks in doing just that and concludes, 'Music is the most powerful agent of education, rivaled by no other, [and it can be shown where music education was missing] that our characters commonly deteriorate if they are left undisciplined, lapsing into base or brutal passions.'

Beginning with the Renaissance we start to find some writers and philosophers willing to defend the emotional side of man against two millennia of attacks against it. An often quoted example, the French Romance, 'The Romance of the Rose,' is found during the 'Pre-Renaissance,' the time when the oppressive clouds of the 'dark ages' begin to fall away during the thirteenth century. Here Reason gives a typically medieval negative assessment of Love.

---

4 The Aristides quotations are quoted in Andrew Barker, *Greek Musical Writings* (Cambridge: Cambridge University Press, 1989), II, 457ff.

> Love is a troubled peace, an amorous war—
> A treasonous loyalty, disloyal faith—
> A fear that's full of hope, a desperate trust—
> A madman's logic, reasoned foolishness—
> A healthy sickness and most languorous health—
> A sadness gay, a frolicsomeness sad—
> A bitter sweetness, a sweet-tasting gall[5]

All of which warnings, the reader is delighted to find, had no effect. In this case, emotion conquered Reason.

> Thus Reason preached, but Love set all at naught;
> For though I heard the sermon word for word
> I took no stock in it, so drawn was I
> To Love, who still my every thought pursued.[6]

During the Renaissance there are a number of fictional works which focus on this same theme, the struggle between Reason and the emotions. In fifteenth-century England we actually find a work by John Lydgate called, 'Reson and Sensuallyte.' A similar contemporary work, one of our favorites, is by Henry Medwall (b. 1461). It is entitled 'Nature,' but has the same theme. Here we find Nature warning man once again to 'Let Reason govern you in every situation.'

But now Sensuality enters and protests to Nature that she should have equal status with Reason. She contends, 'I am the chief perfection of his nature!' Without me, man would have no feeling, he might as well be made of wood or stone.'

> And now you have put me out of his service,
> And have assigned Reason to be his guide
> With Innocence his nurse; thus am I set aside!
>
> You made him lord of all beasts living,
> And nothing worthy, as far as I can see;
> For if there be in him no manner of feeling
> No lively quickness, what kind of lord is he?
> A lord made of rags! or carved from a tree!
> And fares as an image carved from stone
> That can do nothing but stand alone!

'Allow me to have influence with him,' Sensuality pleas with Nature, 'and I will make him governor of the world.'

---

[5] Guillaume de Lorris and Jean de Meun, 'The Romance of the Rose,' trans. Harry Robbins (New York: Dutton, 1962), XXI, 50ff.

[6] Ibid., XXIII.

'No,' says Nature, 'Reason must be preferred,' reminding Sensuality, 'You have brought many men to a wretched end.' 'You should obey me,' Reason says to Sensuality, 'wherever I go.' Sensuality answers, 'No, that I shall never do!'

At length Man decides to subjugate his Sensuality to Reason.

> Reason, Sir, my chief counselor.
> And this, Innocence, my previous nurse,
> And Sensuality, that other, by whom I have power
> To do as all sensuous beasts do.
> But Reason and Innocence, chiefly these two,
> Have the whole rule and governance of me,
> To whom is subdued my Sensuality.

Later another character, Pride, suggests that a 'wild worm' has come into man's head if he thinks he will always be led only be Reason. He doubts that Reason will always endure with man, pointing out that, 'Sensuality … is chief ruler, when Reason is away.'

In Sir Philip Sidney's *The Countesse of Pembrokes Arcadia*, there is an internal masque performed by a group of shepherds under the title, 'The Battle between Reason and Passion.' Here we find such dialog as,

> REASON. Who Passion doth ensue, lives in annoy.
> PASSION. Who Passion doth forsake, lives void of joy …
> ……
> REASON. Yet Passion, yield at length to Reason's stroke.
> PASSION. What shall we win by taking Reason's yoke?

It is also true that in the field of music a 'battle between Reason and Passion' continued throughout much of the Renaissance. In commentary on music this battle usually went under arguments over 'ancient' and 'modern' music. And there were still important philosophers who continued to argue that Reason must rule. The great Dante (1265–1321), for example, made the rather extraordinary statement that the senses 'exist for reason's sake alone.'[7] In one of his poems he even suggests that a sensation such as pain cannot be understood by mere experience, but must be understood by reason as well.[8] His strongest statement supporting the supremacy of Reason comes in another place in his 'Banquet.'

> Things are properly designated by the highest nobility possessed by their form, as man, for instance, is designated by reason and not by the senses or by anything less noble. So when it is said that man lives, this must be understood to mean that he uses his reason, which is the life specific to him and the activity of his most noble part. So anyone who sets reason aside and uses only his sensitive part lives not as a man but as a beast, a point made by the most excellent Boethius when he says: 'He lives as an

---

7   *The Banquet*, trans. Christopher Ryan (Stanford University: Anma Libri, 1989), III, xv, 4.

8   Dante, 'Donne ch'avete intelletto d'armore,' in *Dante's Lyric Poetry*, trans. K. Foster and P. Boyde (Oxford: Clarendon Press, 1967), II.

ass.' I quite agree, for thought is the act proper to reason; animals do not think, because they lack that faculty—a description that fits not only the lower animals but those who have a human appearance but the spirit of a sheep or of some other vile beast.[9]

Dante uses this expression again in his *Divine Comedy*.

> You were not made to live like beasts, but for
> The pursuit of virtue and of knowledge.[10]

His only reservations are two, regarding love:

> Therefore, if my verses are not adequate
> that undertake the praise of her,
> let the infirm intellect be blamed,
> and our speech, which does not have the power
> to recount all that Love speaks forth.[11]

And regarding music,

> Voices sang *Beati pauperes spiritu*,
> In such a way that words could not convey it.[12]

The great Francesco Petrarch (1304–1374), in spite of being a musician as well as a poet of much love poetry, in the Preface to his 'Remedies for Fortune Fair and Foul,' gives us this colorful description of Reason defending us against emotions,

> You should read the book *as if* those four most famous, twin-born passions of the mind, HOPE or DESIRE and JOY, FEAR and SORROW, brought forth at the same time by the two sisters Prosperity and Adversity, fiercely assaulted from all sides the mind of man, and REASON, who governs this citadel, took on all of them at once. In her buckler and helmet, by stratagem and proper force, and, more so, with God's help, she fends off the weapons of the roaring enemies around her.[13]

And in the text which follows, Petrarch, speaking as Reason, points to the location of Reason and the emotions.

---

9   *The Banquet*, II, vii, 3.

10 *Inferno*, XXVI.

11 'Amor che ne la mente mi ragiona,' in Frederick Goldin, *German and Italian Lyrics of the Middle Ages* (Garden City: Anchor Books, 1973), 373.

12 *Purgatory*, XII.

13 'Remedies for Fortune Fair and Foul,' trans. Conrad Rawski (Bloomington: Indiana University Press, 1991), I, Preface, 10.

SORROW: My mind is rent into conflicting parts.

REASON: The philosophers divide the mind into three parts, the first of which they place at the very top, as if in a citadel, that is, in the head. This is the ruler of human life, heavenly, serene, and always close to God, where tranquil, decent intentions dwell. The second part is located in the chest, where anger and malice boil; the third, in the lower parts which house lust and desire.[14]

Perhaps he used this 'geography' of the body to explain for himself those instances when emotions interfered with his speech, as in the following:

But my excessive delight, which is an obstacle to my tongue ...[15]

......

Many times already have I opened my lips to speak, but then my
voice has remained within my breast ...[16]

or when his emotions caused the words to come out wrong.

Sorrow, why do you lead me out of the way to say what I do not wish to say?[17]

In one place Petrarch calls love a 'poison to sound judgment'[18] and he gives many examples of love interfering with Reason.

Love, I transgress and I see my transgression, but I act like a man
who burns with a fire in his breast; for the pain still grows, and
my reason fails and is almost overcome by my sufferings.[19]

......

If to love another more than oneself—if to be always sighing and
weeping, feeding on sorrow and anger and trouble —
If to burn from afar and freeze close by—if these are the causes
that I untune [*distempre*] myself with love, yours will be the blame, Lady,
mine the loss.[20]

......

If my little intellect had been with me at need, and another
hunger had not driven it elsewhere and made it stray ...[21]

---

[14] Ibid., II, lxxv, 171.

[15] 'Quando io v'odo parlar si dolcemente,' in *Petrarch's Lyric Poems*, trans. Robert Durling (Cambridge: Harvard University Press, 1976), 288.

[16] 'Vergognando talor ch' ancor si taccia,' in Ibid., 54.

[17] 'Perche la vita e breve,' in Ibid., 156.

[18] Second letter to Cicero, in *Letters from Petrarch*, trans. Morris Bishop (Bloomington: Indiana University Press, 1966), 18.

[19] 'Amor, io fallo et veggio il mio fallire,' in *Petrarch's Lyric Poems*, 394.

[20] 'S' una fede amorosa, un cor non finto,' in Ibid., 380.

[21] 'Solea de la fontana di mia vita,' in Ibid., 522.

We find a similar stance in his great contemporary, Guillaume de Machaut (1300–1377). While he offers token tribute to the idea that Reason must rule,[22] his more personal illustrations point to the contrary. After a debate over love and its consequences, the character, Loyalty, stipulates, 'A lover would be a fool to listen to you, Reason.'[23] Similarly, in complimenting good speech, Machaut describes it as 'moderate, well-chosen, and appropriate, based wholly on Reason.'[24] But, what happens to Reason-dominated speech when Love is present? It can, Machaut observes, force one,

> to cut short his words and interrupt them with sighs, drawn from the depths of his being, that render him mute and silent, and he has no choice but to remain speechless.

Even the lover's song is interrupted in the same way.

> But some strange heat that turned to cold surprised me and gripped my heart so suddenly that there's no way I could relate how I feel or how it stings me, for I'm hot and cold together and am sweating and shaking at the same time, and I've lost all strength, and was struck speechless in the middle of my song like a dumb beast; wherefore my laughter, my joy, and my song are ended and I must remain silent.[25]

Geoffrey Chaucer (1340–1400) gives an original reason in support of the Church's demand that Reason must rule man. In speaking of marriage, he recommends that in making love with one's wife that one not please her too amorously.

> In mariage, ne nevere mo shal bee,
> That yow shal lette of youre savacion,
> So that ye use, as skile is and reson,
> The lustes of youre wyf attemprely,
> And that ye plese hire nat to amorously,
> And that ye kepe yow eek from oother synne.[26]

This passage reminds us of a place in Tasso where he uses man and wife as metaphors for Reason and emotion.

---

[22] Especially in his poem, 'The Tale of the Alerion.'

[23] Guillaume de Machaut, 'Le Jugement du roy de Behaigne,' trans. James Wimsatt and William Kibler (Athens: The University of Georgia Press, 1988), 154.

[24] Guillaume de Machaut, 'Remede de Fortune,' trans. James Wimsatt and William Kibler (Athens: The University of Georgia Press, 1988), 180.

[25] Ibid., 340ff.

[26] 'The Merchant's Tale,' 1676.

> Women are related to men as desire is to the intellect, and just as desire, which is in itself irrational, is informed by many beautiful and comely virtues when it subjects itself to the intellect, so a woman who obeys her husband adorns herself with virtues that she would not possess if she were rebellious.[27]

Juan Vives (1492–1540), in his famous book on education also addresses the topic of the importance of the rule of Reason. Everyone, he says, would surely agree that the body should obey the mind. Thus it follows that the 'unreasoning impulses' [emotions] must be subjected to Reason as mistress and empress. For Vives it was because of ancient sin that,

> all things were inverted so that man's lower nature desires the higher position for itself; the passions contend for attention in place of Reason; Reason, conquered and overwhelmed is put to silence, and is made the slave to the temerity of the passions.[28]

But for these Renaissance souls, what were they to do, wanting Reason to rule but confronted by emotions like love? The fourteenth-century English theologian and poet, Richard Rolle, recommends that if we concentrate on spiritual things, meditations, sermons and reading holy books, then we experience a form of delight which has none of the 'inordinate stirrings.'[29] For the Spaniard, St. John of the Cross (1542–1591), the solution was simply to erase from the mind all memory of pleasure deriving from appetites, for 'When all things are forgotten, nothing disturbs the peace or stirs the appetites.'[30] Needless to say, he does not recommend any expression of the emotions.

> Never allow yourself to pour out your heart, even though it be but for the space of a creed.[31]

Desiderius Erasmus (1469–1536), in his advice to a young prince, recommended he follow God's example and ignore the emotions. This same passage also reveals Erasmus' level of respect for the common man.

> Although God is swayed by no emotions, he nevertheless orders the world with the greatest good judgment. Following his example in all his actions, the prince must disregard emotional reactions and use only reason and judgment.

---

[27] Torquato Tasso, 'The Father of the Family,' in *Tasso's Dialogues*, trans. Carnes Lord (Berkeley: University of California Press, 1982), 85.

[28] *Vives: On Education*, trans. Foster Watson (Cambridge: University Press, 1913), V, iii.

[29] Richard Rolle, 'Of the Vertu,' in *English Prose Treatises of Richard Rolle* (London: Humphrey Milford, Oxford University Press, 1866, 1921), 14 and 16.

[30] 'The Ascent of Mount Carmel,' in *The Collected Works of St. John of the Cross*, trans. Kieran Kavanaugh and Otilio Rodriguez (Washington, D.C.: Institute of Carmelite Studies, 1979), 222.

[31] 'Maxims and Counsels,' in Ibid., 679.

> Nothing is higher than God, and similarly the prince should be removed as far as possible from the low concerns and sordid emotions of the common people.[32]

For Vives, in his *On Education*, the answer is in using 'practical wisdom,' gained by reading, dialectic, rhetoric and experience, to control the emotions.

> Practical wisdom is the skill of accommodating all things of which we make use in life, to their proper places, times, persons, and functions. It is the moderator and rudder in the tempest of the feelings.[33]

Except for the Puritans, during the Baroque one finds some philosophers more willing to accommodate Reason and the emotions. Saint-Evremond (1610–1703), as a case in point, in a letter to the Mareschal de Crequi, seemed no longer burdened with the idea of making a choice.

> I can say one thing of myself, as extraordinary as true, that I never felt in myself any conflict between Passion and Reason. My Passion never opposed what I resolved out of duty; and my Reason readily complied with what a sense of pleasure inclined me to. I don't aim at praise on account of this easy agreement; on the contrary, I confess I have often been the more vicious for it. Not out of any perverse disposition to evil, but because the vice was entertained as a pleasure, instead of appearing as a crime.[34]

Eventually this accommodation was a matter of age, as he writes another correspondent,

> How unhappy is my condition! I have lost everything on the side of Reason, and I see nothing for me to pretend to on the side of Passion.[35]

From the same perspective of accepting both sides of our nature, it is interesting that he found, and accepted, in the two famous playwrights of his time, Corneille as a representative of emotion and Racine a representative of Reason.

> Corneille is admired for the expression of an heroic grandeur of soul, for the force of the passions, and sublimity of discourse. Racine's merit consists in sentiments which are more natural, in thoughts that are more clear, and in a diction that is more pure, and more easy. The former ravishes the soul, the latter makes a conquest of the mind. The latter gives no room for the reader to censure, the former does not leave the spectator in a condition to examine.[36]

---

32 'The Education of a Christian Prince,' [1516] in *The Collected Works of Erasmus* (Toronto: University of Toronto Press, 1992), XXVII, 221. In his 'A Complaint of Peace Spurned and Rejected by the Whole World,' [Ibid., XXVII, 296], Erasmus again mentions 'the common people, who are swayed by their passions like a stormy sea.'

33 *On Education*, V, i.

34 *The Letters of Saint-Evremond*, ed. John Hayward (Freeport, NY: Books for Libraries Press, 1971), 114.

35 Saint-Evremond, Letter to Duchesse Mazarin, 1676, Ibid., 168.

36 Letter to Duchesse Mazarin, 1676, quoted in Ibid., 298.

The great Francis Bacon (1561–1626), whom Will Durant placed at the head of the Age of Reason,[37] nevertheless accepts emotions and even admits they, like Reason, are capable of good. He finds, however, a third faculty, Imagination, independent of either, but through which both Reason and the emotions operate. Bacon finds Reason consisting of four separate faculties, those to invent, to seek, to judge and to communicate. He also writes of the danger which the affections represent to Reason and in fact suggests that man is only able to function rationally because imagination forms a 'confederacy' with Reason against the affections.[38]

Another great philosopher of this period, David Hume (1711–1776) found the principal role of Reason to be one primarily of identification. No doubt set in motion by Bacon, he now finds seven forms of its activity: resemblance, identity, relations of time and place, proportion in quantity or number, degrees in any quality, contrariety and causation.[39]

Hume raises the entire subject of the emotions to a higher level than any former philosopher, even going so far as to make feeling dominant over ideas. No one had ever before written anything so extraordinary as the following.

> All probable reasoning is nothing but a species of sensation. It is not solely in poetry and music, we must follow our taste and sentiment, but likewise in philosophy. When I am convinced of any principle, it is only an idea, which strikes more strongly upon me. When I give the preference to one set of arguments above another, I do nothing but decide from my feeling concerning the superiority of their influence.[40]

He was also one of the earliest philosophers to point (correctly) to the universality of the basic emotions.

> The minds of all men are similar in their feelings and operations; nor can any one be actuated by an affection, of which all others are not, in some degree, susceptible.[41]

Another who was inclined to raise the emotions to a level above Reason was Voltaire (1694–1778). First, he looked at the long history during which all philosophers, not to mention the Church, insisted that Reason must rule man and he found little to recommend this principle.

> When one considers that Newton, Locke, Clarke, and Leibniz would have been persecuted in France, imprisoned at Rome, and burned at Lisbon, what are we to think of human reason?[42]

---

37 Will Durant, *The Age of Reason Begins* (New York: Simon and Schuster, 1961), 169, 183.
38 *The Works of Francis Bacon* (Cambridge: Cambridge University Press, 1869), VI, 258ff. 299.
39 *A Treatise of Human Nature*, I, iii, section 1.
40 Ibid., I, iii, section 8.
41 Ibid., III, iii, section 1.
42 'Decartes and Newton,' in *The Works of Voltaire* (New York: St. Hubert Guild, 1901), XXXVII, 174.

Further, under 'Abuse of Words,' in his *Philosophical Dictionary*, Voltaire goes to some lengths to demonstrate that language, and books, the traditional centers of Reason, 'rarely give us any precise ideas' and are often taken by the listener in an incorrect sense. As an example he finds it curious that 'the same word (Adoration) that is used both in addressing the Supreme Being and in addressing a mistress.'

Voltaire was also keenly aware that there is more to man than Reason, that there is a feeling side which, in the course of daily actions, may be even more important.

> What will I gain from knowing the path of light and the gravitation of Saturn? These are sterile truths. One feeling is a thousand times more important.[43]

There were some in the Baroque Period who saw an inherent co-ordination between Reason and the emotions. One was Alexander Pope (1688–1744), who in his 'Essay on Man,' could pen this nice thought:

> On life's vast ocean diversely we sail,
> Reason is the [compass], but passion is the gale.

Another who wrote of the co-ordination of Reason and emotion was William Whycherley (1641–1715). His was a rather extraordinary observation for the time:

> It is very rare that Reason cures our passions, but one passion is cured by another. Reason generally places itself on the strongest side, and therefore there can be no violent passion, but has its Reason to authorize it.[44]

Because they form a separate philosophical school during the Baroque, and because their thoughts are in some cases so bizarre, we have not mentioned yet the writings of the Puritan preachers. Robert Burton, in his classic *The Anatomy of Melancholy* (1621), offers little beyond 'weird science' relative to our topic Being limited to the observation of brains in cadavers, he curiously sees a 'fore and hinder' division of the brain, instead of a right and left hemisphere. Like Descartes, he makes the incorrect deduction that the significant action occurs in the spaces between the folds of the brain, rather than in the brain itself. It is into these spaces that 'animal spirits' travel from the heart. And it is in the heart where Burton locates the emotions. The heart, he says,

---

43 Letter to Pierre-Robert Le Cornier de Cideville (February, 1737), in *The Selected Letters of Voltaire*, trans. Richard Brooks (New York: New York University Press, 1973), 63.

44 *The Complete Works of William Wycherley* (New York: Russell & Russell, 1964), IV, 130.

is the seat and fountain of life, of heat, of spirits, of pulse, and respiration: the Sun of our body, the King and sole commander of it: the seat and organ of all passions and affections…by whose motion it is dilated or contracted, to stir and command the humors in the body: as in sorrow, melancholy; in anger, choler; in joy, to send the blood outwardly; in sorrow, to call it in; moving the humors, as horses do a chariot.[45]

The famous preacher, John Bunyan (1628–1688), was not interested in such speculation in traditional anatomy. It is to the soul that he attributes understanding, judgment, the emotions and the senses.[46] Regarding the latter, he categorically states that it is not the body which hears, but the soul—a conclusion he somehow based on Job 4:12, 13:

> Now a word was brought to me stealthily,
> my ear received the whisper of it.
> Amid thoughts from visions of the night …

In a reversal of the position taken by past philosophers, Bunyan gives an example of the 'truth' of the senses being corrupted by Reason. This is the sense of height, as in the distance to heaven which he says 'is obvious to our senses [except] when it is dealt with by our corrupted reason.'[47]

John Donne (1573–1631) arrived by intuition at an absolutely original idea for the time, that it is the heart which rules man. In a treatise known as 'Meditation II,' he calls the heart, and not the brain, the 'Principalitie, and in the Throne, as King, the rest as Subjects.'[48] In another place, he suggests that if Nature explains how we differ in our 'essence,' we would all be alike, whether idiot or 'Wizard,' as we all have the same *kind* of Reason.[49]

For most Puritan philosophers, however, it was still a battle between Reason and the emotions. Joseph Hall (1574–1656), like nearly all clerics before him, warns that the emotions can overwhelm Reason. The emotions he calls the 'secret factors of sin and Satan,' which must be controlled by Reason and religion.

> If there be any exercise of Christian wisdom, it is in the managing of these unruly affections …
> Christianity gives not rules, but power, to avoid this short madness.[50]

---

[45] Robert Burton, *The Anatomy of Melancholy*, ed. Floyd Dell (New York: Tudor Publishing Company, 1938), 133.

[46] 'The Greatness of the Soul,' in *The Works of John Bunyan*, ed. George Offor (London: Blackie and Son, 1853), I, 110ff.

[47] 'The Saints' Knowledge of Christ's Love,' in Ibid, II, 8ff.

[48] John Donne, *Devotions Upon Emergent Occasion*, ed. Anthony Raspa (Montreal: McGill-Queen's University Press, 1975, 56.

[49] John Donne, 'Paradoxes and Problems,' in *Selected Prose*, ed. Helen Gardner (Oxford: Clarendon Press, 1967), 13. Modern clinical findings tend to agree. All on the rational side of us is based on 'spectator' information; everyone agrees $2 + 2 = 4$, etc.

[50] 'Heaven upon earth,' in *The Works of Joseph Hall, D. D.*, ed. Philip Wynter (New York: AMS Press, 1969), VII, 14ff. Joseph Hall (1574–1656) was a bishop in the Church of England.

Robert Burton (1577–1640) also acknowledges the great power, and danger, of the emotions in their capability to overwhelm Reason.

> Good discipline, education, philosophy, divinity, may mitigate and restrain these passions in some few men at some times, but for the most part they domineer, and are so violent, that as a torrent, bears down all before, and overflows his banks, lays bare the fields, lays waste the crops, they overwhelm reason, judgment & pervert the temperature of the body. The chariotuer is run away with, nor does the chariot obey the reins.[51]

James Harrington's utopian *Oceana* (1656) presents a rather simplistic view of man as being torn between his reason and his emotions. In his view, the entire purpose of laws is to prevent man from following his emotions. The reader should perhaps be reminded that this book was written during the Commonwealth Period, when Puritan values were so strongly emphasized.

> The soul of man (whose life or motion is perpetual contemplation or thought) is the mistress of two potent rivals, the one reason, the other passion, that are in continual suit; and, according as she gives up her will to these or either of them, is the felicity or misery which man partakes in this mortal life.
>
> For, as whatever was passion in the contemplation of a man, being brought forth by his will into action, is vice and the bondage of sin; so whatever was reason in the contemplation of a man, being brought forth by his will into action, is virtue and the freedom of soul …
>
> If the liberty of a man consists in the empire of his reason, the absence whereof would betray him to the bondage of his passions, then the liberty of a commonwealth consists in the empire of her laws.[52]

A poem by the severe Puritan, George Wither, finds all of man's ills the result of the victory of the 'monsters' of emotion over Reason.

> Expelling those whom Virtues presence grace,
> And in their steads these hurtful Monsters placed;
> Fond Love, and Lust, Ambition, Enmitie,
> Foolish Compassion, Joy and Jealousy,
> Fear, Hope, Despair, and Sadness, with the Vice
> Called Hate; Revenge, and greedy Avarice,
> Choler, and Cruelty: which I perceived
> To be the only causes Man's bereaved
> Of quietness and rest. Yea, these I found
> To be the principal and only ground
> Of all pernicious mischiefs that now rage,
> Or have disturbed him in any age.
> These losing Reason, their true Prince, began
> To breed disturbance in the heart of Man.[53]

---

51 Robert Burton, *The Anatomy of Melancholy*, 218.
52 Henry Morley, *Ideal Commonwealths* (Port Washington: Kennikat Press, 1968), 192ff.
53 *Works of George Wither* (New York: Franklin, 1967), Spenser Society, Nr. 9, 'Of Man,' 26.

Even John Milton (1608–1674) in his famous 'Paradise Lost' warns, 'Take heed least Passion sway thy Judgment,' and,

> Sensual Appetite, who from beneath
> Usurping over sovereign Reason claimed
> Superior sway.[54]

We might note in passing that while early Church fathers, such as St. Ambroise, warned the Christians against laughter because it was a form of emotion, Milton associated laughter with Reason.[55]

In spite of the warnings of these Puritans of the seventeenth century, not to mention the centuries of similar warnings before, The Enlightenment made possible a new, less Church-dominated perspective. Gradually more trust is found in the emotions, making possible such comments as the one by written by George Washington to Lafayette, 'Democratic States must always *feel* before they can *see*'[56] and the one by Robert Schumann, 'The understanding may err, but not feelings.'[57]

Franz Liszt offered the contention that it is one of the distinctions of music that it bridges this long observed, and feared, gap between Reason and emotion. It is an interesting idea in view of the fact that modern clinical research clearly finds some aspects of music in each of the hemispheres of the brain.

> Music is the intermediary which places sentiment in harmony with intelligence; enabling us to enjoy and love that which intelligence enables us to become acquainted. The Greeks, who were naturally gifted with an incomparable appreciation of the Beautiful, well understood the subtle connecting link provided by music between the perceptible and the impalpable—between that which is understood and that which is felt.[58]

Finally we must mention Herbert Spencer, born in 1820 in England, who was the first important philosopher to discern what modern clinical research has now established, that in fact it is our emotions which determine all our major decisions, not Reason after all. He begins by making an observation which, if one considers the development of the earliest man, must be true, that intelligence and Reason could only have been built upon the earlier foundation

---

[54] 'Paradise Lost,' IX, 1129ff, in *The Works of John Milton*, ed. Frank Patterson (New York: Columbia University Press, 1931–1938), II, 300.

[55] 'The Art of Logic,' I, iii, in Ibid., XI, 31. In another place, he says both anger and laughter are 'rational' faculties. ['Animadversions,' in Ibid., III, 108].

[56] Letter of July 25, 1785.

[57] Schumann's Diary of ca. 1833.

[58] *The Gypsy in Music* (1859).

stones of feelings and the senses.[59] In modern man, Spencer makes a finding that would have shocked, even offended three thousand years of earlier philosophers, that 'The chief component of mind is feeling.'[60]

For Spencer, the proof of the dominance of the emotions was found in something which earlier philosophers *had* observed, the ability of emotions to shut down Reason entirely.

> If altercation rouses extreme anger, the emotion may become so great as even to exclude the power of speech: the thought-element is overwhelmed. Intense alarm may so throw the intellect out of gear as to produce temporary inability to act.[61]

As we have indicated above, Spencer had the courage to conclude what modern research has now established: it is our emotions, not our reason, which drives our choices. Emotions, he says, is that element of thought,

> which thus upon occasion shows itself supreme at all times; for the prevailing emotions, higher or lower, are those components of mind which determine the daily conduct, now dutiful now lax, now noble now base. That part which we ordinarily ignore when speaking of mind is its essential part.[62]

Thus, he concludes,

> The emotions are the masters, the intellect is the servant. The guidance of our acts through perception and reason has for its end the satisfaction of feelings, which at once prompt the acts and yield the energy for performance of the acts.[63]

---

59 Hector Macpherson, *Spencer and Spencerism* (New York: Doubley, Page, & Co., 1900), 110ff.
60 Herbert Spencer, *Facts and Comments* (New York: Appleton & Co., 1902), 36.
61 Ibid., 38.
62 Ibid.
63 Ibid.

Some Early Voices Intuit the Bicameral Mind

We all speak well of our hearts, we none of us dare speak well of our minds.[1]
La Rochefoucauld (1613–1680)

But though I distrust my head, I am always sure of my heart.[2]
Voltaire (1694–1778)

THE PHYSICAL FACT OF OUR BICAMERAL BRAIN has been recognized medically for many centuries. It has only been in recent years that medical research has been able to establish the general functions of the two hemispheres of our brain, a left hemisphere for rational faculties and a right hemisphere for non-rational faculties. While some activities, such as music, employ some functions on both sides, the general rational versus non-rational tendencies are nevertheless now clear. While the physical evidence found by clinical research is new, the fact that man has competing intellectual and emotional faculties has long been a matter of common observation. For example, we trust it is common knowledge that the experience of love, pain or music is not well defined by the English language.

Indeed the manifestations are everywhere. The French word for 'Law,' one of the most conceptual, logical and rational professions, is 'droit' ('right' as in right hand[3]), the significance of which is obvious if the reader remembers that the hemispheres of the brain operate opposite sides of the body. Similarly, the Indians of the American Southwest distinguished between the functions of the hands, the right for writing and the left for music. There are the Hindu notions of *buddhi* and *manas* and the Confucian concepts, found in the ancient book, *I Ching*, which associate the masculine, *Yang*, with the left side of the mind and the feminine, *Yin*, with the right. From this comes our expression, 'I had a yin to …' for those actions for which we lack a good rational explanation.

The previous essay presented early commentary on the relative importance of Reason and emotion, or the rational versus the non-rational sides of man. The purpose here is to provide the reader with a sampling of the views of early philosophers who seemed to recognize our bicameral mind.

To begin with, there were early observers who recognized that something like our twin hemisphere of the brain existed, but were quick to return to the old dogma that Reason must nevertheless rule. For example, among the early Greeks, Epictetus (55–135 AD) was well aware

---

[1] *The Maxims of La Rochefoucauld*, trans. Louis Kronenberger (New York: Random House, 1959), Nr. 98.
[2] Letter to abbe Chaulieu, July 26, 1717.
[3] The same association is true in Spanish.

of the rational and non-rational nature of the person and observed, 'by nothing is the rational creature so distressed as by the irrational.' However, like many early philosophers speculating on how the mind is organized, he arrives at a unique definition. Curiously, a completely rational subject such as grammar he recognizes as something apart from the rational. 'Reason' is something he associates more with the id.

> Of our faculties in general you will find that none can take cognizance of itself; none therefore has the power to approve or disapprove its own action. Our grammatical faculty for instance: how far can that take cognizance? Only so far as to distinguish expression. Our musical faculty? Only so far as to distinguish tune. Does any one of these then take cognizance of itself? By no means. If you are writing to your friend, when you want to know what words to write grammar will tell you; but whether you should write to your friend or should not write grammar will not tell you. And in the same way music will tell you about tunes, but whether at this precise moment you should sing and play the lyre or should not sing nor play the lyre it will not tell you. What will tell you then? That faculty which takes cognizance of itself and of all things else. What is this? The reasoning faculty: for this alone of the faculties we have received is created to comprehend even its own nature; that is to say, what it is and what it can do, and with what precious qualities it has come to us, and to comprehend all other faculties as well.[4]

We are particularly impressed with the insight of Aristides Quintilianus (first to fourth century AD) who not only recognized the rational and non-rational division,

> These, then, are its two aspects, the rational, through which it accomplishes the works of wisdom, and the irrational, through which it engages in the business of the body.[5]

but he also stated that the 'leader and high priest' of the first branch of learning is philosophy and the 'ruler' of the second is music.

Cicero, the Roman (106–43 BC), recognizes two divisions in man, but he does not quite know what to call the non-rational side. One can see here the strong prejudice against everything non-rational which continues to negatively influence society.

> The soul is divided into two parts, one of which partakes of reason, the other does not. So when the instruction that we should rule over ourselves is given, the instruction is that reason should restrain impulsiveness. There is in practically everybody's souls by nature something soft, lowly, abject, nerveless so to speak, and feeble. If there were nothing else, a human being would be the ugliest thing that exists. But at hand is the mistress and queen of all, Reason, which through its own strivings advances forward and becomes perfected virtue. It is man's responsibility to ensure that it rules over that part of the soul which ought to obey.[6]

---

[4] *The Discourses of Epictetus*, trans. P. E. Matheson (New York: Random House, 1957), 224. In another place, p. 372, he says, 'for it is being a child to be unmusical in musical things, ungrammatical in grammar …'

[5] Aristides' discussion begins Book II. Our quotations are from the translation by Andrew Barker, *Greek Musical Writings* (Cambridge: Cambridge University Press, 1989), II, 457ff.

[6] Cicero, *Tusculan Disputations*, II, 47.

In one of the early music treatises, the *Musica Disciplina* of 843 AD, Aurelian of Reome not only finds that music joins 'Reason to the body,' but also finds it more surprising that it is music which connects the rational and non-rational part of us.

> What else is it that binds together the parts of the soul and body of man himself, who, as Aristotle is pleased to put it, has been joined together of the rational and the irrational.[7]

We find an extraordinary insight by the philosopher known as Pico in 1519.

> The intellect does not permit any lower faculty to function in collaboration with it. Rather, whenever anything comes near the intellect and arouses it, the intellect, like a roaring fire, burns it up, and converts it into itself.[8]

He was quite correct: the left hemisphere of our brain tends to completely ignore the mute right hemisphere. The implications of this have had a dramatic influence on civilization. Consider only the fact that the left hemisphere consists primarily of second-hand information; it is not the real us. Yet it tends to ignore the *real* us, the experiential right hemisphere.

Early poets writing of love often found themselves having to sing of both hemispheres, as if they realized that the emotions were fundamentally apart from language. A striking example is found in Dante (1265–1321), who, in the introduction to one of his sonnets, clearly seems aware of the separation of faculties.

> In this sonnet I make two parts of myself in accordance with the way in which my thoughts were divided. One I call *heart*, that is desire; the other *soul*, that is reason; and I relate what one says to the other.[9]

And, when Reason does speak to Desire, it makes reference to the power of the emotions to shut down Reason.

> Who is this one
> that comes with consolation for our mind
> and who, possessing such outrageous strength,
> will not allow another thought to stay?[10]

---

7   Aurelian of Reome, *The Discipline of Music*, trans. Joseph Ponte (Colorado Springs: Colorado College Music Press, 1968), III. The Aristotle reference is apparently to the *Nicomachean Ethics*, I, 13.

8   Giovanni Pico della Mirandola, *Commentary on a Canzone of Benivieni*, trans. Sears Jayne (New York: Peter Lang, 1984), 148.

9   *Vita Nuova*, trans. Mark Musa (Oxford: Oxford University Press, 1992), 76.

10 Ibid., 77.

This must have been impressive, if confusing, to Dante—that feeling could so overpower Reason. In one poem he observes that Love overcomes the intellect like a ray of sunlight overcoming eyes that are weak.[11] He returns to this idea twice in the *Divine Comedy*, a reference at the beginning of *Paradise* again using his terms of desire and intellect.

> As it approaches its desire,
> Our intellect submerges so profoundly
> That our memory is unable to go back.[12]

In the *Inferno*, he speaks of other emotions which have the same power over the intellect.

> Who could ever tell, even in straight prose,
> The full story of the blood and of the wounds
> That I now saw, often though it be told?
> Certainly every tongue would falter, for
> Neither our speech nor our intellect
> Is capable of encompassing so much.[13]

These passages demonstrate that he was clearly aware that there is more to man than Reason.

Another early example of one who was aware of the separate faculties was Geoffrey Chaucer (1340–1400), who, in his 'The Romaunt of the Rose,' observes,

> You must both perceive *and* feel that pride is a sin.[14]

Later in the Renaissance we find the same kind of thought by Guarini (1538–1612):

> My heart and thoughts till now were so much set
> To train that foolish nymph into my net ...[15]

His Spanish contemporary, Cervantes, also recognized love's difficulty in communication:

> Auristela finished her speech and began to weep tears that undid and erased everything she'd just said.[16]

---

[11] 'Amor che ne la mente mi ragiona,' lines 59–60, in Frederick Goldin, *German and Italian Lyrics of the Middle Ages* (Garden City: Anchor Books, 1973), 377.

[12] *Paradise*, I.

[13] *Inferno*, XXVIII.

[14] Line 2240.

[15] Giambattista Guarini, *The Faithful Shepherd* [*Il Pastor Fido*], in *Five Italian Renaissance Comedies* (New York: Penguin Books, 1978), IV, 373.

[16] Miguel de Cervantes, *The Trials of Persiles and Sigismunda*, trans. Celia Weller and Clark Colahan (Berkeley: University of California Press, 1989), II, v.

Juan Vives, in his famous book, *On Education* of 1531, was not only clearly aware of the separate functions of Reason and emotions in the brain, but believed that Reason needed help and understanding in order to hold its own against the emotions.

> All the precepts of Moral Philosophy have been prepared, like an army, to bring support to Reason. Wherefore the whole man must be understood, from within and without. Within the mind are the intellect and the emotions. We must know by what things the emotions are aroused and developed; by what things on the other hand they are restrained, calmed, removed …
>
> Our intellect is enveloped by too dense a darkness for it to see through, for the passions, aroused through sin, have spread a great and most obscuring mist before the eyes of Reason. Reason has need of being clear, and of being as little perturbed as possible.[17]

The problem in trying to have the left hemisphere speak about the experience of love (found in the right hemisphere), something it knows nothing about, of course reflects the independent nature of the two hemispheres. One frequently finds references such as one by Erasmus, who noticed that 'when someone is chattering away, one can not listen to the lute.'[18] Similarly, Martin Luther used to complain about his little son, Hans, singing while he was trying to write.[19]

Here are some similar examples of recognition of the separate hemispheres found in English literature of the Renaissance.

> Robert Greene (1560–1592):
> Can wisdom win the field, when Love is Captain?[20]

> John Lyly (1554–1606):
> I cannot tell what reason it should be,
> But love and reason here do disagree.[21]

> William Shakespeare:
> Ask me no reason why I love you; for though Love use Reason for his physician, he admits him not for his counselor.[22]

---

[17] Vives: On Education, trans. Foster Watson (Cambridge: University Press, 1913), V, iii.

[18] 'The Tongue,' in *The Collected Works of Erasmus* (Toronto: University of Toronto Press, 1992), XXIX, 279.

[19] In a conversation of 1532 reported by Veit Dietrich, in *Luther's Works* (St. Louis: Concordia, 1961), LIV, 21. A comment in the same conversation reveals that Luther understood the left hemisphere knew no emotions. See Ibid., 83.

[20] *Arbasto: The Anatomy of Fortune* [1584], in *The Life and Complete Works of Robert Greene*, ed. Alexander Grosart (New York: Russell & Russell, 1964), III, 197.

[21] John Lyly, *The Maydes Metamorphosis*, IV, i.

[22] *The Merry Wives of Windsor*, II, i, 4.

The accumulation of centuries of common observation resulted in a considerable increase in discussion of the bicameral mind during the Baroque. In addition to the difficulty of communication of feelings through the rational left hemisphere of the brain, the great German philosopher Gottfried Leibniz (1646–1716) added the problem the rational side often has in describing the senses themselves.

> Additional simple primitive terms are all those confused phenomena of the senses which we certainly perceive clearly, but which we cannot explain distinctly, neither define them through other concepts, nor designate them by words.[23]

He struggled with the problem of how the rational mind could have the 'idea,' that is, a rational understanding, of something like emotion.[24] In the end, being a highly rational person himself (a mathematician) he fell back on the old principle that the Reason must rule.

> The highest perfection of man consists not merely in that he acts freely but still more in that he acts with reason. Better, these are both the same thing, for the less anyone's use of reason is disturbed by the impulsion of the affections, the freer one is.[25]

His great contemporary, the French philosopher, Marin Mersenne (1588–1648), speculated on the differing nature of rational and non-rational vocal sounds, that is, the difference between speech and singing. He wonders what would be the nature of speech if a child were reared in an environment which it never heard another human talk, although he doubts such an experiment could ever be made.[26] After much speculation he concludes that the different voices which express 'the passions of the soul' in men and animals are natural, but language itself is artificial.[27] This eventually leads him, in Proposition 12, to wonder if 'the musician can invent the best language of all those by which the conceptions of the mind can be expressed.'[28]

The Frenchman, Blaise Pascal (1623–1662), a brilliant thinker and inventor, seems to have been clearly aware of a bicameral division in the mind and one of his expressions of this is a familiar and widely quoted maxim,

> The heart has its reason, which reason does not know. We feel it in a thousand things.[29]

---

[23] Leibniz, 'An Analysis of the Elements of Language,' in *General Investigations Concerning the Analysis of Concepts and Truths*, trans. Walter O'Briant (Athens: University of Georgia Press, 1968), 33.

[24] Leibniz, 'What is an Idea?' (1678), in *Philosophical Papers and Letters*, ed. Leroy Loemker (Dordrecht: Reidel, 1956), 207.

[25] Leibniz, 'Criticala Thoughts on the General Part of the Principles of Descartes' (1692), 'On Article 37,' in Ibid., 388.

[26] Now such examples have been found, and such children cannot utter intelligible sounds.

[27] Marin Mersenne, Treatise Three, Book One, *Traitez de la Voix, et des Chants*, trans. Edmund LeRoy (New York: Julliard School, unpublished dissertation, 1978), III, i, 10.

[28] There was some discussion of this during the nineteenth century and one Frenchman, François Sudre, apparently had some success in devising a 'musical language.'

[29] Blaise Pascal, *Pensees* (New York: Modern Library, 1941), III, 277.

However, he complicates things when he introduces the term 'intuition,' which we argue, along with 'insight,' is something probably capable in both hemispheres. Nevertheless, here is a nice attempt to personify the two sides as he understood them in this regard.

> Thus it is rare that mathematicians are intuitive, and that men of intuition are mathematicians, because mathematicians wish to treat matters of intuition mathematically, and make themselves ridiculous, wishing to begin with definitions and then with axioms, which is not the way to proceed in this kind of reasoning ...
>
> Intuitive minds, on the contrary, being thus accustomed to judge at a single glance, are so astonished when they are presented with propositions of which they understand nothing, and the way to which is through definitions and axioms so sterile, and which they are not accustomed to see thus in detail, that they are repelled and disheartened.[30]

It is interesting that he attempts to further subdivide the rational mind into two sections.

> There are then two kinds of intellect: the one able to penetrate acutely and deeply into the conclusions of given premises, and this is the precise intellect; the other able to comprehend a great number of premises without confusing them, and this is the mathematical intellect.[31]

We find some additional interesting reflections of our bicameral mind among French writers of the Baroque, first in Charles de Saint-Evremond, in a poem contained in a letter to the Duke of Buckingham (1678), quite correctly suggests that the two hemispheres are inclined to work separately and not together.

> Sometimes let Reason, with a sovereign sway,
> Control all your desires:
> Sometimes let Reason to your heart give way,
> And fan your warmest fires.[32]

Jean de La Bruyere (1645–1696) makes the same point by way of reference to separate famous French playwrights.

> The plays of Corneille occupy one's mind; those of Racine stir one's heart.[33]

At the beginning of this chapter we quoted one of La Rochefoucauld's famous maxims which reflects our bicameral mind. There are two more which perhaps should not be omitted:

> The mind is always the dupe of the heart.[34]

......

---

[30] Ibid., I, i.

[31] Ibid., I, ii.

[32] Quoted in *The Letters of Saint-Evremond*, ed. John Hayward (Freeport, NY: Books for Libraries Press, 1971), 205.

[33] La Bruyere, *Characters*, trans. Jean Stewart (Baltimore: Penguin Books, 1970), 38.

[34] *The Maxims of La Rochefoucauld*, Nr. 102.

> Not all those who know their minds know their hearts as well.[35]

There are two other maxims of his which have a different focus and impress us very much. These two are relevant to the fact that the right hemisphere of our brain is mute and has no language to express itself (except through music). The first of these maxims pictures a right hemisphere communicating in a manner other than through language.

> Tone of voice, look and manner can prove no less eloquent than choice of words.[36]

More extraordinary is his insight that there are forms of understanding unique to the right hemisphere. This is a very correct and valid truth and represents a fundamental part of us that is never approached by the field of education, since society has made the emotions 'off-limits' to teachers.

> Nature would seem to have hidden deep within us talents and abilities we know nothing about; only strong emotion is able to bring them to light, and to give us at times insights beyond the reach of [rational] thought.[37]

We only find one original idea of importance on our subject by the famous Descartes. This is found at the very beginning of his 'Rules for the Direction of the Mind,' where he contends that the hand trained for harp playing, cannot be used for other pursuits, such as agriculture. All this is by way of introducing his observation that it was the arts which convinced the other intellectual disciplines that one must be a specialist in only one subject, devoting his entire life to that alone. Otherwise, he was rather a 'left-brained' man, which we can see clearly in a letter of 1641 to Henricus Regius, a professor of medicine a Utrecht.

> There is only one soul in man, the rational soul; for no actions can be reckoned human unless they depend on reason.

Montesquieu (1689–1755) counters this notion with a wonderful story about a man who had been unable to sleep for thirty-five days. Ordinary physicians, at a loss, proposed to give him opium, but a friend took him to an holistic doctor (a man who 'does not practice medicine, but has a multitude of remedies') who gave him a six-volume study of law. After reading a few pages, the man fell asleep.[38]

This reminds us of another wonderful story, this one by Voltaire. His 'Zadig' (1747) is a tale about a Babylonian philosopher and a wise man who 'knew as much of metaphysics as hath ever been known in any age, that is, little or nothing at all.' This story reflects another aspect of our bicameral mind, the fact that, as each hemisphere controls the opposite side of the

---

35 Ibid., Nr. 103.
36 Ibid., Nr. 249.
37 Ibid., Nr. 404.
38 Montesquieu, *The Persian Letters* (London: Athenaeum, 1901), 269.

body, so each eye feeds into the opposite hemisphere. Thus we must think of the right eye as the rational eye and the left as the eye dealing with our emotional life. With this in mind we return to the beginning of this story when a young man, Zadig, is wounded in the eye. A messenger is sent to Memphis for the famous physician, Hermes, who came with his large retinue. After his examination of Zadig, the doctor observed,

> Had it been the right eye, I could have cured it; but the wounds of the left eye are incurable.

In the English Baroque we find many references to our bicameral brain. Indeed, the great philosopher, David Hume (1711–1776) who once noted,

> Everyone of himself will readily perceive the difference between feeling and thinking.[39]

In Phineas Fletcher's poem, 'The Purple Island,' largely a description of a city as a metaphor for a map of anatomy, we have a curious early description of the twin hemispheres of the brain surrounded by the skull.

> Here all the senses dwell, and all the arts;
> Here learned Muses by their silver spring:
> The Citie severed in two diverse parts,
> Within the walls, and Suburbs neighboring;
> The Suburbs girt but with the common fence,
> Founded with wondrous skill, and great expense;
> And therefore beautie here keeps her chief residence.[40]

A poem by Thomas Sheridan (1687–1738), a priest and schoolmaster, is a remarkable example of someone who had arrived at the bicameral division of the brain purely by intuition. He is absolutely, and astonishingly, correct in his assigning of right or left eye and ear functions vis-a-vis their actual relationship with the brain hemispheres. Indeed, it is difficult to believe this was written before the availability of the results of clinical brain research.

> With my left eye, I see you sit snug in your stall,
> With my right I'm attending the lawyers that scrawl.
> With my left I behold your bellower a cur chase;
> With my right I'm reading my deeds for a purchase.
> My left ear's attending the hymns of the choir,
> My right ear is stunned with the noise of the crier.[41]

Since, as most readers know today, our two hemispheres tend to work separately, and not together, according to which side is best equipped for a particular problem, we should like to include two examples of English writers complaining about the interference of one side or the

---

[39] *A Treatise of Human Nature*, I, i, section 1.

[40] In Frederick Boas, *Giles and Phineas Fletcher Poetical works* (Cambridge: University Press, 1909), II, 54.

[41] Quoted in *The Poetical Works of Jonathan Swift* (London: Bell and Daldy, n.d.), III, 245.

other. Charles Avison (1709–1770), in one place, observes that people sing with more emotion when they visit foreign churches and cannot read the words to the hymns. His point, of course, is that in this case the right hemisphere is not hampered by the left at all.[42]

On the other hand, so to speak, Richard Steele, in the *Spectator* for 24 September 1712, published a fictitious complaint that our emotions carry us away, whereas the sermon is soon forgotten.

> A loose trivial song gains the affections, when a wise Homily is not attended to.

For the nineteenth century we need only point to the experience of the great composers, who also made observations which reflect the recognition of the conflict between the two hemispheres of our brain. Mendelssohn, for example, once noticed that sometimes he became so emotionally involved while he was conducting that he had difficulty in maintaining the beat. In this case, we know conductors use the right hand to give the beat, as it is controlled by the left hemisphere which knows the notation and the numbers of music. When Mendelssohn became emotionally involved, his right hemisphere was interfering with the left hemisphere function. Similarly, Schumann once remarked that when he was absorbed in music he found that he had difficulty remembering his German language!

The musician who wrote most extensively on the subject of our bicameral selves was Richard Wagner and his writings are worthy of thoughtful contemplation, certainly by all musicians. Instead of using terms like left and right (which he had no knowledge of) and rational versus non-rational, he used the terms Understanding versus Feeling, which, of course, match perfectly the primary functions of the two hemispheres of our brain. He makes a number of contentions, beginning with a statement that the musician 'addresses himself to Feeling, and not to Understanding.'[43] And he says if the musician is answered in terms of Understanding, you might as well say he was not understood. One can see right there how shocked he would be if he could observe American music education, which aspires to do just the reverse.

He also wrote in this regard on the subject of the development of modern languages, pointing out that language must have been based on feeling but that it has developed in such a manner that today, 'we speak a language we do not understand with the Feeling [side].'[44] On the other hand, he contends that poetry is impossible unless it passes 'from the Understanding to the Feeling.'[45]

He also attempts to write of music theory in terms of feeling,[46] certainly a foreign concept in modern classrooms. In our view his explanation is not so successful here, but in making the effort he creates a romantic discussion of this left-brain topic which is very refreshing.

---

[42] Charles Avison, *An Essay on Musical Expression* [London, 1753] (New York: Broude Reprint, 1967), 88.

[43] Wagner's Prose Works, trans. William Ashton Ellis (New York: Broude, I, 270ff.

[44] Ibid., II, 230.

[45] Ibid., II, 232.

[46] Ibid., II, 291.

The Secret Agenda: Right-Hand Preference

A wise man's heart inclines him toward the right,
But a fool's heart toward the left.

Ecclesiastes 10:2

IN THE PREVIOUS CHAPTER WE POINTED OUT that man's competing intellectual and emotional faculties have long been a matter of common observation and that subsequent manifestations are everywhere to be seen. Nowhere is this more evident than in references in literature throughout history which point to a right-hand preference. Thus it is a compliment if we say, 'he sat on the right-hand of the king,' but not so if we say, 'he received a left-handed compliment.' And, of course, we shake hands with the right hand and feel awkward if circumstances force us to use the left.

No one can say what the origin of right-hand preference is, but it does not seem adequately explained by the mere fact that ninety percent of persons are born right-handed. Hand preference reflects something else. One theory points to early man and sun worship. It has been pointed out that in the northern hemisphere you have to face south to follow the sun and move from left to right until the sun sets in the west, thus giving moving to the right and the right hand an unconscious significance. Another theory points to early battle. As the heart is on the left side, the left hand must hold the shield while the right hand holds the weapon and is most dominant in subsequent movement.

In our opinion perhaps the reason for right-hand preference lies in the fact that the left hemisphere of the brain (which controls the right-hand) is the only hemisphere which can speak and write. No doubt this fact also helps explain the long tradition among philosophers demanding that the left hemisphere must rule man. Left-brain or right-hand, it is all the same.

We can document this right-hand preference from nearly the beginning of literature. We can see already in Plato (427–347 BC) evidence that the prejudice was so strong that nurses and mothers were active in making sure the child used the right hand. Interestingly, Plato's point was that the difference in the use of the hands should reflect nature and its purpose but whatever this is has been lost as 'we are maimed by the folly of nurses and mothers.'[1] There is a story about Socrates, attributed to Plato by Jean Bodin (1530–1596), which again already clearly establishes a very early right-hand preference.

---

[1] *Laws*, VII, 794e.

> But if a good man has turned to a wrong thought, suddenly he recognizes in the recesses of his soul a teacher and guide who leads him away from the base thought either by the gentlest twitching and humming in his right ear or by a prick, which [Plato] described in these words: 'Cynthius plucks my ear and advises me.' Socrates used to explain that this was done by a friendly demon or rather by an angel who pulled his right ear in assent and his left ear for dissent.[2]

It is also interesting that we find Pliny the Elder, another early writer, in writing of the left-hand uses the word *sinistrae*, which also connotes unlucky or sinister. What one sees here is the left-brain labeling the mysterious and mute right hemisphere.

One of the early Church fathers, St. John Chrysostom (fourth to fifth century AD), paraphrases in one of his sermons a passage in the New Testament, Matthew 25:31–46. Here is this passage in a modern revision[3]:

> When the Son of man comes in his glory, and all the angels with him, then he will sit on his glorious throne. Before him will be gathered all the nations, and he will separate them one from another as a shepherd separates the sheep from the goats, and he will place the sheep at his right hand, but the goats at the left. Then the King will say to those at his right hand, 'Come, O blessed of my Father, inherit the kingdom prepared for you from the foundation of the world …'
>
> Then he will say to those at his left hand, 'Depart from me, you cursed, into the eternal fire prepared for the devil and his angels.'

Talk about incentive to use the right hand! There are more biblical references, by the way. In John 21:14 we have one of the accounts of Jesus appearing to his Disciples after the resurrection. He appears to them by the Sea of Tiberius where the Disciples have been fishing all night but have caught nothing. So Jesus commands them,

> 'Cast the net on the right side of the boat, and you will find some.' So they cast it, and now there were not able to haul it in, for the quantity of fish.

We should perhaps also mention that in Judges 7:20, which describes Gideon's great victory on the field, his men held their torches in their left hands and their trumpets in their right hands. And, similarly, in Revelations 1:16, 'in his right hand he held seven stars.'

Much like God separating the nations right and left, like sheep and goats, an account of Charlemagne (768–814 AD) has him visiting one of the schools he founded and placing the outstanding students on his right hand, praising them, and the unsuccessful students on his left, condemning them.[4]

---

[2] Jean Bodin, *Colloquium of the Seven*, trans. Marion Kuntz (Princeton: Princeton University Press, 1975), 100ff.

[3] All Bible references are from the *Revised Standard Version*.

[4] Einhard and Notker the Stammerer, *Two Lives of Charlemagne*, trans. Lewis Thorpe (Hamondsworth: Penguin Books, 1981), 95.

From the later Middle Ages there is a work by the Churchman, John of Salisbury (first half, twelfth century AD), intended as a treatise of advice for a prince. In a chapter entitled, 'What is the Meaning of Inclining to the Right Hand or the Left, Which is Forbidden to the Prince,' he advises,

> He shall not incline to the right hand nor to the left. To incline to the right hand signifies to insist too enthusiastically on the virtues themselves. To incline to the right is to exceed the bounds of moderation in the works of virtue, the essence of which is moderation …
>
> To incline to the left means to slip or deviate from the way of virtue down the precipices of the vices.[5]

There are some early works of poetry in which a path is described with various features on the right or left. John Lydgate (1370–1450) wrote a poem entitled, 'Reson and Sensuallyte,' in which he argues against Love as an emotion (right hemisphere). He has man take a right-hand path[6] to the (left hemisphere) non-feeling huntress, the goddess Diana. The Italian poet, Ariosto (1474–1533) sings of a similar path:

> The man who leaves this path finds on the right only the beautiful and on the left as much ugliness gathered as the world embraces.[7]

In Don Quijote, by Cervantes, we find,

> When a man doesn't know how to read, or when he's left-handed, it indicates one of two things: either he comes from a very low, a very humble family, or else he's such a wicked rogue that neither good models nor good teaching could have any effect on him.[8]

There are two such references in Erasmus (1469–1536). In a treatise, 'On Good Manners,' Erasmus discusses manners for young people. Among his rules, we find,

> If offering or pouring something see that you do not do it with your left hand.[9]

The second is in his discussion of the proverb, 'Admetus' dirge,' where Erasmus mentions a curious Greek myth regarding Aesculapius, son to Apollo, who studied medicine with Cheiron. Acquiring blood from the veins of the Gorgon, 'he employed blood from the veins on the left side to destroy people, and blood from the right side to save their lives.'[10]

---

[5] *Policraticus*, trans. John Dickinson, in *The Stateman's Book of John of Salisbury* (New York: Russell & Russell, 1963), 43. Similar right-hand prejudice can be found in Bernard of Clairvaux, 'On Conversion,' quoted in *Sermons on Conversion*, trans. Marie-Bernard Said (Kalamazoo: Cistercian Publications, 1981), 162, 166, and 253.

[6] Lines 2724ff.

[7] *The Satires of Ludovico Ariosto*, trans. Peter Wiggins (Athens: Ohio University Press, 1976), 133.

[8] Miguel de Cervantes, *Don Quijote*, trans. Burton Raffel (New York: Norton, 1995), II, xliii.

[9] 'On Good Manners,' [1530] in *The Collected Works of Erasmus* (Toronto: University of Toronto Press, 1992), XXV, 286.

[10] 'Adages,' in Ibid., XXXIII, 302.

In *Henry VI: Part III* (III, I, 43ff), there is a place where Shakespeare associates weeping with the left hand and a smile with the right.

Voltaire (1694–1778) mentions 'the simple and innocent practice yet taught in country places to children—that of kissing their right hands in return for a sugar plum.'[11] He also uses a figure of speech relative to the king of Sweden who 'sometimes ate with King Augustus, whom he had dethroned, and that he always gave him the right hand.'[12] It is also interesting that in one of his essays, Voltaire mentions that the French Academy had actually published a study on the subject of right hand preference, although he saw no potential value in such a study.

> We could have very well dispensed, for instance, with such disquisitions as the origin of the preference due to the right hand over the left.[13]

We see an example of an unfavorable reference to a person in Voltaire, in one of his plays, *The Tatler* (I, ii), where the character, Damis, asks,

> Did you ever remember such a starched, affected, strained, left-handed understanding?

For some reason there was considerable reference to the right-hand preference in England during the Baroque. Among the Puritan preachers we find John Donne praying,

> With thy left hand lay his body in the grave … and with thy right hand receive his soul into thy Kingdom.[14]

And the most famous preacher, John Bunyan, promises those saved will sit at the right hand of God.[15] It is 'on the right hand,' that Christiana and Prudence hear 'a most curious melodious note, with words,' made by birds in Bunyan's *Pilgrim's Progress*.[16]

The greatest pen of the Puritans, John Milton, clearly associated dominance with the right hand as we see in four quotations from his masterpiece, 'Paradise Lost.'.

> … where I shall Reign at thy right hand …[17]

---

[11] *Philosophical Dictionary*, 'Kiss.'

[12] Letter to Marshal Schulenburg [September 15, 1740].

[13] 'The Royal Society and Academies,' in *Works of Voltaire* (New York: St. Hubert Guild, 1901), XXXIX, 100. Voltaire mentions this again in his *Philosophical Dictionary*, under 'Society and Academies.'

[14] John Donne, 'Seventeenth Prayer,' in *Devotions Upon Emergent Occasion*, ed. Anthony Raspa (Montreal: McGill-Queen's University Press, 1975), 90.

[15] 'Saved by Grace,' in *The Works of John Bunyan*, ed. George Offor (London: Blackie and Son, 1853), I, 362.

[16] *Pilgrim's Progress*, in Ibid., III, 205.

[17] 'Paradise Lost,' in *The Works of John Milton*, ed. Frank Patterson (New York: Columbia University Press, 1931–1938), II, 868, in Ibid., II, 68.

> Should intermitted vengeance arm again
> His red right hand to plague us?[18]
>
> … our own right hand
> Shall teach us highest deeds.[19]
>
> … the first assay
> Of this right hand provoked …[20]

In another place, we find,

> Come therefore O thou that hast the seven stars in thy right hand, appoint thy chosen priests according to their Orders.[21]

One passage seems a bit curious to the modern reader, for it is apparent that while Milton employed the right hand for positive purposes he apparently did not realize that the two hemispheres of our brain operate opposite sides of the body. Here he assumes the left hand is associated with the left, or rational, brain.

> Kings most commonly, though strong in Legions, are but weak at Arguments; as they who ever have accustomed from the Cradle to use their will only as their right hand, their reason always as their left.[22]

Finally, those who are confused, says Milton, do not know their right from their left. Writing of tyrants, who, by cunning and dexterity, 'winde themselves by shifting ground into places of more advantage,' Milton concludes 'with them there is no certain hand right or left.'[23]

Among the Jacobean poets there is a poem by Ben Jonson called 'On my First Son,' where we find, 'Farewell, thou child of my right hand.'[24] In this case, the child's name was Benjamin, which in Hebrew means, 'child of the right hand.'

Additional examples of right-hand preference can be seen in Richard Crashaw's poem inspired by Matthew 2:11 (the visit of the three kings to baby Jesus):

> Whether by your eye or by your right hand you honor them …[25]

---

[18] Ibid., II, 44.
[19] Ibid., II, 174.
[20] Ibid., II, 183.
[21] 'Animadversions,' in Ibid., III, 147. Milton appears to have had in mind Revelations 1:16:
  … in his right hand he held seven stars, from his mouth issued a sharp two-edged sword …
[22] 'Eikonoklastes,' Preface, in Ibid., V, 63.
[23] 'The Tenure of Kings,' in Ibid., V, 56.
[24] *The Complete Poetry of Ben Jonson*, ed. William Hunter (New York: Norton, 1963), 20.
[25] 'The Gifts of the Persian Sages,' in *The Complete Poetry of Richard Crashaw*, ed. George Williams (New York: New York University Press, 1972), 280.

and in Abraham Cowley's (1618–1667) discussion of Hazel in his book on plants, where he observes,

> In search of golden mines a Hazle wand
> The wise Diviner takes in his Right-hand.[26]

George Wither (1588–1667), in his book of emblems, entitles one picture, 'The Right-hand way is Virtue's path.' The essence of the poem which follows is that virtue's path is the more difficult. He concludes,

> And, though the Left-hand-way, more smoothness hath,
> Let us go forward, in the Right-hand-path.[27]

There are also examples in this literature of obvious prejudice against the left hand, as for example in Thomas Dekker (b. 1570).

> All the Skies
> Danced to the sounds of several Harmonies;
> Both Angels and Arch-angels loudly sung,
> All Heaven was but One Instrument well strung.
> But They, who on the Left-hand were set by,
> (As Out-casts) shooke and trembled fearefully.[28]

A similar prejudice is expressed by Robert Herrick (1591–1674).

> God has a Right Hand, but is quite bereft
> Of that, which we do nominate the Left.[29]

The only references we have found for right-hand preference by the Jacobean playwrights are by Thomas Dekker. One is from *If This be not a Good Play* (III, ii), where there is a discussion of the right eye being favored over the left. A more conventional example is his *The Wonder of a Kingdom* (IV, iv). A stage direction indicates 'Musicke within,' which is followed by,

> ALPHONSINA. What's the matter sir?
> NICOLETTO. I hear a lute, and sure it comes this way.
> ALPHONSINA. My most loved Lord, step you aside, I would not have you seen for the saving of my right hand.

---

[26] *Of Plants*, in *The Complete Works of Abraham Cowley*, ed. Alexander Grosart (New York: AMS Press, 1967)., I, 276.

[27] Wither, *A Collection of Emblemes* [1635], in *English Emblem Books* (Menston, Yorkshire: Scolar Press, 1968), 160.

[28] Thomas Dekker, 'Dekker his Dreame,' in *The Non-Dramatic Works of Thomas Dekker*, ed. Alexander Grosart (New York: Russell & Russell, 1963), III, 29.

[29] Quoted in L. C. Martin, *The Poetical Works of Robert Herrick* (Oxford: Clarendon Press, 1963), 394.

There are some interesting references to right-hand preference among the Jacobean writers of prose. One is a negative reference, when Thomas Dekker makes mention of 'some left-handed Priest.'[30]

Sir Thomas Browne (1605–1682), in his *Enquiries into Vulgar and Common Errors*, takes a passage in the Old Testament, Ecclesiastes 10:2,

> A wise man's heart inclines him toward the right, but a fool's heart toward the left.

and interprets it to mean one's choice of traveling the right way in the path of virtue or the left road, one of vice.[31] Later in this same book, Browne, who was also a physician, devotes an entire chapter, 'Of the Right and Left Hand,' to the question of the curious priority given the right hand. He begins by representing himself as suspicious of any basis for this prejudice, although he acknowledges several passages in the Old Testament which clearly emphasize the right hand.[32]

He advances several arguments why no basis can be found in Nature for this prejudice, including the fact that no similar preference can be found in other animals, nor is a preference clear in very young children. Most important, he points out that none of the senses honor such a prejudice, nor can he find any meaningful evidence among the internal organs. In the end he finds even the fact that more persons are right-handed to be a matter of custom, and not of nature.

One of the writers of the Restoration in England, Thomas Otway (1652–1685), in speaking of the disappointed lover in his fictional 'Love-Letters,' refers to one of the oldest expressions of the right-hand preference, the place of honor at the right hand.

> … it is like seating me at your Side-table, when I have the best Pretense to your Right Hand at the Feast.[33]

Finally, in Charles Gildon's discussion of the actor's gestures we can see how vividly the tendency toward right-hand preference was felt. He recommends the practice of observing one's own gestures in a mirror, but quickly points out that this practice includes a great disadvantage in the fact that everything is seen backwards. He finds this particularly serious with respect to the hands.

---

[30] Thomas Dekker, 'The Seven Deadly Sinnes of London' (1606), in *The Non-Dramatic Works of Thomas Dekker*, ed. Alexander Grosart (New York, Russell & Russell, 1963), II.

[31] 'Enquiries into Vulgar and Common Errors,' in *Sir Thomas Browne's Works*, ed. Simon Wilkin (London: Pickering, 1836), III, 62.

[32] Ibid., III, 13ff. He also mentions several curious myths, among them that the Amazon women amputated their right breast, for freer use of the bow, and that 'a woman upon a masculine conception advances her right leg.'

[33] Thomas Otway, 'Love-Letters.'

> When you make a motion with your right hand, the reflection makes it seem as done by the left, which confounds the gesture, and gives it an awkward appearance.[34]

Later, we see how extraordinarily important the right-left hand question was to Gildon.

> If an action comes to be used by only one hand, that must be the right, it being indecent to make a gesture with the left alone … When you speak of your self, the right and not the left hand must be applied to the bosom, declaring your own faculties, and passions; your heart, your soul, or your conscience, but this action generally speaking, should be only applied or expressed by laying the hand gently on the breast.[35]

Clearly there is a right-hand preference. What do we take away from this acknowledgment?

The right-hand reflects the left-hemisphere of the brain, the side of the brain which talks and writes. The right-hemisphere of the brain is mute and can communicate only through music, movement (dance) and visual sign-language.

The right-hemisphere, thus not being able to defend its importance to man in speech or language, leaves the left-hemisphere free to emphasize its importance through its representative, 'its hand,' the right-hand.

Who then speaks for the experiential half of ourselves? Musicians, dancers, mimes, painters and sculptors.

---

[34] Charles Gildon, *The Life of Mr. Thomas Betterton, the Late Eminent Tragedian* [1710] (London: Frank Cass Reprint, 1970), 54ff.

[35] Ibid., 74ff.

ously only have a negligible effect on the text, but
PART 3
WHAT MUSIC IS

Music is the Ruler of the Passions of the Soul

*Only Music deserves being extolled as the mistress
and governess of the feelings of the human heart.*
Martin Luther (1538)

Musick is as dangerous as Gun-Powder.
William Congreve (1670–1729)

FOR ANY MUSICIAN, and no doubt most experienced listeners, both the title[1] of this chapter and Luther's observation will seem so obvious as to create wonder why the topic even needs discussion. It is a good question for the association of music and emotion is one of the most ancient of the documented ideas of man. In the Akkadian language, 3,000 BC, the word for music, *nigutu* or *ningutu*, had the connotation of joy or merry-making.[2] In ancient Egypt all music went under the name *hy*, which also meant joy or gladness.[3]

In spite of such ancient tradition, the fact is that the early Christian Church tried with the utmost vigor to remove all emotion from the life of the Christian. They said that emotion is the first step toward sin and so they warned the new Christians not to go to the theater or to sporting events in the arena for emotions are found there. St. Basel warned that a good Christian should not even laugh, for laughing is a form of emotion! Music, which by nature has little purpose other than expressing emotions, they attempted to turn into mathematics. And they left us their notational system which is based on simple arithmetic and has no symbols at all for feeling.

Since the early Church controlled education, and since for centuries Church clerks were the only people in Western Europe who could write, philosophies were put in place which still intrude upon our lives. The way we teach music in the universities is still very much in the footsteps of the Scholastic teachers of the early Church universities. To this day music history texts dealing with the Renaissance and Baroque concentrate on Church music, and thus have provided generations of music students with a very incomplete view of music in society between 1300–1750. Therefore, for a long time there has been some who have continued to think of music as left-hemisphere concepts and mathematics instead of its natural role as a

---

[1] Angelo Berardi, 1681.

[2] Henry G. Farmer, 'The Music of Ancient Egypt,' *New Oxford History of Music* (London: Oxford University Press, 1966), I, 236.

[3] Ibid., I, 262.

voice for the emotions. In the twentieth century, for example, we had fifty years of Twelve-Tone composers who had little desire to communicate emotions to their listeners. They and their music have disappeared without a trace.

In view of this history, we believe it might be well to take a closer look at some of the philosophic thoughts on the relationship of the emotions and music which preceded our time. In earlier essays we have presented some of the debates of the ancient world and the Middle Ages over Reason versus experience and Reason versus emotion. The most influential catalyst for change in Western European music was the rediscovery of the books of the ancient philosophers which the Church had tried to destroy. It was largely the discovery of the role of emotions described by the ancient authors which caused the following Europeans to begin to reconsider their music from the perspective of the ideals of the ancient world. This discussion became Humanism in music, a return of emotions to their ancient and natural purpose in music. And so one finds more and more musicians and philosophers talking about emotion as the Renaissance proceeds. By the beginning of the Baroque the topic had become an obsession and philosophers began to publish theories on exactly how music can communicate specific emotions. These ideas are known as the 'doctrine of affections,' a topic to which we shall devote the following essay.

No period of Western music is so misrepresented in history texts as the Baroque. Who reading these texts would realize that *emotion* was the focus of those musicians? At the same time, these traditional texts have scarcely mentioned the role of improvisation, the opportunity for personal emotional reflection by the performer, during the Baroque, which has led to generations of performances of this music which have been devoid of feeling. It is our belief that very little Baroque music can be performed as it appears on paper. Passages with repeated chords, whole notes and 'alberti bass' figures are signposts calling for improvisation. Without improvisation there is no melody, only grammar. We fail to teach this, yet often whatever the performer plays by way of improvisation, even if nothing more than a diatonic scale it is something more musical than what was written on paper.

During the Middle Ages, because the Church was so powerful and because the Church had placed so much emphasis on Reason, it was difficult for any writer to advance new ideas about the emotions. Nevertheless, common observation began to uncover some things which could not be ignored. First, philosophers were slowly becoming aware that both the emotions and some aspects of music itself seemed to be genetic in character. The first-century philosopher, Longinus, author of the very important treatise, 'On the Sublime,' declares, 'Music is a language which is implanted by nature in man and which appeals not to the hearing only but to the soul itself.'[4] Because of this he has observed that the listener understands music even though he has no training in the art.

---

4   Longinus, *On the Sublime*, trans. W. Rhys Roberts (Cambridge: University Press, 1935), XXXIX, 2.

> For does not the flute instill certain emotions into its hearers and as it were make them beside themselves and full of frenzy, and supplying a rhythmical movement constrain the listener to move rhythmically in accordance therewith and to conform himself to the melody, although he may be utterly ignorant of music?

This is so obvious, writes Longinus, that it is 'folly to dispute' it, for 'experience is proof sufficient.'

Our attention was attracted to the writer known as Aristides Quintilianus, who lived sometime between the first and fourth century AD, and his treatise, *De Musica*,[5] because he promises 'to explain what kinds of melody and rhythm will discipline the natural emotions.' Not only does he promise to set forth the principles written down by the great philosophers, but to reveal to us some of the things they did not write about—those 'esoteric secrets' they reserved 'for their discussions with one another.' He must do this, he says, because now,

> indifference to music (to put it politely) is so widespread, we cannot expect people with only a mild interest in the subject to tolerate being faced with a book in which not everything is explicitly spelled out.

Aristides assigns the emotions to the soul, where he divides them into male and female qualities. This same duality he finds in nature as well, in plants, minerals, and spices, expressed through their qualities of color or texture and their opposites. This duality Aristides finds as well in the simplest elements of music, even in single notes, or sounds. 'Some of them are hard and male, others relaxed and female.' He finds rhythms composed of short syllables are faster and 'more passionate,' those composed only of long syllables are slower and calm and mixtures have the qualities of both. Compound rhythms are more emotional and 'the impression they give is tempestuous, because the number from which they are constructed does not keep the same order of its parts in each position.' Running rhythms inspire us to action, others are supine and flabby.

Since Aristides finds that rhythm is so closely associated with character, it follows that one can judge a person by his manner of walking.

> We find that people whose steps are of good length and equal, in the manner of the spondee, are stable and manly in character: those whose steps are long but unequal, in the manner of trochees or paions, are excessively passionate: those whose steps are equal but too short, in the manner of the pyrrhic, are spineless and lack nobility: while those whose steps are short and unequal, and approach rhythmical irrationality, are utterly dissipated. As to those who employ all the gaits in no particular order, you will realize that their minds are unstable and erratic.

Musical instruments also have character, which explains why a particular listener will 'love and admire the instruments that are suited to them.' Thus he finds the trumpet to be male, because of its vehemence, and the aulos female, 'since it has a mournful and dirge-like sound.'

---

[5] Aristides discussion begins Book II. All our quotations are from the translation by Andrew Barker, *Greek Musical Writings* (Cambridge: Cambridge University Press, 1989), II, 457ff.

Similarly, among the strings, he finds the lyra to be male, because of its extreme deepness and roughness and the *sambyke* to be female, 'since it lacks nobility and incites people to abandonment because of its very high pitch.'

Finally, we note an aesthetic observation by Aristides:

> There are two useful forms of music-making, one valuable for the benefit it brings to the best of men, the other for the harmless relaxation it gives to the common run of mankind, and to anyone there may be still less exalted than they.

The Roman philosopher, Quintilian (30–96 AD) explains that the ability of the orator to communicate emotions to the audience depends on the use of both the voice and the body. Here he recommends to the orator the study of music for learning how this is done.

> Let us discuss the advantages which our future orator may reasonably expect to derive from the study of Music.
>
> Music has two modes of expression in the voice and in the body; for both voice and body require to be controlled by appropriate rules. Aristoxenus divides music, in so far as it concerns the voice, into *rhythm* and *melody*, the one consisting in measure, the latter in sound and song. Now I ask you whether it is not absolutely necessary for the orator to be acquainted with all these methods of expression which are concerned firstly with gesture, secondly with the arrangement of words and thirdly with the inflections of the voice, of which a great variety are required for law practice … It is by the raising, lowering or inflection of the voice that the orator stirs the emotions of his hearers, and the measure, if I may repeat the term, of voice or phrase differs according as we wish to rouse the indignation or the pity of the judge. For, as we know, different emotions are roused even by the various musical instruments, which are incapable of reproducing speech. Further the motion of the body must be suitable and becoming, or as the Greeks call it *eurythmic*, and this can only be secured by the study of music.[6]

The great mathematician, Boethius (475–524), was another who believed that perception through all the senses was something present due to nature and that this genetic information is something different from the 'mind.' He goes even further and states that the genetic aspect makes the power of music inseparable from man himself.

> From all these accounts it appears beyond doubt that music is so naturally united with us that we cannot be free from it even if we so desired.[7]

Aurelian of Reome, of the ninth century, does not address genetics as such, but he was impressed by the fact that music has a universality beyond anything else.

> The very world and the sky above us, according to the doctrine of philosophers, are said to bear in themselves the sound of music. Music moves the affections of men, stimulates the emotions into a different mood. In war it restores the strength of the combatants; and the stronger the blaring of the trumpet, the braver is the spirit made for battle. It influences beasts also, serpents, birds, and dolphins,

---

[6] Quintilian, *The Education of an Orator* (*Institutio Oratoria*), trans. H. E. Butler (London: Heinemann, 1938), I, x, 22.

[7] Boethius, *Fundamentals of Music*, trans. Calvin Bower (New Haven: Yale University Press), I, i.

at its hearing … And what more? The art of music surpasses all other arts. If anyone doubts that the angels, too, in the starry sky, render praises to God with the practice of this discipline, he is not a reader of [the book of Revelations].[8]

In a discussion of two fragments of poetry by Horace[9] by John of Salisbury (twelfth century) we can clearly see that the stage is set for the Renaissance, for Humanism and for the return of emotion as the central element of performance. First there are two points, that Nature has genetically prepared our emotions and, second, that speech is only a surrogate for the emotions.

> Nature first adapts our soul to every
> Kind of fate: she delights us, arouses our wrath,
> Or overwhelms and tortures us with woe,
> After which she expresses these emotions
> Employing the tongue as their interpreter.

It follows that if the musician expects to communicate with his listeners, he must feel the emotion himself.

> If you expect me to weep, then first
> You yourself must mourn.[10]

In the early Renaissance we still find comments which, in the style of the Middle Ages, seem to consider no further than thinking of the emotions in music to be just a matter of making life more bearable. A character in Chaucer's *The Book of the Duchess*, for example, tells us, 'I put my feeling into songs, to gladden my heart.' Perhaps another example of the utilitarian use of the feelings in music is the case of Leonardo da Vinci, who arranged to have music being performed while he painted the *Mona Lisa*.[11]

Another reference to feeling in music in the early Renaissance is quite different as feeling has taken on an importance of its own. John Lydgate (1370–1450), in his poem, 'The Minstrel's answer to Death,' has the minstrel observing that if he is taken from the earth people will continue to dance, but will feel nothing in their heart.

> THIS new daunce is to me so straunge,
> Wonder divers and passingly contrarye;
> The dredefull footyng doth so oft chaunge
> And the measures so oft tymes varye,
> Which now to me is nothyng necessarye.
> If it wer so that I might asterte!

---

8 Aurelian of Reome, *The Discipline of Music*, trans. Joseph Ponte (Colorado Springs: Colorado College Music Press, 1968), XX.

9 Horace's quote may be found in *De Arte Poetica liber*, ed. F. Vollmer (Leipzig, 1925), 108–111, 102, 103.

10 *The Metalogicon*, trans. Daniel McGarry (Berkeley: University of California Press, 1955), 51.

11 Reported by Varsi, quoted in *The Literary Works of Leonardo da Vinci*, ed. Jean Paul Richter (London: Phaidon, 1970), I, 72.

> But many a man, if I shal nought tary,
> Oft daunseth, but nothyng of hert.[12]

As the Renaissance progresses it is not long before we see this return to music's purpose of communicating feeling described in eye-witness reports of actual performance. Stop for a moment and think of lute performances you have heard. Now consider this remarkable passage in Galilei's book on lute intabulation where a lutanist gives a startling description of the emotions capable on the lute. No organist, he says, can approximate the emotions capable on the lute, not even such virtuosi of the organ, such as Claudio di Correggio and Gioseffo Guami,

> not by failure of their art and knowledge but by the nature of the instrument, have not been able, cannot, and never will be able to express the harmonies for *affetti* like *durezza, mollezza, asprezza, dolcezza*—consequently the cries, laments, shrieks, tears, and finally quietude and rage—with so much grace and skill as excellent players do on the lute.[13]

'Shrieks, rage,' this is the Renaissance lute? Perhaps so, for a character in Robert Green's (1560–1592) fictional *Perimedes* is surprised by the emotional power of her own music. She calls for a lute,

> whereupon singing a mere galliard, the thought to beguile such unacquainted passions, but instead finding that music was like trying quench the flame with oil: feeling the assaults to be so sharp as her mind was ready to yield as vanquished: she began with diverse considerations to suppress the frantic affections.[14]

Or consider this art song for voice, an elegy of Magdalene by Michael de Verona. Heinrich Glarean, in his *Dodecachordon* of 1547, an extremely dull and prosaic description of church modes published at a time when the entire practice had virtually ended, nevertheless, when asked for one of his favorite songs suddenly becomes quite emotional as he describes this elegy as,

> possessing great emotion and innate sweetness and tremendous power, so that one really believes he hears the weeping of a woman and her following ... At the end, through a certain confident hope, it rises so magnificently and is lifted to the heights with such tremendous exultation, and then again, as if wearied and self-reproachful for immoderate joy, it falls back into deep and customary weeping.[15]

---

[12] John Lydgate, 'The Daunce of Machabree,' contained at the end of Part III, *Fall of Princes*, ed. Henry Bergen (London: Oxford University Press, 1967), VIII, 1040. This work is ostensibly a translation of Giovanni Boccaccio's *De Casibus Virorum Illustrium*, although Lydgate freely engages in his own commentary and philosophy.

[13] Vincenzo Galilei, *Fronimo* [1584], trans. Carol MacClintock (Neuhasen-Stuttgart: Hanssler-Verlag, 1985), 87.

[14] Robert Greene, *Perimedes* [1588], in *The Life and Complete Works of Robert Greene*, ed. Alexander Grosart (New York: Russell & Russell, 1964), VII, 33.

[15] Glarean, *Dodecachordon*, trans. Clement Miller (American Institute of Musicology, 1965), II, 258ff.

And, of course, the music of no other Italian Renaissance composer was so emotionally charged as that of Gesualdo. If the reader is not familiar with this powerful music, Isacoff summarizes it well.

> His pieces ... reflect the stirrings of an anguished soul. The music is by turns tragic, erotic, and shocking. Tortuous melodies squirm and leap uneasily through convention barriers. Harmonies heave and sigh as they strain to find resolution ... They are stories not of love's ultimate fulfillment, but of relentless yearning—of a heart languishing in the fires of unsated desire—and his music captures that state with remarkable potency.
> It represented everything the Church was hoping to quell.[16]

The great French writer, Michael Montaigne (1533–1592) seemed amazed by the emotional power of the music he was hearing everywhere in society.

> No heart is so flabby that the sounds of our drums and trumpets do not set it ablaze, nor so hard that sweet music does not tickle it and enliven it; no soul is so sour that it does not feel touched by some feeling of reverence when it contemplates the somber vastness of our Churches, the great variety of their decorations and our ordered liturgy, or when it hears the enchantment of the organ and the poised religious harmony of men's voices. Even those who come to scoff are brought to distrust their opinion by a shiver in their heart and a sense of dread.[17]

When one reads first-hand accounts of performances such as the following one by the lute player, Francesco da Milano, one realizes that by the end of the Renaissance the role of emotion in music was understood by all. This could very well be a description of contemplative listeners of our own day.

> The tables cleared, he took up a lute and, as if merely essaying chords, he began, seated near the foot of the table, to strum a fantasy. He had plucked no more than the first three notes of the tune when all the conversation ceased among the festive throng and all were constrained to look there where he was, as he continued with such enchanting skill that little by little, through the divine art in playing that was his alone, he made the very strings to swoon beneath his fingers and transported all who listened into such gentle melancholy that one present buried his head in his hands, another let his entire body slump into an ungainly posture with members all awry, while another, his mouth sagged open and his eyes more than half shut, seemed, one would judge, as if transfixed upon the strings, and yet another, with chin sunk upon his chest, hiding the most sadly taciturn visage ever seen, remained abstracted in all his senses save his hearing, as if his soul had fled from all the seats of sensibility to take refuge in his ears where more easefully it could rejoice in such enchanting symphony.[18]

By Humanism in music we mean the return of the emphasis of communicating emotions as the primary purpose of music. Humanism begins during the Renaissance, it finishes off for good the old Church dogma of music based on mathematics and opens the door for a dramatic period of focus on the emotions in music—the Baroque. Music history texts, based on some

---

16 Stuart Isacoff, *Temperament* (New York: Vintage, 2001), 131.
17 Michel de Montaigne, *Essays*, trans. M. A. Screech (London: Penguin, 1993), II, xii, 670.
18 Pontus de Tyard, *Solitaire second* [1555].

comments by Monteverdi on the 'first practice' and 'second practice,' have told readers that both styles continued during the Baroque. This is true, but it is very misleading to suggest that half the composers were doing one and half the other. The truth is that very few composers continued to write in the old polyphonic Renaissance style and contemporary commentators say over and over again that this old scholastic style is dead.

So enthusiastic were the musicians of the Baroque about the return of emotional emphasis that they tried to study exactly how music communicates emotions. That is, they tried to subject emotions and music to a rational, left-brain kind of analysis and we call their findings the 'Doctrine of Affections.' As always, the rational brain never had much success in describing music, but it makes for some interesting reading which we will present in the following essay. Because national preferences now also become more evident with respect to the role of the emotions in music we will look at the Baroque by the four major geographical areas.

Italy

Perhaps nothing epitomizes the new importance of emotions in performance so well as an eye-witness description of the famous Corelli playing his violin. Stop and think—have you ever seen anyone play Baroque music who looked like this?

> I never met with any man that suffered his passions to hurry him away so much whilst he was playing on the violin as the famous Arcangelo Corelli, whose eyes will sometimes turn as red as fire; his face will be distorted, his eyeballs roll as in an agony, and he gives in so much to what he is doing that he doth not look like the same man.[19]

This extraordinary return to music based on emotions and not on mathematics is also clearly seen at the very beginning of the Baroque with the 'invention' of the new form, opera. The whole point of opera, as envisioned by the committee which founded it, the Camerata, was to create a form more emotionally powerful than mere stage drama. And it is all the more amazing when one remembers that Italy was still otherwise dominated by a very powerful Church.

Already by 1581 Galilei was clearly expressing the goals of the new style. 'True music,' he writes, has a primary purpose 'to express the passions' and, secondarily, 'to communicate these with equal force to the minds of mortals for their benefit and advantage.' The older polyphonic composers, with their 'inviolable laws,' he says, are 'directly opposed to the perfection of the true and best harmonies and melodies.'[20] Finally, he clearly states the goal of the Camerata.

---

[19] François Raguenet, 'Comparison between the French and Italian Music (1702),' trans. Oliver Strunk, *The Musical Quarterly* 32, no. 3 (1946): 419fn.

[20] Quoted in Oliver Strunk, *Source Readings in Music History* (New York: Norton, 1950), 306–7.

> For [polyphony's] sole aim is to delight the ear, while that of ancient music is to induce in another the same passion that one feels oneself.[21]

In short order, the various composers were making similar statements of purpose. Cavalieri, in the preface to his *La rappresentatione di Anima* (1600) says his goal is to 'move listeners to different emotions, such as pity and joy, tears and laughter.'[22] Caccini, in his *Le Nuove Musiche*, writes that the goal of his solo songs was 'to move the emotions of the soul.'[23] Later, he says the singer's duty is to understand the poet's conception and 'imitating them through emotional music and expressing them through emotional singing.'[24]

The immediately following opera composers were true to these goals.

Marco da Gagliano, in the preface to his *Dafne* of 1608, was concerned that the accompanying instruments participated in the emotions of the singers:

> Make sure that the instruments that are to accompany the solo voices are located so that they can see the faces of the performers, in order that by hearing each other better they may perform together.[25]

This same topic was mentioned in 1600, by Emilio de' Cavalieri in the preface to his *Rappresentazione di Anima, et di Corpo*[26] where he recommends the orchestra members changing instruments, according to the emotions, a practice which would explain the very large list of instruments associated with Monteverdi's *Orfeo*.

Before leaving the topic of the theater we might add that perhaps the new emphasis on projecting the emotions, together, no doubt, with the emerging dependence on improvisation, would account for the long rehearsal periods hinted at in the literature. A letter of Monteverdi to Alessandro Striggio in 1620 on the subject of the rehearsals for *Arianna*, tells us that after the singers had learned their parts by memory, *then* the 'five months of strenuous rehearsals took place!' Even a horse ballet given in Vienna in January 1667 required six months of rehearsal!

Monteverdi, in 1638, in making a general comment about the communication of emotions in music, makes a subtle comment on the old scholastic, mathematical polyphonic music of the past.

---

[21] Vincenzo Galilei, *Dialogo della musica antica e della moderna* [1581], quoted in Ibid., 317.

[22] Quoted in Nino Pirrotta and Elena Povoledo, *Music and Theatre from Poliziano to Monteverdi* (Cambridge: Cambridge University Press, 1982), 241.

[23] Giulio Caccini, *Le Nuove Musiche*, ed. H. Wiley Hitchcock (Madison: A-R Editions, 1970), 45.

[24] Ibid., 47.

[25] Quoted in Carol MacClintock, *Readings in the History of Music in Performance* (Bloomington: Indiana University Press, 1979), 190.

[26] Emilio de' Cavalieri, *Rappresentazione di Anima, et di Corpo*, Preface, quoted in Carol MacClintock, *Readings in the History of Music in Performance* (Bloomington: Indiana University Press, 1979), 183.

> I consider the principal passions or emotions of the soul to be three, namely, anger, serenity, and humility. The best philosophers affirm this; the very nature of our voice, with its high, low and middle ranges, shows it; and the art of music clearly manifests it in these three terms: agitated, soft and moderate. I have not been able to find an example of the agitated style in the works of past composers, but I have discovered many of the soft and moderate types.[27]

Marcello, in a letter of 1711, makes a similar comment about older music. He writes that he has tried in his music to lend 'more expression to the words' and refers to the earlier polyphonic style as having a 'natural sterility.'[28] Many similar comments about the new goals of the theater could be quoted, but perhaps they are best summarized by Angelo Berardi, who observed in 1681, 'Music is the ruler of the passions of the soul.'[29]

Galilei's reference, above, to the emotions one feels in oneself is echoed in the contemporary advice to performers. The famous vocal teacher, Tosi, speaks to his students of the voice:

> Oh! how great a master is the heart! Confess it, my beloved singers, and gratefully admit, that you would not have arrived at the highest rank of the profession if you had not been its scholars; admit, that in a few lessons from it, you learned the most beautiful expressions, the most refined taste, the most noble action, and the most exquisite graces: Admit (though it be hardly credible) that the heart corrects the defects of nature, since it softens a voice that's harsh, betters an indifferent one, and perfects a good one: Admit, when the heart sings you cannot dissemble, nor has truth a greater power of persuading.[30]

Also the great violinist, Geminiani, also stresses that the performer must be emotionally inspired and gives wonderful advice on how to begin to achieve this.

> I would besides advise, as well the composer as the performer, who is ambitions to inspire his audience to be first inspired himself, which he cannot fail to be if he chooses a work of genius, if he makes himself thoroughly acquainted with all its beauties; and if while his imagination is warm and glowing he pours the same exalted spirit into his own performance.[31]

It was this great focus on projecting the emotions of the score which made improvisation necessary, as well as freedom in tempo and dynamics and a host of other things not to be found on paper.

---

[27] Monteverdi, *Madrigali guerrieri ed amorosi* [1638], preface, quoted in Sam Morgenstern, *Composers on Music* (New York: Pantheon, 1956), 22.

[28] Benedetto Marcello, letter to Jacopo Perti, October 4, 1711, quoted in Piero Weiss, *Letters of Composers Through Six Centuries*. Philadelphia: Chilton, 1967, 62.

[29] Angelo Berardi, *Ragionamenti Musicali* (Bologna, 1681), 87.

[30] P. F. Tosi, *Observations on the Florid Song* (London: Wilcox, 1743), IX, xliv.

[31] Francesco Geminiani, *A Treatise of Good Taste in the Art of Musick* [1749] (New York: Da Capo Press, 1969), 4.

Germany

Today, as most of us don't recall much of seventeenth-century German opera, one is surprised by the range of emotions expected in a singer by Christoph Bernhard (1627–1692):

> One should take care that the voice is raised in moments of anger, and to the contrary dropped in moments of grief. Pain makes it pause; impatience hastens it. Happiness enlivens it. Desire emboldens it. Love renders it alert. Bashfulness holds it back. Hope strengthens it. Despair diminishes it. Fear keeps it down. Danger is fled with screams. If, however, a person faces up to danger, then his voice must reflect his daring and bravery.[32]

Johann Mattheson gives a similar catalog of emotions in opera,

> [Opera is the best medium of all for expressing] each and every emotion [*Affectus*] since there the composer has the grand opportunity to give free rein to his invention. With many surprises and with as much grace he there can, most naturally and diversely, portray love, jealousy, hatred, gentleness, impatience, lust, indifference, fear, vengeance, fortitude, timidity, magnanimity, horror, dignity, baseness, splendor, indigence, pride, humility, joy, laughter, weeping, mirth, pain, happiness, despair, storm, tranquility, even heaven and earth, sea and hell, together with all the actions in which men participate.[33]

Marpurg also writes of the great range of emotions which a musician must be prepared to deal with and implies that more is needed for good interpretation than the notes on paper, which reminds us of Mahler's famous statement, 'The best things in music are not found in the notes.' For the interpreter to find the composer's emotional intent, if it is not on the page (we have no notational symbols for emotions), Marpurg states that the musician needs powers of intuition.

> All musical expression has an affect or emotion for its foundation ... The musician has therefore a thousand parts to play, a thousand characters to assume at the composer's bidding. To what extraordinary undertakings our passions carry us! He who has the good fortune at all to experience the inspiration which lends greatness to poets, orators, artists, will be aware how vehemently and diversely our soul responds when it is given over to the emotions. Thus to interpret rightly every composition which is put in front of him a musician needs the utmost sensibility and the most felicitous powers of intuition.[34]

Johann David Heinichen (1683–1729) makes the very same point:

> It is impossible to find the tenderness of the soul of music with mere numeric changes of dead notes.[35]

---

[32] Quoted in Ellen Harris, 'Voices,' in *Performance Practice: Music after 1600* (New York: Norton, 1989), 110.

[33] Johann Mattheson, *Das Neu-Eröffnete Orchestre* (Hamburg, 1713), 167ff.

[34] F. W. Marpurg, *Der critische Musicus an der Spree* (Berlin), September 2, 1749.

[35] Johann David Heinichen, *General-Bass Treatise* [1711], quoted in George Buelow, *Thorough-Bass Accompaniment according to Johann David Heinichen* (Ann Arbor: UMI Research Press, 1986), 330.

It is as if Marpurg and Heinichen are mentioning that intuition was rather assumed of German performers of the Baroque. Do we help prepare students for this?

Perhaps another indication of the range of emotions which may have been common to German musicians during the Baroque is found in the definitions of familiar Italian 'tempi' markings. Do we teach *distress* when we teach Adagio?

> An *Adagio* indicates distress; a *Lamento* lamentation; a *Lento* relief; an *Andante* hope; an *Affetuoso* love; an *Allegro* comfort; a *Presto* eagerness ...[36]

In another place Mattheson writes more extensively on emotions in music. Love, he says, is an emotion frequently represented by music and in these cases the composer should 'consult his own experience.' Sadness is second only to love in its use by composers, no doubt, he observes, 'because almost everybody is unhappy.' It is for this reason that sacred music employs this emotion so effectively because it represents the 'penance and remorse, sorrow, contrition, lamentation and the recognition of our misery.'[37]

Here, Mattheson, in acknowledging the difficulty of his subject, makes a comment which reflects on the characteristics of the rational and non-rational hemispheres of the brain. He observes that although the emotions are like a bottomless sea, one can write very little about them.

Mattheson did not attribute as much influence on the emotions to tonality as one might have expected. It is interesting that in his review of tonality[38] he does refer to the association of the old Greek modes with the peoples for whom they were named.

> It is probably that the Dorians had a coarser, more manly, and deeper speaking voice than the Phrygians; and that on the other hand the Lydians sang finer and more effeminately than the others. For the Dorians were a modest, virtuous and peaceful people; the Phrygians however used more noise than foresight; whereas the Lydians, forefathers of the Tuscans, were everywhere described as sensual people.

He also observes that noticeable differences can still be found in the singing of the various areas of Italy during his time, not to mention in other countries. The Mixolydian mode he claims was invented by the lyric poetess, Sappho, to accommodate the fact that she could not sing low enough for the Lydian mode. The voice, Mattheson assures us,

> stemmed from quite natural causes in a young voluptuous widow, since the heat of passion in the long run dries out and contracts certain tubes so that they, especially in the throat, from a lack of sufficient humors cannot stretch adequately enough and cannot produce a low-pitched sound.[39]

---

36 Johann Mattheson, *Der vollkommene Capellmeister* [1739], trans. Ernest Harriss (Ann Arbor: UMI Research Press, 1981), II, xii, 34ff.

37 Ibid., I, iii, 52ff.

38 Ibid., I, ix.

39 Ibid., I, ix, 16ff.

Music is the Ruler of the Passions of the Soul 193

In his survey of tonality, Mattheson calls the long period of the Middle Ages 'the worst and most confused theory on modes that one at any time could have invented.'[40]

Mattheson devotes little space to the theories of tonality of his own era. He points out that music was now based on the triad and then states, based on his own observations, a very important truth which has recently been confirmed by clinical brain research. Basically, it is melody, not harmony, which communicates emotions to the listener. Mattheson writes that,

> the nature and character of each key, namely whether it is happy, sad, lovely, devout, etc., are actually matters of the science of melody.[41]

In his *Neu-Eröffnete Orchestre*, Mattheson discusses in more detail the natural emotions of specific scales, yielding some interesting conclusions.[42] The key of F-sharp minor, for example, he finds,

> is a key characterized by sadness, but a sadness more pensive and lovelorn than tragic and gloomy; it is a key that has about it a certain loneliness, an individuality, a misanthropy.

Mattheson was one of few Baroque writers who reflected some thought on the relationship of emotion and form. First, he finds emotional content in larger formal designs.

> If I hear the first part of a good overture, then I feel a special elevation of soul; the second expands the spirits with all joy; and if a serious ending follows, then everything is brought together to a normal restful conclusion.[43]

In another place, he considers vocal forms and in particular *chant* which he considers the epitome of 'noble simplicity.' Mattheson does not speak much of contemporary church vocal forms here, but does make a remarkably negative reference in passing to the motet style of the sixteenth century.

> [In the motet] there were no passions or affections to be seen for miles; no breaks to be found in the musical rhetoric, indeed rather caesuras in the middle of a word with an adjacent pause; no true melody; no true charm, indeed no meaning: all based on a few words which often meant little or nothing, such as *Salve, Regina Misericordiae*, and the like.[44]

Mattheson adds, in case anyone should think he has been too severe, that he can show contemporary examples of famous composers who are still writing works 'with all the above defects.' How, he wonders, can intelligent composers create such works and call them good?

---

[40] Ibid., I, ix, 23ff.

[41] Ibid., I, ix, 47.

[42] *Das Neu-Eröffnete Orchestre*, 231ff.

[43] *Der vollkommene Capellmeister*, II, xii, 34ff.

[44] Ibid., II, xiii, 72.

He makes this point in another place, now calling the failed composers of the old polyphonic style, *Mathematici*. This passage is especially remarkable for his intuition that this idea might return in the future. It did, of course, with serial music, but Mattheson can rest in peace for that idea also failed.

> I have occupied myself with music, practical as well as theoretical, with great earnestness and ardor for over half a century already: I have also met many very learned *Mathematici* in this not insubstantial time who thought they made new musical wonders out of their old, logical writings; but they have, God knows! always failed miserably. On the other hand, I have quite certainly and very often experienced that not a single famous actor, musician, nor composer, not only in my time but as far as I can remember having read or heard about, has been able to construct even a simple melody which was of any value on the feeble foundations of mathematics or geometry ... What will happen in the future is yet to be seen.

The nature of the *aria* is to express a 'great emotion,'[45] whereas the *cavata* (madrigals, sonnets and poems) aim rather for a 'penetrating observation.' Mattheson's discussion of the *recitative* reflects his concern that it must have as much emotion, with as clearly defined accents, as the principal song. He recognizes its greater rhythmic freedom, but adds 'the recitative has a beat; but it does not use it.'[46]

Mattheson also gives us a wonderful observation which suggests the presence of contemplative listeners at this time in Germany.

> Whoever pays attention can see in the features of an attentive listener what he perceives in his heart.[47]

He also discusses the emotions relative to the style of music used in the church, theater and in the chamber. For example, regarding the use of the instrumental style in the church, Mattheson cautions that such music must have 'a special solemnity and a serious quality ... lest it smack of a loosely-united overture.' But he does not mean by this that instrumental church music must be dark in mood, on the contrary joyful instrumental music can contribute to the atmosphere for devotion.

> Joy does not contradict seriousness; for then all mirth would have to consist of jesting. A cheerful disposition is best disposed for devotion; where such is not to be done mechanically or simply in a trance.

---

45 Ibid., II, xiii, 56, adds that the principal affect of opera is 'intense love.'

> However, it invariably excites a large amount of disquiet and emotionalism with jealousy, sadness, hope, plea, vengeance, rage, fury, etc. I really would seek the most important character of an opera in disquiet itself, if that would not make me suspect.

46 Ibid., II, xiii, 22.

47 Ibid., II, xii, 34ff.

Matheson decided it more important to think of the distinctions 'high, middle and low' styles, or 'noble, moderate or trifling,' than mere classifications of church, theater or chamber. Thus, one can speak of 'high' as meaning something different in different mediums, as for example, 'what is *elevated* in the theater is very different from what is elevated in dinner music.' Or, one can speak of high, medium and low within a single medium. In the case of church music, for example, Mattheson suggests that,

> Divine majesty, heavenly splendor, rapture and magnificence are naturally required for the *elevated* style; Devotion, contemplation, etc., belong to the *middle* style; while Repentance, supplient entreaties, etc., stand under the banner of the *low* style.[48]

This led him to write at more length on the relationship of various emotions and his categories of high, medium and low styles of music. This passage reflects how seriously the entire question of the emotions in music had become.

> Among those emotions which one commonly attributes to the high style are many which do not deserve to be called high at all, in the good sense. For, what can be lower than anger, fear, vengeance, despair, etc. Beating, boasting, snoring is indeed not true nobility. Arrogance is itself only an inflating of the soul, and actually requires more bombast than nobility for expression: now the most haughty are again unfailingly the most angry, in their feelings one debility after another takes the helm. For, though anger will have the *appearance* of being action of a great spirit, still it springs in *fact* from an effeminate heart: one would have to consider it then a special, holy, and just bureaucratic wrath, which nevertheless should punish and discipline, without any indignation.
>
> Great and valiant spirits are forbearing; but small and timid souls can endure nothing. Frivolous people are easily provoked and are as quickly moved to anger, as is the turning around of weathercocks or weather vanes on the roofs. In short, anger is a ridiculous emotion. It sounds quite base and does not entail an elevated presentation.
>
> Fear and fright are indeed probably the most foolish emotions in the world, and really deserve nothing so little as something of the elevated in their expression. Alas! One finds these unfortunate impulses in all creatures, even in those which seem to have no other emotion and are scorned. Nothing can however be lower than miserable human vengeance, which has so little noble in it that it finds a place only in the most depraved hearts.
>
> If we come to despair, then that is the extreme to which fear can lead: hence one would have to set it on the highest peak of sadness if it really is to have something of nobility. The Italians therefore rightly call all malicious and dangerous people, whose spirit is dejected and lost, *Huomini tristi*.
>
> I will meanwhile not deny that something of strength, turbulence, passion and ecstasy is required if one desires to express properly these and similar passions in music; just as the emotions of impetuosity, vengeance, etc., are so constituted that they, according to the difference in station, have the appearance of a high proud quality, although they deny its strength. Here one must also admit that this presumptuous arrogance occasionally requires something of the stately in oratory and music (yet greatly different from the true type); but which is not at all of the mighty, majestic, etc.
>
> Shrieking and grumbling is suitable in anger and quarreling; an uneven, broken, shocking, trembling style in fright; something of daring with vengeance; something frantic with despair; something turgid with arrogance; as long as it did not come out too naturally and arouse disgust: but all of this has nothing to do with the elevated style.

---
[48] Ibid., I, x, 10.

But whoever would want to relegate devotion, patience, diligence, desire, etc., to the middle style might be considered only as moderately devout, moral, patient, diligent and desirous. Indeed, desire corresponds in very many ways with the highest and most emphatic emotion in and outside of the world, namely love, how then can it be relegated to the middle of the road? It is true that desire is according to the nature of the desired object also small or large, high or low, and so on; yet it is the same with almost all emotions.

On the one hand diligence can have much of nobleness, on the other it can have something trifling as the goal. In the last case it would be a work in the dark so to speak (*obscura diligentia*) and would not even deserve to stand in the middle, but rather at the low end. There is nothing at all high-flown about patience, though always something noble: and everyone knows that devotion serves to lift the spirit.

Finally, common dance songs either all, or at least most of them, would indeed have to embody something of the beggarly, slavish, cowardly, disconsolate, base, boorish, stupid, and clumsy, if these qualities of the low style were to be found in them. Low and base are again very different, and if we indeed should exclude from this the most nonsensical peasant dances, though not the clever *Land-Tanze*, *Country Dances*, then for all of that there probably would be no one who would expect beggars in a spirited minuet, slaves in a happy rigaudon, cowards in an heroic entré, despair in a lusty gavotte, or base spirits in a magnificent chaconne.

Drinking songs and lullabies, amorous little pieces, etc., must not always be indiscriminately called trifling: if they are done quite naturally they are often more pleasing and have greater impact than high and mighty concerti and stately overtures. The former no less require their master in their own way than the latter. Yet, what am I to say? Our composers are all kings; or of royal descent... They do not fret over trivialities.[49]

Finally, we wish to include two contemporary observations regarding ideas of Bach on the emotions. A student of Bach reports,

> As concerns the playing of chorales, I was instructed by my teacher Kapellmeister Bach, who is still living, not to play the songs merely offhand but according to the emotions of the words.[50]

Every young music student studies these Bach chorales in his harmony classes, but where is the teacher who discusses the aspect which Bach himself emphasized in the above quotation?

Second, from Forkel we have the interesting insight that even the instrument was a consideration for Bach in this regard.

> Bach preferred the Clavichord to the Harpsichord, which, though susceptible of great variety of tone, seemed to him lacking in soul.[51]

---

49 *Der vollkommene Capellmeister*, I, x, 22ff.
50 Johann Ziegler (1746), quoted in Hans T. David and Arthur Mendel, *The Bach Reader* (New York: Norton, 1966), 237.
51 Quoted in Robert Donnington, *The Interpretation of Early Music* (New York, 1964), 576.

France

During the Baroque in France we find some similar accounts of individual performances by performers filled with emotion. A manuscript by Diderot recounts a performance of opera arias in a café by a singer, the nephew of Rameau. When the young man finished singing one aria, he stood,

> worn out, exhausted, like a man emerging from a deep sleep or a prolonged reverie, he stood motionless, dumb, petrified. He kept looking around him like a man who has lost his way and wants to know where he is. He waited for returning strength and wits, wiping his face with an absent-minded gesture.[52]

A French critic in 1702, similarly described a violinist as one,

> who was so carried away with the piece that he was playing that he not only martyred his instrument but also himself. No longer master of his own being, he became so transported that he gyrated and hopped around like someone overcome by a demon.[53]

An account of a singer finds her to be not a demon, but an Italian!

> She caused a great sensation, but it was short-lived: several people concluded that she could not even sing properly, for this *is quite in the Italian tradition*, and she pulled the most horrible faces. She seemed to be suffering from convulsions.[54]

This last account touches on the most widely discussed topic in contemporary French music criticism. Quite apart from the debate at the time over French vs Italian opera, was the debate over what many Frenchmen heard as excessive emotions in Italian singing. However, there were a number of writers, such as Mersenne, who seem to suggest the native singers should be more like the Italians.

> The Italian [singers] observe several things in their solos of which ours are deprived, since they represent as much as they can the passions and the emotions of the soul and the mind, for example, choler, wrath, spite, rage, lapses of the heart, and several passions, with a violence so peculiar that one would almost judge that they felt the same emotions which they represent when singing, whereas we French are content with charming the ear, and use a constant mildness in our songs, which hinders their vigor.[55]

---

52 Quoted in *Rameau's Nephew and Other Works*, trans. Jacques Barzun (Garden City: Doubleday, 1956), 69.
53 Quoted in Hans-Peter Schmitz, *Die Kunst der Verzierung im 18. Jahrhundert* (Kassel: Barenreiter, 1955), 12.
54 Quoted in David Maland, *Culture and Society in Seventeenth-Century France* (New York: Scribner's, 1970), 80ff.
55 *Marin Mersenne: Fourth Treatise of the Harmonie Universelle*, ed. Robert Williams (Rochester: Eastman School of Music, unpublished dissertation, 1972), IV, vi, 6.

In another place, Mersenne returns to this failure among French singers.

> We must acknowledge that the accents of the passions are lacking most often in French songs, since our singers are content with tickling the ear and with pleasing by their affectations, without concerning themselves with exciting the passions of their listeners, according to the subject and the intention of the text.[56]

Another philosopher, François Raguenet, writing in 1702, recommends the Italian's sincere use of emotions and at the same time gives us an excellent glimpse into the nature of the impact he felt the emotions in music should have on the listener.

> As the Italians are much more brisk than the French, so are they more sensible of the passions and consequently express them more lively in all their productions. If a storm or rage is to be described in a symphony, their notes give us so natural an idea of it that our souls can hardly receive a stronger impression from the reality than they do from the description; everything is so brisk and piercing, so impetuous and affecting, that the imagination, the senses, the soul, and the body itself are all betrayed into a general transport; it is impossible not to be borne down with the rapidity of these movements. A symphony of furies shakes the soul; it undermines and overthrows it in spite of all its care; the artist himself, whilst he is performing it, is seized with an unavoidable agony; he tortures his violin; he racks his body; he is no longer master of himself, but is agitated like one possessed with an irresistible motion.
>
> If, on the other side, the symphony is to express a calm and tranquility, which requires a quite different style, they however execute it with an equal success. Here the notes descend so low that the soul is swallowed with them in the profound abyss. Every string of the bow is of an infinite length, lingering on a dying sound which decays gradually until at last it absolutely expires. Their symphonies of sleep insensibly steal the soul from the body and so suspend its faculties and operations that, being bound up, as it were, in the harmony that entirely possesses and enchants it, it is as dead to everything else as if all its powers were captivated by a real sleep.[57]

There was one French philosopher, Charles Batteux (1713–1780), who could not quite convince himself that the emotions communicated by any of the arts were the real thing. In one place he states these emotions are imaginary, indeed he writes that 'Art is only created to deceive.'[58] In another place he begins with what appears to be genuine acknowledgement of the importance of the emotions communicated in music, only to decide in the last paragraph that they have no significance.

> It is true, you may say, that a melodic line can express certain passions: love, for instance, or joy, or sadness. But for every passion that can be identified there are a thousand others that cannot be put into words.

---

56 Ibid., IV, vi, 8. Mersenne, aware of the inherited problem we have of a notational system without symbols for emotions, suggests some alternatives, such as a series of up to eight dots over each note to represent specific emotions or the use of different colors by the composer in his manuscript.

57 Francois Raguenet, 'Parallele des Italiens et des Francais,' (1702), in Oliver Strunk, *Source Readings in Music History* (New York: Norton, 1950), 478ff.

58 Charles Batteux (1713–1780), *Les beaux-arts reduits a un meme principe* [Paris, 1746], quoted in Peter le Huray and James Day, *Music and Aesthetics in the Eighteenth and Early-Nineteenth Centuries* (Cambridge: Cambridge University Press, 1981), 48.

> That is indeed so, but does it follow that these are pointless? It is enough that they are felt; they do not have to be named. The heart has its own understanding that is independent of words. When it is touched it has understood everything. Moreover, just as there are great things that words cannot reach, so there are subtle things that words cannot capture, above all things that concern the feelings.
>
> We may conclude then that although music may be the most exactly calculated art in respect of its tones, and the most geometrically structured in respect of its consonances, even with these qualities it may well have no significance whatever. The analogy might be with a prism, which produces the finest colors but no picture, or with a color keyboard the colors and color sequences of which might amuse the eye, but which would certainly weary the mind.[59]

There was no doubt in the mind of David de Flurance Rivault that the emotions in music were real.

> A well-measured voice can rejoice an afflicted person ... The voice can sometimes bring forth contentment and love; sometimes it can carry away the minds of the hearers to rage and fury: and then again quieten these fumes and calm impassioned souls.[60]

There can be found indications that some felt the emotions in music were genetically implanted. Even Batteux wrote that while ordinary speech is invented by institutions, gesture and music 'contain a language that we all know upon being born.'[61] Du Bos (1670–1742) agreed:

> All these sounds, as we have already shown, have a wonderful power to move us because they are the signs of the passions that are the work of nature herself, from whence they have derived their energy. Spoken words, on the other hand are only arbitrary symbols of the passions. The spoken word only derives its meaning and value from man-made conventions and it has only limited geographical currency.[62]

Perhaps it was another facet of the same suspicion, that there was something natural or genetic about music, that we begin to see even among the French, who loved to analyze and create rules for all the arts, a tendency now by some to suggest that in the end it might be OK to forget the rules in favor of the stronger claims of nature and emotional communication. We see this in Brossard's advice to singers:

> This is a manner of singing which holds as much of declamation as of song, as if one declaimed in singing, or as if one sang in declaiming, hence where one has more attention to expressing the passion than to following exactly a timed measure.[63]

---

59 Ibid., 50.

60 'L'art d'embellir,' quoted in Frances Yates, *The French Academies of the Sixteenth Century* (Nendeln: Kraus, 1968), 280, fn. 5.

61 Batteux, *Les beaux-arts reduits a un meme principe*, 260ff.

62 Jean-Baptiste Du Bos, *Reflexions critiques sur la posie et sur la peinture* [Paris, 1719], quoted in Peter le Huray and James Day, *Music and Aesthetics in the Eighteenth and Early-Nineteenth Centuries* (Cambridge: Cambridge University Press, 1981), 18.

63 Sebastien de Brossard, Dictionaire de Musique (Paris, 1703), 'Recitativo.'

Something of this nature was no doubt intended by Couperin when he observed,

> The fact is we write a thing differently from the way in which we execute it.[64]

Rameau makes this point several times, first with regard to composing:

> While composing music is not the time to recall the rules which might hold our genius in bondage. We must have recourse to the rules only when our genius and our ear seem to deny what we are seeking.[65]

Rameau was absolutely correct that the listener as well must not hear the rules, not listen to music with the left hemisphere, so to speak.

> We must not think but let ourselves be carried away by the feeling which the music inspires; without our thinking at all, this feeling will become the basis of our judgment.[66]
>
> ......
>
> To enjoy the effects of music fully, we must completely lose ourselves in it; to judge it, we must relate it to the source through which we are affected by it. This source is nature. Nature endows us with the feeling that moves us in all our musical experiences; we might call her gift *instinct*. Let us allow instinct to inform our judgments, let us see what mysteries it unfolds to us before we pronounce our verdicts.[67]

ENGLAND

In England during the Baroque we do not find the same degree of enthusiasm in the discussion of music and emotion as we do on the continent. Samuel Butler, in his character sketch of a typical musician, makes identity with the emotions a form of treason.

> Is his own Siren, that turns himself into a beast with musick of his own making. His perpetual study to raise *passion* has utterly debased his *reason*; and as music is wont to set false values upon things, the constant use of it has rendered him a stranger to all true ones ... This puts him into the condition of a traitor ... And therefore a musician, that makes it his constant employment, is like one that does nothing but make love, that is half mad, fantastic and ridiculous to those that are unconcerned. Cupid strings his bow with the strings of an instrument, and wounds hearts through the ear.[68]

---

[64] François Couperin, *L'Art de toucher* [Paris, 1717] (reprinted Wiesbaden: Breitkopf & Hartel, 1933), 23.

[65] Rameau, *Le Nouveau Systeme de musique theorique* [1726], quoted in Morgenstern, *Composers on Music* (New York: Pantheon, 1956), 41.

[66] Jean Philippe Rameau, *Observations sur notre instinct pour la musique et sur son principe*, in Morgenstern, *Composers on Music*, 44.

[67] Jean Philippe Rameau, *Le Nouveau Systeme de musique theorique*, 43.

[68] Samuel Butler, *Characters*, 'A Musitian.'

We are surprised to find the great philosopher, Hobbes, in his *The Leviathan*, in which he attempts to organize all 'subjects of knowledge,' separate music and emotion entirely. Music, he says, is the study of sounds, but the study of the emotions is Ethics![69]

But for William Congreve (1670–1729) there was no question about the power of the emotions in music. 'Musick,' he concluded, 'is as dangerous as Gun Powder.'[70] James Harris (1709–1780) also makes a simple acknowledgement to the power of music to excite the emotions.

> There are various affections which may be raised by the power of music. These are sounds to make us cheerful, or sad; martial or tender; and so of almost every other affection which we feel.[71]

Lord Chesterfield, who did not particularly respect music to begin with, reminds his son that the communication of emotion in music requires a faithful performance.

> The best compositions of Corelli, if ill executed and played out of tune, instead of touching, as they do when well performed, would only excite the indignation of the hearers, when murdered by an unskilled performer.[72]

One subject which does receive more attention in England than on the continent is the notion that individual instruments may be associated with individual emotions. The well-known John Dryden (1631–1700), in his most famous Ode, the 'A Song for St. Cecilia's Day, 1687,' after declaring, 'What Passion cannot Musick raise and quell!,' presents a remarkable survey of the emotional qualities which he associates with various musical instruments, expressed in his most vivid choice of words.

> The TRUMPETS loud clangor
> Excites us to arms
> With shrill notes of anger …
>
> ……
>
> The double double double beat
> Of the thundering DRUM …
>
> ……
>
> The soft complaining FLUTE
> In dying Notes discovers
> The woes of hopeless lovers,
> Whose dirge is whispered by the warbling LUTE.
>
> ……
>
> Sharp VIOLINS proclaim
> Their jealous pangs, and desperation,
> Fury, frantick indignation,
> Depth of pains, and height of passion …

---

69 *The Leviathan*, I, ix.

70 'Amendments of Mr. Collier,' in *The Complete Works of William Congreve* (New York: Russell & Russell, 1964), III, 206.

71 *Three Treatises* (1744, on music, painting and poetry), VI, iff.

72 Earl of Chesterfield, letter to his son, July 9, 1750.

A humorous examination of the emotional character of various instruments is found in the *Tatler* for 1 April 1710. Addison mentions a painting, *The Consort of Musick*, by Zampieri, which pictured famous painters, each holding an instrument which corresponded to their character. Addison then speculates how the various instruments might also serve as metaphors for styles of conversation, in the process offering his view of the individual character of the various instruments. The percussion, for example, he finds are like 'Blusterers in Conversation,' with lots of noise but 'seldom any wit, humor, or good breeding.' Nevertheless they are appropriate to the ignorant and to ladies of little taste. The lute he considers the opposite to the percussion, having a soft sound, 'exquisitely sweet, and very low, easily drowned in a multitude of instruments.' The lute, then, corresponds to 'men of fine genius, uncommon reflection, great affability … and good taste.'

The trumpet, an instrument he finds of 'no compass of Musick, or variety of sound,' having only four or five notes, although it is pleasing enough, he equates with the gentleman of fashionable education and breeding, yet who are shallow, with weak judgment and little understanding.

Regarding the violin, it is interesting that Addison first thinks of its use in improvisation.

> Violins are the lively, forward, importunate wits, that distinguish themselves by the flourishes of imagination, sharpness of repartee, glances of satyr, and bear away the upper part in every consort. I cannot however but observe, That when a man is not disposed to hear Musick, there is not a more disagreeable sound in harmony than that of a violin.

Addison associates every sensible, 'true-born Britain' with the Bass-Viol, as 'Men of rough sense, and unpolished parts … but who sometimes break out with an agreeable bluntness, unexpected wit, and surly pleasantry.' Musically, he finds this instrument one which 'grumbles in the bottom of the consort, with a surly masculine sound, strengthens the harmony, and tempers the sweetness of the several instruments that play along with it.'

The 'Rural Wits,' which he associates with horns, he is not quite sure should be permitted in polite society. The bagpipe, with its perpetual repetition of a few notes over a drone, he associates with the 'dull, heavy, tedious story-tellers.'

The above comments, Addison admits, are concerned only with 'male instruments,' the female ones he promises to discuss in a later issue. In the meantime, however, he warns the reader to,

> make a narrow search into his life and conversation, and upon his leaving any company, to examine himself seriously, whether he has behaved himself in it like a drum or trumpet, a violin or a Bass-Viol; and accordingly endeavor to mend his Musick for the future.

As he promised, Addison discusses the 'female' instruments in his issue of 11 April 1710. The flute he finds an instrument with small compass, sweet and soft, which lulls and soothes the ear and raises 'a most agreeable passion between transport and indolence.' This reminds him of the conversation of a 'mild and amiable woman, that has nothing in it very elevated, or at the same time any thing mean or trivial.' The flageolet, on the other hand, is like a young lady 'entertaining the company with tart ill-natured observations, pert fancies, and little turns which she imagined to be full of life and spirit.' Curiously, Addison also considers the oboe to be part of the flute family.

> I must here observe that the Hautboy is the most perfect of the flute-species, which, with all the sweetness of the sound, has a greater strength and variety of notes; though at the same time I must observe, that the hautboy in one sex is as scarce as the harpsichord in the other.

The 'Prude,' characterized by 'the gravity of her censures and composure of her voice,' he associates with the 'ancient serious matron-like instrument the Virginal.' The 'Romantic instrument called a Dulcimer,' he finds a pleasant rural instrument, as is also the hornpipe, while the Welsh harp is a 'Female Historian.' It is interesting that he includes among the female instruments, the timpani.

> But the most sonorous part of our consort was a She-Drum, or (as the vulgar call it) a Kettle-Drum, who accompanied her discourse with motions of the body, tosses of the head, and brandishes of the fan. Her Musick was loud, bold and masculine. Every thump she gave alarmed the company, and very often set somebody or other in it a blushing.

The obsession of the Baroque musicians and philosophers on the subject of music communicating emotions in a stroke cleared away a thousand years' efforts by the Church to make music instead a branch of mathematics. Now the stage was set for the most emotion filled masterpieces ever composed, the music of the Classical Period and the nineteenth century. By the nineteenth century hardly anyone could question the powerful association between the emotions and music.[73] The greatest minds now offer testimony to the fact that emotion is the central purpose of music. Let them speak for themselves:

Berlioz:
   The prevailing characteristics of my music are passionate expression, intense ardor, rhythmical animation, and unexpected turns.[74]

Liszt:
   Music embodies feeling.[75]

Chopin:
   A long time ago I decided that my universe will be the soul and heart of man.[76]

---

73   A few philosophers were still inclined to think of the emotions as somewhat vague (Hegel) or just mere sensation (Kant).
74   *Memoirs*.
75   'Berlioz and his "Harold" Symphony,' *Neue Zeitschrift für Musik* (1855) XLIII.
76   Letter to Delphine Potocka. Chopin's last words were reported to be, 'Play Mozart in memory of me.'

Verdi:
  I should compose with utter confidence a subject that set my blood going, even though it were condemned by all other artists as anti-musical.[77]

Paul Dukas:
  Be it laughter or tears, feverish passion or religious ecstasy, nothing, in the category of human feelings, is a stranger to music.[78]

Max Reger:
  Music, in and by itself, should generate a flow of pure emotion without the least tinge of extraneous rationalization.[79]

Ravel:
  Music, I feel, must be emotional first and intellectual second.[80]

Wagner:
  Music is the speech of Passion.[81]

Leo Tolstoy:
  Music is the shorthand of emotion.[82]

Clara Schumann, on Brahms:
  It is really moving to see him sitting at the piano, with his interesting young face which becomes transfigured when he plays.[83]

Arthur Rubinstein:
  When I play, I make love—it is the same thing.[84]

Tchaikovsky:
  Here are things which can bring tears to our eyes. I will only mention the adagio of the D minor string quintet. No one else has ever known as well how to interpret so exquisitely in music the sense of resigned and inconsolable sorrow. Every time Laub played the adagio I had to hide in the farthest corner of the concert-room, so that others might not see how deeply this music affected me.[85]

---

[77] Letter of 1854.

[78] Quoted in Nat Shapiro, *An Encyclopedia of Quotations About Music* (New York: Da Capo, 1978), 194.

[79] Letter to Adalbert Lindner (June 6, 1891)

[80] Quoted in Shapiro, *An Encyclopedia of Quotations About Music*, 197.

[81] Wagner, 'Judaism in Music.'

[82] Quoted in Shapiro, *An Encyclopedia of Quotations About Music*, 199.

[83] Clara Schumann, Diary (September, 1853)

[84] *Arthur Rubinstein—Love of Life* (film, 1975).

[85] Letter to von Meck, March 16, 1878.

Kierkegaard:
> I am in love with Mozart like a young girl. Immortal Mozart! I owe you everything; it is thanks to you that I lost my reason, that my soul was awestruck in the very depths of my being ... I have you to thank that I did not die without having loved.[86]

Some three thousand years of experience were not enough to discourage radical new departures during the twentieth century. One new school of composers championed 'objective' music, which had never ever existed before. Their credo was that music can be understood only as C♯s and B♭s, and some significant voices attempted to make their case.

Stravinsky:
> I consider that music is, by its very nature, powerless to express anything at all, whether a feeling, an attitude of mind, a psychological mood, a phenomenon of nature, etc ... If, as is nearly always the case, music appears to express something, this is only an illusion, and not a reality.[87]

Hindemith:
> Music cannot express the composer's feelings.[88]

What can one say about such comments? In part they represent a brief moment when some composers were trying to make music rational and like many musicians today no doubt they felt obligated to discuss music in rational terms. Their own music, of course, is often quite emotional. So, what were they thinking? We choose to ignore what they say, but praise their music.

One topic, while by no means new, began to receive more attention during the late nineteenth and twentieth centuries. This is the ethical question regarding the assimilation of the music by the performer, that is, does the listener hear the composer's emotions or the performer's? The issue is this: Beethoven is dead and cannot speak for himself, other than the notes on paper he has left behind—notes written in a notational system which lacks any symbols for the emotions. Therefore, if Beethoven is to come alive he can only do so through the live performer. This only happens if the performer becomes the music, if the present-tense emotions become his, and cannot happen if the performer merely reproduces what is on paper.

The great conductor, Herbert von Karajan, addressed the solution of this problem by quoting a story told him by a priest who had studied the Buddhist faith in the Far East.

> One day a young man went to the guru to seek his help. The guru sent him into his hut to meditate on his parents. The young man came out again. He couldn't concentrate. The guru v suggested he mediate on a rose. Again, failure. So the guru asked him, 'What is the thing that is dearest to you?' And the young man said it was a buffalo that lived on his farm. 'So, go into my hut and meditate on that,' said the guru. After a very long time the young man had not reappeared. Eventually the guru

---

[86] *Either/Or* (1843).

[87] *Chronicle of My Life* (English edition), 91ff.

[88] *A Composer's World*.

was so worried he called into the hut to see what was happening. The young man said he was fine. 'So why do you not come out?' asked the guru. 'I have the problem,' the young man replied, 'that I cannot maneuver my horns through your narrow door.'[89]

What this means in music and how the performer accomplishes this is a topic addressed by Bruno Walter.

> If a pianist, in Beethoven's E-flat major Concerto, wishes to put himself fully at the service of Beethoven's genius ... this does not imply an act of servile self-negation. On the contrary, he will only be successful in his endeavor if he freely unfolds his own self, to the limits of its capacity. In brinigng to life the fire, the grace, the melancholy, the passion of the composer's work, what can he call upon but his own fire, his own grace, melancholy and passions?[90]

The French composer, Charles Gounod, suggests the performer becomes one with the ideas of the composer.

> The conductor is the ambassador of the master's thought; he ... ought to be the living expression, the faithful mirror, the incorruptible depositary of it.[91]

Von Karajan advised that the conductor must be able to 'see yourself in a great work of art.'[92] Carlo Maria Giulini agreed.

> An interpreter, in the moment he is involved in a great expression of art, becomes himself the composer.

None of these great artists, of course, believed that the resultant emotions were found anywhere but in the music itself. But, taking that as the starting point, one might ask, are there limits to the emotions an interpreter can find in a score? The answer appears to be only the limits of the interpreter's own insight and experience. As an illustration of what a great artist can find in the score, consider the following thoughts by Wagner upon reflecting on a single fermata symbol in the fifth symphony of Beethoven.

> Now let us suppose the voice of Beethoven to have cried from the grave to a conductor: 'Hold thou my fermata long and terribly! I wrote no fermata for jest or from bepuzzlement, haply to think out my further move; but the same full tone I mean to be squeezed dry in my Adagio for utterance of sweltering emotion, I cast among the rushing figures of my passionate Allegro, if need be, a paroxysm of joy and horror. Thus shall its life be drained to the last blood-drop; then do I part the waters of my ocean, and bare the depths of its abyss; or curb the flocking herd of clouds, dispel the whirling web of mist, and open up a glimpse into the pure blue firmament, the sun's irradiate eye. For this I set

---

89 Richard Osborne, *Conversations with Von Karajan* (New York: Harper & Row, 1989), 103.

90 Bruno Walter, *Of Music and Music-Making* (New York: Norton, 1957), 23.

91 *Memoires.*

92 *Conversations with Von Karajan*, 126.

fermate in my Allegros, notes entering of a sudden, and long held out. And mark thou what a definite thematic aim I had with this sustained E-flat, after a storm of three short notes, and what I mean to say by all the like held notes that follow.'[93]

---

[93] *Wagner's Prose Works*, trans. William Ashton Ellis (New York: Broude), IV, 312.

On the Doctrine of the Affections

All musical expression has an affect or emotion for its foundation.
F. W. Marpurg (1749)

*Music of all the arts has the most influence on the passions
and the legislator should give it the greatest encouragement.*
Napoleon

THE INTELLECTUAL SUBJECT known as 'The Doctrine of the Affections' is primarily associated with German music theorists of the Baroque. It was above all a manifestation of Humanism in music, the movement to return music to its ancient role of expressing emotion and away from the fifteen centuries of Church dogma which associated music instead with mathematics.

Humanism in music had its roots in the rediscovery during the late Middle Ages of the 'lost' writings by the ancient Greek and Roman philosophers, which the Church had attempted to destroy but which had survived in Arabic translations. Following this one can trace growing interest in, and enthusiasm for, the role of emotions in music during the Renaissance and an almost total absorption with this idea during the Baroque (modern music history texts notwithstanding). The Doctrine of the Affections was part of this last chapter, the Baroque, and it was a study which attempted to discover exactly, in a physical sense, how music communicated specific emotions to the listener.

As the philosophers who promoted Humanism in music frequently based their ideas on the ancient writers, so too did those whom we associate with the doctrine of the affections. For this reason, it might be helpful for the modern reader if we briefly review some of the weird-science—excuse us, physiological terms—which they discussed.

Hippocrates (fifth century BC) of the Greek island of Cos, the traditional 'Father of Medicine,' believed that man's health was influenced by four fluids, known as the 'Humors,' blood, phlegm, choler (yellow bile) and melancholy (black bile).[1] It was his idea that good health resulted in a balance of these four fluids. If there was an imbalance, then he treated the patient with broth of lizard, goat eye or whatever he deemed necessary to bring the fluids into balance.

The Roman doctor, Galen (130–201 AD) extended the idea of the four fluids by concluding they also influenced the man's personality. Thus he equates 'blood' with a sanguine personality, amorous, happy, one who enjoys laughter, music and has a passionate and generous disposition; phlegm (phlegmatic), one who is sluggish, dull, pale and cowardly; choler, or choleric,

---

[1] These fluids were also associated by the basic elements so important to even earlier philosophers, hence blood = air, phlegm = water, yellow bile = fire and black bile = earth.

a violent person quick to anger and melancholy, a melancholic or depressed, gluttonous, lazy and sentimental personality. Now the concept became known as the 'Four Temperaments,' instead of the 'Humors.' It was the doctor's job, if he found an imbalance, to treat through the use of emetics, cathartics, purgatives or by bloodletting. These views were held for centuries. George Washington was subjected to bloodletting, and was killed by the procedure because his doctor mistakenly thought the human body held twelve instead of six quarts.

During the next fifteen centuries there were numerous new 'sciences' which branched off from the 'Temperaments.' One of the evolutions of this theory in the eighteenth century was the quack-science of 'phrenology,' founded by Franz Joseph Gall (1758–1828). Through this 'science' the practitioner concluded the dominant personality traits were reflected in the shape of the skull. The practice of this study resulted in Haydn, Mozart and Beethoven being buried without their heads!

One evolution of the Temperaments was to combine them with astrology, with three zodiac symbols assigned to each temperament.

Another label frequently used by the proponents of the doctrine of the affections was 'the Passions.' This idea had its origin in the philosophy of the ancient Stoics.[2] After first dividing human ends into the good and the bad, the Stoics found four basic passions: desire, fear, delight and distress. Secondary passions were related to these four, for example under desire we find anger, sexual desire and love of riches, etc. For the Stoics these passions were actual movements of the soul and that the soul was a physical entity which could be explained by physical characteristics. The Stoic sought to be free of the passions through his control of the movements of the soul.

The Medieval Church tied this idea to the basic emotions, finding among the 'concupiscible appetite' joy or delight, sadness, desire, aversion or abhorrence and love and hatred, and among the 'irascible appetite,' hope and despair, courage and fear and anger. The Church, of course, taught that the duty of the Christian was to keep the passions under subjugation.

As we have mentioned above, the Doctrine of the Affections is associated with the Baroque Period. However, a few Renaissance references suggest that the basic ideas were being discussed earlier. We must assume that the 'humors' were sufficiently known to the theater audience that Lope de Vega could make fun of them in his *Fuente Ovejuna*:

BARRILDO. There's no such thing as love.
LAURENCIA. In general? That's too sweeping.
BARRILDO. Yes, and stupid.
   The world itself could never last without it.
MENGO. I can't philosophize—wish I could read!
   But if the elements from which our bodies
   draw sustenance—phlegm, melancholy, blood,
   and choler too—are in perpetual conflict,
   it stands to reason.

---

[2] For more, see Plato 'Meno,' 87cff and 'Euthydemus,' 278eff.

> BARRILDO. Mengo, all the world,
>   here and up there, is perfect harmony,
>   and harmony is love, for love is concord.³

The French philosopher, Jean Bodin (1530–1596) was particularly interested in the influence of geography on the humors. In one place, speaking of the black bile, he makes a reference to music therapy in Germany.

> In Lower Germany there are almost none who are mad from black bile, but rather from blood; this type of lunacy the common man calls the disease of St. Vitus, which impels them to exultation and senseless dancing. Musicians imitate this on the lyre; afterwards they make use of more serious rhythms and modes, doing this gradually until by the gravity of the mode and the rhythm the madmen are clearly soothed.⁴

The Italian philosopher, Girolamo Cardano (1501–1576), represents an early example of one attempting to associate specific musical gestures with specific emotions.

> The first rule of artistic music: there is nothing more efficacious for pleasure than proper imitation. It has three parts: manner [*modus*], sense [*sensus*], and sound [*sonus*]. These three do not always coincide. For example, if one imitates the song of small birds, it is not necessary to imitate the sense, for their chirping has no meaning, but only their sound and manner …
>
> We imitate by sense when there is great emotion, such as in the four moods of sorrow, joy, tranquility, and excitement …
>
> A mood of commiseration proceeds in music in slow and serious notes by dropping downward suddenly from a high range. This imitates the manner of those who weep, for at first they wail in a very high and clear voice and then they end by dropping into a very low and rather muffled groan.⁵

The German philosopher, Henry Agrippa (1486–1536), found it quite logical to associate the humors with the 'music of the spheres.'

> Moreover, they that followed the number of the elements, did affirm, that the four kinds of music do agree to them, and also to the four humors, and did think the Dorian music to be consonant to the Water and phlegm, the Phrygian to choler and Fire, the Lydian to blood and Air, the mixed-Lydian to melancholy and Earth: others respecting the number and virtue of the heavens, have attributed the Dorian to the Sun, the Phrygian to Mars, the Lydian to Jupiter, the mixed-Lydian to Saturn, the hypo-Phrygian to Mercury, the hypo-Lydian to Venus, the hypo-Dorian to the Moon, the hypo-mixed-Lydian to the fixed stars …⁶

---

3   Act I, 79.

4   Jean Bodin, *Method for the Easy Comprehension of History*, trans. Beatrice Reynolds (New York: Columbia University Press, 1945), 103.

5   Clement Miller, *Hieronymus Cardanus, Writings on Music* (American Institute of Musicology, 1973), 142ff.

6   Henry Cornelius Agrippa, *De occulta Philosophia*, II, xxv. The best modern edition, which is highly recommended, is Donald Tyson, *Three Books of Occult Philosophy* (St. Paul: Llewellyn Publications, 1993).

The most original writing of the seventeenth century on the Doctrine of the Affections occurred in France, by two very well-known writers. First, Martin Mersenne (1588–1648), author of the virtual encyclopedia, *Harmonie universelle* (1636), in his second treatise, *Traite de mechanique*, takes the basic idea of the doctrine of affections and expands it to include a discussion of music and taste in foods.

> We shall commence with tastes, the most agreeable of which must correspond to the octave. These are the sweet tastes which are found in honey, sugar, flowers of honeysuckle …
>
> The fatty or greasy taste corresponds to the perfect fifth, since, with the exception of the sweet, it is the most agreeable taste.
>
> The perfect fourth is comparable to the salty taste, for the salty taste is disagreeable in combination with the sweet, as is the perfect fourth when it is joined with the octave. If the perfect fourth is joined with the perfect fifth, however, it is agreeable, as is the salty taste with the fatty …
>
> The astringent taste corresponds to the major third, and the insipid taste to the minor third. These two consonances combine well with the octave, as do the astringent and insipid tastes with the sweet. The gentle impression which the astringent and insipid tastes make on the gustatory sense is similar to that which the major or minor third takes on the ears. Although they can be mixed with the salty, the astringent and insipid tastes do not combine so well with the fatty. Similarly the major or minor third combines better with the perfect fourth than with the perfect fifth. When the major or minor third combines with the perfect fourth, it forms the major or minor sixth. The sixths, however, are less agreeable than the thirds. Just as the thirds do not contain the octave or the perfect fifth, so the astringent and insipid tastes do not partake of the sweet or the fatty.
>
> The major sixth corresponds to the sour taste, and the minor sixth with the acid taste. Just as the major sixth combines well with the minor third and the minor sixth with the major third, so the sour can be joined with the insipid and the acid with the astringent. Such taste combinations ought to result in the sweet taste, just as the major sixth combines with the minor third to form the octave and the minor sixth combines with the major third to form the octave. The octave thus formed, however, lacks the perfect fifth, just as the corresponding taste combinations lack the fatty taste.
>
> The sharp taste can be combined with the sour, such as wine with pepper, and that the sharp and sour agree with the tasteless and the sweet. Just as the two sixths agree with the octave and the perfect fifth. The two sixths can not be joined with the perfect fourth, just as the two aforesaid tastes can not be agreeably combined with the salty.
>
> The bitter taste is like the whole-tone. It is always disagreeable. The tastes of all fruits begin with bitterness, as one experiences with unripe fruits. So, too, songs often begin with the whole-tone. The whole-tone is never more disagreeable than in combination with the octave, and the bitter is never more disagreeable than in combination with the sweet.
>
> On the other hand, the bitter is never more agreeable than in combination with the salty, just as the whole-tone is never more agreeable than in combination with the perfect fourth so as to create the perfect fifth. For this reason certain people prefer the taste of salty olives to that of pheasants.[7]

Mersenne was also interested in the relationship of color to emotion.

> It should be noticed here that songs are similar to the nuances of colors, which follows the idea of not being able to pass from one extremity to another without passing through a central shade. That is why one can be instructed in making good songs by the consideration of the nuances, for as one has

---

7   Marin Mersenne, *Harmonie Universelle*, II, ii. English translation is taken from John Egan (Bloomington: Indiana University, unpublished dissertation, 1962).

seven intervals, or eight sounds in the octave, so one takes seven or eight colors for each shade, as is seen in the shade of purple, blue, and chartreuse, or lemon yellow. In this way one can compare each song to each color …

One can add that if songs are made of the twelve tones in the octave, one has also twelve colors, and that a shade may have as many colors as the octaves do sounds, or intervals, for each may be divided into an infinity of degrees.

One can be instructed by an analogy to other things. Simple tones compare to simple colors. Intervals of sounds compare to mixtures of the colors, and the songs to paintings.[8]

Regarding color, it is interesting that Mersenne thought it might be helpful if the composer arranged to have his music actually printed in color to help identify the emotions he had in mind. Therefore, the diatonic, a joyful set of intervals, might be printed in black; the chromatic, whose half-steps arouse sad, amorous, and ravishing feelings, could be printed in red; and the enharmonic, since it is particularly fitting 'for ravishing the mind in the contemplation of heavenly things,' could be reproduced in blue.

Mersenne also assigned significant responsibility to the performer for the communication of the emotions in music to the listener. Since Mersenne was primarily interested in song, his discussion centers on the singer.

> The Italian [singers] observe several things in their solos of which ours are deprived, since they represent as much as they can the passions and the affections of the soul and the mind, for example, choler, wrath, spite, rage, lapses of the heart, and several passions, with a violence so peculiar that one would almost judge that they felt the same affections which they represent when singing, whereas we French are content with charming the ear, and use a constant mildness in our songs, which hinders their vigor.[9]

We find the most interesting comments by Mersenne on the subject of the performer are those which deal with the problem of the emotions and their actual notation symbols. He wishes for a notational system which was more helpful and he is correct: we do not have a single written symbol which is addressed to feeling!

> There are a number of passions which we can make appear in singing, for which we have not yet devised symbols, such as the great *exclamations* of Italian airs, and the representations of lapses of the heart. It appears that if the circumflex accent had not been used for the double-flagged notes...it would be suitable for representing these great cries and excesses of the voice, since it is composed of the acute and the grave accent, just as the exclamation of despair and of pain is composed of a cry of the voice and a small rest which descends to the third, the fourth, the minor sixth, or other intervals, according to its magnitude and the strength of the voice which sings …
>
> We lack symbols to represent the notes or syllables which we should sing more strongly, as we have some bowing strokes much stronger than others. Since the voice has as many degrees of force as of intervals, we can divide this force into eight degrees, as we divide heat and the other qualities, so that the first degree is suitable for expressing very weak echoes, and the other seven degrees designate the different degrees of the most vehement passions up to the eighth, which will represent the great-

---

[8] III, ii, 6.

[9] IV, vi, 6.

est exclamation which can be made, such as that of despair and of any great pain of the mind or the body, such as we can imagine that of Esau when he roared and cried when demanding the benediction of his father Isaac. These different degrees of force can be designated by numbers, or by as many dots or accents. Since, however, they have already been used for other purposes, there would be need to add new symbols, although if we retain the ordinary usage of notes, which carry the value of time with them, numbers can serve to indicate the differences of force of the voice.[10]

It seems clear that at least part of Mersenne's introduction to the Doctrine of the Affections came from the writings of Pontus de Thyard (1521–1605), who was the 'theorist in residence' of Baïff's Academy, for he specifically quotes from his writings on this subject.

Pontus de Thyard also speaks thereof in his second *Solitaire*, in which he says that the agreement of the four humors is called health and the discord thereof is called sickness. The changeability of the pulse attests to this; it is like the master of the music of the human body. Philosophers have considered three kinds of movement in the spirit, namely, desire or concupiscence, ire, and reason, which produce an intellectual harmony in man when they accord with the will of God. Otherwise they yield a very disagreeable dissonance.

Desire has three divisions. Ire has four, and reason has seven. The divisions are called virtues. The first division of desire is Temperance, which despises the voluptuous. The second division is Continence, which suffers failure and poverty without tiring. The third division of desire is Shame, which rejects any rejoicing over the voluptuous.

Ire has four divisions, namely, Clemency, Courage or Assurance, Fortitude, and Constancy.

Reason has seven divisions, namely, Understanding, Perspicacity, Curiosity, Counsel or Consideration, Wisdom, Prudence, and Experience.

Temperance taken from the ternary of the perfect fourth, Fortitude drawn from the quaternary of the perfect fifth, Prudence drawn from the septenary of the octave, and Justice taken from the perfect consonance (inasmuch as it unites the powers of body and soul) make the perfect quaternary of the Pythagoreans, in which all the perfect consonances can be found.[11]

In this same place, Mersenne also paraphrases Ptolemy, concluding,

There are certain sounds which excite some to voluptuousness, others to pity and mercy, and still others to rage and ecstasy. The passions of the soul are changed according to the sounds, songs, and modes which are used.[12]

Mersenne begins the discussion of his own theories on the relationship of music and the temperaments with a number of general observations on the nature of the emotions and music. He begins by considering the 'voices of animals,' which he finds serve to 'signify the passions of the soul, but does not always signify the temperament of the body.'

---

[10] IV, vi, 7. An error in Mersenne's original publication incorrectly numbers the propositions from this point on, beginning with 8, instead of 7.

[11] II, iii.

[12] II, iii.

> Experience points out [that] ... birds, dogs, and other animals make another sound when angered than when complaining, or when sick than when well again and in good health. For bile makes the voice high, melancholy and phlegm make it low, and the bloody humor renders it tempestuous. Thus the height is compared to fire, depth to earth and water and tempestuousness to air.[13]

Mersenne concludes that pitch itself is not an infallible indication of temperament, in either man or animal. However,

> As for the other qualities of the voice, such as sharpness, sweetness and agility, they seem to be able to give us more certain indications of temperament. For those who speak swiftly and brusquely are ordinarily testy, and those who speak slowly are melancholy. But those who speak moderately are cheerful and of a good temperament.
>
> ......
>
> One can say in general the hardest and roughest voices are the most appropriate for signifying the passions, and griefs and displeasure; and the sweetest voices are most appropriate for the amorous passions, and that the great cries best represent the great sorrows and sadnesses.

Now Mersenne begins to wonder if it might be more effective in expressing our feelings, if we substituted singing for speech. In fact, he concludes that 'song seemingly is more appropriate and natural for expressing the passions.'

> For the song of an interval of a second is appropriate for expressing sadness and that of a third is appropriate for expressing joy. And if one were to examine the nature of all intervals, one would find the conformity they have with each thing, such that he could enjoy them in place of our ordinary speech for making us understand and for expressing the nature of things.

But, he admits, that persons with limited vocal resources would thus have trouble expressing themselves.[14]

It would seem a given conclusion to a seventeenth-century philosopher such as Mersenne that 'happy' songs should be more agreeable to the listener than sad ones. But to his astonishment, he found the opposite was sometimes the case!

> Nevertheless all musicians are of contrary opinion, and the listeners who sing confess that they receive more pleasure from sad and languishing songs, than from gay ones ...
>
> However one can first consider that men have much more melancholy and phlegm than bile, and they embrace the earth more than air, or the skies, and the gay airs being of an aerial nature, representing fire, are not so suitable to the nature of men as the sad and languishing songs which represent the earth, melancholy, and phlegm. I have proved in the 31 propositions of the 'Book of Sounds' that the high sounds are more agreeable than the low ones, because they partake more of the nature of air and fire. This does not mean however that sad songs must be less agreeable than gay ones. But the rea-

---

[13] III, i, 7.

[14] In III, i, 36, Mersene offers a remedy for clearing the throat, a potion of the 'grain of ground cole-wort mixed with sugar, or with Spanish licorice, or with tobacco syrup.' He adds, 'I leave out all the extraordinary remedies and many ways that actors and preachers use to preserve their voices.'

son is not enough, since one meets bilious men, who are pleased with sad songs, as well as melancholy ones, in a way that it is necessary to take the nature of the sad songs in mind, since some listeners differ in their opinion.

It is necessary to consider the nature of sad airs, which consist of several things, for the melody of sad airs represents languor and sadness by its continuation, by its weakness and its trembling. The half-tones and sharps represent the tears and complaining because of their small intervals which mean weakness. The small intervals which are made in rising or falling are similar to children, to the old, and to those who arise from a long illness, who cannot walk in large steps …

And then when one takes a long time to shift from interval to interval that shows a great weakness, which makes its impression in the soul of the listener … Gay songs are so rapid, that one has not as much time to notice them, since they do not remain long enough in one place to make an impression on the soul. I do not wish to speak here of the text which augments sadness, when it makes us review the unhappy accidents of life with which we have been tormented, since sad airs can exist without words.

However, it is necessary to notice that all men are more subject to sadness than to joy, for if each one could reflect on the actions that he does, or on his thoughts, he would find a dozen of the sad ones for each gay one. Sadness fell upon us after the original sin, and is natural to us. In contrast, joy comes to us by accident, as happens in joyous gatherings, where each one forces himself to give pleasure to his companion (which he does not always succeed) and there are many who have laughed while the heart was sad. But it seems that often one lets himself follow the common opinion that there are sad songs, and that one should say they are gay, since they bring contentment to the listeners. Many times musicians call songs sad when in reality they are not, but rather they fit the voice of those who lament, particularly well.

What is this pleasure derived from sad things? How is it engendered in listeners? I would say only that there are two types of sadness, one moral, because its motifs are drawn from deprivation, the other is natural, and comes from the melancholic humor, or from the phlegmatic, when one has sinned to excess. Sad songs do not engender either, but leave the listener in whatever humor he was previously in. If we use reason, we see that the melancholiacs derive more pleasure from gay songs than from sad ones, since the brusque and lively movements of the chansons are more suitable for dissipating excessive humor of melancholy, rather than the slow and languishing movements of lamentations. One is cured by the contrary of his ailments, if we believe Hippocrates rather than Paracelsus, who believed that people are cured by similar things.[15]

Mersenne now extends this discussion of a man's temperament to include the subject of laughing. First the interesting observation is made that all laughter uses one or other of the five vowels (Ha, Ha, Ha; He, He, He, etc). From this the following discussion ensues.

Now since a greater ardor is necessary for moving the wings of the lungs when the laugh is made on *a*, it can be said that those who form *a* while laughing have more ardor than those who form *o* and *i*, and that *e* signifies a greater ardor than *u*. *A* shows the moistness and facility that the glottis has in opening, and, consequently, that one is full-blooded. But *e*, *o*, and *i* show its dryness and that those who form these letters while laughing are of a cold and dry temperament. Just as the vowel *u* signifies that one is cold and moist, the vowels *i* and *o* show that one is hot, dry, and bilious. *E* signifies melancholy, and *u* signifies phlegm, and those who form the said letters while laughing are subject to the maladies deriving from these humors, or are appropriate to the virtues that these same humors favor. This is why I conclude that *a* and *o* signify audacity and liberality when they are made by a

---

[15] III, ii, 26.

quick movement, and that *e* and *u* signify avarice; that those who form *a* and *o* are loved by those who form *e* and *i*, who look for ardor to be perfected and conserved; and that those who form the same letter are loved reciprocally because of the resemblance; that those who form *a* and *o* have a quicker and sharper mind; and that those who form *e* have better memory and less imagination, and that they are more opinionated; that the vowels *i* and *u* show a short life and the others a long life; such that the spring of his life who forms *a* lasts 25 years, which he similarly confers to the summer, autumn, and winter of life.[16]

Mersenne's own special area of interest, within the general topic of music and the emotions, was the relationship of the vocal accents of speech and the melodic accents he heard musicians add to the music and how these might be related to the 'temperaments' and the 'humors.' He begins by considering the use of accent in general.

> With regard to the ordinary accents of which the Greeks, the Latins, and the other nations speak, they admit only three, namely, the grave, the acute, and the circumflex, or the accents of grammar, rhetoric, and music.[17]

Mersenne now wonders if the individual use of these accents may identify 'the temperament and humor.' First, he points out that one can easily identify persons from different parts of France merely by their accents. To him it followed that,

> Experience teaches that those who are hasty and abrupt in their actions and who are easily upset have an abrupt and high accent, and that those who are gloomy have a low, slow, and heavy one. Just as there are quite as many temperaments and different humors as there are men, likewise there are just as many different accents and different manners of speaking ... This can apparently arise only from the difference of their humors and the diversity of their organs, which arises from the difference of their temperaments.[18]

Mersenne now offers the proposition: 'The accent of which we speak here is an inflection or modification of the voice or the word with which we express the passions and the affections naturally or artificially.' He then sets forth in some detail his own theory that 'Each passion and affection of the soul has its proper accents by which its different degrees are explained.'

> Every day we experience that choler is expressed by an accent different from that of admiration or sorrow. If we follow the division which philosophers make of the passions of the soul, we shall establish eleven kinds of accents. For they admit eleven passions, namely, six in the concupiscible appetite, which resides on the right side of the heart, or in the liver, as the Platonists wish, and five in the irascible appetite, which is on the left side of the heart, or in the gall, or in other places according to this Latin distich,
>
> *The heart savors and the lung speaks, the gall awakens wrath,*
> *The spleen causes laughter, the liver urges love.*[19]

---

[16] III, i, 46.

[17] IV, vi, 10.

[18] IV, vi, 11.

[19] Cor sapit, et pulmo loquitur, sel commovet iras, Splen ridere facit, cogit amare iecur.

The first passion of the concupiscible appetite, or of concupiscence, is love, which is the root of all the passions. For we do not hate anything except when we believe that it is opposed and is contrary to that which we love. Thus all the disorder of the passions arises from love, which is divided into desire and joy, according to the different movements which it gives to the soul.

Hatred is opposed to love, and has its advancement in flight and in sorrow. Thus the six passions can be reduced to these two capital ones, since they are an advancement of love and of hatred, and since we do not desire anything, or rejoice in anything other than those we love, just as we shun nothing and grieve at no things other than those we hate.

Hope, boldness or daring, choler, fear, and despair belong to the irascible appetite ...

We can conclude from this that the ancients established these four passions, namely, joy, pain, fear, and hope, as the four elements, or the four humors, of the appetite which we have in common with the animals. We can, however, admit love and hatred instead of joy and pain. We must see in what the movement of these passions consists before establishing certain accents for them.

In the first place, the heart enlarges, blossoms out, and opens in joy and hope, just as heliotrope, roses, and lilies do in the presence of the sun. It is from this that the complexion of the face is rosy, because of the vital spirits which the heart sends above. Thus if joy is so great that the heart remains without a great enough quantity of these spirits, we faint, and sometimes die laughing.

On the contrary, when sorrow is excessive, the same spirits withdraw to the heart in too great a multitude, and smother it, since it can no longer move nor open. Thus these two passions are like the ebb and flow of the sea. For joy is like the flow which brings a great quantity of stones, shells, and fish to the shore of the sea, and joy brings a quantity of blood and spirits to the face and the other parts of the body. Fear and pain, however, are like the ebb, which withdraws that which was gathered. For fear and terror render the face pale and the countenance bleak and hideous by withdrawing the blood and the spirits, and cause melancholy to corrupt the little blood which remains in the veins, and fills the imagination with frightful dreams. It is necessary, therefore, that the accents with which we express the different affections and passions of the soul be different, and that some of them imitate and represent the flow of spirits and blood, and others the ebb, that the former be quick, lively, cheerful, and similar to the flowers and odors of spring, and the latter be similar to rain, snow, winter, and all that is disagreeable, that the former be similar to consonances and ensemble pieces, and the latter to dissonances and disturbing noises, and finally, that the former have as many perfections as the latter have imperfections.

We must see whether it is possible to establish four principal accents according to these four different passions. For the accents of which we speak here can be called the word or discourse of the passions, just as words and ordinary discourse are called the discourse of the mind, which partakes more of artificial means than of nature, just as that of the passions partakes more of nature than of artificial means. Consequently, the latter is less subject to concealment than the former. With regard to the accent of joy, it is certain that it is different from that of sorrow. That of joy, however, includes that of desire and love, just as the triangle includes two right angles, and just as the rational soul includes the sensitive and the vegetative. This accent is cheerful, pleasant, and quite agreeable, and can be divided into as many other accents as there are different degrees of joy and love.

The accent of sorrow is slow, gloomy, and troublesome. That of hatred is more violent, and approaches that of indignation, which is contained in that of choler. With regard to the accent of flight, it is related to that of fear, and that of desire is like that of hope. The accent of despair follows that of sorrow, just as that of boldness follows that of hope and desire. It is difficult, however, to express all these accents.[20]

---

[20] IV, vi, 13.

The final sentence, above, reflects the fact that Mersenne realized that his ideas were far too complex to be notated in either speech or music. He therefore urges that the time has come to invent new symbols for the 'passions.' To be sufficient to express the necessary range of emotions, Mersenne finds the need for nine new symbols. He expresses this in the proposition, 'All the accents which we use to express the three passions to which we have related the others have need of nine different characters to be explained and understood, namely, three for the three degrees of choler, and just as many for the degrees of love and of sorrow.'

> The first degree of choler is noted in the voice when it rises a little higher and when we speak with more vehemence. If we touch the pulse, we shall quickly judge that the heart beats more swiftly or more strongly. We must observe, however, whether this pulsation is sesquialtera that of the natural pulsation, or whether it observes some other proportion, in order to establish the first degree of choler and to have its internal character by the movements of the pulse or by that of the respiration, and its external character by the height or force and speed of the voice.
>
> Since this accent originates from the bile, we could represent this first degree of choler by one dot of flame or of fire, or by some other symbol which designates how many degrees it must raise or strengthen and hasten the word to the first degree of choler. This could perhaps be done with flagged notes and the *fredons* of music.
>
> The second degree of choler gives a stronger blow to the reason, which begins to yield to passion. It can be explained by two dots of flame. If the pulse of the first degree of choler is sesquialtera that of the natural, the pulse of the second degree will be double in swiftness the natural, and consequently, sesquiteria that of the pulsation which the second degree makes, for the double ratio is composed of the sesquialtera and the sesquitertia. We must, nevertheless, note that the natural pulsation does not pass at once to the second degree, nor does that of the second degree to that of the third. It is enough, however, to have established the final point of these degrees, which we can reach either all at once, or by several intervals, just as we can go from the lower sound to the fifth without using degrees, or with the ordinary degrees.
>
> The third degree of choler which ascends to wrath, can be represented by a flame with three dots. The pulsation of the heart will be triple that of the natural, either in speed or force, or in both. We can relate to this the range of the voice which in pain rises more than a twelfth from the tone of the ordinary word which is used without passion, to the cry of wrath and despair. For if the voice ascends higher, it becomes raucous and disagreeable and should be called a squeal rather than a human voice. Thus those who have arrived at this degree no longer say a word, or if they talk or cry out, they lower the tone. Moreover, it is difficult, and perhaps naturally impossible, for the pulse to beat more than three times more swiftly in choler than outside of it. Since, however, we must avoid as much as possible the innovation of symbols, an acute accent can designate the first degree of choler, two the second, and three the third. If we wished to use specific letters, they can carry with them any point or sign we wish, by which those who read the discourse will be warned that it is necessary to pronounce the end or some other part of the sentence with the first, the second, or the third accent of choler.
>
> The same thing must be said of the accents of the passion, of joy, and of sorrow, which have their beginnings, advancements and endings, as do choler, illnesses, and the other things of this world, although the pulse and the voice of these two passions are not as easy to explain as those of choler. We can, nevertheless, establish accents and symbols for them in proportion of those of choler.
>
> Some have believed that the passions change the weight of the body, and that the man in choler is lighter by eight pounds per hundred than when he is sorrowful, by a thirteenth when he is in the final degree of choler, and by a twenty-fifth when he is extremely joyous. These remarks, or rather

these imaginations, however, are quite false, for inflammation and death bring a greater alternation to beasts and the human body than do all the passions of the soul of the body. Nevertheless, the living body is not lighter than the dead one, nor the warm and inflamed breast than the cold one, as we have experimented quite exactly.[21]

Next he considers to what degree the various 'passions' he has been discussing can be expressed in musical notation and he finds the problem much more difficult than in the case of speech.

> This is quite difficult to explain, so much so because it appears that music desires a certain delicacy and agreeableness which cannot be compatible with the vehemence and severity of the passions, particularly with choler. For with regard to the accents of sorrow and pain, it is easy to make them by means of the semitone which the voice forms when yearning. This is almost the only accent in French songs, in which we sometimes mix also the accents of joy, love, and hope, appropriately enough. The Italians, however, have more vehemence than we do for expressing the strongest passions of choler with their accents, particularly when they sing their verses for the theater to imitate the scenic music of the ancients. The accent of choler is made by rushing the final syllables, and by strengthening the last sounds. If we reflect upon the elevation of the voice, we shall note that it is often raised an entire tone, a third, and a fourth, when pronouncing the final syllable of words which are used in choler and sometimes by the same intervals or by the diapente when sustaining the voice on the antepenultimate syllable. The manners in which choler is expressed, however, are so diverse that there is almost no interval at all which it does not use, according to its different degrees and the other passions which accompany it. Thus the musician should consider the time, the place, the characters, and the subject for which the accent should be made, in order that he indicate it on the syllable which the voice should sustain, and which it should raise and strengthen.
>
> I have noted that the tone of voice of choler often ascends an entire octave or more all at once. This is difficult to perceive, unless we try to place these intervals into music by forming the same intervals slowly, and little by little, so that the imagination might have the time to understand the interval of choler. The same thing must be said of the accent of spite, displeasure, and the other passions, which will often be found on a tone of voice much higher than we believe, although it is also made sometimes on the same pitch by striking it more strongly and more quickly.
>
> I leave the investigation of symbols necessary to indicate this passion and the others, to composers who desire to write songs in which nothing is lacking, and particularly, who have the intent to accent them in all kinds of ways. This will give such a charm and such an air to the songs and the solos, that all who hear them will acknowledge that they are animated and full of vigor and spirit, of which they are devoid without these accents. Composers can be instructed in this by considering the striking of chamades, charges on the drum, and those of trumpets, whose last sounds of each beat represent choler by the promptness and the force of the blow of the stick or the tongue. With regard to the promptness, we have flagged or double-flagged and triple-flagged notes, which are quick enough to indicate the speed of all the degrees of the most rapid passions, just as we have those of sixteen, twelve, eight, six, four, three, and two beats, which are slow enough to indicate the listlessness of the greatest sorrows. Thus we are only lacking symbols which designate the impetuosity, the vigor, and the force of these passions. For example, we can designate the first degree with the same mark by which we indicate the first minutes, namely, by this small straight line, /, by the second by the sign of the seconds, //, the third by the sign of the thirds, ///, etc. Those who teach singing, however, should show all these different degrees of the passions to children, just as they teach them cadences and

---

[21] IV, vi, 15.

various passages and trills, so that they might be lacking in nothing to accent all the syllables and the notes indicated by the composer, who should strive for a knowledge of the movements and degrees of each passion, in order to represent them as simply as possible.

If the composer of songs judges that he cannot form the accents of the passions with the ordinary intervals of the diatonic and chromatic, that is, with the music which we ordinarily use, it is easy for him to use the enharmonic dieses which I have explained in Book Three, and in those on lutes and the organ. For example, if he finds that the major third is too small to express some passion and its accent, he can increase it by any diesis he wishes, that is, by the one which makes only a quarter tone, or by that which makes a third of a tone, or by any other interval he judges suitable for his intent. I have wished to add to this so that we might not think that the Greeks have had, or were able to have, any other degrees or intervals than those which we can use just as well as they did in all kinds of situations, without there remaining any reason for us to doubt that they were able to write better songs than ours, particularly if we accommodate to them all which we have said.[22]

Mersenne now turns to the role of rhythm in the communication of emotions in music. In the following proposition, the word 'movement' is used to refer to emotional character, not speed or as a term to distinguish part of a larger form as we use the term today.

Rhythmics is an art which considers movements and which regulates their succession and their mixture to excite the passions and to maintain them, and to increase, decrease, or calm them.[23]

He begins here a discussion of the application of the Greek rhythmic modes to composition, but he admits it is difficult 'to prescribe what the succession of these movements should be to excite the listeners to the given passion.' It is equally difficult to persuade composers to observe these, not only because they find the application of these modes result in tedious rhythms, but because they would prefer to write what comes to them solely from their imagination.

The second French philosopher who wrote at length on aspects of the Doctrine of the Affections was René Descartes (1596–1650). Although his analytical style induces the reader to hope for interesting insights, unfortunately most of his conclusions are only weird-science. After presenting the definition of human passions as 'something which moves the soul to want the things for which they prepare the body,'[24] Descartes concludes there are only six principal ['primitive'] passions: wonder, love, hatred, desire, joy and sadness. All others are contained in these, or composed of them.[25]

Wonder, is a 'sudden surprise of the soul' which causes it to devote unusual attention to objects that 'seem to it unusual and extraordinary.' Since this passion is concerned primarily with knowledge, it is not accompanied by changes in the heart or blood. A stronger form of

---

[22] IV, vi, 16.

[23] IV, vi, 18.

[24] 'The Passions of the Soul,' xl, li.

[25] Ibid., lxixff.

Wonder, astonishment, has an added element of surprise which 'causes the spirits in the cavities of the brain to make their way to the place where the impression of the object of wonder is located.' Descartes observes,

> Although it is only the dull and stupid who are not naturally disposed to wonder, this does not mean that those with the best minds are always the most inclined to it.

Excessive Wonder may become a habit, he notes, when we fail to correct it.

Regarding Love and Hatred, he writes,[26]

> Love is an emotion of the soul caused by a movement of the [animal] spirits, which impels the soul to join itself willingly to objects that appear to be agreeable to it. And hatred is an emotion caused by the spirits, which impels the soul to want to be separated from objects which are presented to it as harmful.

Descartes distinguishes between benevolent love (a wish for the well-being of the object) and concupiscent love (to desire the object) and notes that there is an abundance of passions which are also associated with love: the desire of the ambitious for glory, the miser for money, the drunkard for wine, etc. He also associates affection, friendship and devotion with whether we esteem the object as less, equal or more than ourselves.

Desire is a passion in which an agitation of the soul caused by the animal spirits disposes the soul to wish, in the future, for something agreeable.[27] Descartes finds there is no single opposite for Desire, but that there are many kinds: curiosity for knowledge, desire for glory, desire for vengeance, etc.

Joy and Sadness,[28] he defines as follows:

> Joy is a pleasant emotion which the soul has when it enjoys a good, which impression in the brain represent to it as its own.... Sadness is an unpleasant listlessness which affects the soul when it suffers discomfort from an evil or deficiency which impressions in the brain represent to it as its own.

Next Descartes explains the physical manifestation associated with these basic passions,[29] excepting Wonder which is located only in the brain. In the case of Love,

> the pulse has a regular beat, but is much fuller and stronger than normal; we feel a gentle heat in the chest; and the digestion of food takes place very quickly in the stomach. In this way this passion is conducive to good health.

---

26 Ibid., lxxixff.

27 Ibid., lxxxviff.

28 Ibid., xciff.

29 Ibid., xcviiff.

In Hatred,

> the pulse is irregular, weaker and often quicker; we feel chills mingled with a sort of sharp, piercing heat in the chest; and the stomach ceases to perform its function, being inclined to regurgitate and reject the food we have eaten, or at any rate to spoil it and turn it into bad humors.

In Joy,

> the pulse is regular and faster than normal, but not so strong or full as in the case of love; we feel a pleasant heat not only in the chest but also spreading into all the external parts of the body along with the blood which is seen to flow copiously to these parts; and yet we sometimes lose our appetite because our digestion is less active than usual.

In Sadness,

> the pulse is weak and slow, and we feel as if our heart had tight bonds around it, and were frozen by icicles which transmit their cold to the rest of the body. But sometimes we still have a good appetite and feel our stomach continuing to do its duty, provided there is no hatred mixed with the sadness.

Desire,

> agitates the heart more violently than any other passion, and supplies more spirits to the brain. Passing from there into the muscles, these spirits render all the senses more acute, and all the parts of the body more mobile.

Descartes now elaborates on the physical manifestations associated with the passions.[30] We will cite, as an example, only those associated with Love.

> These observations, and many others that would take too long to report, have led me to conclude that when the understanding thinks of some object of love, this thought forms an impression in the brain which directs the animal spirits through the nerves of the sixth pair to the muscles surrounding the intestines and stomach, where they act in such a way that the alimentary juices (which are changing into new blood) flow rapidly to the heart without stopping in the liver. Driven there with greater force than the blood from other parts of the body, these juices enter the heart in greater abundance and produce a stronger heat there because they are coarser than the blood which has already been rarefied many times as it passes again and again through the heart. As a result the spirits sent by the heart to the brain have parts which are coarser and more agitated than usual; and as they strengthen the impression formed by the first thought of the loved object, these spirits compel the soul to dwell upon this thought. This is what the passion of love consists in.

In a letter to Pierre Chanut, French ambassador to Sweden, Descartes acknowledges the genetic nature of the emotions, but contends that the prenatal fetus has only four 'passions,' joy, love, sadness and hatred. It was the unconscious retention of the confused prenatal emotions which complicated our judgments of the passions in later life, Descartes suggested.

---

30 Ibid., ciiff.

> Those four passions, I think, were the first we felt, and the only ones we felt before our birth. I think they were then only sensations or very confused thoughts, because the soul was so attached to matter that it could not do anything except receive impressions from the body ... Before birth love was caused only by suitable nourishment, which entered in abundance into the liver, heart, and lungs and produced an increase of heat: this is the reason why similar heat still always accompanies love, even though it comes from other very different causes ... The other bodily conditions which at the beginning of our life occurred with these four passions still accompany them. It is because of these confused sensations of our childhood, which continue connected to the rational thoughts by which we love what we judge worthy of love, that the nature of love is difficult for us to understand.[31]

In his treatise, 'The Passions of the Soul,' Descartes contends that every passion of the soul is usually accompanied by an action in the body.[32] In his 'Compendium of Music,' he appears to have this in mind when he offers some observations on the physical manifestations of musicians while performing.

> Few are aware how in music with diminution [*musica valde diminuta*], employing many voices, this time division is brought to the listener's attention without the use of a beat [*battuta*]; this, I say, is accomplished in vocal music by stronger breathing and on instruments by stronger pressure, so that at the beginning of each measure the sound is produced more distinctly; singers and instrumentalists observe this instinctively, especially in connection with tunes to which we are accustomed to dance and sway. Here we accompany each beat of the music by a corresponding motion of our body; we are quite naturally impelled to do this by the music. For it is undoubtedly true that sound strikes all bodies on all sides, as one can observe in the case of bells and thunder ... Since this is so, and since, as we have said, the sound is emitted more strongly and clearly at the beginning of each measure, we must conclude that it has greater impact on our spirits, and that we are thus roused to motion. It follows that even animals can dance to rhythm if they are taught and trained, for it takes only a physical stimulus to achieve this reaction.[33]

Descartes adds only a few more observations on the relationship of music and the communication of emotions. Slower tempi, he suggests, 'arouses in us quieter feelings such as languor, sadness, fear and pride.' Faster tempi arouses 'faster emotions, such as joy.'[34]

We are disappointed that Descartes elected not to speculate more, in his music treatise, on the role of emotions. This disappointment is increased by curiosity when he mentions in passing that he would like to 'discuss the various powers which the consonances possess of evoking emotions,' but that the topic exceeds the scope of his treatise.

We find relative little pertaining to the Doctrine of the Affections by English writers of the Baroque. Robert Burton, in his famous *The Anatomy of Melancholy* (1621) offers the following definitions of the 'humors':

---

[31] Letter to Chanut, February 1, 1647.
[32] 'The Passions of the Soul,' ii.
[33] 'Compendium of Music,' trans. Walter Robert (American Institute of Musicology, 1961), 14ff.
[34] Ibid., 15.

> A humor is a liquid or fluent part of the body, comprehended in it, for the preservation of it; and is either innate or born with us, or adventitious and acquisite ...
>
> *Blood* is a hot, sweet, temperate, red humor, prepared in the *meseraick* veins, and made of the most temperate parts of the *chylus* in the liver, whose office is to nourish the whole body, to give it strength and color, being dispersed by the veins through every part of it. And from it *spirits* are first begotten in the heart, which afterwards by the *arteries* are communicated to the other parts.
>
> *Pituita*, or phlegm, is a cold and moist humor, begotten of the colder parts of the *chylus* (or white juice coming out of the meat digested in the stomack) in the liver; his office is to nourish and moisten the members of the body, which, as the tongue, are moved, that they be not over dry.
>
> *Choler* is hot and dry, bitter, begotten of the hotter parts of the *chylus*, and gathered to the gall: it helps the natural heat and senses, and serves to the expelling of excrements.
>
> *Melancholy*, cold and dry, thick, black, and sour, begotten of the more faeculent part of nourishment, and purged from the spleen, is a bridle to the other two hot humors, *blood* and *choler*, preserving them in the blood, and nourishing the bones. These four humors have some analogy with the four elements, and to the four ages in man.

We might also mention here that John Donne (1573–1631) makes a rare association between the color of clothes and the 'affections.'

> For we, when we are melancholy, wear black; when lusty, green; when forsaken, tawny; pleasing our own inward affections.[35]

With the work of William Harvey, in his *Lectures on the Whole of Anatomy* (1616), we finally begin to see the curtains of truth rise and the beginning of the end of the long period of weird-science with respect to the operation of the body. He acknowledges the past beliefs of his profession,

> Medical Schools admit three kinds of spirits; the natural spirits flowing through the veins, the vital spirits through the arteries, and the animal spirits through the nerves ...[36]

but he acknowledges that in his personal clinical studies he has been unable to find these 'animal spirits,' etc.

> We have found none of all these spirits by dissection, neither in the veins, nerves, arteries, nor other parts of living animals.

One of the earliest of the Baroque Germans to write about the Doctrine of the Affections was Athanasius Kircher (1601–1680), who spent most of his life in Rome. His greatest accomplishment was his *Musurgia Universalis* (Rome, 1650), a massive encyclopedia of music. Of the ten books which make up this work, Book Seven, 'Diacritical,' is devoted to an attempt to classify musical styles. First he discusses 'individual styles,' which presumes one's preference in music is based on the 'humors.' After turning to 'national styles,' Kircher attempts a third type of classification based on function. Here one finds eight headings of which the last one is,

---

[35] John Donne, 'Paradoxes and Problems,' in *Selected Prose*, ed. Helen Gardner (Oxford: Clarendon Press, 1967), 12.

[36] *The Works of William Harvey*, ed. Robert Willis (Reprinted New York: Johnson Reprint Corp., 1965), 116ff.

> *Stylus dramaticus* or *Stylus recitativus*, recitative style for the representation of any of the so-called affections, or for abrupt changes of affection through sudden alternations in tonality, the so-called *Stylus metabolicus*.

Athanasius Kircher introduced his belief that the humors indigenous to a person explained his preferences in music as follows:

> Melancholy people like grave, solid, and sad harmony; sanguine person prefer the *hyporchematic* style (dance music) because it agitates the blood; choleric people like agitated harmonies because of the vehemence of their swollen gall; martially inclined men are partial to trumpets and drums and reject all delicate and pure music; phlegmatic persons lean toward women's voices because their high pitched voice has a benevolent effect on phlegmatic humor.[37]

He began by determining that there are eight basic emotions which music can affect: love, grief or pain, joy, exultancy, rage or indignation, compassion or tears, fear or distress, presumption or audacity and admiration or astonishment.[38] Kircher attempted to identify the power of music at work through descriptive, and even subjective, language. For the first emotion, love [*paradigma affectus amoris*] he finds in a madrigal by Gesualdo intervals which languish and syncopations which express 'the syncope of the languishing heart.' The second emotion, grief or pain [*paradigma affectus dolorosi*] he illustrates by describing the lament of Jephtha's daughter in an oratorio by Carissimi.

> Giacomo Carissimi, a very excellent and famous composer ... through his genius and the felicity of his compositions, surpasses all others in moving the minds of listeners to whatever affection he wishes. His compositions are truly imbued with the essence and life of the spirit. Among numerous works of great worth, he has composed the dialogue of *Jephte* ... After the recitative with which he ingeniously and subtly expresses the jubilant welcome accorded Jephtha by his daughter (who celebrates the victories and triumphs of her father in a joyous dance, accompanied by all sorts of musical instruments), Carissimi depicts, by means of a sudden change of mode, the dismay into which Jephtha has been plunged by this unexpected meeting with his only begotten daughter, against whom he has taken an irrevocable vow, and whom he despairs of being able to save. Joy thus gives way to the opposing affections of sorrow and grief. This is followed by the six-voice lament of the daughter's virgin companions, which Carissimi composes with such skill that you would swear you could hear their sobbings and lamentations.

The German who wrote most extensively on the doctrine of the affections was Johann Mattheson (1681–1764). There is no doubt that Mattheson believed the central purpose of music, after praising God, was the communication of feeling. The whole question of the 'passions,' Mattheson suggests, is perhaps more the province of the philosopher than the Kapellmeister, but on a practical level it is fundamental to composer and performer if they are to communi-

---

[37] Athanasius Kircher (1602–1680), *Musurgia Universalis*, quoted in Paul Henry Lang, 'Musical Thought of the Baroque: The Doctrine of Temperaments and Affections,' in William Hays, ed., *Twentieth-Century Views of Music History* (New York: Scribner's, 1972), 195.

[38] *Musurgia Universalis*, I, Bk. I, iii, 6.

cate with the listener.[39] He discusses the doctrine of affections under the caption, 'Concerning Sound and the Natural Sciences of Music,'[40] and as is typical for him it is an highly organized and thoughtful exposition.

56. Since joy is an expansion of our vital spirits, it follows sensibly and naturally that this affect is best expressed by large and expanded intervals.
57. Sadness is a contraction of those same subtle parts of our bodies. It is, therefore, easy to see that the narrowest intervals are the most suitable.
58. Love is a diffusion of the spirits. Thus, to express this passion in composing, it is best to use intervals of that nature.
59. Hope is an elevation of the spirit; despair, on the other hand, a casting down of the same.

Here Mattheson discusses love at more length, 'since love is so prevalent in music.' He points out that desire cannot be separated from love, nor can yearning, wishing and wanting. He concludes by saying the composer must use his own experience here, or 'if he has no experiences or strong feelings of his own in this noble passion, he had best leave the subject alone.'

66. Sadness is a quite important emotion. In sacred works, where this emotion is most moving and beneficial, it rules all these: penance, remorse, sorrow, dejection, complaint, and the recognition of our misery. Most people prefer to hear sad rather than happy music because almost everybody is unhappy.
68. Like love, sadness must be felt and experienced more than any other emotion if one wishes to represent it musically.
72. Pride, haughtiness, arrogance, etc., all have their respective proper musical color as well. Here the composer relies primarily on boldness and pompousness. He thus has the opportunity to write all sorts of fine-sounding musical figures that demand special seriousness and bombastic movement. They must never be too quick or falling, but always ascending.
73. The opposite of this sentiment lies in humility, patience, etc., treated in music by abject [*erniedrigenden*] sounding passages without anything that might be elevating. The latter passions, however, agree with the former in that none of them allow for humor and playfulness.
74. Stubbornness is an emotion that is entitled to its own place in musical speech. It can be represented by means of so-called *capricci* or strange inventions. These may be written by introducing certain dogged passages in one or the other part and resolving not to change them, cost what it may. The Italians know a kind of counterpoint they call *perfidia* which, in a sense, belongs here.
75. As far as anger, heat, revenge, rage, fury, and all other such violent emotions are concerned, they are far more suitable to all sorts of musical inventions that the gentle and agreeable passions, which must be treated with more refinement. It is not enough, however, to rumble along, to make a lot of noise, and to go at a fast clip; notes with many tails will not suffice, contrary to the opinion of many peoples. Each of these harsh characteristics demands its own particular treatment and, despite strong expression, must have a proper singing quality. This is our general rule that should never be forgotten.

---

39 Johann Mattheson, *Der vollkommene Capellmeister* [1739], trans. Ernest Harriss (Ann Arbor: UMI Research Press, 1981), I, iii, 52ff.

40 Ibid. Here we use the translation by Hans Lenneberg in the *Journal of Music Theory*, April, 1958.

76. Music, like poetry, occupies itself a great deal with jealousy. Since this state of emotion is a combination of seven passions, namely, mistrust, desire, revenge, sadness, fear, and shame, which go along with the main emotion, burning love, one can easily see why it gives rise to many kinds of musical invention. All of these, in accordance with nature, must aim at restlessness, vexation, anger, and mournfulness.
77. Hope is an agreeable and pleasing thing. It consists of joyous wishing which, along with some courage, occupies the spirit. As a result, this affect demands the loveliest conduct of melody and the sweetest combination of sounds in the world. These, as it were, are spurred on by resolute wishes in such a way that, even though happiness is only moderate, courage nevertheless enlivens and cheers up everything. This results in the best joining and uniting of sounds in all of music.
80. Despair, which is the extreme to which cruel fear can drive us, requires, as one can readily imagine, the strangest extremes of sound for its natural expression. It can thus lead to very unusual passages and to the strangest, wildly disordered sequences of notes.

Mattheson now discusses a long list of musical forms with respect to their characteristic emotions. One of the more interesting of these is his characterization of the new church concerto, familiar to us today in the works of Gabrieli. He mentions the large orchestral forces used in this form and which, in fact,

> often carried to such excess that it resembles a table laid for show rather than to satisfy hunger. Everyone can easily guess that contests, as in all concertos—from which, in fact, they derive their name—are not lacking. Thus jealousy and revenge, envy and hatred, and other such passions are represented in the concerto.

Mattheson also discusses the use of rhythm here, suggestions for creativity when a composer can't think what to write or how to begin and finally attempts to make correspondence between rhetoric and music. Here is an example,

81. *Locus exemplorum* is presumably to be interpreted as imitation of other composers. One must, however, choose only the best examples and change them so that they will not just be copied or stolen. When all has been said, it must be admitted that this source is used most frequently. As long as it is done modestly, it need not be condemned. Borrowing is permissible; the loan, however, must be returned with interest; ie., one must work out and dispose the borrowed material in such ways that it will gain a better and more beautiful appearance than it had in the composition from which it came.

The one musician during the Baroque who voiced doubt about the entire significance of the Doctrine of the Affections was Johann David Heinichen (1683–1729). He was particularly concerned about preserving the artistic choice in the composer, not leaving it in the hand of the theorists. He even goes so far as to suggest that there might be circumstances, in the case of music for the theater, where the composer might elect to compose music reflecting a different emotion than that called for in the text.

> I would never suggest to anyone to fill up the theatrical style with too many serious inventions ... For pathetic, melancholic, and phlegmatic music (in so far as it is based on tenderness and good taste) is effective in the church and chamber styles; but it is not well suited to the theatrical style, and

one uses serious pieces simply for judicious [variety]. And if their lordships, the poets, overload us with pathetic and sorrowful arias, we [the composers] must try to sweeten these either with mixed inventions or effective accompaniments; or in those arias containing a double emotion, one turns the invention more gradually to the lively element rather than the serious one. Thus, for example, with the melancholy of love, one should rather express the pleasantness of love and not the blackness of melancholy ... In summary, the theatrical style for the most part requires something moving or adroit, though I should not call it simply merry. For merry music in itself can easily degenerate into barbarism and is unpleasant to sensitive ears.[41]

Heinichen also questions whether there can be any meaningful association between emotions and tonality. This relationship, one of the most fundamental questions in early philosophy, had long been assumed to be an important key to how emotions affect the listener. The long history of this idea in literature left Heinichen somewhat ambivalent. He appears to want to believe that keys have certain emotional qualities, but he immediately casts doubt on the general idea by pointing out that the *real* emotional meaning is found in the actual *music* the composer writes.

> The aria begins in E♭; for this reason, however, the invention need not be sad, serious, or plaintive, for brilliant concerti as well as joyous arias in certain cases can be composed with the greatest effect in this beautiful key. Furthermore, the previous examples ... clearly show that one can express the same words and emotions in various and, according to the old theory, opposing keys. For that reason, what previous theorists have written and rewritten about the properties of the modes are nothing but trifles, as if one mode could be merry, another sad, a third pious, heroic, war-like, etc.

He continues by noting that even if this were true, it would be rendered void by the conflicting tuning systems and lack of agreement on a standardized pitch. Following this, he concludes,

> In my opinion, the ancient theorists erred in their research of modal characteristics, in the same way as we continue to err today in judging a musical work. If we, for example, find for this or that key ... one or more beautifully tender, plaintive, or serious arias, we prefer to attribute the fine impression of the aria to the key itself and not to the excellent ideas of the composer; and we immediately establish a *proprietas modi*, as if contrary words and emotions could not be expressed in this key. This, however, is worse than wrong, as can be proved to the contrary by a thousand beautiful examples. In general, one can say that one key is more suitable than another for expressing emotions. Thus in the practice today using well-tempered scales, the keys indicated with two and three sharps or flats are particularly beautiful and expressive in the theatrical style ... Yet, to specify this or that key especially for the emotion of love, sadness, joy, etc., is not good. Should someone object at this point and say that D, A, B♭ major are much more suited to raging music than the calmer scales of A minor, E minor, and similar ones, then this actually does not prove the *proprietas modorum* even if it were so, but it depends on the inclination of the composer. For we have heard famous composers write the saddest and tenderest music in D, A, and B♭ major, etc., whereas in A minor, E minor, C minor; and in similar scales we have heard the most powerful and brilliant music.[42]

---

[41] Johann David Heinichen, *General-Bass Treatise* [1711], quoted in George Buelow, *Thorough-Bass Accompaniment according to Johann David Heinichen* (Ann Arbor: UMI Research Press, 1986), 282.

[42] Ibid., 283.

Regarding the Doctrine of the Affections, to the extent that one means developing specific formulas or rules for expressing specific emotions through composition, Heinichen says, 'forget it.' He reports that no one has any interest in that idea at all, not 'even the slightest introduction' to the subject.

> What a bottomless ocean we still have before us merely in the expression of words and the affections in music. And how delighted is the ear, if we perceive in a refined church composition or other music how a skilled virtuoso has attempted here and there to move the feelings of an audience through his *galanterie* and other devices that express the text, and in this way to find successfully the true purpose of music. Nevertheless, no one wants to search deeper into this beautiful musical *Rhetorica* and to invent good rules. What could one not write about musical taste, invention, accompaniment, and their nature, differences, and effects? But no one wants to investigate the matters aiming at this lofty practice or to give even the slightest introduction to it.[43]

In retrospect, it is clear that Heinichen was correct. Some philosophers were excited about theories of the Doctrine of the Affections, but they do not appear to have influenced actual composition. Composers during the Baroque were certainly interested in communicating strong emotions through their music, but they arrived at this result through the heart and not by following someone's rules. Of course, generally speaking, it was always the case that composers composed music and the theorists and philosophers came along *later* and issued their contentions. It has rarely worked the other way around. In addition, as we know from clinical brain research today, if not from common observation, theorists and philosophers use rational left-hemisphere language, something which is not particularly conversant with the right-hemisphere realm of the experience of music and the emotions.

It is for these reasons that one finds little more than a passing reference to the Doctrine of the Affections in standard music history texts which deal with Renaissance or Baroque music. One might as well conclude the whole subject is one without merit. However, that being said, one is left with some unsettling perceptions. Modern clinical research has proven that a certain affinity with particular melodic patterns seems to be genetic. If that is the case, perhaps there is indeed some ancient connection between melodic patterns and specific emotions. One recent writer whom we believe has very successfully explored this idea is Deryck Cooke and we highly recommend his book.[44]

In addition we are not yet comfortable with writing off the idea that tonality may be related to emotion. Certainly, from a *rational* perspective, when one considers the absence among all countries before the twentieth century of agreed common pitch (such as A = 440), the idea that a particular key should communicate a specific emotion to everyone in every country makes no sense. Nevertheless, common experience suggests that perhaps once again rational explanation (left-hemisphere) may not quite explain *musical* experience. For example, modern theorists explain that the distinction between major keys is merely a different starting point,

---

43 Ibid., 326. In a footnote, Heinichen observes that some attempts at expressing emotions in music sound mannered and make people laugh. Thus, he says, 'a mighty chasm stretches between knowledge and ability.'

44 Deryck Cooke, *The Language of Music* (Oxford: Clarendon Paperbacks, 1959), see pp. 113ff.

followed by identical organizations of half and whole-steps. That is true, as a rational fact. But is there a musician anywhere who would not confess that the key of F Major *sounds* somehow different from the key of G major? Does the key of A Major communicate the same feeling as Ab Major? Can one imagine Beethoven's A Major Symphony transposed and performed in Ab Major? Would the feeling, even of the opening bars, be changed?

Perhaps we may yet have more to learn.

Music is Truth

> *Music is a form of beauty.*
> Music Educators National Conference (1991)
>
> *Anyone who still hasn't got past the stage of the beauty of music knows nothing about music ... Music is Truth.*
> Sergiu Celibadache (1989)

THE REAL SECRET TO THE POWER OF MUSIC is that it is the expression of experiential Truth dealing with feeling. It is only the left hemisphere of man's brain which is capable of lying, thus making suspect all reading, writing, speech, history, poetry, oratory and theater. But, the right hemisphere of our brain, the domain of the experiential nature of music, does not lie and has no equivalent of 'No.'[1] This is clear to everyone in the example of love. You can use the left brain (speech, thought) in trying to talk yourself in or out of your feelings of love, but it is always quite clear to yourself what those feelings *really* are. And so it is with music, as was accurately observed by Confucius (551–479 BC) in a treatise on music:

> Music is the one thing in which there is no use trying to deceive others or make false pretenses.

And Robert Schumann once noted,

> Understanding may err, but not feelings.[2]

The agent that makes Truth in music so powerful to the listener is the fact that the communication is always first person present tense, it occurs live, lock-step in time with the listener. In the performance of music, the listener *experiences* the music immediately and has an *instantaneous* connection with the inner artistic idea of the composer.[3] This is an important distinction between music and painting or sculpture. The observer of a canvas first employs *exclusively* the eye. If he is going to be successful in going beyond this to see and communicate with the inner artistic idea of the artist, he must make a *shift* from vision to mental contemplation. In other words, he must get past the experience of the eye before he can get to the experience of the artist. It is this delay, this circumnavigation which robs art and sculpture of the power of music.

---

[1] A discussion of the clinical research can be found in Robert Ornstein, *The Right Mind* (New York: Harcourt Brace, 1997), 93.

[2] Robert Schumann's Diary, ca. 1833.

[3] W. H. Auden observed, 'A verbal art like poetry is reflective; it stops to think. Music is immediate, it goes on to become.' Quoted in George Marek, *Schubert* (Viking, 1985), 5.

But there are additional important distinctions. First, the art work of the painter is 'frozen' in time. In this way it is like a photograph. If you think of someone you know well, you can 'see' in your mind much of his features. But if you happen to have a photograph of that person, when you look at that a much more vivid picture of the person comes to mind. But the picture *never becomes the real person*. A recording of music, by the way, is analogous with a photograph.

Another important distinction lies in the nature of the existence of the art work. A finished canvas exists as a work of art even if it is hanging in a closed museum where no one can see it. A composition, on the other hand, exists as genuine music *only* in performance, which implies the presence of a listener—as there would be no purpose in a performance if there were no one to hear it. Therefore in a musical performance the listener is not an observer at all, but a *participant* in a live aesthetic experience. And in this regard let us remember that a single wealthy individual can own a canvas of Leonardo, and keep it secret from the public if he so desires, but no one owns Beethoven. Music, as is appropriate for a form of Truth, belongs to all mankind.

Among the early Greek philosophers Plato (427–347 BC) make three important points which most of the following philosophers would agree. First, he sets music apart from the other arts and theater as, he says, these are only 'imitations' of the real thing. He seemed to understand that music was not an imitation of something, nor a symbol of something, but the *real thing* expressed from composer to musician or listener. This is why, he points out, that a singer cannot be fooled, he knows immediately if a composition is good or bad and if the composer has a 'good or bad soul.'[4]

Second he, as with so many early philosophers, makes the connection between music and the divine. Speaking of the poets, whom let us not forget were musicians who sang their works before the public, Plato observes,

> For poets are a divine race, and often in their strains, by the aid of the Muses and the Graces, they attain Truth.[5]

He follows this with the suggestion that music was genetically given to man by the gods.

> And did we not say that the sense of harmony and rhythm spring from this beginning among men, and that Apollo and the Muses and Dionysus were the Gods whom we had to thank for them?

The third, and most important, point which Plato makes is the distinction between entertainment music and that aesthetic music which represents Truth. He condemned those who had allowed music to fall to the level of mere entertainment, 'ignorantly affirming that music

---

4   *Laws*, 812b and following.

5   *Laws*, 682.

has no truth … and can only be judged by the pleasure of the public.'[6] Quite the contrary, he contends that 'being pleasant' is not an appropriate criterion for selecting music for performance or for judging the value of music.

> AN ATHENIAN STRANGER. When anyone says that music is to be judged by pleasure, his doctrine cannot be admitted; and if there be any music of which pleasure is the criterion, such music is not to be sought out or deemed to have any real excellence, but only that other kind of music which is an imitation of the Good, and bears a resemblance of its original.
> CLEINIAS. Very true.
> AN ATHENIAN STRANGER. And those who seek for the best kind of song and music ought not to seek for that which is pleasant, but for that which is True.[7]

Aristides Quintilianus, who lived sometime during the first four centuries AD, was not so strict as Plato, believing that music could give pleasure and still be true to its basic purpose.

> We should not avoid song altogether just because it gives pleasure. Not all delight is to be condemned, but neither is delight itself the objective of music. Amusement may come as it will, but the aim set for music is to help us toward virtue.[8]

It is interesting that he also wrote directly to the point of why music is so potent in its communication of emotions, because the emotion expressed in the music is identical with that felt within the listener (due to the genetic similarity in all men with respect to the basic emotions).

> Music persuades most directly and effectively, since the means by which it makes its imitation [*mimesis*] are of just the same kind as those by which the actions themselves are accomplished in reality.

The ancient Romans, who in general were more interested in entertainment than the Greeks, do not speak of this topic much. The Roman philosopher, Quintilian (30–96 AD) in the course of a discussion of oratory, seemed to believe that all the arts dealt with Truth. He observed that since all art must be based on direct perception, 'Art can never deal in false ideas.'[9]

Cicero (106–43 BC) rarely discusses or praises music at all, but we do find one interesting passage. Many early philosophers who comment on oratory point out that the successful orator is one who gets the crowd excited, even if what he says is completely untrue. Cicero, on this subject, seems to suggest that musicians are true to themselves, without regard to the audience, while the orator is the reverse. He phrased it this way:

---

6   Ibid., 656d.

7   Ibid., 668b.

8   Aristides, *De Musica*, Book II. All our quotations are from the translation by Andrew Barker, *Greek Musical Writings* (Cambridge: Cambridge University Press, 1989).

9   Quintilian, *The Education of an Orator* (*Institutio Oratoria*), trans. H. E. Butler (London: Heinemann, 1938), II, xvii, 17.

> Can it be that while the aulos players and those who play the lyre use their own judgment, not that of the crowd, … the [orator], endowed with a far greater skill, searches out not what is most true, but what the crowd wants?[10]

This reminds us of a comment by Mendelssohn, 'the public is more attracted by outward show than by Truth.'[11]

The poets of the early Christian Era contribute some interesting comments on Truth in music. The fourth-century poet, Ausonius, using the name of one of the Greek gods of music, writes 'Phoebus bids us speak truth.'[12] But, he points out, Truth in music is not found in the externals.

> Because with purchased books thy library is crammed, dost think thyself a learned man and scholarly, Philomusus? After this sort thou wilt lay up strings, keys, and lyres, and, having purchased all, tomorrow thou wilt be a musician.[13]

If the reader recalls that all early poetry was sung, and therefore usually cataloged under music, he will find interesting the suggestion by Sidonius, fifth century, that if there be Truth in music, it follows that it must reflect his own life as well.

> As for me, my anxiety absolutely forbids me to make the content of my poetry different from the content of the life I lead.[14]

This suggestion that the music and the musician are to some degree inseparable reminds us of a comment by Boethius (475–524 AD). Boethius, the famous mathematician, when speaking of 'Truth' was speaking of rational, or intellectual, truth. Nevertheless, he sets music apart with an observation which is near to the meaning of 'Truth' as others use it in regard to music.

> There happen to be four mathematical disciplines [arithmetic, music, geometry, and astronomy], the other three share with music the task of searching for truth; but music is associated not only with speculation but with morality as well.[15]

---

[10] *Tusculan Disputations*, V, 104.

[11] Letter to Conrad Schleinitz, Berlin, August 1, 1838.

[12] *Ausonius*, trans. Hugh G. Evelyn White (London: Heinemann, 1921), II, 17. One fifth-century poet, Julianus, City Prefect of Rome, found, on the other hand, that the public did not always want the truth.

> The flame that gives life to Art was my gift, and now from Art and fire I get the semblance of ceaseless pain. Ungrateful of a truth is the race of mankind. [*The Greek Anthology*, trans. W. R. Paton (London: Heinemann, 1918), V, 87.]

[13] 'To Philomusus a Grammar Master,' in Ibid., II, 161.

[14] *Sidonius Poems and Letters*, trans. W. B. Anderson (Cambridge: Harvard University Press, 1965), II, 443.

[15] Boethius, *Fundamentals of Music*, trans. Calvin Bower (New Haven: Yale University Press), I, i.

As the Medieval Period progressed there were still occasional references in poetry to Truth in music. Two eighth-century examples from England are interesting. The poem, 'The Wonders of Creation,' suggests that it is the aspect of Truth in music which helps man understand life.

> It is, thinking man, an obvious example
> to every one who by wisdom
> can comprehend in his mind all the world,
> that long ago men, well-advised people,
> could often utter and say a truth
> in the art of song, by means of lays,
> so that most of mankind, by always asking
> and repeating and remembering,
> gained knowledge of the web of mysteries.[16]

Another poet declares he can write only of Truth in his songs,

> Let none of human kind imagine,
> that I of lying words compose my lay,
> or write my verse![17]

During the years of the 'Pre-Renaissance,' the twelfth and thirteenth centuries, one finds many references in the secular songs to the Truth being communicated by the singer/composer. In one example by Vogelweide (ca. 1170–1230), he says that the Truth in his song is so obvious that only someone with no experience in love could possible misunderstand it.

> Many there are that mock my pain,
> And ever say that 'tis not truly from the heart I sing;
> These but spend their breath in vain,
> Since they can never yet have known love's joy and suffering;
> And so it is they judge me wrong:
> Whoever knows
> All that from true love flows,
> Would not misunderstand my song.[18]

With the growing movement toward a return to the importance of emotions in music, and departing from the Church's one thousand years of pretending that music was a branch of mathematics, it is perhaps fitting that the Renaissance begins with an extraordinary insight by a man born in 1300, Johannes de Grocheo. In his *De Musica*, he observes that not only is music used to express the feelings of the composer or musician, but that music is the means by which

---

[16] *The Exeter Book* (Oxford University Press, 1958), II, xiv, 8ff.
[17] 'The Phoenix,' Ibid., II, iv, 546ff.
[18] *Selected Poems of Walter von der Vogelweide*, trans. W. Alison Phillips (London: Smith, Elder, & Co., 1896), 43.

the 'practical' part of the brain 'explains and exposes its functions.'[19] This is an amazing early reference to the actual fact that the right hemisphere of the brain is otherwise mute. He is saying that music is the only means that we have for understanding the nature of Truth as it exists in the right hemisphere. We are reminded of a similar remark in Sir Philip Sidney's (1554–1586) *The Countesse of Pembrokes Arcadia*, where we find,

> Then she remembered this song, which she thought took a right measure of her present mind.[20]

In the early Renaissance we find some remarkable references to Truth on our experiential or emotional side. In Boccaccio a character says 'don't listen to the words of my song. Listen to what the feeling reveals when I sing it.'

> Love, heed not what my voice sings, but rather how much my heart, your subject, is filled with desire.[21]

A passage with the same meaning is also found in Machaut:

> And if it please you, my dear lady, to consider the last little song I sang, of which I composed both words and music, you can easily tell whether I'm lying or speaking the truth.[22]

There are two comments by Chaucer which are worthy of consideration relative to our topic. In one place, after concluding that Beauty is something which cannot be described in words, Chaucer offers a definition for Beauty that it is Truth. 'Truth,' he says, 'is the crown of Beauty'[23] We believe he was also thinking along these lines when he wrote, 'Nature does not lie.'[24] Music may not lie, but performers can be something else, as we see in a Greek proverb quoted by Erasmus called, 'Singers tell many lies.' In addressing to singers the objections often directed toward orators, he says,

> It comes from the fact that singers, whose only object is to delight and give pleasure, produce for the most part what redounds to the credit of the audience [even though it is not true]; for nothing is more solemn than the truth, or more agreeable than flattery.[25]

---

[19] Johannes de Grocheo, *De Musica*, trans. Albert Seay (Colorado Springs: Colorado College Music Press, 1967), 9.

[20] Sir Philip Sidney, *The Countesse of Pembrokes Arcadia*, in *The Prose Works of Sir Philip Sidney*, ed. Albert Feuillerat (Cambridge: Cambridge University Press, 1962), I, Book II, xxv.

[21] *L'Ameto*, trans. Judith Serafini-Sauli (New York: Garland, 1985), 40.

[22] Guillaume de Machaut, 'Remede de Fortune,' trans. James Wimsatt and William Kibler (Athens: The University of Georgia Press, 1988), 374.

[23] 'A Complaint unto Pity,' 75.

[24] 'The Parliament of Birds,' 629.

[25] 'Adages,' in *The Collected Works of Erasmus* (Toronto: University of Toronto Press, 1992), XXXIII, 128.

Perhaps the erudite Erasmus had in mind that line from one of the books left out of the modern bible, 'Use not much the company of a woman that is a singer.'[26]

During the Baroque we find an interesting reference to our subject in a poem by Antonio Abbatini in which he provides a first-hand description of one of the early academies. He describes a period of discussion and argument after which a period of three hours is set aside during which time each man exposes his real character before all through performance.

> Then to the harpsichord the company transfers,
> and each man takes upon himself to show, with song
> and sound, his virtue, which binds the heart and soul.[27]

There are several other similar comments from this period which make the same point, that words are somehow inadequate but that music expresses the real thing. The French philosopher, Jean-Baptiste Du Bos (1670–1742) thought the key to the power of music lay in the fact that its sounds came directly from nature, whereas language can only be the *symbol* of the real thing.

> All these sounds have a wonderful power to move us because they are the signs of the passions that are the work of nature herself, from whence they have derived their energy. Spoken words, on the other hand, are only arbitrary symbols of the passions.[28]

A passage in Calderon's *Life is a Dream* (II, i) makes the same point. Here, Astolfo observes,

> Tell the eyes
> In their music to keep better
> Concert with the voice, because
> Any instrument whatever
> Would be out of tune that sought
> To combine and blend together
> The true feelings of the heart
> With the false words speech expresses.

The famous vocal teacher, Tosi, reminds his students that if they sing from the heart the listener will understand it is true.

> Oh! how great a master is the heart! Confess it, my beloved singers, and gratefully admit, that you would not have arrived at the highest rank of the profession if you had not been its scholars … Admit, when the heart sings you cannot dissemble, nor has truth a greater power of persuading.[29]

---

[26] Ecclesiasticus 9:4.

[27] Quoted in Lorenzo Bianconi, *Music in the Seventeenth Century*, trans. David Bryant (Cambridge: Cambridge University Press, 1989), 290ff.

[28] 'Reflexions critiques sur la poesie et sur la peinture' (Paris, 1719), quoted in Peter le Huray and James Day, *Music and Aesthetics in the Enghteenth and Early Nineteenth Centuries* (Cambridge: Cambridge University Press, 1981), 18.

[29] P. F. Tosi, *Observations on the Florid Song* (London: Wilcox, 1743), IX, xliv.

Finally, from the Baroque we also like the thought by the mathematician, Gottfried Leibniz (1646–1716), that while painting makes the truth clear, music makes it believable.

> It is as in painting and music, which are [also] abused, one of which often represents grotesque and even hurtful imaginations, and the other softens the heart, and the two amuse in vain; but they can be usefully employed, the one to render the truth clear, the other [music] to make it effective.[30]

Here are two nineteenth-century quotes on Truth:

> The first universal characteristic of all great art is tenderness, as the second is truth.
> *John Ruskin, 1859*

> It is the glory and good of art
> That art remains the one way possible
> Of speaking the truth.
> *Robert Browning,*
> *'The Ring and the Book,' 1868*

During the nineteenth century we also begin to find the use of the word, 'soul,' rather than 'Truth.' But the intent is often the same, a reference to the real meaning coming from deep inside oneself, as we read in Schumann:

> Music is to me the perfect expression of the soul.[31]

It was surely something like this, the revelation of the soul, that the great Arthur Rubinstein had in mind, and not what the phrase has come to mean today—'playing the notes accurately,' when he remarked, 'A concert is the moment of truth.'[32]

In more recent times there have still been occasional philosophers who have labored to make the Truth in art return to the world of Reason. Hegel, for example, in his 'The Science of Beauty,' tries to make 'beauty' and 'truth' understandable only as an *idea*,

> Beautiful is the Idea of the beautiful. This means that beautiful must be grasped as Idea, and if the Idea is a representation of truth, then the Idea is both true and beautiful.[33]

Of course it is possible to talk about the Truth in music as being an idea, or some other rational construction, but if one does that one misses the real value which this kind of Truth offers mankind. Here are three quotations which are much more to the real point:

---

[30] Leibniz, *New Essays Concerning Human Understanding*, trans. Alfred Langley (La Salle: Open Court Publishing Company), 1949, III, x, 34. Here he also still classifies poetry as music, 'rhetoric and music.'

[31] Letter to his Mother, Leipzig, August 9, 1832.

[32] Quoted in Robert Jacobson, *Reverberations* (1974).

[33] Georg Wilhelm Friedrich Hegel, *Aesthetics: Lectures on Fine Art* (Oxford: Clarendon Press, 1975), 106.

> Music whispers to us dim secrets that startle our wonder as to who we are.
> *Emerson*

> [Music] shuts us off from the outer world, as it were, to let us gaze into the inmost Essence of ourselves....
> *Wagner*[34]

> You use a glass mirror to see your face; you use works of art to see your soul.
> *George Bernard Shaw*[35]

And this is the great opportunity for music education, the opportunity to be the only teachers in the school building who have the tools to reach the *real* student. But, music educators are not taught to understand this and they continue down the road no student is interested in, devoting themselves to the grammar of music, talking *about* music. They aspire to make music like the rest of the curriculum, like English, Geography, Math and History.

But these kinds of subjects have nothing to do with the real student. These kinds of subjects only bombard the student with external facts, outside the experience of the student as an unique, individual person, which the student is then advised to add to his mental database. 'Two plus two is four, Memorize that!'

But music is different. Music deals with Truth at the individual level, the *real* student. Since music is not taught this way in school, and thus is of little value in helping the student discover who he is, his only hope is to figure it out by himself. Some have been fortunate enough to do this, as was the case with Wagner, when one day walking 'aimlessly in the country side of Italy,'

> I suddenly realized my own nature; the stream of life was not to flow to me from without, but from within.[36]

---

34 Quoted in Wagner's Prose Works, trans. William Ashton Ellis (New York: Broude), V, 77.
35 *Back to Methuselah*, 1921.
36 Richard Wagner, *My Life* (New York: Tudor, 1936), 603.

On Music as the Language of Truth

Music is a language without words.
Martin Luther

The primal organ of utterance of the inner man is music.
Richard Wagner

VIRTUALLY ALL PHILOLOGISTS TODAY AGREE that before there was language, man communicated through musical sounds. What do they mean? Paleontologists, judging by changes which occurred in the shape of the human skull formation with respect for room for modern vocal cords, generally hold that language as we know it was not possible before 250,000 BC. Music, meaning the voice and instruments made from natural objects, is presumed to be much older. In any case, the overtone series, the single natural law of physics upon which all music is based, was present far before man himself. Whatever prior creature had ears to hear, heard sounds organized according to the overtone series.

The musical sounds early man made were, it seems reasonable to suppose, emotional utterances using the five basic vowel sounds—much like what a dog does. This was the very point made by one of the many writers who have speculated on the idea that musical communication came before language, Richard Wagner!

> The primal organ of utterance of the inner man, however, is music, as the most spontaneous expression of the inner feeling stimulated from without. A mode of expression similar to that still proper to the beasts was alike first employed by man (and this we can demonstrate at any moment by removing from our language its dumb articulations [consonants] and leaving nothing but the open sounds of the vowels). In these vowels, if we think of them as stripped of their consonants, and picture to ourselves the manifold and vivid play of inner feelings, with all their range of joy and sorrow, we shall obtain an image of man's first emotional language; a language in which the stirred and high-strung Feeling could certainly express itself through nothing but a combination of ringing tones, which altogether of itself must take the form of Melody. His melody, which was accompanied by appropriate bodily gestures in such a way as the gestures would also appear a simultaneous inner expression, and from these gestures we get rhythm.[1]

Voltaire, having much the same viewpoint, differed in that he proposed that it was the addition of gesture to these sounds which created the first step from these sounds toward the earliest language.

---

[1] *The Prose Works of Richard Wagner* (New York: Broude), II, 224ff.

> May we not, without offending anyone, suppose that the alphabet originated in cries and exclamations? Infants of themselves articulate one sound when an object catches their attention, another when they laugh, and a third when they are whipped, which they ought not to be ...
>
> From exclamations formed by vowels as natural to children as croaking is to frogs, the transition to a complete alphabet is not so great as may be thought. A mother must always have said to her child the equivalent of come, go, take, leave, hush!, etc. These words represent nothing; they describe nothing; but a gesture makes them intelligible.[2]

With the five basic vowel sounds, early man expressed a variety of emotions and emotional reactions to his world. These five basic vowel sounds not only continue today as a fundamental part of every language on earth, but we as individuals also carry significant remnants of early man's musical communication. When we become excited, the voice rises in pitch. This comes from early man. Every sentence we utter has melodic contour and it is this melodic contour which clarifies the meaning of the sentence. We create emphasis for a specific spoken word by raising the pitch. We call it *accent* and again it comes to us from the singing of early man, as suggested by Roger Bacon (b. ca. 1214):

> For accent is a kind of singing; whence it is called accent from *accino*, *accinis* [I sing, thou singest], because every syllable has its own proper sound either raised, lowered, or composite, and all syllables of one word are adapted or sung to one syllable on which rests the principal sound. Thus length and shortness and all other things required in correct pronunciation are reduced to music.[3]

The communication of emphasis by raising the voice must be very ancient.

Another example of the influence music had on developing languages is the entire realm of meter and governance of time. In his treatise on mathematics, Roger Bacon maintains that the theologian must have training in music in order to understand the Scriptures.[4] Aside from the numerous references to music itself in the Old Testament, Bacon points to the many kinds of meters found in the old Hebrew text. Here he notes that while the grammarian may teach the practical rules, only Music gives 'the reasons and theories' for these meters. In the same manner, he points to the issue of pronunciation, as the Scripture is filled with 'accents, longs, shorts, colons, commas, and period.'

> All these belong causally to music, because of all these matters the musician states the reason, but the grammarian merely the fact.

Eventually a means of notating music was developed. A Church mathematician known as John (ca. 1100 AD) argues for the need for this notation.

---

[2] *Philosophical Dictionary*, 'The Alphabet.'

[3] *The Opus Majus of Roger Bacon*, trans. Robert Burke (New York: Russell & Russell, 1962), I, 259ff.

[4] 'Mathematics,' in Ibid., I, 259.

> Music is one of the seven liberal arts—and a natural one, as are the others. Thus we sometimes see jongleurs and actors who are absolutely illiterate composing pleasant-sounding songs. But just as grammar, dialectic, and the other arts would be considered vague and chaotic if they were not committed to writing and made clear by precepts, so it is with music.[5]

While he acknowledges the jongleurs managed to compose and perform quite well without theoretical knowledge, he argues that one cannot really be called a musician unless one can read notation and, by implication, understand the theory behind it. One can learn to read music, if one 'devotes unremitting labor to it and perseveres without pausing or wearying.' A singer who cannot read music he compares to 'a drunken man who does indeed get home but does not in the least know by what path he returns.'[6] Finally, he concludes that the musician who performs without reading or understanding theory is 'a beast by definition.'

We have only a dim idea of language before the age of writing (ca. 3,000 BC), but it seems reasonable to us to suppose that the further back you go, the closer you get to early man's musical-emotional utterances. But one wonders what were the intermediate steps on the way to modern language? Perhaps there was a step represented by the Rhapsodist. If only we could hear once again this artist who performed before the advent of the written form of the Greek language. Plato, in *Ion*, describes him as a kind of musician, performing epic poetry in something in between music and speech, and discusses the emotional impact he had on his listeners. Because of him for two millennia poetry would be sung and not recited. Perhaps a last remnant of this was the 'canting' heard by the underworld of London in the eighteenth century. Thomas Dekker, in an essay of lowlife in London, describes canting as follows:

> This word *canting* seems to be derived from the Latin verbe (*canto*) which signifies in English, to sing, or to make a sound with words, that is to say to speake. And very aptly may *canting* take his *derivatio a cantando*, from singing, because amongst these beggarly consorts that can play upon no better instruments, the language of *canting* is a kinde of musicke, and he that in such assemblies can *cant* best, is counted the best Musician.[7]

Perhaps some clues of intermediate steps might be found in the history of oratory. Numerous early treatises not only speak of relationships with music but emphasize the relationship of movement and emotion. The oratory treatises emphasize the importance of communicating emotion to the listener, something, ironically, early music treatises almost never do.

When written languages first appear they were essentially primitive pictures, that is the symbol for house looked like a house. This was not only natural, but effective for man's experience corresponded with the written language. Eventually this form of writing became too complicated and so symbolic writing began. In this form of writing a relatively small num-

---

[5] John, 'On Music,' 51, in *Hucbald, Guido, and John on Music*, trans. Warren Babb (New Haven: Yale University Press, 1978), 51.

[6] Ibid., 52.

[7] Thomas Dekker, 'Lanthorne and Candle-Light' [1609], *The Non-Dramatic Works of Thomas Dekker*, ed. Alexander Grosart (New York, Russell & Russell, 1963), III, 194.

ber of symbols (as in the alphabet) can be combined to form unlimited words. However, the problem this created meant that now man's experience was no longer connected to the written form. The letters, 'C–A–T,' have nothing about them to resemble a cat. Thus learning a language now became a separate step, as was the experience of Plutarch (46–119 AD).

> Upon which that which happened to me, may seem strange, though it be true; for it was not so much by the knowledge of words, that I came to understanding of things, as by my experience of things I was enabled to follow the meaning of words.[8]

Having a language which is by its very nature something separate from the experiential side of ourselves, the *real us*, causes problems in communication. Already in the fifth century BC, the philosopher Gorgias argued that Reason must be based solely on language because the information gained through the senses cannot be communicated through language.

> For how could any one communicate by word of mouth what he has seen? And how could that which has been seen be indicated to a listener if he has not seen it? For just as the sight does not recognize sounds, so the hearing does not hear colors but sounds; and he who speaks, speaks, but does not speak a color or a thing. When, therefore, one has not a thing in the mind, how will he get it there from another person by word or any other token of the thing except by seeing it, if it is a color, or hearing it, if it is a noise? For he who speaks does not speak a noise at all, or a color, but a word; and so it is impossible to conceive a color, but only see it, nor a noise, but only to hear it.[9]

But, if that is not bad enough, St. Basil (4th century) reminds us that language fails even to communicate very well our rational left hemisphere of the brain.

> Even when I was writing to your Eloquence, I knew well that every theological expression is less than the thought in the mind of the speaker and less than the interpretation desired by him who seeks, because speech is in some way too weak to serve perfectly our thoughts.[10]

Exactly like early philosophers, we today find ourselves observers of numerous situations in which two people seem to have difficulty communicating through their common language. Why is this? Conceptual information (left hemisphere of the brain) should be *perfectly* capable of communication through conceptual symbolic language, providing the speaker/writer is capable of using this symbolic language correctly, and the listener/reader has an equal background in the subject and understands the agreed conventional meaning of the symbolic language. But, as Voltaire points out, this 'agreed conventional meaning' fails in common usage. Under 'Abuse of Words,' in his *Philosophical Dictionary*, he goes to some lengths to demonstrate

---

8 'Life of Demosthenes.'

9 Quoted in Giovanni Reale, *A History of Ancient Philosophy* (Albany: State University of New York Press, 1987), 167.

10 St. Basil, 'Letter to Gregory of Nazianzus,' in *Letters of Saint Basil*, trans. Sister Agnes Way (New York: Fathers of the Church, 1951), I, 20.

that language, and books, 'rarely give us any precise ideas' and are often taken by the listener in an incorrect sense.[11] In this regard, he mentions that he finds it curious that 'the same word (Adoration) that is used in addressing the Supreme Being is also used in addressing a mistress.'

> We not infrequently go from hearing a sermon, in which the preacher has talked of nothing but *adoring* God in spirit and in truth, to the opera, where nothing is to be heard but *the charming object of my adoration*, etc.[12]

The *problem*, as Voltaire indirectly suggests, is that the speaking/writing part of us, the left hemisphere, cannot express *non*-rational concepts very well, as anyone knows who has ever tried to write a love letter. This is *why* we have retained, since earliest man, a separate non-rational language, which we call *Music*. Among the other gifts we possess from early man is a certain amount of genetic, universal musical information and genetic universal forms (and gestures) of the basic emotions. Languages are very recent in the history of man and they exist in the left hemisphere of the brain as dictionaries with agreed upon usages. But these languages carry no feeling.[13] When we speak, feeling is added by the emotional content in the right hemisphere. In other words, feelings are *natural*. Language is *artificial*. Voltaire goes further and suggests that feelings are more important even than scientific facts.

> What will I gain from knowing the path of light and the gravitation of Saturn? These are sterile truths. One feeling is a thousand times more important.[14]

The inability of language to convey feeling is why music is so necessary as a special language for feeling. During the long centuries when the Church controlled what could be published in books, little can be found on this subject since the Church had taken a position of trying to eliminate emotion from the life of the Christian. But with the dawn of the Renaissance, so characterized by the return of the importance of feelings, one finds frequent references to the failure of language in describing feeling, together with observations on the importance of music to take over that function. Guillaume de Machaut (1300–1377), for example, describes good speech as 'moderate, well-chosen, and appropriate, based wholly on Reason.'[15] But, what happens to Reason-dominated speech when Love is present? It can, Machaut observes, force one,

> to cut short his words and interrupt them with sighs, drawn from the depths of his being, that render him mute and silent, and he has no choice but to remain speechless.

---

[11] *Philosophical Dictionary*, 'The Alphabet.' Franz Liszt in a letter to Richard Wagner of June 8, 1854, writes,
   ... the real kernel of people's phrases has not been, and cannot be, clearly expressed.
[12] Ibid.
[13] 'If only words were not so cold!,' Letter of Mendelssohn to his family, London, Nov. 6, 1829.
[14] Letter to Pierre-Robert Le Cornier de Cideville (February, 1737.
[15] Guillaume de Machaut, 'Remede de Fortune,' trans. James Wimsatt and William Kibler (Athens: The University of Georgia Press, 1988), 180.

His great countryman of the following generation, Froissart (1333–1405), made a similar complaint:

> Pleasure sets him on fire so forcefully
> And true love has such power over him
> That, when he wishes to express his feelings,
> He cannot move his mouth or bring forth words.[16]

But what Machaut could not express in words, he found he *could* express through music.

> So I decided that I would compose, according to my feelings towards you and in praise of you, a lai, a *complainte*, or original song; for I did not dare or know how to tell you otherwise how I felt, and it seemed to be better to tell in my new song what was oppressing and wringing my heart than to try by some other method.[17]

Furthermore, Machaut points out that it is in the *music*, not the words of the song, that his beloved will discover Truth.[18]

> And if it please you, my dear lady, to consider the last little song I sang, of which I composed both words and music, you can easily tell whether I'm lying or speaking the truth.[19]

In Italy, in Giovanni Boccaccio (1313–1375), we find the identical thought, 'listen to the music, not the words' if you want to know the truth!

> Love, heed not what my voice sings (the words), but rather how much my heart, your subject, is filled with desire.[20]

These kinds of observations continued as the Renaissance progressed. Erasmus, in a poem of 1504, cries, 'My tongue is not adequate to my feelings,'[21] and in an unusually obsequious paper praising Archduke Philip, he pretends that it is the strong feelings of joy which prevent him from communicating his thoughts.

> Something strange has just happened: now I have reached the point where not even the most carefully chosen words could have been sufficient, even ordinary language suddenly fails me. It seems almost phenomenal, but the richness of my material is overwhelming my natural talent, the throng of events chokes and strangles the flow of my eloquence, and this strange and unwonted force of

---

[16] 'Chanson Royale,' in *The Short Lyric Poems of Jean Froissart*, ed. Kristen Figg (New York: Garland Publishing, 1994), 211.
[17] 'Remede de Fortune,' 368.
[18] And he is quite correct, only the left hemisphere of the brain is capable of lying.
[19] 'Remede de Fortune,' 374.
[20] *L'Ameto*, trans. Judith Serafini-Sauli (New York: Garland, 1985), 40.
[21] 'A Congratulatory Poem [for] Prince Philip, Upon his Happy Return,' in *The Collected Works of Erasmus* (Toronto: University of Toronto Press, 1992), LXXXV, 139.

happiness, which does not permit silence, at the same time cuts off my power of speech. I have no idea what this can be, unless it must be what the tragic poet expressed so elegantly: light feelings can speak, strong feelings have no voice.[22]

Michel Montaigne (1533–1592), who was generally critical of academic education, points out that it is difficult to *talk* about the really important things in *any* art form.

> Take an arts professor; converse with him. Why is he incapable of making us feel the excellence of his arts?[23]

But of all the sixteenth-century writers, the one who felt most strongly that music was a special language of feeling was Martin Luther. In 1538 Luther wrote the preface for a collection of part-songs based on the suffering and death of Jesus. In addition to mentioning the emphasis on music in the Old Testament, together with his own awe of the art, Luther touches on the most fundamental purpose of music, to express feelings.

> Here ought one to speak of the use one might make of so great a thing, but even this use is so infinitely manifold that it is beyond the reach of the greatest eloquence of the greatest orators. We are able to adduce only this one point at present, namely, that experience proves that, next to the Word of God, only music deserves being extolled as the mistress and governess of the feelings of the human heart.

Luther expands his testimonial to music's ability to express feeling in his preface to Rhau's *Symphoniae iucundae*, published in the same year. He could not be more correct when he says 'music is a language [of feelings] without words.' And notice he calls music the 'mistress and governess of the emotions which as masters govern men.' There in a sentence is what should be the purpose and curriculum of music education.

> Here it must suffice to discuss the benefit of this great art. But even that transcends the greatest eloquence of the most eloquent, because of the infinite variety of its forms and benefits. We can mention only one point (which experience confirms), namely, that next to the Word of God, music deserves the highest praise. She is a mistress and governess of those human emotions which as masters govern men or more often overwhelm them. No greater commendation than this can be found—at least not by us. For whether you wish to comfort the sad, to terrify the happy, to encourage the despairing, to humble the proud, to calm the passionate, or to appease those full of hate—and who could number all these masters of the human heart, namely, the emotions, inclinations, and affections that impel men to evil or good?—what more effective means than music could you find? …
>
> Thus it was not without reason that the fathers and prophets wanted nothing else to be associated as closely with the Word of God as music. Therefore, we have so many hymns and Psalms where message and music join to move the listener's soul, while in other living beings and [sounding] bodies music remains a language without words.

---

[22] 'Panegyric for archduke Philip,' [1503] in Ibid., XXVII, 67. The 'tragic poet' is Seneca, *Phaedra*, 607.
[23] Michel de Montaigne, *Essays*, trans. M. A. Screech (London: Penguin, 1993), III, viii, 1050.

The Baroque Period was obsessed with music's ability to communicate feeling and from this time forward there is much commentary. Johann Scheibe wrote in 1739,

> Music which does not penetrate the heart or the soul ...
> Is quite dead, and lacks spirit and vitality.[24]

A more typical expression of this purpose during the Baroque is given by Georg Muffat, in his *Florilegia* (1695). He writes that he has given each suite the name of 'some state of the affections which I have experienced,' namely, Piety, The Joys of the Hopeful, Gratitude, Impatience, Solicitude, Flatteries, and Constancy.

Johann Mattheson wrote extensively on performance practice and about the 'Doctrine of Affections,' a label given to the theory of the expression of feelings through music. In one place he notes that although the emotions are like a bottomless sea, one can write very little about them (in words).[25] He also adds that he regrets that some composers fail to express feelings through their music. He finds the reason for this must be in the fact that they do not know their own desires or what they actually wanted to achieve. But this failure has significant implications for the listener.

> Is it then astonishing that with pieces thus formed, where true natural theory of sound together with the pertaining science of human affections are completely absent, merely the ears of the poor, simple, and self-righteous listeners are tickled, but their hearts and minds are not aroused in proper measure.[26]

The German Baroque philosopher who gave the most thought to our present topic was the great mathematician, Gottfried Wilhelm Leibniz (1646–1716). It frustrated him that he could not explain in scientific terms what thought itself is.

> Thought is a sensible quality either of the human intellect or of something 'I know not what' within us which we observe to be thinking. But we cannot explain what it is to think any more than what [the color] white is.[27]

It did seem obvious to Leibniz that speech itself must be an important key to the function of the thought process. For this reason he speculated rather broadly on the origin of speech, on the chronological development of the parts of language and, for example, which came

---

[24] Poem in honor of the publication of Johann Mattheson, *Der vollkommene Capellmeister* [1739], trans. Ernest Harriss (Ann Arbor: UMI Research Press, 1981), 74.

[25] *Der volkommene Capellmeister*, I, iii, 83, 88.

[26] Ibid., I, iii, 89.

[27] Leibniz, 'A New Method for Learning and Teaching Jurisprudence' (1667), I, xxxiv, in *Philosophical Papers and Letters*, ed. Leroy Loemker (Dordrecht: Reidel, 1956), 89.

first, proper or generic names.[28] After noting that monkeys have the physical components for speech, but do not speak, Leibniz considered the possibility, as did Voltaire and others at this time, of creating a new language consisting of musical tones.

> We must also consider that we could *speak*, ie., makes ourselves understood by the sounds of the mouth without forming articulate sounds, if we availed ourselves of musical *tones* for this effect; but more art would be necessary to invent a *language of tones*, whilst that of words may have been formed and perfectly gradually by persons who found themselves in a state of natural simplicity. There are, however, people like the Chinese, who by means of tones and accents vary their words, of which they have only a small number.[29]

We have mentioned above the Rhapsodist of ancient Greece, a performer employing something between speech and music. We might add here that we have wondered if the ancient Chinese language with its great vocal variety might offer us an insight into the long lost art of the Rhapsodist.

Leibniz continues by also mentioning the difficulty of describing in words the objects of our senses,

> Additional simple primitive terms are all those confused phenomena of the senses which we certainly perceive clearly, but which we cannot explain distinctly, neither define them through other concepts, nor designate them by words.[30]

or feeling,

> I admit that men frequently happen to be wrong when indeed they discuss seriously and speak in accord with their feeling.[31]

As was the case for many philosophers before our modern clinical understanding of our bicameral mind, the chief obstacle for Leibniz was trying to fit everything into 'one' mind. This, as was so often the case with previous philosophers, resulted in minimizing the importance of feelings as a genuine form of knowing. Leibniz, like the old Church philosophers, consequently gives a certain sinister cast to emotions.

---

[28] Curiously, among his various speculations, the one obvious factor which apparently did not occur to Leibniz at all was the fact that all languages use the same five vowel sounds. In his discussion of a few vowel sounds he does refer to Johann Becan (1518–1572) a Belgian scholar who believed that Adam spoke German!

[29] Leibniz, *New Essays Concerning Human Understanding* [1704], trans. Alfred Langley (La Salle: The Open Court Publishing Company, 1949), III, i, 1. Leibniz himself was inclined to believe that mathematics was the universal language and in a treatise 'The Art of Discovery' (1685) he suggests that a way might be found for mathematics to express basic grammar, etc.

[30] Leibniz, 'An Analysis of the Elements of Language,' in *General Investigations Concerning the Analysis of Concepts and Truths*, trans. Walter O'Briant (Athens: University of Georgia Press, 1968), 33.

[31] Leibniz, *New Essays Concerning Human Understanding*, III, x, 13.

> The highest perfection of man consists not merely in that he acts freely but still more in that he acts with reason. Better, these are both the same thing, for the less anyone's use of reason is disturbed by the impulsion of the emotions, the freer one is.[32]

The French Baroque philosophers gave considerable thought to, and left important papers on, the power of music to communicate feeling. Jean-Baptiste Du Bos (1670–1742) viewed everything from the aesthetic perspective of Nature. It is a particularly accurate and important point he makes when he reminds his readers that spoken words are mere symbols of emotion, but carry no actual emotional content in themselves. Sung words, on the other hand, carry the direct emotional meaning of the music. He believed this ancient emotional communication might well be thought of as 'the work of nature herself,' as we have discussed above.

> Just as the painter imitates the forms and colors of nature so the musician imitates the tones of the voice—its accents, sighs and inflections. He imitates in short all the sounds that nature herself uses to express the feelings and passions. All these sounds, as we have already shown, have a wonderful power to move us because they are the signs of the passions that are the work of nature herself, from whence they have derived their energy. Spoken words, on the other hand are only arbitrary symbols of the passions. The spoken word only derives its meaning and value from man-made conventions and it has only limited geographical currency.[33]

Du Bos makes another very important aesthetic point: what matters in music composition is the communication of feeling, 'the language of nature and the passions.' The ability to do this he calls 'genius.' This is not to be confused with the grammar of music, musical theory or the art of composition.

> Just as some people are more attracted to the color of pictures than to the expression of passions, so others are only sensible to the pleasures of melody or even to the richness of harmony, and pay not the slightest attention to whether the melody is an effective imitation, or care whether it is consonant with the words to which it is set. Such people do not require the composer to match his melodic lines to the feelings that the words suggest, but are content that his melodies should be pleasing, and even singular. As far as they are concerned it is enough that the occasional word in a recitative shall be treated expressively. There are far too many musicians who are of this mind, and who act as though music were incapable of anything more …
>
> Musical compositions that fail to move us can unequivocally be equated with pictures that have no merit other than their coloring, or with poems that are no more than well-constructed verses. In poetry and painting, technical excellence must serve to express the insights of genius, and to reveal those imaginative beauties that constitute the imitation of nature. In the same way, harmonic richness and variety, ornamentation and melodic originality must be used solely to create and embellish the musical imitation of the language of nature and the passions. The science of composition is, so

---

32 Leibniz, 'Criticala Thoughts on the General Part of the Principles of Descartes' (1692), 'On Article 37,' in *Philosophical Papers and Letters* (Dordrecht: Reidel, 1956), 388.

33 Jean-Baptiste Du Bos, *Reflexions critiques sur la poesie et sur la peinture* [Paris, 1719], quoted in Peter le Huray and James Day, *Music and Aesthetics in the Eighteenth and Early-Nineteenth Centuries* (Cambridge: Cambridge University Press, 1981), 18.

to speak, the servant which the genius of the musician must keep under his thumb, just as the poet of genius must control his talent for writing verse … Genius is essential to expression, whereas even without genius, it is still possible to compose scholarly music and to produce excellent rhymes.[34]

Another very important French philosopher, Charles Batteux (1713–1780), left a brilliant discussion of man's forms of communication. He begins with the definition, 'Men have three means of expressing their ideas and their feelings: speech, the tone of the voice, and gesture.'[35] In defining how these three differ, he begins with two extraordinary deductions, which have since been confirmed in clinical research: that emotions are genetic and that through music they speak directly to the listener without the aid of Reason, which is to say, the left hemisphere of the brain. When he says 'music is a dictionary of plain nature,' we again think of early man.

> Speech expresses passion only by means of the ideas to which the feelings are tied, and as though by reflection. Tone and gesture reach the heart directly and without any detour. In a word, speech is a language of institution, which men have formed for communicating their ideas more distinctly: gestures and tones are like the dictionary of plain nature; they contain a language that we all know upon being born and of which we make use to announce everything that is related to our needs and to the conservation of our being: also they are vivid, short, energetic. What better basis for the arts, whose object is to move the soul, than a language all of whose expressions are rather those of humanity itself than those of men![36]

Batteux next draws a distinction between the purpose of music and poetry.

> From which I conclude first: That the principal object of music and of dance should be the imitation of feeling or of passions: instead of which that of poetry is principally the imitation of actions.[37]
>
> ……
>
> Thus poetry having chosen speech, which is most particularly the language of the mind, and music and dance having taken for themselves, the one the tones of the voice, and the other the movements of the body, and these two sorts of expressions being dedicated above all to feeling, true poets have had to attach themselves above all to actions and to discourse, and true musicians to feelings and to passions.[38]

Saint-Evremond was a rare Baroque philosopher who found no interest in opera and it is from this point of view that he agrees with the above point by Batteux.

---

34 Ibid., 21ff.

35 Charles Batteux, *Les beaux-arts reduits a un meme principe* [Paris,1746], quoted in Peter le Huray and James Day, *Music and Aesthetics in the Eighteenth and Early-Nineteenth Centuries* (Cambridge: Cambridge University Press, 1981), 260.

36 Ibid., 260ff.

37 Ibid.

38 Ibid., 262.

254 Part 3: What Music Is

> There is nothing so ridiculous as having an action sung, whether it be the deliberation of a Council, the giving of orders in battle, or anything else. Where the Gods are concerned there may be singing: every Nation has worshiped them in song, and chanted their praises. We can sing what we feel and suffer, for grief and affection are naturally expressed by a kind of tender and melancholy song. But our actions require no other expression but the spoken word.³⁹

But Batteux would have clarified this by adding that in opera it is the communication of feelings we are interested in, not the actions of the plot.⁴⁰

Batteux concludes his discussion with a marvelous testimonial to the fact that the importance of music, the feelings, cannot be communicated in words.

> It is true, you may say, that a melodic line can express certain passions: love, for instance, or joy, or sadness. But for every passion that can be identified there are a thousand others that cannot be put into words.
>
> That is indeed so, but does it follow that these are pointless? It is enough that they are felt; they do not have to be named. The heart has its own understanding that is independent of words. When it is touched it has understood everything. Moreover, just as there are great things that words cannot reach, so there are subtle things that words cannot capture, above all things that concern the feelings.⁴¹

The famous Descartes contributed nothing of interest on the subject of music as a language, although he agreed that the purpose of music was 'to arouse various emotions in us.'⁴² Voltaire left several poems which mention the power of music to express emotions and one of these reminds the listener that 'The ear's a passage to the heart.'⁴³

The well-known English writer, Roger North (1653–1734) includes the communication of emotion as part of the purpose of music. When he writes that to understand good music we must look to Nature itself, he is, of course, thinking of emotion.

> Therefore in order to find the criteria of Good Music we must look into Nature itself, and the truth of things. Music hath two ends. First to please the sense, and that is done by the pure Dulcor of harmony, which is found chiefly in older music ... Secondly, to move the emotions, or excite the passion; and that is done by measures of time joined with the former [the emotions].⁴⁴

The English philosopher of the Baroque who was most thoughtful on the nature of communication through music was Charles Avison (1709–1770). He mentions something that only a very few prior philosophers had, that it is somehow the nature of music itself that it only communicates *positive* emotions.

---

39 Saint-Evremond, Letter to d'Hervart, February, 1675, quoted in *The Letters of Saint-Evremond*, ed. John Hayward (Freeport, NY: Books for Libraries Press, 1971), 161ff.

40 Batteux, *Les beaux-arts reduits a un meme principe*, 263.

41 Ibid.,50

42 'Compendium of Music,' trans. Walter Robert (American Institute of Musicology, 1961), 11.

43 'The Answer.' See also his poems 'The Maid of Orleans.' 'The Nature of Pleasure' and 'The Henriade.'

44 Quoted in John Wilson, *Roger North on Music* (London: Novello, 1959), 291ff.

> I would appeal to any man, whether ever he found himself urged to acts of selfishness, cruelty, treachery, revenge, or malevolence by the power of musical sounds? Or if he ever found jealousy, suspicion, or ingratitude engendered in his breast, either from harmony or discord? I believe no instance of this nature can be alleged with truth. It must be owned, indeed, that the force of music may urge the passions to an excess, or it may fix them on false and improper objects, and may thus be pernicious in its effects: But still the passions which it raises, though they may be misled or excessive, are of the benevolent and social kind, and in their intent at least are disinterested and noble.[45]

He immediately recognizes that some readers might consider the emotions of terror and grief to be an exception to what he has just written. But, no,

> terror raised by musical expression is always of that grateful kind, which arises from an impression of something terrible to the imagination, but which is immediately dissipated, by a subsequent conviction, that the danger is entirely imaginary … As to grief, it will be sufficient to observe that as it always has something of the social kind for its foundation, so it is often attended with a kind of sensation, which may with truth be called pleasing.

Avison makes another, and very important, point. What we call today, 'text-painting,' is not an example of music communicating feeling. This is more like metaphor and detracts from the genuine expression of emotions which is the nature of music.

> What then is the composer, who would aim at true musical expression, to perform? I answer, he is to blend such an happy mixture of melody and harmony, as will affect us most strongly with the passions or affections which the poet intends to raise: and that, on this account, he is not principally to dwell on particular words in the way of imitation, but to comprehend the poet's general drift or intention … If he attempts to raise the passions by imitation, it must be such a temperate and chastised imitation, as rather brings the object before the hearer, than such a one as induces him to form a comparison between the object and the sound. For, in this last case, [the listener's] attention will be turned entirely on the composer's art, which must effectually check the passion. The power of music is, in this respect, parallel to the power of eloquence: if it works at all, it must work in a secret and unsuspected manner.[46]

One English theorist, Thomas Mace (1613–1709), when he considered the confusion of languages on earth, and the fact that this condition would only be multiplied in Heaven, wondered if perhaps music would be the language of communication there.

> And I am subject to believe (if in Eternity we shall make use of any languages, or shall not understand one another, by some more spiritual conveyances, or infusions of perceptions, than by verbal language) that music itself may be that eternal and celestial language.[47]

---

[45] Charles Avison, *An Essay on Musical Expression* [London, 1753] (New York: Broude Reprint, 1967), 2ff. Of course, he had not heard the pop music of our era!

[46] Ibid., 69ff. In a footnote, Avison reflects that the 'wonderful effects' attributed to the ancient Greek composers must have been due to 'the pure simplicity of melody.'

[47] Thomas Mace, *Musick's Monument* [1676] (Paris: Editions du Centre National de la Recherche Scientifique, 1966), 272.

We have mentioned above some of the characteristics of the 'music' of early man which is with us still in our spoken languages. The English philosopher William Shenstone (1714–1763), a man of perceptive intelligence, was of the opinion that perhaps it is the genetic music in us which determines our preferences in literary authors. After reading his comments, it occurred to us that instead of saying language developed *after* music, perhaps we should say language is a form *of* music.

> It may in some measure account for the difference of taste in the reading of books, to consider the difference of our ears for music. One is not pleased without a perfect melody of style, be the sense what it will. Another, of no ear for music, gives to sense its full weight without any deduction on account of harshness.
>
> Harmony of period and melody of style have greater weight than is generally imagined in the judgment we pass upon writing and writers. As proof of this, let us reflect, what texts of scripture, what lines in poetry, or what periods we most remember and quote, either in verse or prose, and we shall find them to be only musical ones.[48]

In this regard he adds later,

> I have sometimes thought Virgil so remarkably musical, that were his lines read to a musician, wholly ignorant of the language, by a person of capacity to give each word its proper accent, he would not fail to distinguish in it all the graces of harmony.[49]

The famous Lord Chesterfield points to the purpose of the communication of emotions, but conditions this on the premise of accuracy in performance.

> The best compositions of Corelli, if ill executed and played out of tune, instead of touching, as they do when well performed, would only excite the indignation of the hearers, when murdered by an unskilled performer.[50]

There are, of course, many passing references by English writers to the power of communication through music. Two we give as representatives of many more. First, from Sonnet II by John Milton (1608–1674), a tribute to the power of music,

> When, beautiful, thou speakest, or, in mood of happiness, sing in such guise that the hardest and wildest oak is moved to feeling, one must guard the gateways to ear and eye.

Second, a powerful reference to music of grief found in *Antonio and Mellida* (IV, i), by the playwright, John Marston (1575–1634):

> I prithee sing, but mark my words
> Let each note breathe the heart of passion,
> The sad extracture of extremest grief.

---

48 William Shenstone, *Men and Manners* (Boston: Houghton Mifflin, 1927), 49.

49 Ibid., 73.

50 Earl of Chesterfield, letter to his son, July 9, 1750.

> Make me a strain speak groaning like a bell
> That tolls departing souls;
> Breathe me a point that may enforce me weep,
> To wring my hands, to break my cursed breast,
> Rave, and exclaim, lie grovelling on the earth,
> Straight start up frantic, crying, Mellida!
> Sing but, 'Antonio hath lost Mellida,'
> And thou shalt see me like a man possess'd
> Howl out such passion, that even this brinish marsh
> Will squeeze out tears from out his spongy cheeks:
> The rocks even groan, and—prithee, prithee sing.`

By the arrival of the nineteenth century the arguments of these early philosophers were confirmed time and time again. We need not repeat the arguments at length, but for the interest of the reader we shall provide some representative quotations. We begin with the employment of music when language fails.

When Langauge Fails

Franz Liszt:

> When one is at a loss what to say or write, well—one tries to help oneself with music.[51]

Richard Wagner:

> It is a truth forever, that where the speech of man stops short, there Music's reign begins.[52]

Hans Christian Anderson:

> Where words fail, music speaks.

Leo Tolstoy:

> Music is the shorthand of emotion. Emotions which let themselves be described in words with such difficulty, are directly conveyed to man in music, and in that is its power and significance.[53]

Victor Hugo:

> To sing seems a deliverance from bondage. Music expresses that which cannot be said, and which cannot be suppressed.

---

[51] Letter to Adelheid von Schorn, Rome, Sept. 15, 1877.
[52] Wagner, 'A Happy Evening.'
[53] Quoted in Nat Shapiro, *An Encyclopedia of Quotations About Music* (New York: Da Capo, 1978), 199.

Robert Ingersoll:

> Language is not subtle enough, tender enough to express all we feel, and when language fails, the highest and deepest longings are translate into music.

We add now some similar quotations on the general nature of music as a language of feeling.

On Music as a Language of Feeling

Robert Schumann:

> Music is to me the perfect expression of the soul.[54]
>
> ......
>
> Schubert unburdened his heart on a sheet of music paper, just as others leave the impression of passing moods in their journals. His soul was so steeped in music that he wrote notes where others use words.[55]

Hector Berlioz:

> The prevailing characteristics of my music are passionate expression, intense ardor, rhythmical animation, and unexpected turns.[56]

Paul Dukas:

> Be it laughter or tears, feverish passion or religious ecstasy, nothing, in the category of human feelings, is a stranger to music.[57]

Max Reger:

> Music, in and by itself, should generate a flow of pure emotion without the least tinge of extraneous rationalization.[58]

Maurice Ravel:

> Music, I feel, must be emotional first and intellectual second.[59]

---

[54] Letter to his mother, Leipzig, May 8, 1832.

[55] Letter to Friedrich Wieck, Heidelberg, Nov. 6, 1829.

[56] *Memoirs.*

[57] Quoted in Shapiro, *An Encyclopedia of Quotations About Music*, 194.

[58] Letter to Adalbert Lindner (June 6, 1891)

[59] Quoted in Shapiro, *An Encyclopedia of Quotations About Music*, 197.

Frederick Delius:

> Music is an outburst of the soul.[60]

Felix Mendelssohn:

> Music is a distinct language which speaks clearly.[61]
>
> ……
>
> People usually complain that music is so ambiguous; that it is so doubtful what they ought to think when they hear it; whereas everyone understands words. With me it is entirely the reverse. And not only with regard to an entire speech, but also with individual words; these, too, seem to me to be so ambiguous, so vague, and so easily misunderstood in comparison with genuine music, which fills the soul with a thousand things better than words. The thoughts which are expressed to me by a piece of music which I love are not too indefinite to be put into words, but on the contrary too definite.[62]

Modest Mussorgsky:

> Music is a means of communicating with people, not an aim in itself.

Edward MacDowell:

> Music … is a language, but a language of the intangible, a kind of soul-language.[63]

Richard Wagner:

> Music is the speech of Passion.[64]
>
> ……
>
> Music, who speaks to us solely through quickening into articulate life the most universal concept of the inherently speechless Feeling.[65]

Bruno Walter:

> At no time and in no place has music been merely playing with sounds. The vibrations themselves which we perceive as musical sounds are not exclusively material in nature—emotional elements are active in them, lending inner meaning and coherence to the sound phenomenon: only thus can the successive and simultaneous arrangement of notes become a musical language whose eloquence speaks to the human soul.[66]

---

[60] Ibid., 11.
[61] Letter to Carl Zelter, Rome, June 31, 1831.
[62] Letter to Marc Andre Souchay (October 5, 1842).
[63] *Critical and Historical Essays* (1912).
[64] Wagner, 'Judaism in Music.'
[65] *Richard Wagner's Prose Works* (New York: Broude Brothers), V, 77.
[66] Bruno Walter, *Of Music and Music-Making* (New York: Norton, 1957), 65.

We need also to recommend to the reader Wagner's essay on Beethoven[67] in which he pays homage to Schopenhauer's discussion of music as a language of feeling. The key points Schopenhauer makes are:

1. His wonder at the fact that music is a language immediately intelligible by everyone.
2. Music does this directly with no need of any aid from the intellect.
3. Music is an Idea unto itself and is not a part of something else.
4. Music cannot strictly be set forth in logical terms [music theory!] and the essence of music cannot be understood through any mere *objective* knowledge [such as drawing Roman numerals beneath the chords].

This final point that Wagner draws from the philosophy of Schopenhauer is what lies at the heart of the failure of modern American music education.

Finally we have mentioned above several philosophers who went so far as to propose the possibility of using music to replace ordinary international languages. This idea was particularly current in France where Descartes, Chenier, Nodier, Chabanon, De Vismes and J.-J. Rousseau in particular, began to speculate on the possibility of an international language based on music. An article by Voltaire, in his *Dictionnaire philosophique*, will provide the reader with the general line of thought among these various philosophers.

> There is no complete language which has the power to express all of our ideas and feelings, whose nuances are very numerous and imperceptible.
>
> No one can express precisely the degree of feeling that he feels. One is obliged, in consequence, to use a general name, such as love or hate, for thousands of different kinds of love and hate—everyone would be different. It is the same for pain and pleasure. All languages are imperfect, as we are …
>
> Languages have all been made successively [over time], and by degrees, according to our needs. It is the instinct common to all men which made the first grammar, without being aware of it. The Laplander, the Blacks, as well as the Greeks, needed to be able to express the past, present and future; and they did it, but not because they ever had meetings of logicians to create a language. No one ever created an absolutely regular language …
>
> Of all the languages of Europe, the French language must be the most general, because it is the most proper for conversation: its character is in common with the people who speak it …
>
> The most beautiful language should be the one which can express the weakest and most impetuous movements of the soul. It will be the one which most resembles music.

As extraordinary as this idea may seem, of having music replace ordinary languages, there was one Frenchman, Jean-François Sudre who, if we can believe contemporary press accounts of his live demonstrations, apparently succeeded. Sometime before 1819, Sudre, a music teacher, designed a system of notation whereby numbers were assigned to pitches, but this seems to have had little immediate success.

His next invention was quite different, a kind of Morse code consisting of four pitches (*sol, ut, mi and sol*) intended to be played by a trumpet for use in the military. His system was a competitor of the newly developed telegraph, which at this time consisted of long wires leading to

---

[67] *Richard Wagner's Prose Works*, V, 65ff.

a hill top where a device contained large letters of the alphabet. The field commander would send signals over the wires and the required letters would pop up to be read by the soldiers in the field. Since Sudre's system was designed to be heard, not requiring the wires, etc., he called his system *Téléphonie* or *Télégraphe Acoustique*. It was the first coining of the word telephone!

The *Téléphonie* was given a field test on the Champ-de-Mars in 1829 before a number of generals. A general would give an order such as 'Start to march at 4:00 in the morning,' and Sudre's trained trumpeter would play the appropriate sequences of four pitches. Another trained trumpeter at the opposite end of the field immediately translated the sounds correctly for a general standing beside him.[68]

This was the first of many trials for both the army and navy and they always ended with a recommendation to the government to adapt Sudre's system because it was a noticeable improvement over the ancient system of trumpet calls ('charge,' 'retreat,' etc.). In addition the government requested several tests before the Institute de France. One in 1833 included among the Jury the leading composers of Paris: Cherubini, Lesueur, Berton, Boieldieu, Auber and Paer. They enthusiastically endorsed the system. A similar test in 1852 included on the jury the composers Auber, Halevy, Adam, Carafa, Onslow and Thomas. One demonstration in 1835 in the hall of the Conservatoire was heard by Berlioz, who wrote,

> For the second time, day before yesterday, we have seen and heard M. Sudre …
> We have seen the telegraph of M. Sudre function, and we predict the ruin of all the present telegraphs of day and night. All of the diplomatic notes will be transmitted in musical notes …
> To sing out of tune would now become a capital sin like the lie, a crime against the nation like perjury.[69]

During this time Sudre was requesting a modest payment from the government to reveal the secret of his system, patriotically resisting firm offers from Germany to buy the system for their military. But the government never responded, in spite of the frequent commissions who enthusiastically endorsed the various trials.

Growing weary of the military ever adopting his system, Sudre moved on to grander plans—a system whereby five pitches (and later up to seven) could reproduce everything necessary for ordinary communication in the French language. Now he developed a dictionary of nearly thirteen thousand combinations of five pitches, organized by tonal centers. For example, the key center of D included household items, the key of B included all government vocabulary and the key of G included the fine arts and science. Thus, in the key of G, 'flute' was *sol, re, do, me* and 'oboe' was *sol, re, do, fa*, etc. Eventually he made corresponding dictionaries in ten other languages including Arabic and Chinese!

---

[68] In Germany, one B. C. A. Weyrich published in Leipzig in 1830 a similar system of which we know nothing. He called it *Die Instrumentation-Sprechkunst oder Anleitung durch instrumentaltone alle Nachrichten in die Ferne zu geben, sowloll in Frieden als in Kriege, beim Civil und Military, auf dem Lande und Meere.*

[69] Vert-Vert, January 27, 1835.

It staggers the imagination to suppose anyone could learn thousands of combinations of five pitches, but Sudre and his students regularly demonstrated in public this new system, now called the Universal Musical Language. Typically Sudre would be on stage next to a blackboard which would be turned so only the audience could see it. A member of the audience would contribute a phrase of French written on paper, which Sudre would then write on the board for all to see. Then he would play his musical translation on his violin whereupon a student trained in the system would hear Sudre's playing from a distant closed room and would then enter the auditorium and invariably announce the very French phrase written on the blackboard. It never failed!

Sudre demonstrated his new Universal Musical Language in numerous public venues, in France, Belgium and in England. All were described in detail in the press. In a typical summation the *Le Temps* of 27 February 1835, wrote,

> It was a curious thing to see the master dictate on his violin various successive notes which the student translated so rapidly on the blackboard in words of the common language. The phrase had been given extemporaneously by the spectators, and no one could be tempted to suspect in all of this any sort of trickery [*charlatanisme*].

In the summer of 1835 Sudre made a demonstration in London presided over by the president of the Royal Society of London. The *Morning Herald* reported,

> Mr. Children, secretary of the Royal Society, was present at this reception, as well as chevalier Bernardi, a scholar of Romance Languages, who had written the phrases which were dictated by His Highness in Hebrew, Greek, Italian, French, Spanish, German, English, Swedish and Dutch. Despite the difficulties in inflections and aspirations of all these different languages, M. Sudre, by means of his instrument, communicated them with a precision which was all the more surprising when one considers that the young student, who had been placed at the end of the long gallery of the magnificent library of His Highness, repeated them exactly even though he did not know any of the languages.[70]

Sudre, stubbornly and yet understandably, steadfastly refused to reveal the key to how his system worked in the hope the government would eventually award him the commensurate grant of fifty thousand francs which a government commission had recommended. The government never did and Sudre died without revealing the key to his system.[71] We should like to close this part of the story with a quotation from another review by Hector Berlioz about Sudre's system, because it is also a wonderful tribute to Berlioz' own extraordinary foresightedness.[72] Having written articles for years in support of the acceptance of Adolph Sax, who was also rejected at every turn, Berlioz begins with a sad reflection on the fate of inventors.

---

[70] A great number of such reviews are reproduced in David Whitwell, *La Téléphonie and the Universal Musical Language* (Austin: Whitwell Publishing, 2012), www.whitwellbooks.com..

[71] A variation on his system based on the human hand and intended for the deaf and blind actually had some success during the following years in institutions for such students.

[72] *Journal des Debats*, November 17, 1849.

And yet the *téléphonie* method has not yet been adopted officially, and the fifty thousand francs have not been given over, and the poor inventor, in order to live, is driven to the last expediencies. If he is not indeed driven mad, he will die of hunger, and it is a true scandal whose causes the Assembly of the Representatives will shortly be called upon to examine.

But this is the fatal law to which the unfortunate, bent under the weight of a new idea, have, in all times and in all places, been subjected. Two years have not passed when they wrote before, here, very seriously to prove the impossibility of the use of the electric telegraph and the absurdity of the attempts made for its application. Yet, today human thought circulates lightening fast from one end of Europe to the other, and in the northern half of America, by means of this simple wire, so ridiculed, whose conduction power (they said) would be paralyzed by the simple contact with a magpie. Napoleon did not recognize the future of steam, and Fulton, in his eyes, was only a fool, whose claims and experiments obsessed him.

Shortly, we will have the repetition of the same spectacle for a discovery even more important, that of the directing of lighter-than-air craft by means of a combination of propellers and inclined planes. Obviously, the latter, once demonstrated and put into usage, the relations of the diverse peoples who make up the large human family will be entirely changed; an immense revolution will be accomplished whose fortunate consequences are incalculable. This is precisely why the audacious mechanic who wishes to give man wings capable of defying the winds and swooping over the storms will experience a stronger and more obstinate resistance. He will be ruined, he will die in harness; he expects to, he is prepared for it. But navigation of the aerial ocean will nonetheless be opened to us sooner or later, and our descendants will be astonished then, because a corner of the veil had already been lifted, that their fathers, doubting for centuries the solution to the problem, should have been so seemingly determined to prowl the terrestrial crust like the most infirm animals.

Time is a great teacher, it is true, but man is a very stupid student.

And so it would seem that Sudre's amazing discovery came and disappeared without leaving a trace on civilization. But, maybe not. The first thing we thought of when, in the National Library in Paris, we saw examples of Sudre's system of nouns represented by a few pitches, and especially the transpositions, such as *do, mi, sol* for 'God 'and *sol, me, do* for 'Devil,' was the *leitmotiv* system of Richard Wagner.

Wagner was in residence in Paris in 1839–1842,[73] a time when Sudre was still conducting his public demonstrations. As witnessed by the leading composers who participated in the several commissions which studied Sudre's system, not to mention the very idea of the system itself, one may reasonably assume that the Universal Musical Language was much discussed among the musicians of Paris, not to mention the leading composers who had served as adjudicators on the government studies of the new system. Wagner was an intellectual with very broad interests, as is documented by the diverse topics contained in his numerous prose articles. It is impossible to believe that Wagner could have been living in the center of Paris for nearly three years and not have attended one of the public demonstrations of the Universal Musical Language by Sudre.

---

[73] In visiting Paris today, the reader can stay in one of the (small) rooms Wagner lived in, Room Nr. 55 in the Hotel du Quai Voltaire, 19, Quai Voltaire, 75007 Paris.

Could Sudre's system have been the inspiration for Wagner's *leit-motiv* system? There were earlier examples of the use of a single melody to personify a character in works by Weber and in Berlioz, but no one has ever believed these cases were related to Wagner's idea. Wagner himself never answered when asked where he got the idea for his *leit-motivs*, so we will never be able to determine if Sudre's system is where he got his inspiration. But it would be nice to think that Sudre's life was not lived in vain and that his rejected Universal Musical Language was a seed that blossomed into some of the world's greatest music.

Due to modern clinical research on the brain we know today that language is located primarily in the left hemisphere and the experiential side of us, including music, is based primarily in the right hemisphere. The right hemisphere is mute, thus the evolution of man has developed special languages for communicating this other side of himself. Of these, music is by far the most powerful.

The real purpose of music, then, is to communicate feelings. Everyone knows this. Even 'normal' people untrained in music know this. Every child knows this. If there was ever a 'core subject' this is it—helping students to get to know themselves as individuals, in particular their individual emotional templates. It was the fundamental reason for music in education from the time of Plato until 1957.

Since 1957 this timeless educational obligation American schools have chosen not to meet. American music educators have elected instead to allow the music of the street form the character and the emotional templates of our children. The results are evident.

The End of Music: Catharsis (Know Thyself)

> Tragedy, then, is an imitation of an action that is serious, complete, and of a certain magnitude; in language embellished with each kind of artistic ornament, the several kinds being found in separate parts of the play; in the form of action, not of narrative; through pity and fear effecting the proper catharsis [*katharein*] of these emotions. By 'language embellished,' I mean language into which rhythm, harmony and song enter. By 'the several kinds in separate parts,' I mean, that some parts are rendered through the medium of verse alone, others again with the aid of song.
>
> Aristotle

THE ABOVE PARAGRAPH BY ARISTOTLE, found in his *Poetics*, is one of the most famous paragraphs in art history.[1] His fundamental purpose was to define for the playwright the elements necessary to create the highest form of drama, Tragedy, as opposed to Epic productions which had more of an entertainment character. In reading of the elements which make up Tragedy the modern reader is probably most surprised by the frequent mention of music as performing a fundamental role, for in the modern productions of these famous ancient Greek plays there is no music at all.

In addition to having in mind the obvious constituent parts of Tragedy, such as plot, character, language, etc., Aristotle famously goes one step beyond the play itself to consider what it meant to the audience, what is the audience left with when the performance of the play is finished? It is for this part of his distinction between Tragedy and Epic productions that he uses the word *catharsis*. In doing so he creates a new branch of philosophy, with catharsis becoming the cornerstone for drama criticism of the following three thousand years in determining the essential distinction between tragedy and comedy. In the study of the aesthetics of music, following the lead of drama criticism very closely, the result of catharsis in the listener is the fundamental distinction between art music, or aesthetic music, and entertainment music.

What did Aristotle mean by this word, *catharsis* [*katharein*]? First, as the reader can see in the famous paragraph above, it is the effect of 'pity and fear' in the audience member. A better modern translation of these two terms might be 'empathy and introspection.' It is clear that when Aristotle uses the word, 'pity,' he means 'empathy,' as we can see in a passage from his treatise on rhetoric.

> Pity may be defined as a feeling of pain caused by the sight of some evil, destructive or painful, which befalls one who does not deserve it, and which we might expect to befall ourselves or some friend of ours, and moreover to befall us soon.

---

[1] *Poetics*, 1449b.24. The work is incomplete and the sections which discussed the use of music in tragedy, in particular, are lost. Later speculation on what the role of music really was in Greek Tragedy led to the creation of opera.

As an illustration, the observer sees on the stage a character who is contemplating incest, the observer realizes he holds some similar thoughts, he sees the gods punish the character on the stage and with introspection he concludes 'that could happen to me.' As a result his bad thoughts are purged, he feels better as a person as a result. He has experienced catharsis. In fact, if one looks in a dictionary for the definition of 'catharsis' one finds 'purging of the emotions,' in the sense of replacing one bad emotion with a good or better one. Thus one can understand that in the field of drama criticism, most later philosophers, such as Corneille, Racine and Lessing, understood Aristotle to mean by catharsis, in the case of the tragedy, that the play had an ethical or moral end.

It seems apparent, by the way, that this experience, if not the name 'catharsis,' had earlier roots in the cult-religious myths of ancient Greece. Plato, for example, had earlier described something of this sort relative to ritual dance.

> The emotion both of the Bacchantes and of the children is an emotion of fear, which springs out of an evil habit of the soul. And when someone applies external agitation to emotions of this sort, the motion coming from without gets the better of the terrible and violent internal one, and produces a peace and calm in the soul, and quiets the restless palpitation of the heart, which is a thing much to be desired, sending the children to sleep, and making the Bacchantes, although they remain awake, to dance to the pipe with the help of those gods to whom they offer acceptable sacrifices, and producing in them a sound mind, which takes the place of their frenzy.[2]

In the context of the new field of Aesthetics which was founded on Aristotle's famous paragraph above, and the focus of later drama criticism, perhaps a more modern analogy with going to the cinema will demonstrate the application of the word 'catharsis.' One goes to the cinema with friends and during the film we are totally involved, we laugh, we cry. But as soon as the film ends, on the way out of the theater we immediately begin talking with our friends about other things, school, boy/girl friends and jobs, etc. On another occasion we go with friends to the cinema and when the film ends no one says a word, sometimes for a long time. We wish we could just sit there and that they would not turn on the lights. In the first example we were entertained. We were totally involved, but unaffected. In the second example the film reached us on a *deeper* level. It did not just 'bounce off.'[3] The observer experienced catharsis.

Aristotle's philosophical idea of catharsis, of purging the emotions and replacing them with good ones, takes on real significance for the modern reader when he discusses this idea in an earlier treatise, *Politics*, for now the subject is music. Here he extends the value of this experience in music by considering two new areas, music for education and music for leisure time.

For music education Aristotle makes a specification which is followed by all later philosophers: only by using the *best* music does the process of catharsis take on a valuable end. Since the object is for the student to model the best of what is available, 'we must use those that express the best character, but we may use melodies of action and enthusiastic melodies for

---

[2] Laws. 791.

[3] The reader will easily recall similar examples of both experiences following concerts.

concerts where other people perform.' Next, Aristotle establishes an important principle, one that Wagner would later write about in discussing how music, when it leaves the stage, affects the numerous individual members of the audience. The belief of both Aristotle and Wagner is that the general nature of an emotion (Wagner calls it the quintessence of an emotion) is shared by all listeners, but each individual listener, based on his own past experience, will understand that emotion on an *individual* level. Aristotle describes the educational end of this emotional catharsis when the student listener is brought back 'to a normal condition as if they had been medically treated and undergone a purge.' Aristotle's text from the *Politics*, reads,

> We say, however, that music is to be studied for the sake of many benefits and not of one only. It is to be studied with a view to education, with a view to a catharsis—we use this term without explanation for the present; when we come to speak of poetry, we shall give a clearer account of it—and thirdly with a view to the right use of leisure and for relaxation and rest after exertion. It is clear, then, that we must use all the modes, but not all in the same way. For educational purposes we must use those that express the best character, but we may use melodies of action and enthusiastic melodies for concerts where other people perform. For every feeling that affects some souls violently affects all souls more or less; the difference is only one of degree. Take pity and fear, for example, or again enthusiasm. Some people are liable to become possessed by the latter emotion, but we see that, when they have made use of the melodies which fill the soul with orgiastic feeling, they are brought back by these sacred melodies to a normal condition as if they had been medically treated and undergone a purge [catharsis, *katharein*]. Those who are subject to the emotions of pity and fear and the feelings generally will necessarily be affected in the same way; and so will other men in exact proportion to their susceptibility to such emotions. All experience a certain purge [*katharein*] and pleasant relief. In the same manner cathartic melodies give innocent joy to men.[4]

Although the early Christian Church attempted to discourage the new Christians from attending the theater as part of its campaign to remove emotions from their daily life and the Church's efforts to destroy Pagan literature, including Plato, Aristotle and the rest of the 'pagan' philosophers, nevertheless theater itself continued as did the teachings of Aristotle regarding Tragedy. We will trace some of the later discussions and definitions of catharsis in order for the reader to see some of the permutations and additions to Aristotle's new philosophy of aesthetics.

St. Augustine, who in his youth had some acting experience, as a later Churchman paints his understanding of catharsis with the brush of the Church's view of the theater as a sinful place.[5]

> Stage plays also carried me away, full of images of my miseries, and of fuel to my fire. Why is it, that man desires to be made sad, beholding doleful and tragical things, which yet himself would by no means suffer? Yet he desires as a spectator to feel sorrow at them, and this very sorrow is his pleasure. What is this but a miserable madness? For a man is the more affected with these actions, the less free he is from such emotions. Howsoever, when he suffers in his own person, it is styled misery; when he compassionates others, then it is mercy. But what sort of compassion is this for feigned and scenical

---

4   *Politics*, VIII: 7; 1341b35–1342a8. This translation is by J. Burnet.

5   Due to the Church, we know almost nothing of theater during the time Augustine lived.

passions? For the auditor is not called on to relieve, but only to grieve: and he applauds the actor of these fictions the more, the more he grieves. And if the calamities of those persons (whether of old times, or mere fiction) be acted in such a way, that the spectator is not moved to tears, he goes away disgusted and criticizing; but if he be moved to passions, he stays intent, and weeps for joy ...

I, miserable, then loved to grieve, and sought out what to grieve at, when in another's and that feigned and personated misery, that acting best pleased me, and attracted me the most vehemently, which drew tears from me.[6]

Eustache Deschamps, student of the great fourteenth-century French poet and musician, Machaut, speaks of the importance of hearing music renewing the spirit in terms of the poor tired scholar!

Music is the final, and the medicinal science of the seven [liberal] arts; for when the heart and spirit of those applied to the other arts ... are wearied and vexed with their labors, Music, by the sweetness of her science and the melodiousness of her voice, sings them her delectable and pleasant melodies with her six notes in thirds, fifths, and octaves. These she performs sometimes with *orgues* and *chalumeaux* [shawms] by blowing with the mouth and touching with the fingers; otherwise with the *harpe, rebebe, vielle, dou aine*, with the noise of *tabours*, with *fleuthes*, and other musical instruments, so much so that by her delectable melody the hearts and minds of those who were fatigued, weighed down, and troubled with the said arts by thought, imagination or labor are revived and restored.[7]

A similar passage is found in fifteenth-century France by Jean de Gerson. This reference is unique in its interesting and curious reference to bells [*campanulae*] used in melodies, in particular as heard 'arranged in certain clocks.'

By these our inner dispositions of mind may be improved and stimulated, for it has been proved that he whose mind is agitated, weakened or tardy rejoices wholly in himself when this celebrated sound is made ... This is the profusion of inestimable joy[8]

The most important Renaissance writer to write of catharsis was the great theorist, Johannes Tinctoris (1435–1511). In writing of the composers he most respected (Dufay, Dunstable and Okeghem, etc.) he describes himself after hearing their music as being 'more refreshed and wiser.'[9] This new phrase, 'to be refreshed,' is one that will be used frequently to describe catharsis during the German Baroque. As for becoming 'wiser,' we trust Tinctoris was thinking of the introspection aspect of Aristotle's definition of catharsis. In this same pas-

---

[6] *The Confessions*, Book III.

[7] Eustache Deschamps, 'L'Art de Dictier,' quoted in Christopher Page, 'Machaut's "Pupil" Deschamps on the Performance of Music,' *Early Music* 5, no. 4 (1977): 488ff, doi: 10.1093/earlyj/5.4.484

[8] Jean de Gerson, 'Tractatus de Canticis,' trans. Christopher Page, in 'Early fifteenth-century instruments in Jean de Gerson's Tractatus de Canticis,' *Early Music* 6, no. 3 (1978): 348, doi: 10.1093/earlyj/6.3.339

[9] *The Art of Counterpoint*, trans. Albert Seay (American Institute of Musicology, 1961), 14ff.

sage Tinctoris lists additional affects which music can have on the listener: music delights God, it excites the soul to piety, it elevates the mind, it makes work easier and it increases convivial pleasures.[10]

During the Renaissance several Italian writers speak of catharsis and they all focus on the 'purge' character of its definition. Torquato Tasso, for example, uses the expression, 'drawing the mind out of itself,' as a synonym of 'purge.' He is writing of the old Greek modes and, like Aristotle, he finds the very ones which accomplish this end in the theater and in the church are the very ones considered too 'powerful' for use in the education of children.

> The Phrygian and Lydian modes, and the one formed by combining them [Mixolydian] are much more desirable in tragedy and the canzone as in these they can move the mind and, so to speak, draw it out of itself. But they are not suitable for instruction …
>
> Since music was invented not merely to entertain idleness or as a medicine and catharsis for the mind but for instruction as well … a solemn and steady music like the Doric [Dorian] will serve the heroic poem better than any other.[11]

An important Italian writer on the Renaissance theater was Antonio Sebastiano, known as Minturno, Bishop of Ugento, who had represented that town in the council of Trent. In his *The Art of Poetry* (1563) he first paraphrases the part of Aristotle's definition of tragedy which deals with catharsis.[12] In Minturno's words, Tragedy arouses,

> feelings of pity and terror, tending to purge the mind of the beholder of similar passions, to his delight and profit.[13]

Later he emphasizes the educational purpose of drama, saying that 'the ennobling or purification of manners is the end toward which all effort is directed.'

Minturno returns to catharsis, giving one of the most extended definitions to be found in early Italian literature and offers an analogy with art of the physician. The terror and pity which the observer experiences in tragedy, he contends,

> frees us most pleasantly from similar passions, for nothing else so curbs the indomitable frenzy of our minds. No one is so completely the victim of unbridled appetites, that, being moved by fear and pity at the unhappiness of others, he is not impelled to throw off the habits that have been the cause of such unhappiness. And the memory of the grave misfortunes of others not only renders us more ready and willing to support our own; it makes us more wary in avoiding like ills. The physician who with a powerful drug extinguishes the poisonous spark of the malady that afflicts the body, is no more powerful than the tragic poet who purges the mind of its troubles through the emotions aroused by his charming verses.[14]

---

[10] Quoted in Gustav Reese, *Music in the Renaissance* (New York: Norton, 1959), 146.

[11] Tasso, *Discourses on the Heroic Poem*, trans. Mariella Cavalchini (Oxford: Clarendon Press, 1973), 199.

[12] He said dramatic works should be no less than three hours in length and no more than four.

[13] Ibid., 58.

[14] Ibid., 58ff.

The prolific Italian writer, Girolamo Cardano (1501–1576) gives the phrase, 'cleansing of the spirit,' as a synonym of 'purge' in his definition of the parts of music. His reference to education and teachers imply that some catharsis related activities were in use.

> Music's usefulness is divided into three parts, for it pertains to instruction and study, or to the cleansing of the spirit, or to spending time pleasurably in leisure, tranquility, and freedom from the pressure of more serious matters. It is often said that emotions in music reflect weakened and enervated morals, but I believe such emotions consist of gentle virtues, and correspond to those more appropriate to action and also to those most divine virtues suitable for intellectual endeavor. Accordingly music celebrates those moral virtues which are especially appropriate to that useful quality which pertains to learning. Teachers and disciplinarians have agreed on the expiative and purgative force of strong emotions. When these emotions subside they may become excessively reversed and softened by giving way especially to emotions of misery and pity, causing dejection and depression. Music also proposes to fill such moods with a certain innocuous pleasure.[15]

Finally among the Italians, there was the very conservative counter-Reformation Church philosopher, Giordano Bruno (b. 1548).[16] He left an allegorical reference to catharsis and extended its range to include arithmetic and geography.

> Jove ordered his first-born, Minerva, to hand him the box he kept under the pillow on his bed, after which he drew forth nine boxes containing nine collyria, prescribed to purge the human mind in respect both to its knowledge and to its disposition. And to begin with he gave three of them to the first three Muses, [Arithmetic, Geometry and Music], saying to them: 'Here for you is the best unguent with which you will be able to purge and make clear your perceptive virtue as regards the number, the size and the harmonious proportion of sensible things.'[17]

We find only two references to catharsis by Renaissance Spanish writers. First, the great drama theorist, Ludovico Castelvetro, in his *Poetics* of 1570, after observing that 'tragedy can have either a happy or a sorrowful ending, as can comedy,' then qualifies this statement by pointing out that catharsis can occur only with a sad ending.

> Tragedy without a sad ending cannot excite and does not excite, as experience shows, either pity or fear.[18]

The great Spanish playwright, Miquel de Cervantes (1547–1616) has a character in his *The Trials of Persiles and Sigismunda* make a reference to a characteristic of catharsis, that one can have a satisfying feeling even though the story is sad.

---

[15] Quoted in Clement Miller, *Hieronymus Cardanus, Writings on Music* (American Institute of Musicology, 1973), 105.

[16] While he reads very conservative today, the Church at the time considered him too liberal and burned him at the stake.

[17] Giordano Bruno, *The Expulsion of the Triumphant Beast*, trans. Arthur Imerti (New Brunswick: Rutgers University Press, 1964), 181ff [II, iii].

[18] Ibid., 65.

> 'If this weren't more a time to be moaning than singing, I'd easily prove the truth of this to you. But if things improve and my tears have a chance to dry, I'll sing, and while they may not be happy songs, at least they can be sad dirges that will cast their spell as they're sung and make you happy as you cry over them.'[19]

The greatest playwright of the sixteenth century, Shakespeare, like Eustache Deschamps, wrote of music refreshing the mind of the student. In *The Taming of the Shrew*, when Lucentio, in criticizing a pretended music teacher, observes,

> Preposterous ass, that never read so far
> To know the cause why music was ordained!
> Was it not to refresh the mind of man
> After his studies or his usual pain?[20]

Finally, there is one Renaissance reference to catharsis which we really like. It is found in the music treatise, *Musica* (1537), by the German theorist Nicholaus Listenius, who was a student at Wittenberg when Luther was there. In this work he first defines music in the two familiar academic categories, the theoretical and practical (performance). The listener, he says, should be left with 'something more,' than the performance itself.

> Practical, whose goal is doing, is that which delights not only in the intricacies of skill, but extends into performance itself, leaving out no part of the act of performance. Hence the practical musician, who teaches others something more than the recognition of art, trains himself in it for the goal of any performance.

He employs this phrase again in a passage where he adds a third part to the medieval definition of music. In addition to the theoretical and the practical, he now adds what he calls the 'poetic.' By this he is thinking of the meaning left with the listener when the performance is concluded. This he calls '*total* performance.' It is most important and enlightening that he also observed in passing that the practical and the poetic always include the theoretical, 'but the reverse is not true.' When he says here that the total performance 'leaves something more' after the conclusion of the performance, he is speaking of catharsis exactly in the sense of our cinema analogy above.

> Poetic is that which is not content with just the understanding of the thing nor with only its practice, but which leaves something more after the labor of performance, as when music or a song of musicians is composed by someone whose goal is total performance and accomplishment. It consists of making or putting together more in this work which afterwards leaves the work perfect and absolute, which otherwise is artificially like the dead.

---

[19] *The Trials of Persiles and Sigismunda*, III, iv.
[20] *The Taming of the Shrew*, III, i, 9ff.

The marriage of the first great composer of the German Baroque, Heinrich Schütz, was celebrated in a poem by Conrad Bayer, which makes a passing reference to music 'renewing the heart and mind.'

> Music, sweet harmony,
> Over all the elements
> Rightly art thou exalted;
> Nothing can be compared to thee.
> To God's own praise and honor
> Dost thou most rightly turn,
> His fame to magnify.
>
> The human voice and song
> And sound of instrument
> Are pleasing thus to God;
> And in the whole wide world,
> Nothing doth please man more,
> Renew the heart and mind
> And drive away all sadness.[21]

In a previous essay we have documented the fact that the Baroque musician was obsessed with finding ways to communicate emotion through music. The composers shared this new emphasis on emotions with the other musicians as is illustrated in Johann Scheibe's poem of 1739, 'Music which does not penetrate the heart or soul … is quite dead.'[22] Composers now began to add forewords and dedications to their scores which clearly gave catharsis as the goal of their music. Thus we find in the score of Bach's *Clavier Übung*, Part III, and also in the 'Goldberg Variations,' a statement to the effect that his purpose was to 'refresh the spirits' of the listener. Similarly, when Bach was looking into a position in Halle, he was sent a contract which specified that the church music should have the result that 'the members of the Congregation shall be the more inspired and refreshed in worship.'[23]

We can document this transformation in the foreword of Georg Muffat's *Auserlesene Instrumental-Music* (1701). First, he explains that in his previous collections he has sought to draw 'liveliness and grace' from the 'Lullian well.' In other words, previously he wrote in the French style, whose goal contemporaries often referred to as 'tickling the ears.' Now, in the present collection Muffat says his goal is to present 'certain profound and unusual affects of the Italian manner.' The purpose of this music, as he makes very clear, is what we would call 'concert music' in the modern sense. That is, serious music intended for the contemplative listener. Muffat expresses it this way:

---

[21] Quoted in Hans Moser, *Heinrich Schütz* (St. Louis: Concordia, 1936), 104.

[22] Poem in honor of the publication of Johann Mattheson, *Der vollkommene Capellmeister* [1739], trans. Ernest Harriss (Ann Arbor: UMI Research Press, 1981), 74.

[23] Quoted in Hans T. David and Arthur Mendel, *The Bach Reader* (New York: Norton, 1966), 65.

> These concerti, suited neither to the church … nor for dancing … [are] composed only for the express refreshment of the ear.

French music was little affected by the movements in the rest of Europe until late in the Baroque. Comments by French philosophers, however, suggest that they were moving toward the equivalent of catharsis in other fields. Blaise Pascal (1623–1662), for example, contends that the emotions employed by the orator should result in the awakening and contemplation of the listener's own emotions. His final line we quote here is a perfect illustration of the educational value in having students get to know 'great minds.'

> When a natural discourse paints a passion or an effect, one feels within oneself the truth of what one reads, which was there before, although one did not know it. Hence one is inclined to love him who makes us feel it, for he has not shown us his own riches, but ours.[24]

Charles de Marguetel de Saint-Denis, sieur de Saint-Evremond (1610–1703) gives his own definition of catharsis as part of his discussion of the end, or purpose, of tragedy.

> We ought, in tragedy, before all things whatever, to look after a greatness of soul well expressed, which excites in us a tender admiration. By this sort of admiration our minds are sensibly ravished, our courage elevated, and our souls deeply affected.[25]

The only English philosopher during the Baroque who mentioned the phenomenon of catharsis in music was Francis Hutcheson (1694–1746) in his *Essay on the Nature and Conduct of the Passions and Affections* (1742). His discussion is disappointing, however, as it reflects the 'stiff upper-lip' of English high society and their public lack of enthusiasm toward the emotions.

> There is also another charm in Musick to various persons, which is distinct from the harmony, and is occasioned by its raising agreeable passions. The human voice is obviously varied by all the stronger passions; now when our ear discerns any resemblance between the melody of the composition [*Air of a Tune*], whether sung or played upon an instrument, either in its time, or modulation, or any other circumstance, to the sound of the human voice in any passion, we shall be touched by it in a very sensible manner, and have Melancholy, Joy, Gravity, Thoughtfulness excited in us by a sort of *Sympathy* or *Contagion*.

It is ironic that this tepid discussion of catharsis came at the same time and place as the music of Henry Purcell, who wrote some of the most emotionally powerful music of the seventeenth century.

The one subject not mentioned in the preceding two thousand years of philosophical thought is popular music. In the case of producing catharsis, entertainment music does not work because by its very nature it does not reach us at deeper levels. And it is for the same reason that during this same long period there was no mention of popular music used for educational purposes.

---

[24] Blaise Pascal, *Pensees* (New York: Modern Library, 1941), I, xiv.

[25] Quoted in Barrett Clark, *European Theories of the Drama* (New York: Crown Publishers, 1959), 167.

Plato, still thinking of the association of music and religion, set the tone when he observed,

> Most persons say, that the excellence of music is to give pleasure to our souls. But this is intolerable and blasphemous.[26]

Plato's principal concern was that amusement in any form, aside from the immediate pleasure, had a potential for harming the soul.

> SOCRATES. I would have you consider … whether there are not other similar activities which have to do with the soul—some of them activities of art, making a provision for the soul's highest interest; others despising the interest, and as in the parallel case considering only the pleasure, of the soul, and how this may be acquired, but not considering what pleasures are good or bad, and having no other aim but to afford gratification, whether good or bad. In my opinion, Callicles, there are such activities, and this is the sort of thing which I term flattery, whether concerned with the body or the soul or anything else on which it is employed with a view to pleasure and without any consideration of good and evil.[27]

And, of course it followed that Plato was especially concerned over the potential for harm of entertainment within the educational environment.

> Then, I said, our guardians must lay the foundations of their fortress in music?
> Yes, he said; the lawlessness of which you speak too easily steals in.
> Yes, I replied, in the form of amusement, and as though it were harmless.
> Why, yes, he said, and harmless it would be; were it not that little by little this spirit of license, finding a home, imperceptibly penetrates into manners and customs; whence issuing with greater force it invades contracts between man and man, and from contracts goes on to laws and constitutions, in utter recklessness, ending at last, Socrates, by an overthrow of all rights, private as well as public.
> Is that true? I said.
> That is my belief, he replied.
> Then, as I was saying, our boys should be trained from the first in a stricter system, for if childish amusement becomes lawless, it will produce lawless children, who can never grow up into well-conducted and virtuous citizens.[28]

And this is the point where every intelligent citizen needs to consider the nature of music education in the United States. The first question must be: Is the purpose of music education to heighten the intellectual awareness of my child or to entertain him? The subsequent question should be: Should catharsis be at the center of music education? Enabling the student to get to know, experience and heighten his own emotional make up is something that music can do that no other core subject can do.

---

[26] *Laws.*, 655d.

[27] *Gorgias*, 501b.

[28] *Republic*, IV, 424d.

This potential, together with the gifts handed us by modern clinical brain research, should have been the catalyst for a Renaissance in music education, making music teachers among the most valued faculty members in the school. This is precisely because we can educate the half of the brain which the rest of education ignores. To date this has not happened because we have been blinded by the 'conceptual' theories of the doctors of education, educational theories which are easy to test but have nothing to do with real music, and by a turn to entertainment music in the classroom in the desperate search for popularity, the quiet hand-maiden of educational accountability.

Three millennia of philosophers and modern Nobel Prize winning medical research have made perfectly clear the inherent values of music education. When will we connect the dots?

Bibliography

CHAPTER 1 ANCIENT VOICES ASK: WHAT IS MUSIC

Aristotle. *Nicomachean Ethics*.
Aristoxenus. *The Elements of Harmony*. Translated by Henry S. Macran. Hildesheim: Georg Olms Verlag, 1974.
Aurelian of Reome. *The Discipline of Music*. Translated by Joseph Ponte. Colorado Springs: Colorado College Music Press, 1968.
Bacon, Roger. *The Opus Majus of Roger Bacon*. Translated by Robert Burke. New York: Russell & Russell, 1962.
Boethius. *Fundamentals of Music*. Translated by Calvin Bower. Haven: Yale University Press.
Browne, Thomas. *Sir Thomas Browne's Works*. Edited by Simon Wilkin. London: Pickering, 1836.
Carpenter, Nan Cooke. *Music in the Medieval and Renaissance Universities*. Norman: University of Oklahoma Press, 1958.
Cassiodorus, 'On Dialectic,' in *An Introduction to Divine and Human Readings*. Translated by Leslie Jones. York, Octagon Books, 1966.
Johannes de Grocheo. *De Musica*. Translated by Albert Seay. Colorado Springs: Colorado College Music Press, 1967.
Listenius, Nicolaus. *Musica*. Translated by Albert Seay. Colorado Springs: Colorado College Music Press, 1975.
Marchetto of Padua. *Lucidarium*. Translated by Jan W. Herlinger. Chicago: University of Chicago Press, 1985.
Mattheson, Johann. *Der vollkommene Capellmeister* [1739]. Translated by Ernest Harriss. Ann Arbor: UMI Research Press, 1981.
Mersenne, Marin. *Harmonie universelle* [1636], Treatise Three, Book Two ('Second Book of Songs') of the *Traitez de la Voix et des Chants*. Translated by Wilbur F. Russell. Princeton: Westminster Choir College, unpublished dissertation, 1952.
Plato. *Laws*.
———. *Phaedo*.
———. *Politica*.
———. *Prior Analytics*.
———. *Symposium*.
———. *Timaeus*.
Sextus Empiricus, 'Against the Musicians,' in *Against the Professors*. Translated by R. G. Bury. Cambridge: Harvard University Press, 1949.

St. Augustine. *On Music*. Translated by Robert Taliaferro in *Writings of Saint Augustine*. New York: Fathers of the Church.

St. Bernard. *De Revisione Cantus Cistercienis*. Translated by Francisco Guentner. American Institute of Musicology, 1974.

Wagner, Richard. *Richard Wagner's Prose Works*. Translated by William Ashton Ellis. New York: Broude.

Wilson, John. *Roger North on Music*. London: Novello, 1959.

Chapter 2 On the Ancient Gods of Music

Athenaeus. *Deipnosophistae*.

Chamberlin, Henry H. *Last Flowers*. Cambridge: Harvard University Press, 1937.

Clement of Alexandria. *The Miscellanies*. Translated by William Wilson. Edinburgh: T & T Clark, 1884i.

Dryden, John. *The Works of John Dryden*. Edited by Edward Hooker. Berkeley: University of California Press, 1956.

Engel, Carl. *The Music of The Most Ancient Nations*. London: Reeves, 1909.

Farmer, Henry G., 'The Music of Ancient Mesopotamia,' in *The New Oxford History of Music*. London: Oxford University Press, 1966.

Herodotus. *The History of Herodotus*. Translated by David Grene. Chicago: University of Chicago Press, 1987.

Manniche, Lise. *Music and Musicians in Ancient Egypt*. London: British Museum Press, 1991.

Oldham, John. *The Works of John Oldham*. London: Bettenham.

Ovid. *Amores*.

———. *The Love Poems*.

———. *Metamorphoses*.

Pope, Alexander. 'Ode on St. Cecilia's Day,' in *The Works of Alexander Pope*. New York: Gordian Press, 1967.

Sendrey, Alfred. *Music in the Social and Religious Life of Antiquity*. Rutherford: Fairleigh Dickinson University Press, 1974.

Statius. *Thebaid*.

Tibullus. *Poems*.

Chapter 3 On Ancient Muses and Myths

Athenaeus. *Deipnosophistae*.

Ausonius. *Ausonius*. Translated by Hugh G. Evelyn White. London: Heinemann, 1921.

Capella, Martianus. *Martianus Capella and the Seven Liberal Arts*. Translated by William Harris Stahl and Richard Johnson. New York: Columbia University Press, 1977.

Cassiodorus. *Variae*. Translated by Thomas Hodgkin. London: Frowde, 1886.

Chappell, W. *The History of Music*. London: Chappell.

Erasmus, Desiderius. *The Collected Works of Erasmus*. Toronto: University of Toronto Press, 1992.
Gesta Romanorum. Translated by Charles Swan. London: C. and J. Rivington, 1824.
Horace. *Odes*.
Lucian. *Icaromenippus*.
Martin, L. C. *The Poetical Works of Robert Herrick*. Oxford: Clarendon Press, 1963.
Milton, John. *The Works of John Milton*. Edited by Frank Patterson. New York: Columbia University Press, 1931–1938.
Nagy, Gregory. *Pindar's Homer*. Baltimore: Johns Hopkins University Press, 1982.
Ovid. *Metamorphoses*.
Philetaerus. *The Aulos Lover*, quoted in Athenaeus.
Pliny the Elder. *Natural History*.
Seneca. *Hippolytus*.
———. *Medea*.
Strabo. *The Geography of Strabo*. Translated by Horace L. Jones. Cambridge: Harvard University Press, 1960.
Tertullian, 'Spectacles,' in *Disciplinary, Moral and Ascetical Works*. Translated by Rudolph Arbesmann. New York: Fathers of the Church, 1959.
Tibullus. *Poems*.
Virgil. *Georgics*.
Voltaire. *The Works of Voltaire*. New York: St. Hubert Guild, 1901.

CHAPTER 4 ON DIVINE INSPIRATION

Cicero. *De Divinatione*.
———. *Tusculan Disputations*.
Clement of Alexandria. *Miscellanies*. Translated by William Wilson. Edinburgh: T. & T. Clark, 1884.
Genealogia Deorum Gentilium, quoted in *Boccaccio on Poetry*. Translated by Charles Osgood. New York: The Liberal Arts Press, 1956.
Goldin, Frederick. *Lyrics of the Troubadours and Trouveres*. Garden City: Anchor Books.
Horace. *Epistles*.
———. *Satires*.
———. *Odes*.
Joannes Scotus Eriugena. *Periphyseon on the Division of Nature*. Translated by Myra Uhlfelder. Indianapolis: Bobbs-Merrill, 1976.
Nichols, Stephen. *The Songs of Bernart de Ventadorn*. Chapel Hill: The University of North Carolina Press, 1965.
Origen. *De Principiis*. Translated by Frederick Crombie, in *The Writings of Origen*. Edinburgh: T. & T. Clark, 1871.

Ovid. *Amores*.
———. *Letters*.
———. *Metamorphoses*.
———. *The Art of Love*.
Press, Alan. *Anthology of Troubadour Lyric Poetry*. Austin: University of Texas Press, 1971.
Propertius. *Poems*.
Saint Justin Martyr. *The Monarchy or The Rule of God*. Translated by Thomas B. Falls. New York: Christian Heritage, Inc.
Sharman, Ruth. *The Cansos and Sirventes of the Troubadour Giraut de Borneil*. Cambridge: Cambridge University Press, 1989.
Tibullus. *Poems*.
Vagabond Verse. Translated by Edwin H. Zeydel. Detroit: Wayne State University Press, 1966,
Van der Werf, Hendrik. *The Chansons of the Troubadours and Trouvères*. Utrecht: A. Oosthoek, 1972.
Virgil. *Georgics*.

CHAPTER 5 IS MUSIC MATH?

Aristotle. *Metaphysics*.
Aurelian of Reome. *The Discipline of Music*. Translated by Joseph Ponte. Colorado Springs: Colorado College Music Press, 1968.
Bacon, Roger. *The Opus Majus of Roger Bacon*. Translated by Robert Burke. New York: Russell & Russell, 1962.
Boethius. *Fundamentals of Music*. Translated by Calvin Bower. New Haven: Yale University Press.
Cannon, Beekman. *Johann Mattheson, Spectator in Music*. Archon Books, 1968.
Carpenter, Nan Cooke. *Music in the Medieval and Renaissance Universities*. Norman: University of Oklahoma Press, 1958.
Cassiodorus. *The Letters of Cassiodorus*. London: Frowde, 1886.
Coclico, Adrian. *Musical Compendium*. Translated by Albert Seay. Colorado Springs: Colorado College Music Press, 1973.
David Hans T. and Arthur Mendel. *The Bach Reader*. New York: Norton, 1966.
Empiricus, Sextus. *Against the Professors*. Translated by R. G. Bury. Cambridge: Harvard University Press, 1949.
Erasmus, Desiderius. *The Collected Works of Erasmus*. Toronto: University of Toronto Press, 1992.
Galilei, Vincenzo. *Fronimo* [1584]. Translated by Carol MacClintock. Neuhasen-Stuttgart: Hanssler-Verlag, 1985.
Johannes Cochlaeus. *Tetrachordum Musices*. Translated by Clement Miller. American Institute of Musicology, 1970.

Johannes de Grocheo. *De Musica*. Translated by Albert Seay. Colorado Springs: Colorado College Music Press, 1967.

Leibniz, Gottfried. *Leibniz Selections*. Edited by Philip Wiener. New York: Scribner's, 1951.

Matthéson, Johann. *Das Neu-Eröffnete Orchestre*. Hamburg, 1713.

———. *Der vollkommene Capellmeister* [1739]. Translated by Ernest Harriss. Ann Arbor: UMI Research Press, 1981.

Miller, Clement. *Hieronymus Cardanus, Writings on Music*. American Institute of Musicology, 1973.

Newton, Isaac. *The Correspondence of Isaac Newton*. Cambridge: University Press, 1959.

Nicholas of Cusa. *Compendium*. Translated by William Wertz, Jr., in *Toward a New Council of Florence*. Washington, D.C.: Schiller Institute, 1993.

Strunk, Oliver. *Source Readings in Music History*. New York: Norton, 1950.

Tinctoris. *Concerning the Nature and Propriety of Tones*. Translated by Albert Seay. Colorado Springs, 1976.

———. *Proportionale Musices*. Albert Seay in *Journal of Music Theory* 1 (1957): 22–75.

Vives, Juan. *Vives: On Education*. Translated by Foster Watson. Cambridge: University Press, 1913.

Weiss, Piero. *Letters of Composers Through Six Centuries*. Philadelphia: Chilton, 1967.

CHAPTER 6 IS MUSIC: THEORY OR PERFORMANCE?

Blunt, Anthony. *Artistic Theory in Italy, 1450–1600*. Oxford: Clarendon Press, 1959.

Boethius. *Fundamentals of Music*. Translated by Calvin Bower. New Haven: Yale University Press.

Bottrigari, Hercole. *Il Desiderio*. Translated by Carol MacClintock. American Institute of Musicology, 1962.

Carpenter, Nan Cooke. *Music in the Medieval and Renaissance Universities*. Norman: University of Oklahoma Press, 1958.

Coclico, Adrian. *Musical Compendium*. Translated by Albert Seay. Colorado Springs: Colorado College Music Press, 1973.

Couperin, François. *L'Art de toucher*. Paris, 1717, reprinted Wiesbaden: Breitkopf & Härtel, 1933.

Da Vinci, Leonardo. *The Literary Works of Leonardo da Vinci*. Edited by Jean Paul Richter. London: Phaidon, 1970.

Dictionary of Musical Terms. Translated by Carl Parrish. New York: Free Press of Glencoe, 1963.

Gaffurio, Franchino. *The Practica musicae of Franchinus Gafurius*. Translated by Irwin Young. Madison: University of Wisconsin Press, 1969.

Giustiniani, Vicenzo. *Discorso sopra la Musica* [ca. 1628]. Translated by Carol MacClintock. American Institute of Musicology, 1962.

Hucbald, 'Melodic Instruction' in *Hucbald, Guido, and John on Music*. Translated by Warren Babb. New Haven: Yale University Press, 1978.

John, 'On Music,' in *Hucbald, Guido, and John on Music*. Translated by Warren Babb. New Haven: Yale University Press, 1978.

Marchetto of Padua. *Lucidarium*. Translated by Jan W. Herlinger. Chicago: University of Chicago Press, 1985.

Mattheson, Johann. *Das Neu-Eroffnete Orchestre*. Hamburg, 1713.

Ornithoparchus, Musicae active mirologus and Dowland, Introduction: Containing the Art of Singing. New York: Dover, 1973.

Peacham, Henry. *The Complete Gentleman*. Edited by Virgil Heltzel. Ithaca: Cornell University Press, 1962.

Petrarch. *Remedies for Fortune Fair and Foul*. Translated by Conrad Rawski. Bloomington: Indiana University Press, 1991.

St. Augustine. *On Music*. Translated by Robert Taliaferro in *Writings of Saint Augustine*. New York: Fathers of the Church.

Tinctoris. *Concerning the Nature and Propriety of Tones*. Translated by Albert Seay. Colorado Springs, 1976.

Voltaire. *The Works of Voltaire*. New York: St. Hubert Guild, 1901.

Wagner, Richard. *The Prose Works of Wagner*. Translated by William Ashton Ellis. New York: Broude.

Wilson, John. *Roger North on Music*. London: Novello, 1959.

Zarlino, Gioseffo. *On the Modes*. Translated by Vered Cohen. New Haven: Yale University Press, 1983.

———. *The Art of Counterpoint*. Translated by Guy Marco and Claude Palisca. New Haven: Yale University Press, 1968.

Chapter 7 Early Voices Argue: Reason versus Experience

Aquinas, Thomas. *Commentary on the Metaphysics of Aristotle*. Translated by John Rowan. Chicago: Henry Regnery, 1961.

Aristotle. *Posterior Analytics*. Translated by Hugh Tredennick. Cambridge: Harvard University Press, 1960.

Bacon, Roger. *The Opus Majus of Roger Bacon*. Translated by Robert Burke. New York: Russell & Russell, 1962.

Boccaccio, Giovanni. *The Fates of Illustrious Men*. Translated by Louis Hall. New York: Ungar, 1965.

Boethius. *Consolatione Philosophiae*. Translated by Samuel Fox. London: George Bell, 1895.

Cardano, Girolamo. *The Book on Games of Chance*. Translated by Sydney Gould. New York: Dover, 1953.

Clark, Barrett. *European Theories of the Drama*. New York: Crown, 1959.

Da Vinci, Leonardo. *The Literary Works of Leonardo da Vinci*. Edited by Jean Paul Richter. London: Phaidon, 1970.

Democritus, in Milton C. Nahm. *Selections from Early Greek Philosophy*. New York: Appleton-Century-Crofts, 1964.

Descartes, René. *Descartes Philosophical Letters*. Translated by Anthony Kenny. Oxford: Clarendon Press, 1970.

Fenelon. *The Adventures of Telemachus, Son of Ulysses*. London: Garland Publishing, 1979.

Johannes de Grocheo. *De Musica* [ca. 1300]. Translated by Albert Seay. Colorado Springs: Colorado College Music Press, 1967.

Lope de Vega. *The Knight from Olmedo*. Translated by Jill Booty, in *Lope de Vega, Five Plays*. New York: HIll and Wang, 1961.

Montaigne, Michel. *Essays*. Translated by M. A. Screech. London: Penguin, 1993.

Ore, Oystein. *Cardano The Gambling Scholar*. New York: Dover, 1953.

Plato. *Republic*.

Reale, Giovanni. *A History of Ancient Philosophy*. Albany: State University of New York Press, 1987.

Rojas, Fernando. *Celestina*. Translated by James Mabbe. New York: Applause Publishers, 1986.

Strunk, Oliver. *Source Readings in Music History*. New York: Norton, 1950.

Erasmus, Desiderius. *The Collected Works of Erasmus*. Toronto: University of Toronto Press, 1992.

St. John of the Cross. *The Collected Works of St. John of the Cross*. Translated by Kieran Kavanaugh and Otilio Rodriguez. Washington, D.C.: Institute of Carmelite Studies, 1979.

Voltaire. *The Works of Voltaire*. New York: St. Hubert Guild, 1901.

Walton, Izaak. *The Compleat Angler*. London: Oxford University Press, 1935.

CHAPTER 8 EARLY VOICES STRUGGLE TO EXPLAIN THE EMOTIONS

A Woman's Life in the Court of the Sun King. Translated by Elborg Forster. Baltimore: Johns Hopkins University Press, 1984.

Agrippa. *De occulta philosophia* in Donald Tyson, *Three Books of Occult Philosophy*. St. Paul: Llewellyn Publications, 1993.

Anglicus, Bartholomew. *Medieval Lore*. Translated by Robert Steele. London: Stock, 1893.

Aquinas. Thomas. *Summa Contra*.

———. *Summa Theologiae*.

———. *Summa Theologiae*.

Aristides. *Greek Musical Writings*. Translated by Andrew Barker. Cambridge: Cambridge University Press, 1989.

Aristotle. *Ethica Nicomachea*.

———. *On Interpretation*. Translated by Harold P. Cook. Cambridge: Harvard University Press, 1962.

Bacon, Francis. *The Works of Francis Bacon*. Cambridge: Cambridge University Press, 1869.
Bacon, Roger. *The Opus Majus of Roger Bacon*. Translated by Robert Burke. New York: Russell & Russell., II, 786.
Burton, Robert. *The Anatomy of Melancholy*. Edited by Floyd Dell. New York: Tudor Publishing Company, 1938.
Cicero. *De Finibus*.
———. *De Officiis*.
———. *Tusculan Disputations*.
de Machaut, Guillaume. *Le Livre du Voir-Dit de Guillaume de Machaut*. Paris: Paulin Paris, 1875.
———. *Remede de Fortune*. Translated by James Wimsatt and William Kibler. Athens: The University of Georgia Press, 1988.
Descartes, René. *The Philosophical Writings of Descartes*. Translated by John Cottingham, Robert Stoothoff and Dugald Murdoch. Cambridge: Cambridge University Press, 1985.
Erasmus, Desiderius. *The Collected Works of Erasmus*. Toronto: University of Toronto Press, 1992.
Galen. *On the Passions and Errors of the Soul*. Translated by Paul W. Harkins. Columbus: Ohio State University Press.
Gower, John. *The Voice of One Crying*. Translated by Eric Stockton in *The Major Latin Works of John Gower*. Seattle: University of Washington Press, 1962.
Gracian. *A Pocket Mirror for Heroes*. Translated by Christopher Maurer. New York: Currency Doubleday, 1996.
Hall, Joseph. *The Works of Joseph Hall, D. D.* Edited by Philip Wynter. New York: AMS Press, 1969.
Harvey, William. *The Works of William Harvey*. Edited by Robert Willis. New York: Johnson Reprint Corp., 1965.
Hucbald, Guido, and John on Music. Translated by Warren Babb. New Haven: Yale University Press, 1978.
John of Salisbury. *The Metalogicon*. Translated by Daniel McGarry. Berkeley: University of California Press, 1955.
Locke, John. *The Works of John Locke*. Aalen: Scientia Verlag, 1963.
Longinus. *On the Sublime*. Translated by W. Rhys Roberts. Cambridge: University Press, 1935.
Montaigne, Michel. *Essays*. Translated by M. A. Screech. London: Penguin, 1993.
Plutarch. *Life of Pericles*.
Pope, Alexander. *The Works of Alexander Pope*. New York: Gordian Press, 1967.
Prior, Matthew. *The Literary Works of Matthew Prior*. Oxford: Clarendon, 1959.
Quintilian. *The Education of an Orator (Institutio Oratoria)*. Translated by H. E. Butler. London: Heinemann, 1938.
Rojas, Fernando. *La Celestina*. J. M. Cohen. New York: New York University Press, 1966.
Seneca. *De Tranquillitate Animi*.

Shenstone, William. *Letters of William Shenstone*. Minneapolis: University of Minnesota Press, 1939.
———. *Men and Manners*. Boston: Houghton Mifflin, 1927.
St. Augustine. *The Confessions*.
———. *The Free Choice of the Will*. Translated by Robert P. Russell. Washington, D.C.: The Catholic University of America Press.
St. John of the Cross. *The Ascent of Mount Carmel*, in *The Collected Works of St. John of the Cross*. Translated by Kieran Kavanaugh and Otilio Rodriguez. Washington, D.C.: Institute of Carmelite Studies, 1979.
Saint-Simon. *The Memoirs of the Duke of Saint-Simon*. Translated by Bayle St. John. London: George Allen, 1926.
Swift, Jonathan. *The Prose Works of Jonathan Swift*. Oxford: Blackwell, 1957.
Zwingli, Ulrich. 'Refutation of the Tricks of the Baptists' [1523], in *Ulrich Zwingli, Selected Works*. Edited by Samuel Jackson. Philadelphia: University of Pennsylvania Press, 1901.

CHAPTER 9 ON ANIMALS AND MUSIC

'The Story of the Volsungs and Niblungs.' Translated by Eir'kr Magnœsson and William Morris in *Epic and Saga*, volume 49, *The Harvard Classics*. New York: Collier, 1910.
Aelianus, Claudius. *Of the Characteristics of Animals*.
Aeschylus. *The Seven Against Thebes*.
Aesop. Translated by Lloyd W. Daly. New York: Yoseloff, 1961.
Agrippa, Henry Cornelius. *Of the Vanitie and Uncertaintie of Arts and Sciences*. Edited by Catherine Dunn. Northridge: California State University, Northridge Press, 1974.
Augustine. *On Music*. Translated by Robert Taliaferro in Writings of Saint Augustine. New York: Fathers of the Church.
Burton, Elisabeth. *The Pageant of Elisabethan England*. New York: Scribner's.
Cassiodorus, 'On Music,' in *An Introduction to Divine and Human Readings*. Translated by Leslie Jones. New York: Octagon Books, 1966.
Chaucer, Geoffrey 'The Squire's Tale.'
———. *The Book of the Duchess*.
de Quevedo, Francisco. 'Letrilla burlesca,' in *An Anthology of Spanish Poetry*. Edited by John Crow. Baton Rouge: Louisiana State University Press, 1979.
Erasmus, Desiderius. *The Collected Works of Erasmus*. Toronto: University of Toronto Press, 1992.
Euripides. *Helen*.
The Exeter Book (eighth century). Oxford University Press, 1958.
Giustiniani, Vicenzo. *Discorso sopra la Musica* [ca. 1628]. Translated by Carol MacClintock. American Institute of Musicology, 1962.
The Greek Anthology. Translated by W. R. Paton. Cambridge: Harvard University Press, 1939.

Herodotus. *The Histories*. New York: Penguin, 1977.
Jones, Paul. *The Household of a Tudor Nobleman*. Urbana, 1918.
Kircher, Athanasius. *Musurgia universalis* [1650]. Translated by Frederick Crane (unpublished dissertation, State University of Iowa, 1956.
Longus. *Daphnis and Chloe*. Translated by Paul Turner. London: Penguin Books, 1956.
Machaut, Guillaume de. 'Le Jugement du roy de Behaigne.' Translated by James Wimsatt and William Kibler. Athens: The University of Georgia Press, 1988.
———. *Musikalische Werke*. Edited by Friedrich Ludwig. Leipzig, 1926.
Magnus, Albertus. *De animalibus*. Translated by James Scanlan. Binghamton, NY: Medieval & Renaissance Texts, 1987.
Menestrier, Claude. *Des Ballets anciens et modernes, selon les regles du Theatre* (Paris, 1682.
Milton, John. *The Works of John Milton*. New York: Columbia University Press, 1931–1938.
Molina. *Damned for Despair*.
Montaigne, Michael. *Essays*. Translated by M. A. Screech. London: Penguin, 1993.
Pliny the Elder. *Natural History*.
Plutarch. *The Banquet of the Seven Wise Men*.
Polybius. *On the Characteristics of Animals*.
———. *The Rise of the Roman Empire*. New York: Penguin, 1981.
Prato, Giovanni. *Paradiso degli Alberti* [1389].
Saint Ambrose. 'Six Days of Creation: Five,' in *Hexameron, Paradise, Cain and Abel*. Translated by John J. Savage. New York: Fathers of the Church, 1961.
Shakespeare. *A Midsummer Night's Dream*.
Sidney, Philip. *The Countesse of Pembrokes Arcadia*, in *The Prose Works of Sir Philip Sidney*. Edited by Albert Feuillerat. Cambridge: Cambridge University Press, 1962.
Strabo. *The Geography of Strabo*. Translated by Horace L. Jones. Cambridge: Harvard University Press, 1960.
Voltaire. *The Works of Voltaire*. New York: St. Hubert Guild, 1901.

CHAPTER 10 IS MAN RULED BY REASON OR EMOTION?

Bacon, Francis. *The Works of Francis Bacon*. Cambridge: Cambridge University Press, 1869.
Barker, Andrew. *Greek Musical Writings*. Cambridge: Cambridge University Press, 1989.
Bunyan, John. *The Works of John Bunyan*. Edited by George Offor. London: Blackie and Son, 1853.
Burton, Robert. *The Anatomy of Melancholy*. Edited by Floyd Dell. New York: Tudor Publishing Company, 1938.
Cicero. *De Finibus*.
———. *De Officiis*.
———. *Tusculan Disputations*.
Dante. *Inferno*.

Dante. *The Banquet.*
Donne, John. *Devotions Upon Emergent Occasion.* Edited by Anthony Raspa. Montreal: McGill-Queen's University Press, 1975.
Donne, John. *Selected Prose.* Edited by Helen Gardner. Oxford: Clarendon Press, 1967.
Durant, Will. *The Age of Reason Begins.* New York: Simon and Schuster, 1961.
Erasmus, Desiderius. *The Collected Works of Erasmus.* Toronto: University of Toronto Press, 1992.
Goldin, Frederick. *German and Italian Lyrics of the Middle Ages.* Garden City: Anchor Books, 1973.
Hall, Joseph. *The Works of Joseph Hall, D. D.* Edited by Philip Wynter. New York: AMS Press, 1969.
Lorris, Guillaume and Jean de Meun. *The Romance of the Rose.* Translated by Harry Robbins. New York: Dutton, 1962.
Machaut, Guillaume. *Le Jugement du roy de Behaigne and Remede de Fortune.* Translated by James Wimsatt and William Kibler. Athens: The University of Georgia Press, 1988.
Macpherson, Hector. *Spencer and Spencerism.* New York: Doubley, Page, & Co., 1900.
Milton, John. *The Works of John Milton.* Edited by Frank Patterson. New York: Columbia University Press, 1931–1938.
Morley, Henry. *Ideal Commonwealths.* Port Washington: Kennikat Press, 1968.
Petrarch. *Letters from Petrarch.* Translated by Morris Bishopo. Bloomington: Indiana University Press, 1966.
———. *Petrarch's Lyric Poems.* Translated by Robert Durling. Cambridge: Harvard University Press, 1976.
———. *Remedies for Fortune Fair and Foul.* Translated by Conrad Rawski. Bloomington: Indiana University Press, 1991.
Rolle, Richard. *English Prose Treatises of Richard Rolle.* London: Humphrey Milford, Oxford University Press, 1866, 1921.
Saint Evremond. *The Letters of Saint-Evremond.* Edited by John Hayward. Freeport, NY: Books for Libraries Press, 1971.
St. John of the Cross. *The Collected Works of St. John of the Cross.* Translated by Kieran Kavanaugh and Otilio Rodriguez. Washington, D.C.: Institute of Carmelite Studies, 1979.
Spencer, Herbert. *Facts and Comments.* New York: Appleton & Co., 1902.
Tasso, Torquato. *Tasso's Dialogues.* Translated by Carnes Lord. Berkeley: University of California Press, 1982.
Vives, Juan. *Vives: On Education.* Translated by Foster Watson. Cambridge: University Press, 1913.
Voltaire. *The Selected Letters of Voltaire.* Tranlsated by Richard Brooks. New York: New York University Press, 1973.
Voltaire. *The Works of Voltaire.* New York: St. Hubert Guild, 1901.
Wither, George. *Works of George Wither.* New York: Franklin, 1967.

Wycherley, William. *The Complete Works of William Wycherley*. New York: Russell & Russell, 1964.

Chapter 11 Some Early Voices Intuit the Bicameral Mind

Arbasto: The Anatomy of Fortune (1584), in *The Life and Complete Works of Robert Greene*. Edited by Alexander Grosart. New York: Russell & Russell, 1964.

Aristotle. *Nicomachean Ethics*.

Aurelian of Reome. *The Discipline of Music*. Translated by Joseph Ponte. Colorado Springs: Colorado College Music Press, 1968.

Avison, Charles. *An Essay on Musical Expression* [London, 1753]. New York: Broude Reprint, 1967.

Barker, Andrew. *Greek Musical Writings*. Cambridge: Cambridge University Press, 1989.

Boas, Frederick. *Giles and Phineas Fletcher Poetical Works*. Cambridge: University Press, 1909.

Cervantes, Miguel. *The Trials of Persiles and Sigismunda*. Translated by Celia Weller and Clark Colahan. Berkeley: University of California Press, 1989.

Cicero. *Tusculan Disputations*.

Dante. *Inferno*.

———. *Paradise*.

———. *Vita Nuova*. Translated by Mark Musa. Oxford: Oxford University Press, 1992.

Epictetus. *The Discourses of Epictetus*. Translated by P. E. Matheson. New York: Random House, 1957.

Erasmus, Desiderius. *The Collected Works of Erasmus*. Toronto: University of Toronto Press, 1992.

Giovanni Pico della Mirandola. *Commentary on a Canzone of Benivieni*. Translated by Sears Jayne. New York: Peter Lang, 1984.

Goldin, Frederick. *German and Italian Lyrics of the Middle Ages*. Garden City: Anchor Books, 1973.

Guarini, Giambattista. *The Faithful Shepherd* [*Il Pastor Fido*] in *Five Italian Renaissance Comedies*. New York: Penguin Books, 1978.

Hume, David. *A Treatise of Human Nature*.

La Bruyere. *Characters*. Translated by Jean Stewart. Baltimore: Penguin Books, 1970.

La Rochefoucauld. *The Maxims of La Rochefoucauld*. Translated by Louis Kronenberger. New York: Random House, 1959.

Leibniz, Gottfried. 'An Analysis of the Elements of Language,' in *General Investigations Concerning the Analysis of Concepts and Truths*. Translated by Walter O'Briant. Athens: University of Georgia Press, 1968.

———. 'What is an Idea?' (1678), in *Philosophical Papers and Letters*. Edited by Leroy Loemker. Dordrecht: Reidel, 1956.

Luther, Martin. *Luther's Works*. St. Louis: Concordia, 1961.

Mersenne, Marin. Treatise Three, Book One, *Traitez de la Voix, et des Chants*. Translated by Edmund LeRoy. New York: Julliard School, unpublished dissertation, 1978.
Montesquieu. *The Persian Letters*. London: Athenaeum, 1901.
Pascal, Blaise. *Pensees*. New York: Modern Library, 1941.
Saint-Evremond. *The Letters of Saint-Evremond*. Edited by John Hayward. Freeport, NY: Books for Libraries Press, 1971.
Swift, Jonathan. *The Poetical Works of Jonathan Swift*. London: Bell and Daldy, n.d.
Vives, Juan. *Vives: On Education*. Translated by Foster Watson. Cambridge: University Press, 1913.
Wagner, Richard. *Wagner's Prose Works*. Translated by William Ashton Ellis. New York: Broude.

Chapter 12 The Secret Agenda: Right-hand Preference

Ariosto, Ludovico. *The Satires of Ludovico Ariosto*. Translated by Peter Wiggins. Athens: Ohio University Press, 1976.
Bernard of Clairvaux. *Sermons on Conversion*. Translated by Marie-Bernard Said. Kalamazoo: Cistercian Publications, 1981.
Bodin, Jean. *Colloquium of the Seven*. Translated by Marion Kuntz. Princeton: Princeton University Press, 1975.
Browne, Thomas. *Sir Thomas Browne's Works*. Edited by Simon Wilkin. London: Pickering, 1836.
Bunyan, John. *The Works of John Bunyan*. Edited by George Offor. London: Blackie and Son, 1853.
Cervantes, Miguel. *Don Quijote*. Translated by Burton Raffel. New York: Norton, 1995.
Cowley, Abraham. *The Complete Works of Abraham Cowley*. New York: AMS Press, 1967.
Crashaw, Richard. *The Complete Poetry of Richard Crashaw*. Edited by George Williams. New York: New York University Press, 1972.
Dekker, Thomas. *The Non-Dramatic Works of Thomas Dekker*. Edited by Alexander Grosart. New York, Russell & Russell, 1963.
Dickinson, John. *The Stateman's Book of John of Salisbury*. New York: Russell & Russell, 1963.
Donne, John. *Devotions Upon Emergent Occasion*. Edited by Anthony Raspa. Montreal: McGill-Queen's University Press, 1975.
Einhard and Notker the Stammerer. *Two Lives of Charlemagne*. Translated by Lewis Thorpe. Hamondsworth: Penguin Books, 1981.
Erasmus, Desiderius. *The Collected Works of Erasmus*. Toronto: University of Toronto Press, 1992.
Gildon, Charles. *The Life of Mr. Thomas Betterton, the Late Eminent Tragedian* [1710]. London: Frank Cass Reprint, 1970.
Jonson, Ben. *The Complete Poetry of Ben Jonson*. New York: Norton, 1963.

Martin, L. C. *The Poetical Works of Robert Herrick*. Oxford: Clarendon Press, 1963.

Milton, John. *The Works of John Milton*. Edited by Frank Patterson. New York: Columbia University Press, 1931–1938.

Plato. *Laws*.

Voltaire. *Works of Voltaire*. New York: St. Hubert Guild, 1901.

Wither, Geroge. *A Collection of Emblemes* [1635]. *English Emblem Books*. Menston, Yorkshire: Scolar Press, 1968.

Chapter 13 Music is the Ruler of the Passions of the Soul

Aristides in Andrew Barker. *Greek Musical Writings*. Cambridge: Cambridge University Press, 1989.

Aurelian of Reome. *The Discipline of Music*. Translated by Joseph Ponte. Colorado Springs: Colorado College Music Press, 1968.

Berardi, Angelo. *Ragionamenti Musicali*. Bologna, 1681.

Boethius. *Fundamentals of Music*. Translated by Calvin Bower. New Haven: Yale University Press.

Brossard, Sebastien. *Dictionaire de Musique* (Paris, 1703).

Buelow, George. *Thorough-Bass Accompaniment according to Johann David Heinichen*. Ann Arbor: UMI Research Press, 1986.

Caccini, Giulio. *Le Nuove Musiche*. Edited by H. Wiley Hitchcock. Madison: A-R Editions, 1970.

Cavalieri, Emilio. *Rappresentazione di Anima, et di Corpo*, Preface, quoted in Carol MacClintock, *Readings in the History of Music in Performance*. Bloomington: Indiana University Press, 1979.

Congreve, William. *The Complete Works of William Congreve*. New York: Russell & Russell, 1964.

Couperin, François. *L'Art de toucher* (Paris, 1717), reprinted Wiesbaden: Breitkopf & Hartel, 1933.

David, Hans T. and Arthur Mendel. *The Bach Reader*. New York: Norton, 1966.

da Vinci, Leonardo. *The Literary Works of Leonardo da Vinci*. Edited by Jean Paul Richter. London: Phaidon, 1970.

Diderot, Denis. *Rameau's Nephew and Other Works*. Translated by Jacques Barzun. Garden City: Doubleday, 1956.

Donnington, Robert. *The Interpretation of Early Music*. New York, 1964.

Farmer, Henry G. 'The Music of Ancient Egypt,' *New Oxford History of Music*. London: Oxford University Press, 1966.

Galilei, Vincenzo. *Fronimo* [1584]. Translated by Carol MacClintock. Neuhasen-Stuttgart: Hanssler-Verlag, 1985.

Geminiani, Francesco. *A Treatise of Good Taste in the Art of Musick* [1749]. New York: Da Capo Press, 1969.

Glarean. *Dodecachordon*. Translated by Clement Miller. American Institute of Musicology, 1965.
Greene, Robert. *The Life and Complete Works of Robert Greene*. Edited by Alexander Grosart. New York: Russell & Russell, 1964.
Harris, Ellen. 'Voices,' in *Performance Practice: Music after 1600*. New York: Norton, 1989.
Huray, Peter and James Day. *Music and Aesthetics in the Eighteenth and Early-Nineteenth Centuries*. Cambridge: Cambridge University Press, 1981.
Isacoff, Stuart. *Temperament* (New York: Vintage, 2001.
John of Salisbury. *The Metalogicon*. Translated by Daniel McGarry. Berkeley: University of California Press, 1955.
Liszt, Franz. 'Berlioz and his "Harold" Symphony,' *Neue Zeitschrift für Musik* (1855).
Longinus. *On the Sublime*. Translated by W. Rhys Roberts. Cambridge: University Press, 1935.
Lydgate, John, 'The Daunce of Machabree,' in *Fall of Princes*. Edited by Henry Bergen. London: Oxford University Press, 1967.
MacClintock, Carol. *Readings in the History of Music in Performance*. Bloomington: Indiana University Press, 1979.
Maland, David. *Culture and Society in Seventeenth-Century France*. New York: Scribner's, 1970.
Marpurg, F. W. *Der critische Musicus an der Spree*. Berlin, 1749.
Mattheson, Johann. *Das Neu-Eröffnete Orchestre*. Hamburg [1713].
———. *Der vollkommene Capellmeister* [1739]. Translated by Ernest Harriss. Ann Arbor: UMI Research Press, 1981.
Mersenne, Marin. *Fourth Treatise of the Harmonie Universelle*. Edited by Robert Williams. Rochester: Eastman School of Music, unpublished dissertation, 1972), IV.
Montaigne, Michel. *Essays*. Translated by M. A. Screech. London: Penguin, 1993.
Morgenstern, Sam. *Composers on Music*. New York: Pantheon, 1956.
Osborne, Richard. *Conversations with Von Karajan*. New York: Harper & Row, 1989.
Pirrotta, Nino and Elena Povoledo. *Music and Theatre from Poliziano to Monteverdi*. Cambridge: Cambridge University Press, 1982.
Pontus de Tyard. *Solitaire second* (1555).
Quintilian. *The Education of an Orator (Institutio Oratoria)*. Translated by H. E. Butler. London: Heinemann, 1938.
Raguenet, François. 'Comparison between the French and Italian Music (1702).' Translated by Oliver Strunk. *The Musical Quarterly* 32, no. 3 (1946): 411–436.
Rameau. *Le Nouveau Systeme de musique theorique* [1726], quoted in Morgenstern, *Composers on Music*. New York: Pantheon, 1956.
Schmitz, Hans-Peter. *Die Kunst der Verzierung im 18. Jahrhundert*. Kassel: Barenreiter, 1955.
Shapiro, Nat. *An Encyclopedia of Quotations About Music*. New York: Da Capo, 1978.
Strunk, Oliver. *Source Readings in Music History*. New York: Norton, 1950.
Tosi, P. F. *Observations on the Florid Song*. London: Wilcox, 1743.

Wagner, Richard. *Wagner's Prose Works.* Translated by William Ashton Ellis. New York: Broude.

Walter, Bruno. *Of Music and Music-Making.* New York: Norton, 1957.

Weiss, Piero. *Letters of Composers Through Six Centuries.* Philadelphia: Chilton, 1967.

Yates, Frances. *The French Academies of the Sixteenth Century.* Nendeln: Kraus, 1968.

Chapter 14 On the Doctrine of the Affections

Agrippa, Henry Cornelius. *De occulta Philosophia.* Edited by Donald Tyson, in *Three Books of Occult Philosophy.* St. Paul: Llewellyn Publications, 1993.

Bodin, Jean. *Method for the Easy Comprehension of History.* Translated by Beatrice Reynolds. New York: Columbia University Press, 1945.

Cooke, Deryck. *The Language of Music.* Oxford: Clarendon Paperbacks, 1959.

Descartes, René. *Compendium of Music.* Translated by Walter Robert. American Institute of Musicology, 1961.

Donne, John. 'Paradoxes and Problems,' in *Selected Prose.* Edited by Helen Gardner. Oxford: Clarendon Press, 1967.

Hays, William, ed. *Twentieth-Century Views of Music History.* New York: Scribner's, 1972.

Harvey, William. *The Works of William Harvey.* Edited by Robert Willis. Reprinted New York: Johnson Reprint Corp., 1965.

Heinichen, Johann David. *General-Bass Treatise* [1711], quoted in George Buelow, *Thorough-Bass Accompaniment according to Johann David Heinichen.* Ann Arbor: UMI Research Press, 1986.

Mattheson, Johann. *Der vollkommene Capellmeister* (1739). Translated by Ernest Harriss. Ann Arbor: UMI Research Press, 1981.

Mersenne, Marin. *Harmonie Universelle.* Translated by John Egan. Bloomington: Indiana University, unpublished dissertation, 1962.

Miller, Clement. *Hieronymus Cardanus, Writings on Music.* American Institute of Musicology, 1973.

Chapter 15 Music is Truth

Ausonius. *Ausonius.* Translated by Hugh G. Evelyn White. London: Heinemann, 1921.

Barker, Andrew. *Greek Musical Writings.* Cambridge: Cambridge University Press, 1989.

Bianconi, Lorenzo. *Music in the Seventeenth Century.* Translated by David Bryant. Cambridge: Cambridge University Press, 1989.

Boccaccio. *L'Ameto.* Translated by Judith Serafini-Sauli. New York: Garland, 1985.

Boethius. *Fundamentals of Music.* Translated by Calvin Bower. Haven: Yale University Press.

Cicero. *Tusculan Disputations.*

Erasmus, Desiderius. *The Collected Works of Erasmus.* Toronto: University of Toronto Press, 1992.

The Exeter Book. Oxford University Press, 1958.
The Greek Anthology. Translated by W. R. Paton. London: Heinemann, 1918
Hegel, Gerog Wilhelm Friedrich. *Aesthetics: Lectures on Fine Art*. Oxford: Clarendon Press, 1975.
Huray, Peter and James Day. *Music and Aesthetics in the Enghteenth and Early Nineteenth Centuries*. Cambridge: Cambridge University Press, 1981.
Johannes de Grocheo. *De Musica*. Translated by Albert Seay. Colorado Springs: Colorado College Music Press, 1967.
Leibniz, Gottfried Wilhelm. *New Essays Concerning Human Understanding* [1704]. Translated by Alfred Langley. La Salle: The Open Court Publishing Company, 1949.
Machaut, Guillaume. *Remede de Fortune*. Translated by James Wimsatt and William Kibler. Athens: The University of Georgia Press, 1988.
Marek, George. *Schubert*. Viking, 1985.
Ornstein, Robert. *The Right Mind*. New York: Harcourt Brace, 1997.
Plato. *Laws*.
Quintilian. *The Education of an Orator (Institutio Oratoria)*. Translated by H. E. Butler. London: Heinemann, 1938.
Sidney, Philip. *The Countesse of Pembrokes Arcadia*, in *The Prose Works of Sir Philip Sidney*. Edited by Albert Feuillerat. Cambridge: Cambridge University Press, 1962.
Sidonius. *Sidonius Poems and Letters*. Translated by W. B. Anderson. Cambridge: Harvard University Press, 1965.
Tosi, P. F. *Observations on the Florid Song*. London: Wilcox, 1743.
Vogelweide, Walter von der. *Selected Poems of Walter von der Vogelweide*. Translated by W. Alison Phillips. London: Smith, Elder, & Co., 1896.
Wagner, Richard. *My Life*. New York: Tudor, 1936.
———. *Wagner's Prose Works*. Translated by William Ashton Ellis. New York: Broude.

Chapter 16 Music as the Language of Truth

Avison, Charles. *An Essay on Musical Expression* [London, 1753]. New York: Broude Reprint, 1967.
Bacon, Roger. *The Opus Majus of Roger Bacon*. Translated by Robert Burke. New York: Russell & Russell, 1962.
Boccaccio. *L'Ameto*. Translated by Judith Serafini-Sauli. New York: Garland, 1985.
Dekker, Thomas. *The Non-Dramatic Works of Thomas Dekker*. Edited by Alexander Grosart. New York, Russell & Russell, 1963.
Descartes, René. *Compendium of Music*. Translated by Walter Robert. American Institute of Musicology, 1961.
Erasmus, Desiderius. *The Collected Works of Erasmus*. Toronto: University of Toronto Press, 1992.

Froissart, Jean. *The Short Lyric Poems of Jean Froissart*. Edited by Kristen Figg. New York: Garland Publishing, 1994.

Hucbald, Guido, and John on Music. Translated by Warren Babb. New Haven: Yale University Press, 1978.

Huray, Peter and James Day. *Music and Aesthetics in the Eighteenth and Early-Nineteenth Centuries*. Cambridge: Cambridge University Press, 1981.

Saint-Evremond. *The Letters of Saint-Evremond*. Edited by John Hayward. Freeport, NY: Books for Libraries Press, 1971.

Leibniz, Gottfried. 'An Analysis of the Elements of Language,' in *General Investigations Concerning the Analysis of Concepts and Truths*. Translated by Walter O'Briant. Athens: University of Georgia Press, 1968.

———. *Philosophical Papers and Letters*. Edited by Leroy Loemker. Dordrecht: Reidel, 1956.

———. *New Essays Concerning Human Understanding* [1704]. Translated by Alfred Langley. La Salle: The Open Court Publishing Company, 1949.

Mace, Thomas. *Musick's Monument* [1676]. Paris: Editions du Centre National de la Recherche Scientifique, 1966.

Machaut, Guillaume. *Remede de Fortune*. Translated by James Wimsatt and William Kibler. Athens: The University of Georgia Press, 1988.

Mattheson, Johann. *Der vollkommene Capellmeister* [1739]. Translated by Ernest Harriss. Ann Arbor: UMI Research Press, 1981.

Montaigne, Michel. *Essays*. Translated by M. A. Screech (London: Penguin, 1993.

Plutarch. *Life of Demosthenes*.

Reale, Giovanni. *A History of Ancient Philosophy*. Albany: State University of New York Press, 1987.

Shapiro, Nat. *An Encyclopedia of Quotations About Music*. New York: Da Capo, 1978.

Shenstone, William. *Men and Manners*. Boston: Houghton Mifflin, 1927.

St. Basil, 'Letter to Gregory of Nazianzus,' in *Letters of Saint Basil*. Translated by Sister Agnes Way. New York: Fathers of the Church, 1951.

Voltaire. *Philosophical Dictionary*.

Wagner, Richard. *Wagner's Prose Works*. Translated by William Ashton Ellis. New York: Broude.

Walter, Bruno. *Of Music and Music-Making* (New York: Norton, 1957.

Wilson, John. *Roger North on Music*. London: Novello, 1959.

The End of Music: Catharsis—Know Thyself!

Aristotle. *Poetics*.

———. *Politics*.

Bruno, Giordano. *The Expulsion of the Triumphant Beast*. Translated by Arthur Imerti. New Brunswick: Rutgers University Press, 1964.

Clark, Barrett. *European Theories of the Drama*. New York: Crown Publishers, 1959.
David, Hans T. and Arthur Mendel. *The Bach Reader*. New York: Norton, 1966.
Mattheson, Johann. *Der vollkommene Capellmeister* [1739]. Translated by Ernest Harriss. Ann Arbor: UMI Research Press, 1981.
Miller, Clement. *Hieronymus Cardanus, Writings on Music*. American Institute of Musicology, 1973.
Moser, Hans. *Heinrich Schütz*. St. Louis: Concordia, 1936.
Pascal, Blaise. *Pensees*. New York: Modern Library, 1941.
Plato. *Gorgias*.
———. *Laws*.
———. *Republic*.
Reese, Gustav. *Music in the Renaissance*. New York: Norton, 1959.
St. Augustine. *The Confessions*.
Tasso. *Discourses on the Heroic Poem*. Translated by Mariella Cavalchini. Oxford: Clarendon Press, 1973.
Tinctoris, Johannes. *The Art of Counterpoint*. Translated by Albert Seay. American Institute of Musicology, 1961.

About the Author

Dr. David Whitwell is a graduate ('with distinction') of the University of Michigan and the Catholic University of America, Washington DC (PhD, Musicology, Distinguished Alumni Award, 2000) and has studied conducting with Eugene Ormandy and at the Akademie für Musik, Vienna. Prior to coming to Northridge, Dr. Whitwell participated in concerts throughout the United States and Asia as Associate First Horn in the USAF Band and Orchestra in Washington DC, and in recitals throughout South America in cooperation with the United States State Department.

At the California State University, Northridge, which is in Los Angeles, Dr. Whitwell developed the CSUN Wind Ensemble into an ensemble of international reputation, with international tours to Europe in 1981 and 1989 and to Japan in 1984. The CSUN Wind Ensemble has made professional studio recordings for BBC (London), the Köln Westdeutscher Rundfunk (Germany), NOS National Radio (The Netherlands), Zürich Radio (Switzerland), the Television Broadcasting System (Japan) as well as for the United States State Department for broadcast on its 'Voice of America' program. The CSUN Wind Ensemble's recording with the Mirecourt Trio in 1982 was named the 'Record of the Year' by The Village Voice. Composers who have guest conducted Whitwell's ensembles include Aaron Copland, Ernest Krenek, Alan Hovhaness, Morton Gould, Karel Husa, Frank Erickson and Vaclav Nelhybel.

Dr. Whitwell has been a guest professor in 100 different universities and conservatories throughout the United States and in 23 foreign countries (most recently in China, in an elite school housed in the Forbidden City). Guest conducting experiences have included the Philadelphia Orchestra, Seattle Symphony Orchestra, the Czech Radio Orchestras of Brno and Bratislava, The National Youth Orchestra of Israel, as well as resident wind ensembles in Russia, Israel, Austria, Switzerland, Germany, England, Wales, The Netherlands, Portugal, Peru, Korea, Japan, Taiwan, Canada and the United States.

He is a past president of the College Band Directors National Association, a member of the Prasidium of the International Society for the Promotion of Band Music, and was a member of the founding board of directors of the World Association for Symphonic Bands and Ensembles (WASBE). In 1964 he was made an honorary life member of Kappa Kappa Psi, a national professional music fraternity. In September, 2001, he was a delegate to the UNESCO Conference on Global Music in Tokyo. He has been knighted by sovereign organizations in France, Portugal and Scotland and has been awarded the gold medal of Kerkrade, The Netherlands, and the silver medal of Wangen, Germany, the highest honor given wind conductors in the United States, the medal of the Academy of Wind and Percussion Arts (National Band Association) and the highest honor given wind conductors in Austria, the gold medal of the Austrian Band Association. He is a member of the Hall of Fame of the California Music Educators Association.

Dr. Whitwell's publications include more than 127 articles on wind literature including publications in Music and Letters (London), the London Musical Times, the Mozart-Jahrbuch (Salzburg), and 52 books, among which is his 13-volume *History and Literature of the Wind Band and Wind Ensemble* and an 8-volume series on *Aesthetics in Music*. In addition to numerous modern editions of early wind band music his original compositions include 5 symphonies.

David Whitwell was named as one of six men who have determined the course of American bands during the second half of the 20th century, in the definitive history, *The Twentieth Century American Wind Band* (Meredith Music).

A doctoral dissertation by German Gonzales (2007, Arizona State University) is dedicated to the life and conducting career of David Whitwell through the year 1977. David Whitwell is one of nine men described by Paula A. Crider in *The Conductor's Legacy* (Chicago: GIA, 2010) as 'the legendary conductors' of the 20th century.

> 'I can't imagine the 2nd half of the 20th century—without David Whitwell and what he has given to all of the rest of us.' Frederick Fennell (1993)

About the Editor

CRAIG DABELSTEIN began studying the piano at age seven and took up the saxophone at age twelve. Mr Dabelstein has Bachelor of Arts (Music) and Bachelor of Music degrees from the Queensland Conservatorium of Music, where he majored in the performance of classical saxophone repertoire. He also has a Graduate Diploma of Learning and Teaching and a Graduate Certificate in Editing and Publishing from the University of Southern Queensland.

He has held the principal alto and tenor saxophone chairs in the Australian Wind Orchestra and has been an augmenting member of the Queensland Philharmonic Orchestra, the Queensland Symphony Orchestra, and the Queensland Pops Orchestra. For many years he was also a member of the Queensland Saxophone Quartet.

He has been a casual conductor of the Young Conservatorium Symphonic Winds, and has previously been a saxophone teacher at the Queensland Conservatorium of Music. He is a regular conductor of the Queensland Wind Orchestra, having served as their artistic director and chief conductor from 2004 to 2009.

Craig Dabelstein is a research associate for the *Teaching Music Through Performance in Band* series of books, contributing analyses to volumes 7, 8, 1 (rev. edn), and the *Solos with Wind Band Accompaniment* volume. He served as the copyeditor and layout designer of the *Australian Clarinet and Saxophone Magazine* from 2007 to 2009 and he has written many CD and book reviews for *Music Forum* magazine. He is the editor of the second editions of the books by Dr. David Whitwell including *A Concise History of the Wind Band*, *Foundations of Music Education*, *Music Education of the Future*, *The Sousa Oral History Project*, *Wagner on Bands*, *Berlioz on Bands*, *The Art of Musical Conducting*, and the *Aesthetics of Music* series (8 volumes) and *The History and Literature of the Wind Band and Wind Ensemble* series (13 volumes). From 1994 to 2012 he was a staff member at Brisbane Girls Grammar School. He now teaches woodwinds and conducts bands at St. Joseph's College, Gregory Terrace, Brisbane, Australia.

www.ingramcontent.com/pod-product-compliance
Lightning Source LLC
Chambersburg PA
CBHW081347230426
43667CB00017B/2746